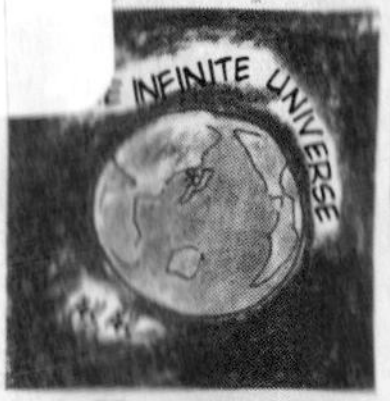
INFINITE UNIVERSE

樋口大輔

One of my ambitions is now fulfilled. Viva! Volume 10!! We're in double digits!! I did it! Great job, Higuchi. As a matter of fact, I have a grand ambition which I've had since I decided to become a manga artist. I want to draw manga that will influence the lives of the reader even if just a little. How presumptuous of me! Ha ha! But I will do it! Facing the 21st century, I'm getting carried away and publicly declaring my ambition!

- Daisuke Higuchi

Daisuke Higuchi's manga career began in 1992 when the artist was honored with third prize in the 43rd Osamu Tezuka Award. In that same year, Higuchi debuted as creator of a romantic action story titled ***Itaru***. In 1998, ***Weekly Shonen Jump*** began serializing ***Whistle!*** Higuchi's realistic soccer manga became an instant hit with readers and eventually inspired an anime series, debuting on Japanese TV in May of 2002.

WHISTLE!
VOL. 10: BROTHERHOOD

The SHONEN JUMP Manga Edition

STORY AND ART BY
DAISUKE HIGUCHI

English Adaptation/Drew Williams
Translation/Naomi Kokubo
Touch-up Art & Lettering/Jim Keefe
Cover, Graphics & Layout/Sean Lee
Editor/Andy Nakatani

Managing Editor/Elizabeth Kawasaki
Director of Production/Noboru Watanabe
Vice President of Publishing/Alvin Lu
Vice President & Editor in Chief/Yumi Hoashi
Sr. Director of Acquisitions/Rika Inouye
Vice President of Sales & Marketing/Liza Coppola
Publisher/Hyoe Narita

Printed in the U.S.A.

Published by VIZ Media, LLC
P.O. Box 77010
San Francisco, CA 94107

SHONEN JUMP Manga Edition
10 9 8 7 6 5 4 3 2 1
First printing, March 2006

WHISTLE!™

Vol. 10

Brotherhood

Story and Art by
Daisuke Higuchi

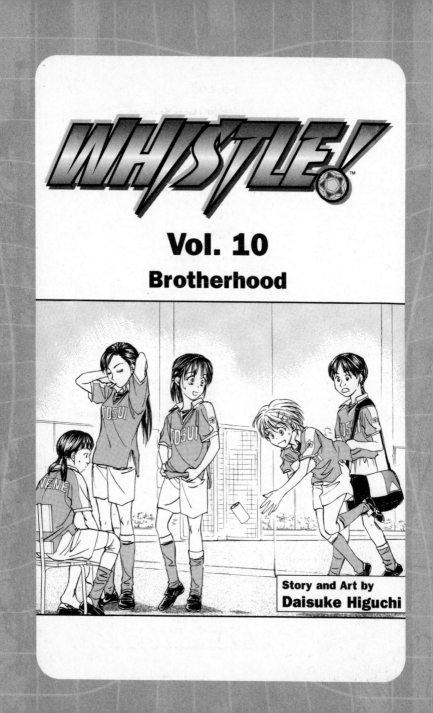

CHARACTERS

SHŌ KAZAMATSURI

● JOSUI JUNIOR HIGH SOCCER TEAM FORWARD

KŌ KAZAMATSURI

YŪKO KATORI

TATSUYA MIZUNO

● JOSUI JUNIOR HIGH SOCCER TEAM MIDFIELDER

SOUJŪ MATSUSHITA

FORMER JAPAN LEAGUE PLAYER

JOSUI JUNIOR HIGH COACH

SHIGEKI SATŌ

JOSUI JUNIOR HIGH SOCCER TEAM

FORWARD

TSUBASA SHIINA

HIBA JUNIOR HIGH SOCCER TEAM

CENTER BACK

To realize his dream, Shō Kazamatsuri, a bench warmer at soccer powerhouse Musashinomori, transferred to Josui Junior High so he could play the game he loves.

Things started looking up for Josui after Soujū Matsushita, a former Japan League player, took on the coaching duties, and now Josui seems to improve every time they play a match. In the third game of the district primary tournament, Josui defeated Rakuyō Junior High after a fierce battle in the rain.

Morale is at an all-time high for the Josui soccer team, but dark clouds are on the horizon! Unless every player gets at least an average score on the final exams, the school will eliminate the soccer team!!

STORY

WHISTLE!

**Vol. 10
BROTHERHOOD**

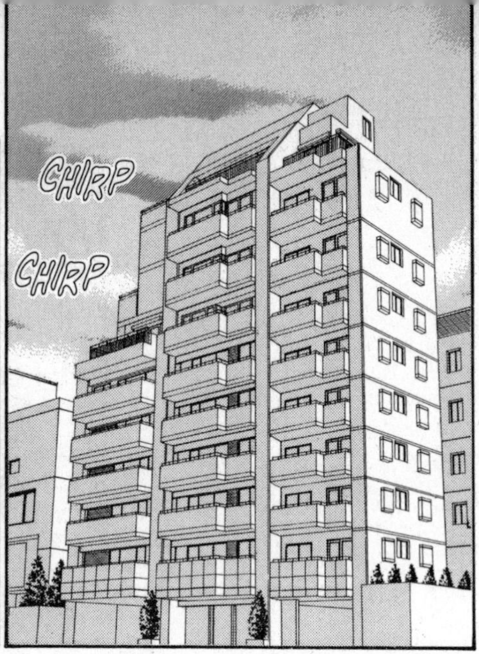
CHIRP
CHIRP
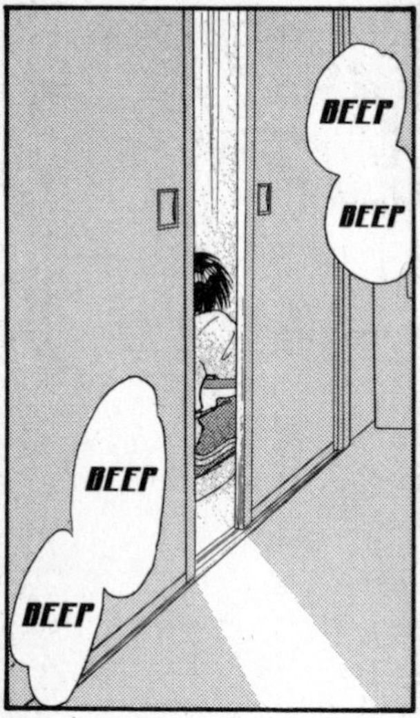
BEEP
BEEP
BEEP
BEEP

STAGE.81 Checking Out Hiba Junior High

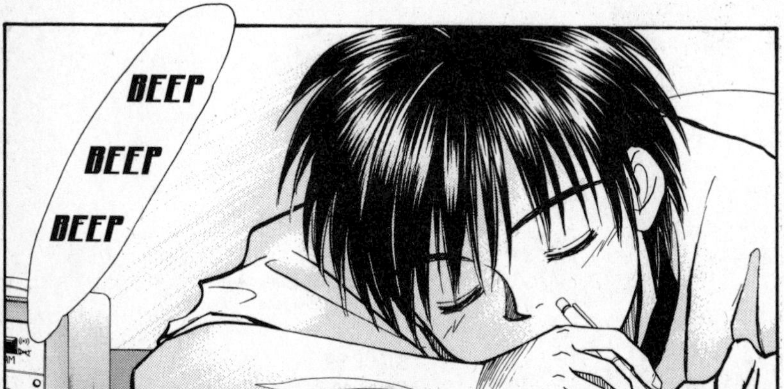
BEEP
BEEP
BEEP

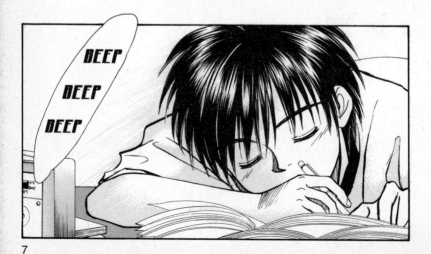

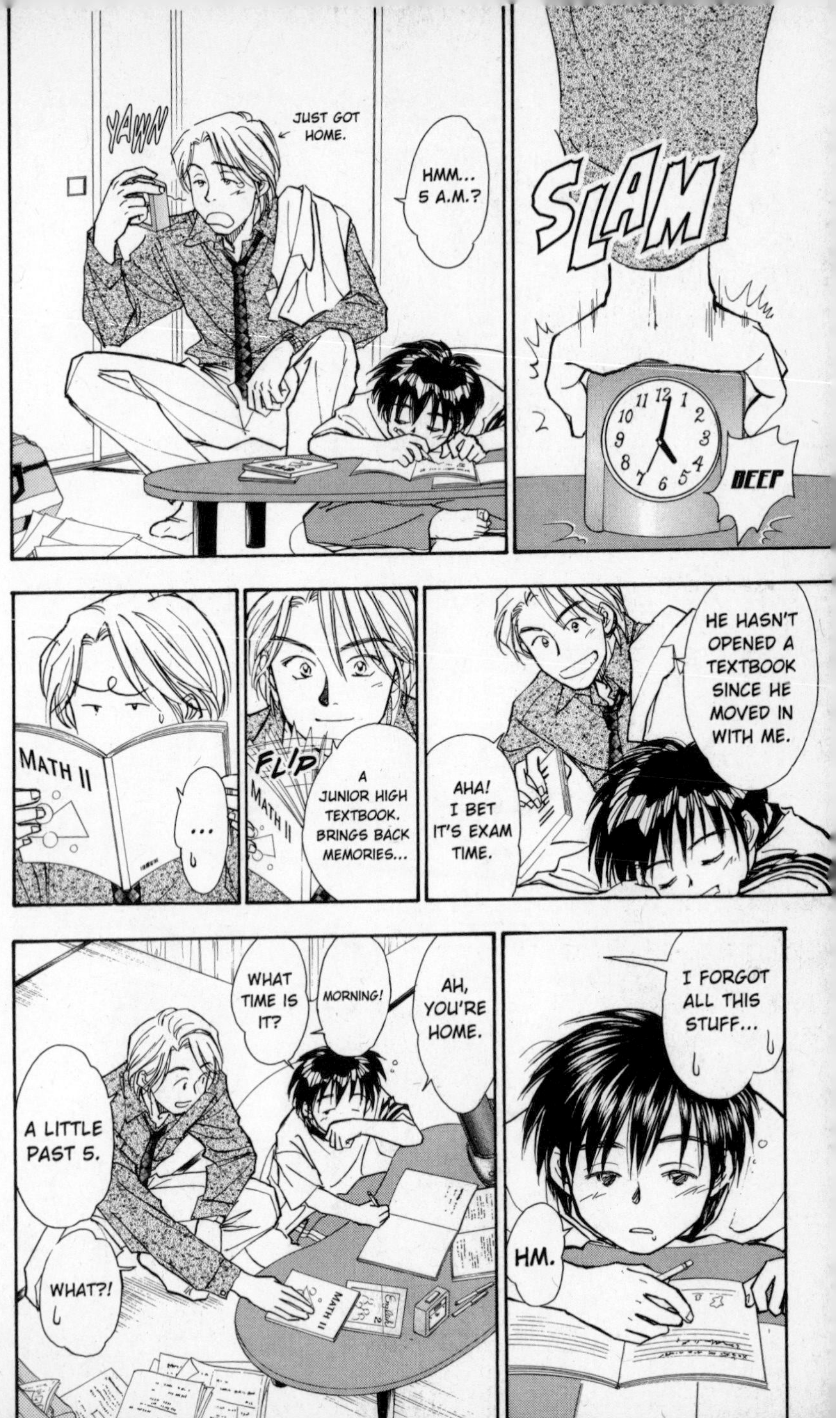
SLAM
BEEP
YAWN
JUST GOT HOME.
HMM... 5 A.M.?
HE HASN'T OPENED A TEXTBOOK SINCE HE MOVED IN WITH ME.
AHA! I BET IT'S EXAM TIME.
FLIP
A JUNIOR HIGH TEXTBOOK. BRINGS BACK MEMORIES...
MATH II
MATH II
...
I FORGOT ALL THIS STUFF...
HM.
AH, YOU'RE HOME.
MORNING!
WHAT TIME IS IT?
A LITTLE PAST 5.
WHAT?!
MATH II

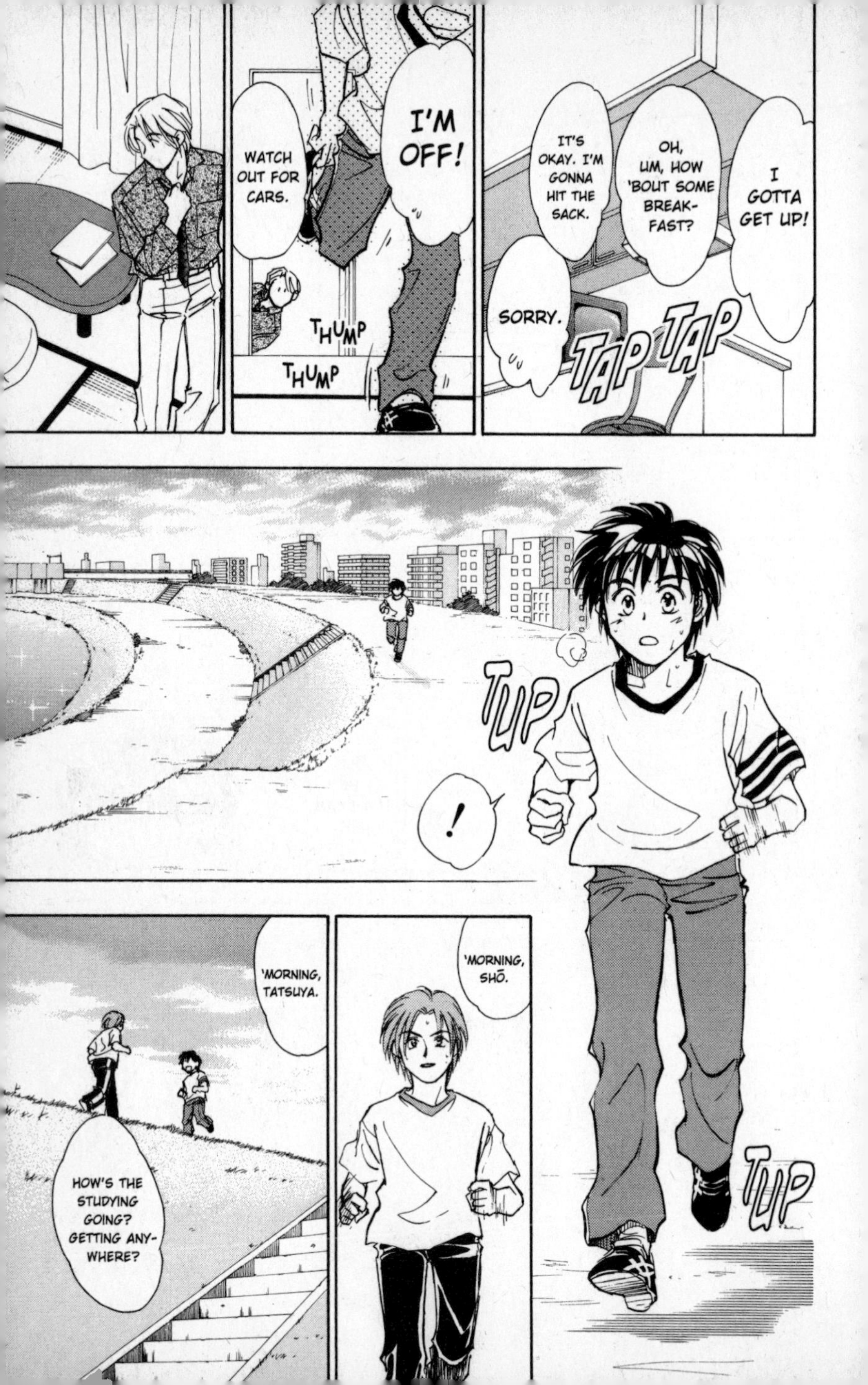
I GOTTA GET UP!
OH, UM, HOW 'BOUT SOME BREAK-FAST?
IT'S OKAY. I'M GONNA HIT THE SACK.
SORRY.
TAP TAP
I'M OFF!
WATCH OUT FOR CARS.
THUMP
THUMP
TUP
!
TUP
'MORNING, SHŌ.
'MORNING, TATSUYA.
HOW'S THE STUDYING GOING? GETTING ANY-WHERE?

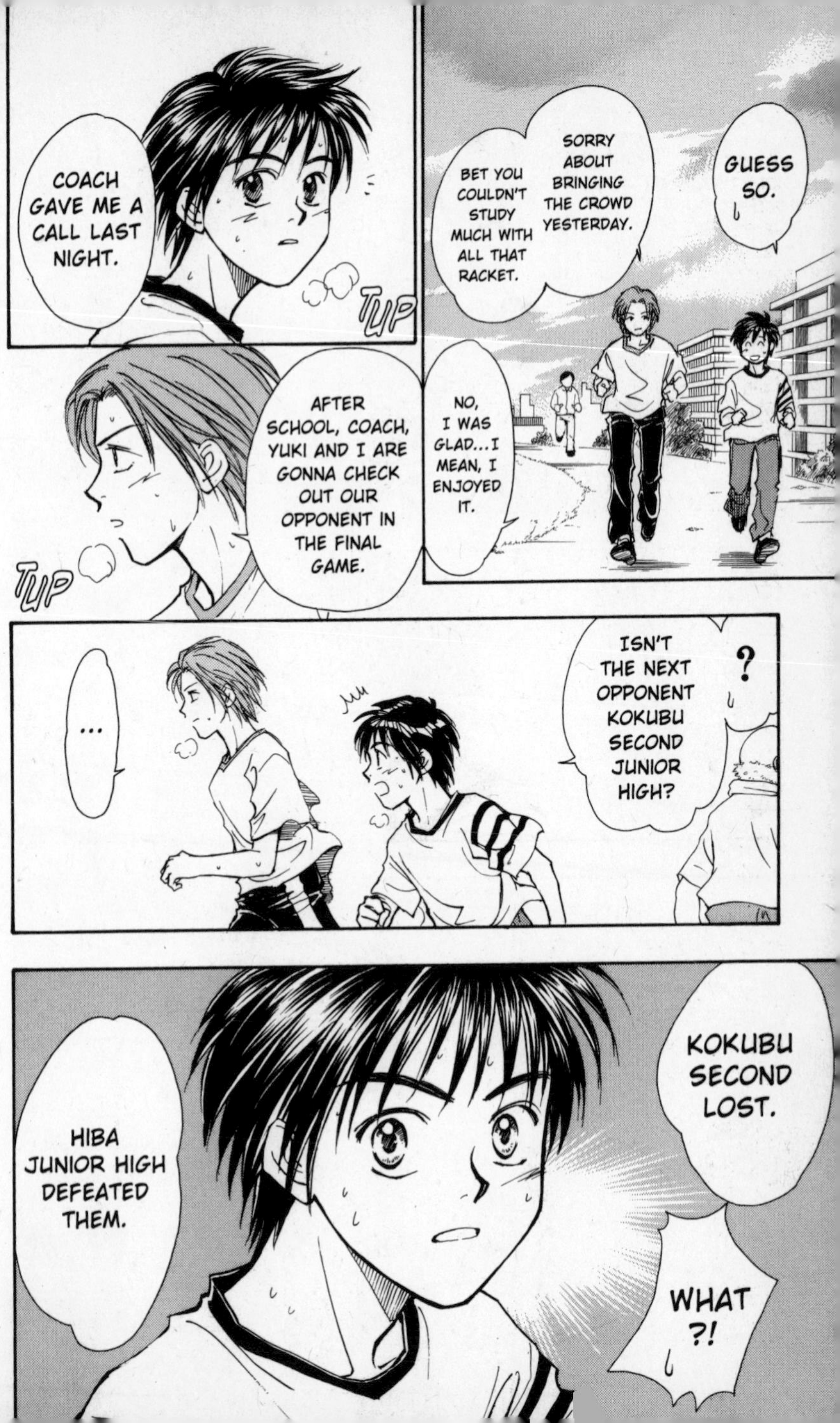
GUESS SO.
SORRY ABOUT BRINGING THE CROWD YESTERDAY.
BET YOU COULDN'T STUDY MUCH WITH ALL THAT RACKET.
NO, I WAS GLAD... I MEAN, I ENJOYED IT.
COACH GAVE ME A CALL LAST NIGHT.
TUP
AFTER SCHOOL, COACH, YUKI AND I ARE GONNA CHECK OUT OUR OPPONENT IN THE FINAL GAME.
TUP
?
ISN'T THE NEXT OPPONENT KOKUBU SECOND JUNIOR HIGH?
...
KOKUBU SECOND LOST.
HIBA JUNIOR HIGH DEFEATED THEM.
WHAT ?!

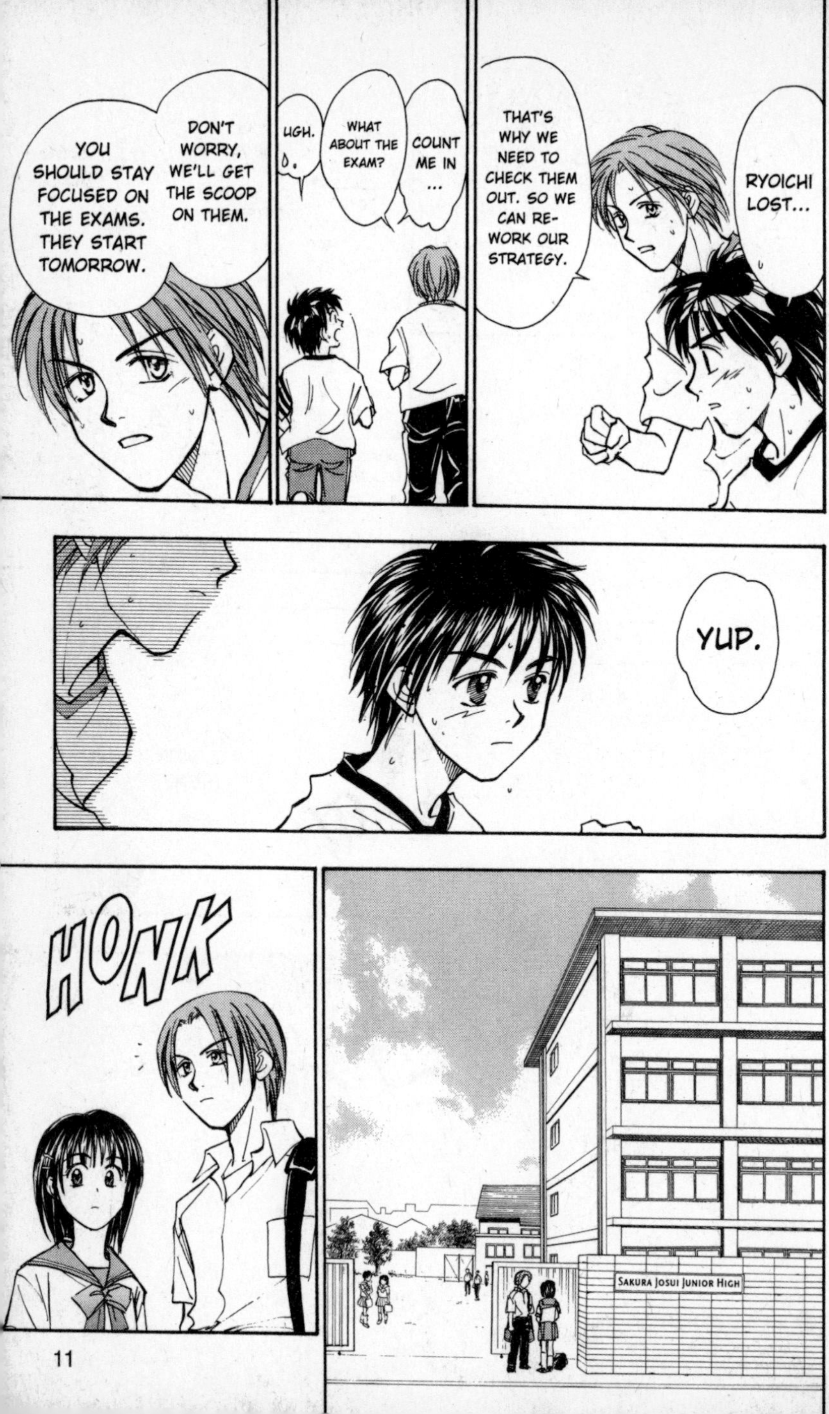

RYOICHI LOST...
THAT'S WHY WE NEED TO CHECK THEM OUT. SO WE CAN RE-WORK OUR STRATEGY.
COUNT ME IN ...
WHAT ABOUT THE EXAM?
UGH.
DON'T WORRY, WE'LL GET THE SCOOP ON THEM.
YOU SHOULD STAY FOCUSED ON THE EXAMS. THEY START TOMORROW.
YUP.
SAKURA JOSUI JUNIOR HIGH
HONK

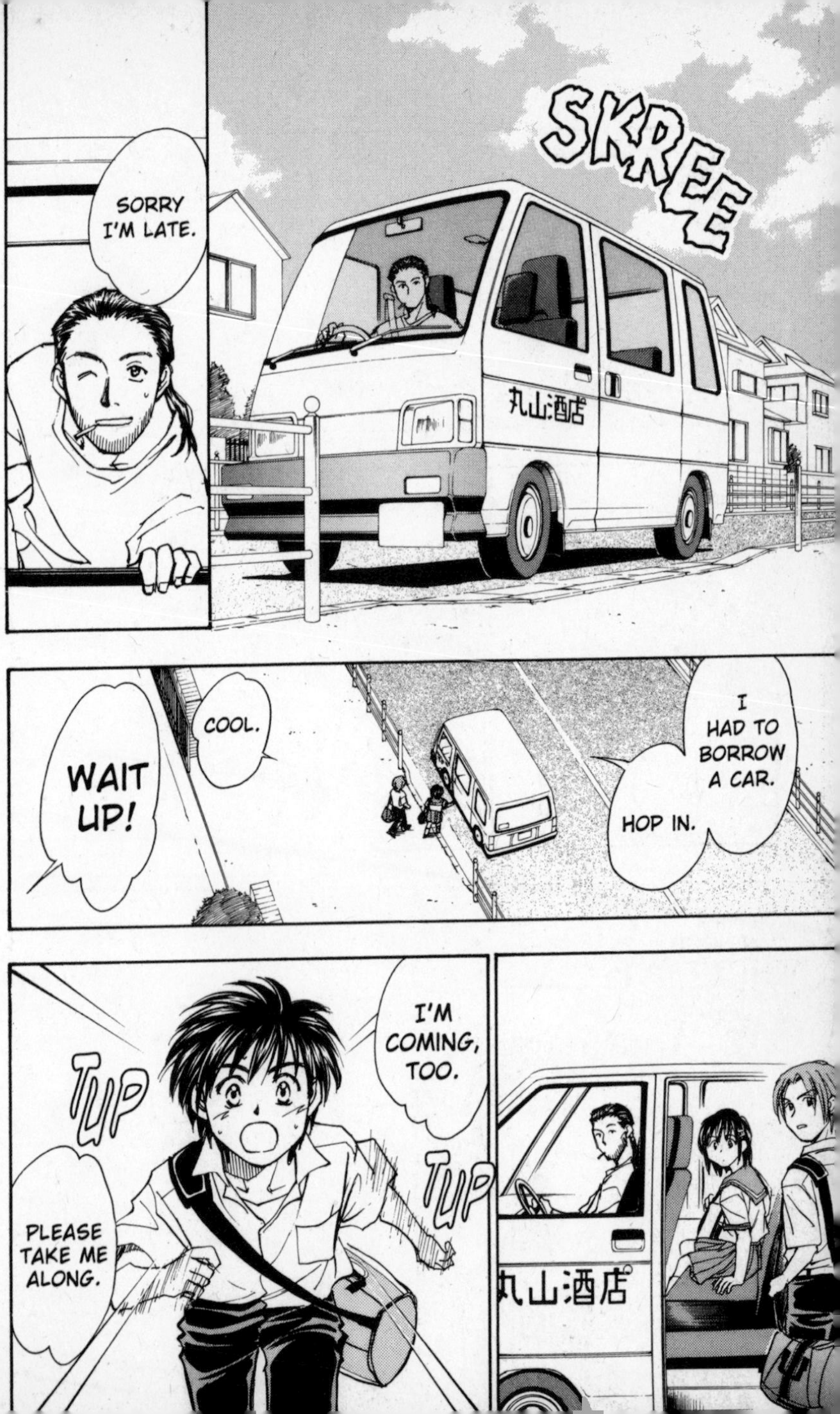
SKREE
丸山酒店
SORRY I'M LATE.
I HAD TO BORROW A CAR.
HOP IN.
COOL.
WAIT UP!
丸山酒店
I'M COMING, TOO.
TUP
TUP
PLEASE TAKE ME ALONG.

READ THIS WAY

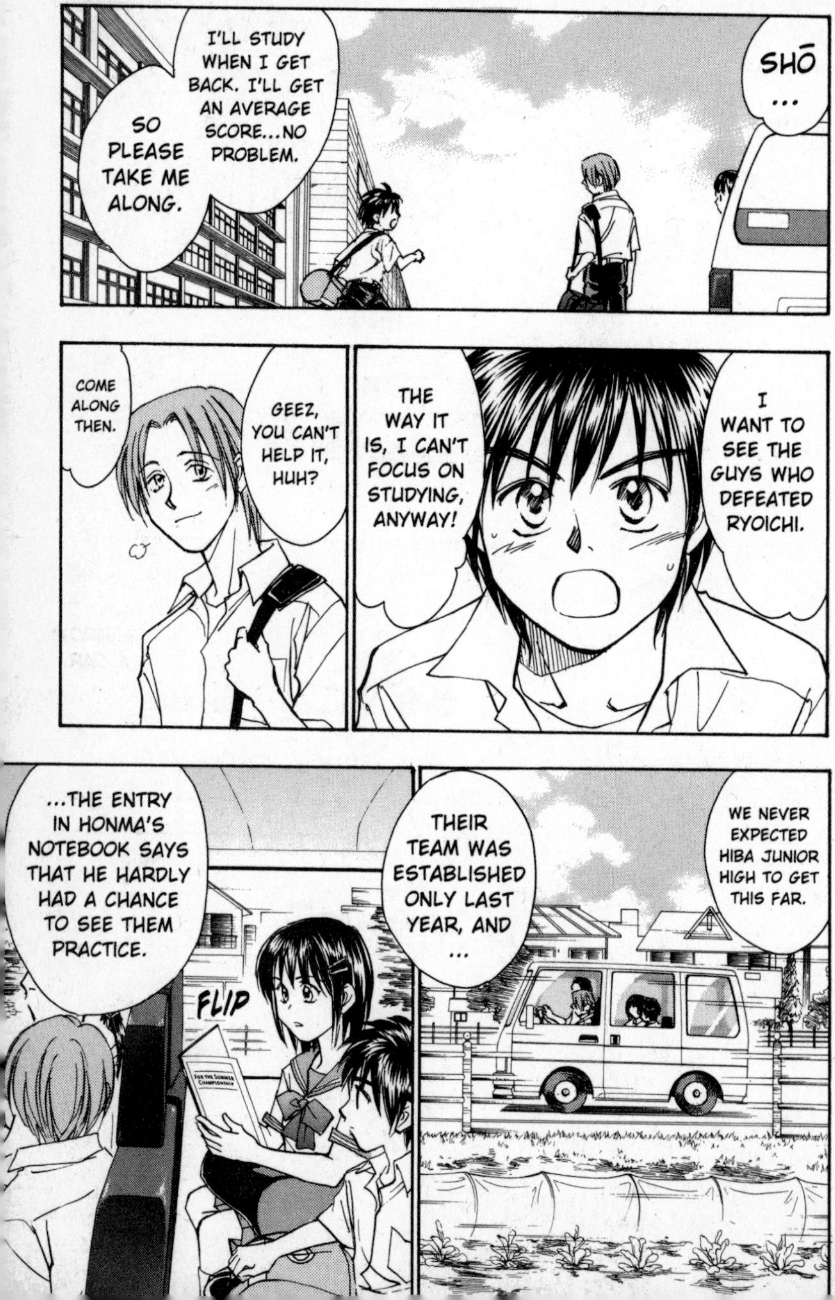
SHŌ ...
I'LL STUDY WHEN I GET BACK. I'LL GET AN AVERAGE SCORE...NO PROBLEM.
SO PLEASE TAKE ME ALONG.
I WANT TO SEE THE GUYS WHO DEFEATED RYOICHI.
THE WAY IT IS, I CAN'T FOCUS ON STUDYING, ANYWAY!
GEEZ, YOU CAN'T HELP IT, HUH?
COME ALONG THEN.
WE NEVER EXPECTED HIBA JUNIOR HIGH TO GET THIS FAR.
THEIR TEAM WAS ESTABLISHED ONLY LAST YEAR, AND ...
...THE ENTRY IN HONMA'S NOTEBOOK SAYS THAT HE HARDLY HAD A CHANCE TO SEE THEM PRACTICE.
FLIP
FOR THE SUMMER CHAMPIONSHIP

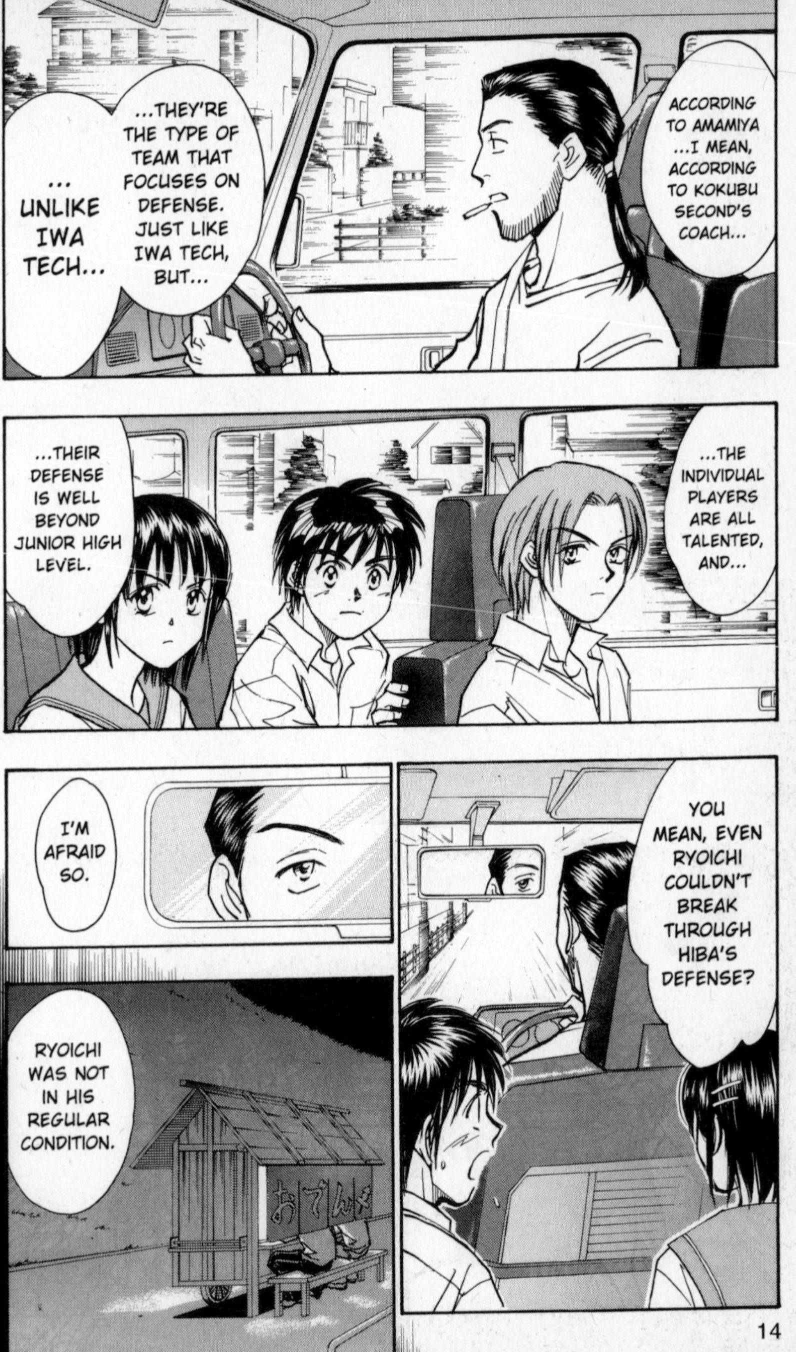
ACCORDING TO AMAMIYA ...I MEAN, ACCORDING TO KOKUBU SECOND'S COACH...
...THEY'RE THE TYPE OF TEAM THAT FOCUSES ON DEFENSE. JUST LIKE IWA TECH, BUT...
... UNLIKE IWA TECH...
...THE INDIVIDUAL PLAYERS ARE ALL TALENTED, AND...
...THEIR DEFENSE IS WELL BEYOND JUNIOR HIGH LEVEL.
YOU MEAN, EVEN RYOICHI COULDN'T BREAK THROUGH HIBA'S DEFENSE?
I'M AFRAID SO.
RYOICHI WAS NOT IN HIS REGULAR CONDITION.

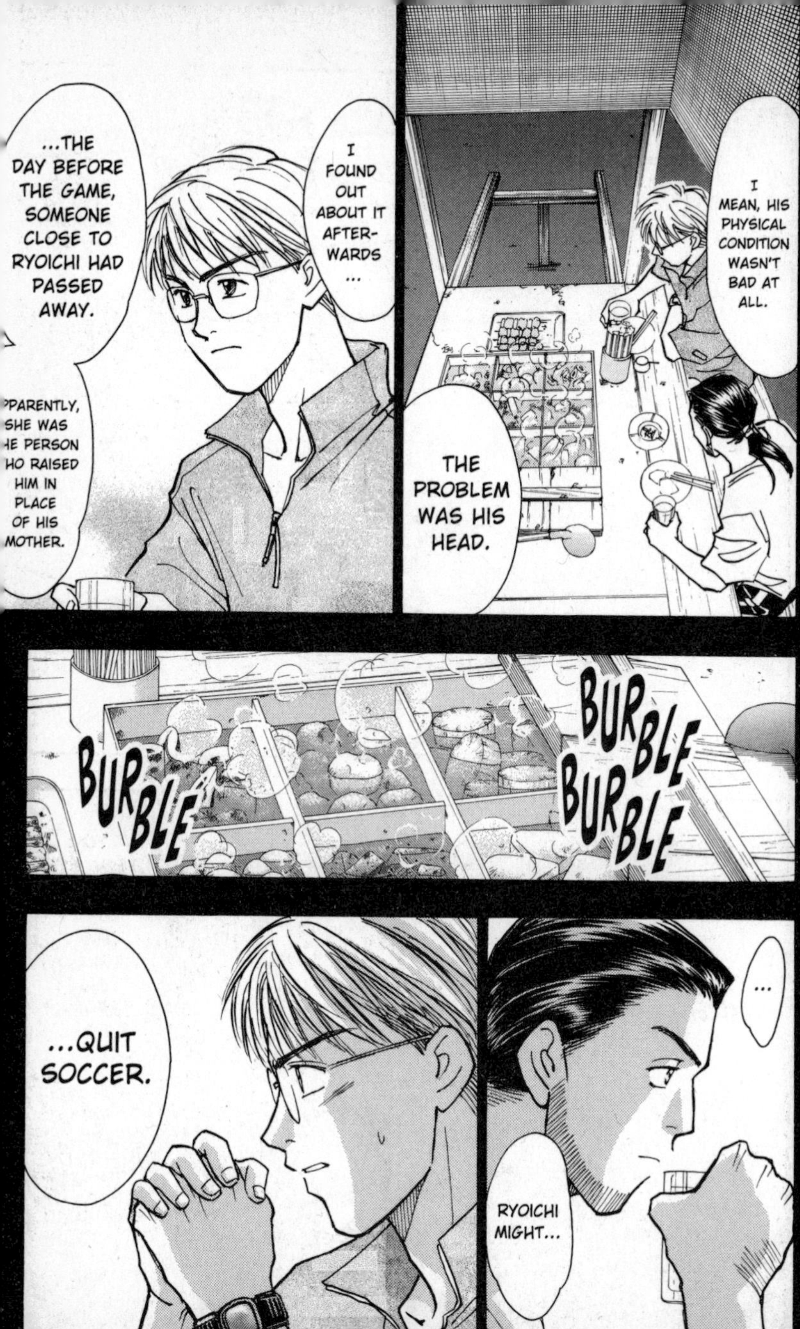
I MEAN, HIS PHYSICAL CONDITION WASN'T BAD AT ALL.
THE PROBLEM WAS HIS HEAD.
I FOUND OUT ABOUT IT AFTER-WARDS ...
...THE DAY BEFORE THE GAME, SOMEONE CLOSE TO RYOICHI HAD PASSED AWAY.
PPARENTLY, SHE WAS HE PERSON HO RAISED HIM IN PLACE OF HIS MOTHER.
BURBLE BURBLE
BURBLE
...
RYOICHI MIGHT...
...QUIT SOCCER.

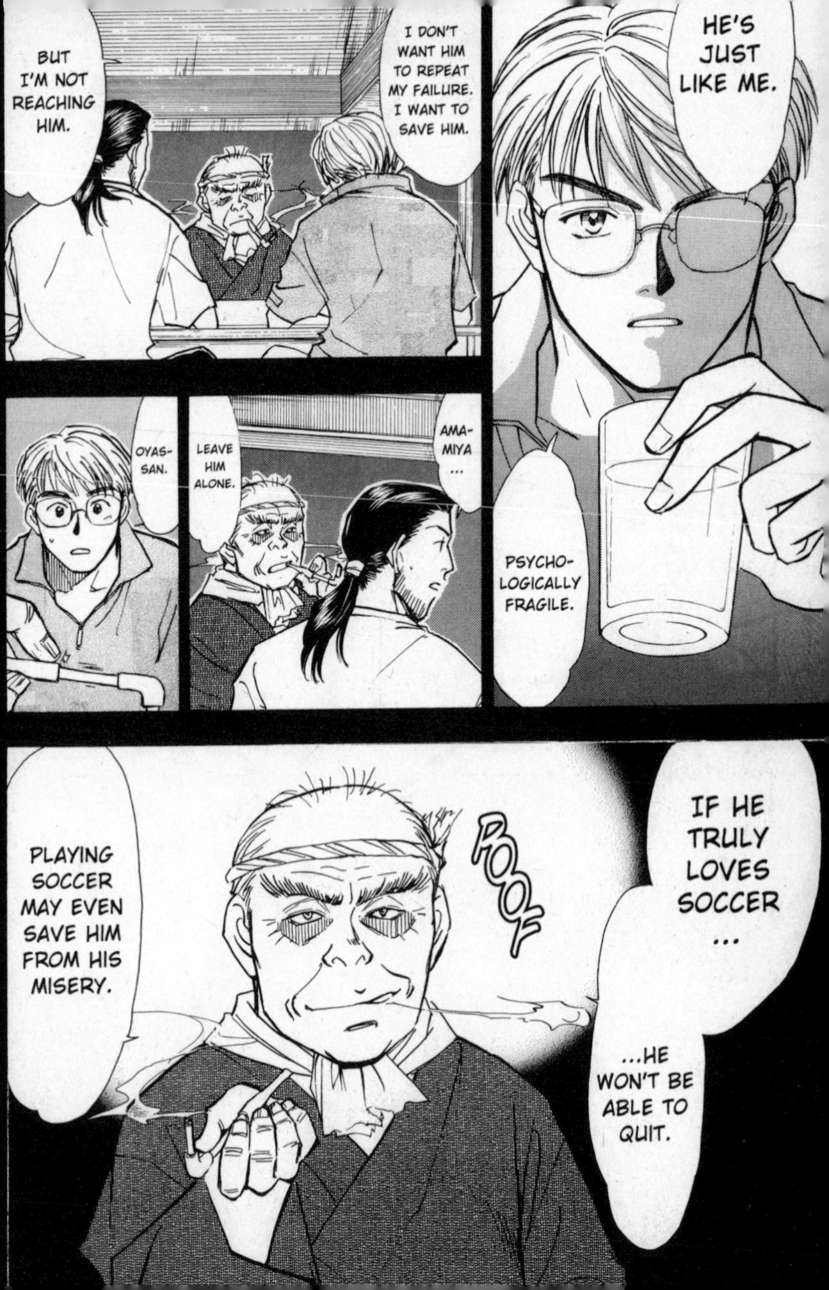
HE'S JUST LIKE ME.
PSYCHO-LOGICALLY FRAGILE.
I DON'T WANT HIM TO REPEAT MY FAILURE. I WANT TO SAVE HIM.
BUT I'M NOT REACHING HIM.
AMA-MIYA...
LEAVE HIM ALONE.
OYAS-SAN.
IF HE TRULY LOVES SOCCER...
...HE WON'T BE ABLE TO QUIT.
POOF
PLAYING SOCCER MAY EVEN SAVE HIM FROM HIS MISERY.

READ THIS WAY

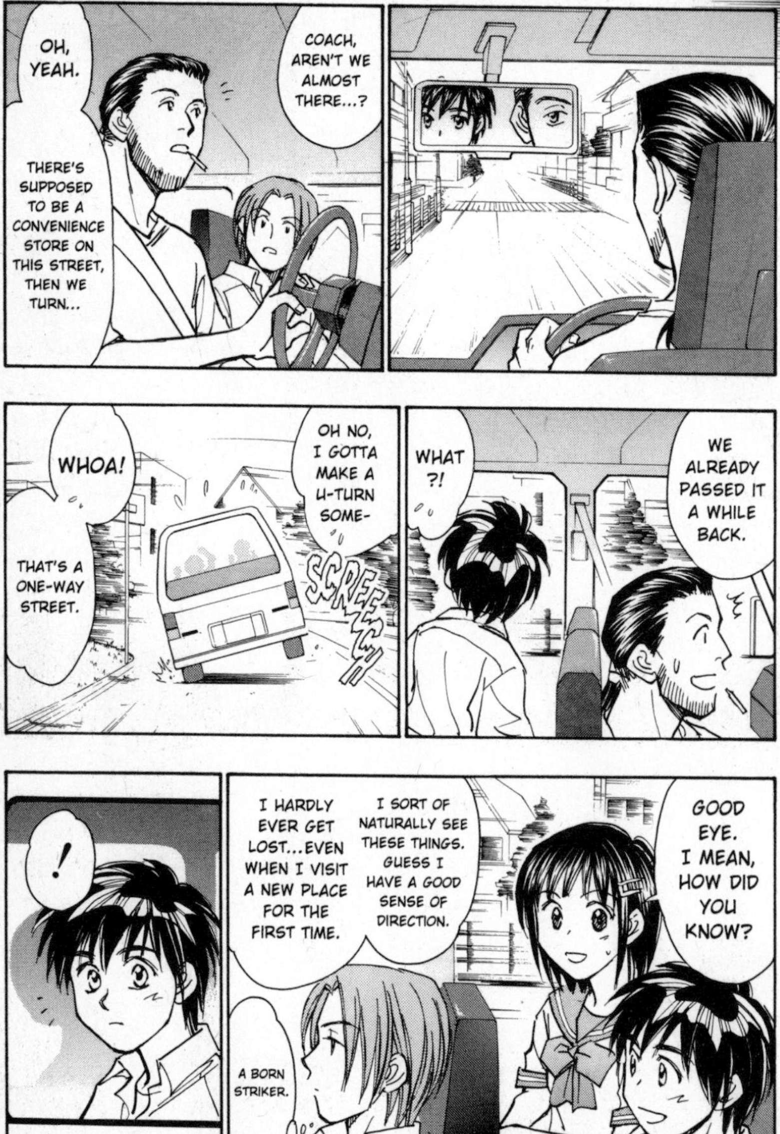
COACH, AREN'T WE ALMOST THERE...?
OH, YEAH.
THERE'S SUPPOSED TO BE A CONVENIENCE STORE ON THIS STREET, THEN WE TURN...
WE ALREADY PASSED IT A WHILE BACK.
WHAT?!
OH NO, I GOTTA MAKE A U-TURN SOME-
SCREEECH
WHOA!
THAT'S A ONE-WAY STREET.
GOOD EYE. I MEAN, HOW DID YOU KNOW?
I SORT OF NATURALLY SEE THESE THINGS. GUESS I HAVE A GOOD SENSE OF DIRECTION.
I HARDLY EVER GET LOST...EVEN WHEN I VISIT A NEW PLACE FOR THE FIRST TIME.
A BORN STRIKER.
!

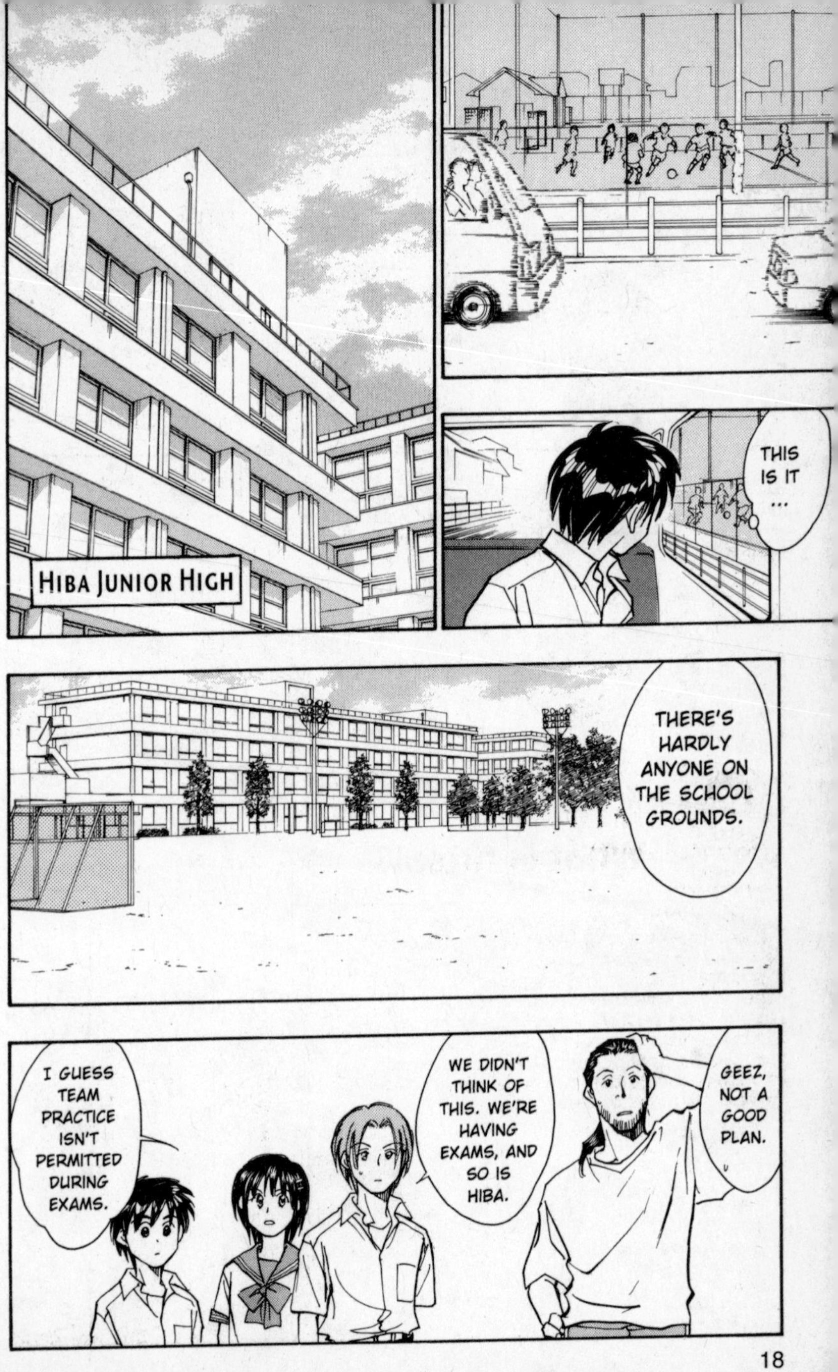
THIS IS IT ...
HIBA JUNIOR HIGH
THERE'S HARDLY ANYONE ON THE SCHOOL GROUNDS.
GEEZ, NOT A GOOD PLAN.
WE DIDN'T THINK OF THIS. WE'RE HAVING EXAMS, AND SO IS HIBA.
I GUESS TEAM PRACTICE ISN'T PERMITTED DURING EXAMS.

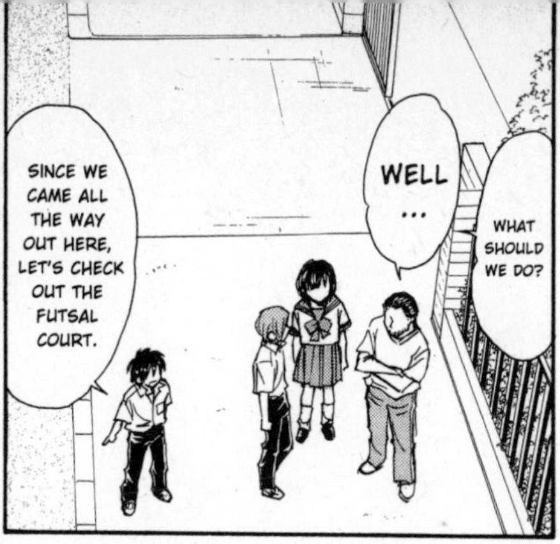
WELL ...
WHAT SHOULD WE DO?
SINCE WE CAME ALL THE WAY OUT HERE, LET'S CHECK OUT THE FUTSAL COURT.

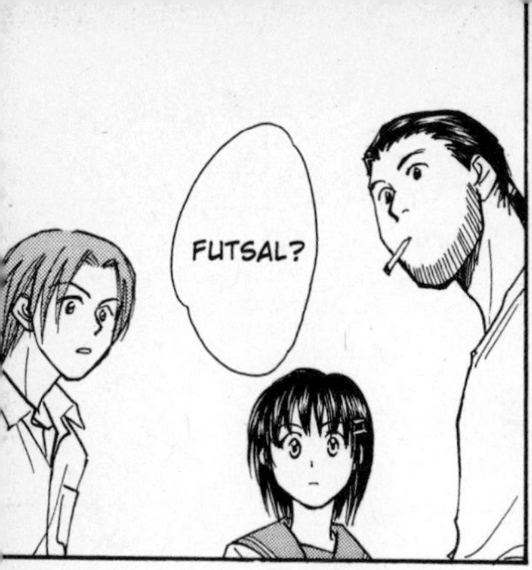
FUTSAL?

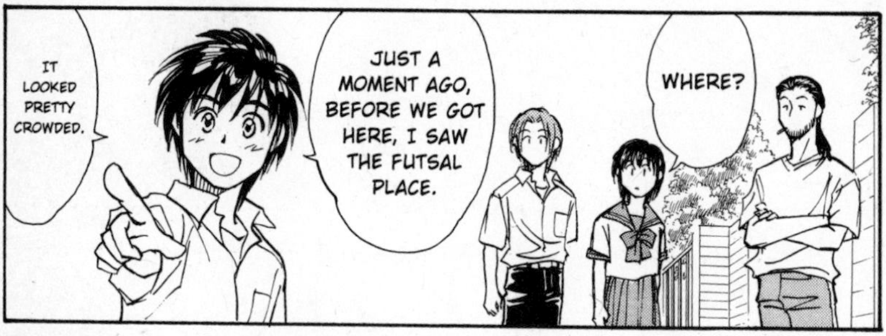
WHERE?
JUST A MOMENT AGO, BEFORE WE GOT HERE, I SAW THE FUTSAL PLACE.
IT LOOKED PRETTY CROWDED.

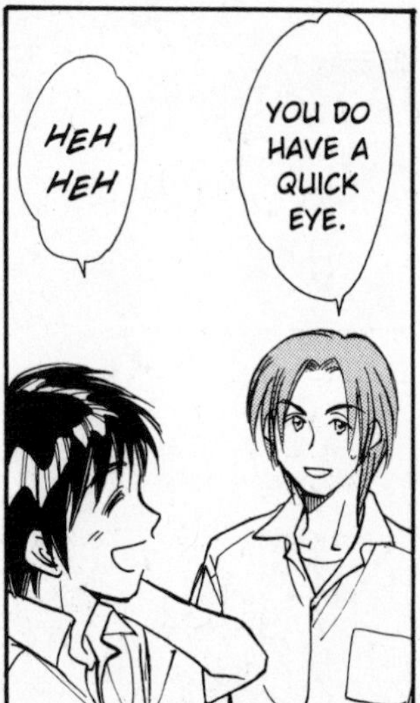
YOU DO HAVE A QUICK EYE.
HEH HEH

Tacchan's One Point Lesson

What is futsal?

SIMPLY PUT, IT'S A MINI SOCCER GAME PLAYED BY TEAMS OF FIVE, INCLUDING THE KEEPER. THE J-LEAGUE IS MAKING A BIG EFFORT TO PROMOTE THE SPORT. FOR INTERNATIONAL CHAMPIONSHIP PLAY, THE PITCH SIZE IS SET AT APPROXIMATELY 20 METERS BY 40 METERS. THE RULES ARE SOMEWHAT DIFFERENT FROM SOCCER: INSTEAD OF USING THROW-INS, FUTSAL USES KICK-INS, AND BOTH SLIDE TACKLING AND SHOULDER CHARGING ARE FORBIDDEN. THE BIGGEST DIFFERENCE IS THAT THERE IS NO OFFSIDES RULE.

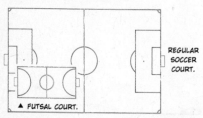

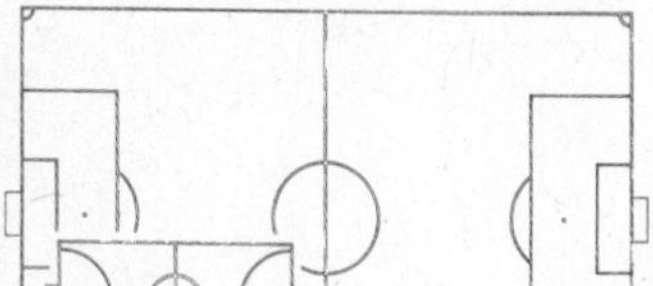
▲ FUTSAL COURT.

REGULAR SOCCER COURT.

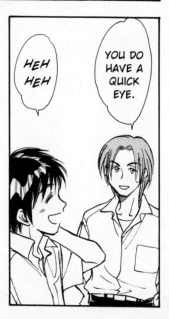

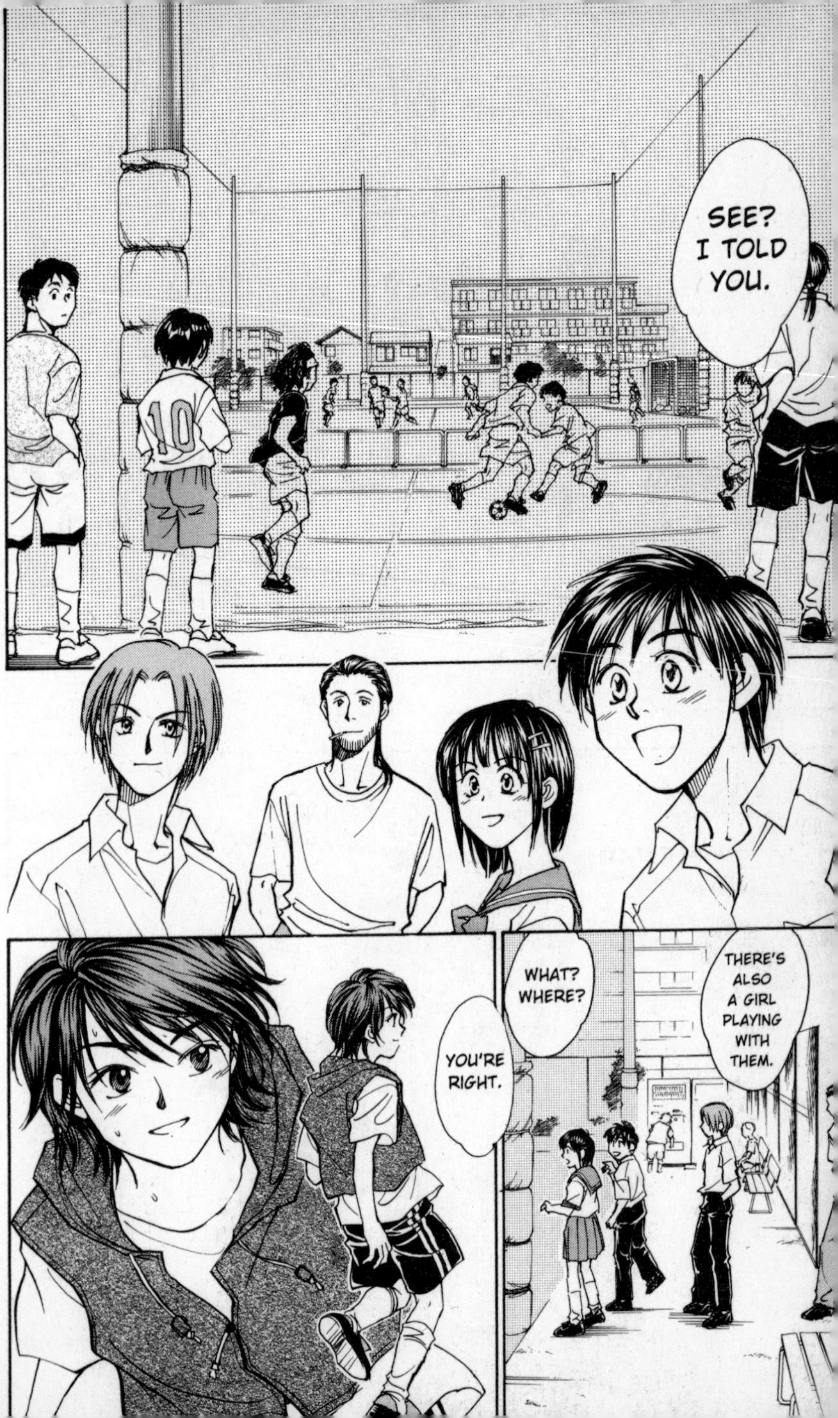
SEE? I TOLD YOU.
THERE'S ALSO A GIRL PLAYING WITH THEM.
WHAT? WHERE?
YOU'RE RIGHT.

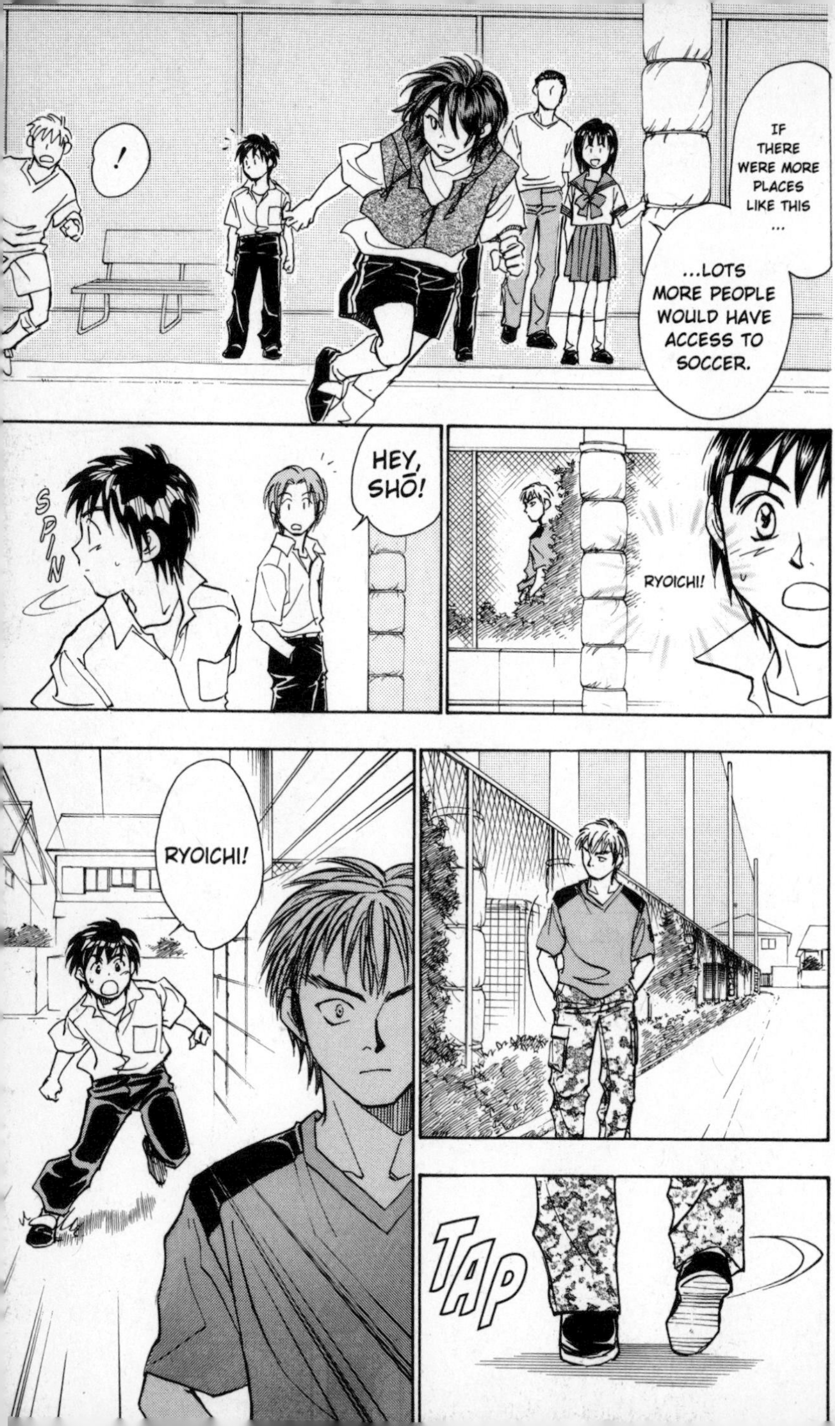
IF THERE WERE MORE PLACES LIKE THIS ...
...LOTS MORE PEOPLE WOULD HAVE ACCESS TO SOCCER.
!
RYOICHI!
HEY, SHŌ!
SPIN
TAP
RYOICHI!

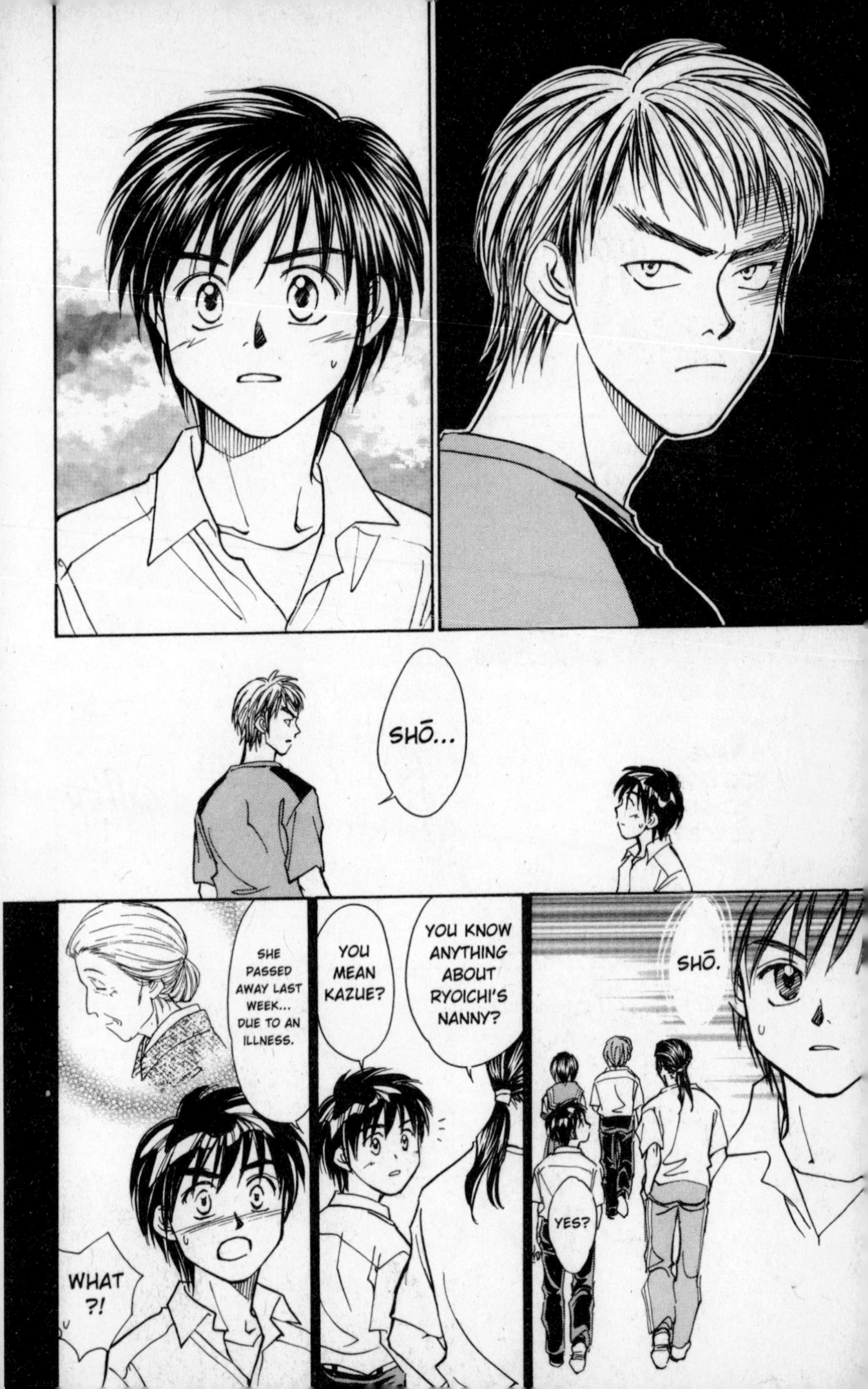
SHŌ...
SHŌ.
YES?
YOU KNOW ANYTHING ABOUT RYOICHI'S NANNY?
YOU MEAN KAZUE?
SHE PASSED AWAY LAST WEEK... DUE TO AN ILLNESS.
WHAT ?!

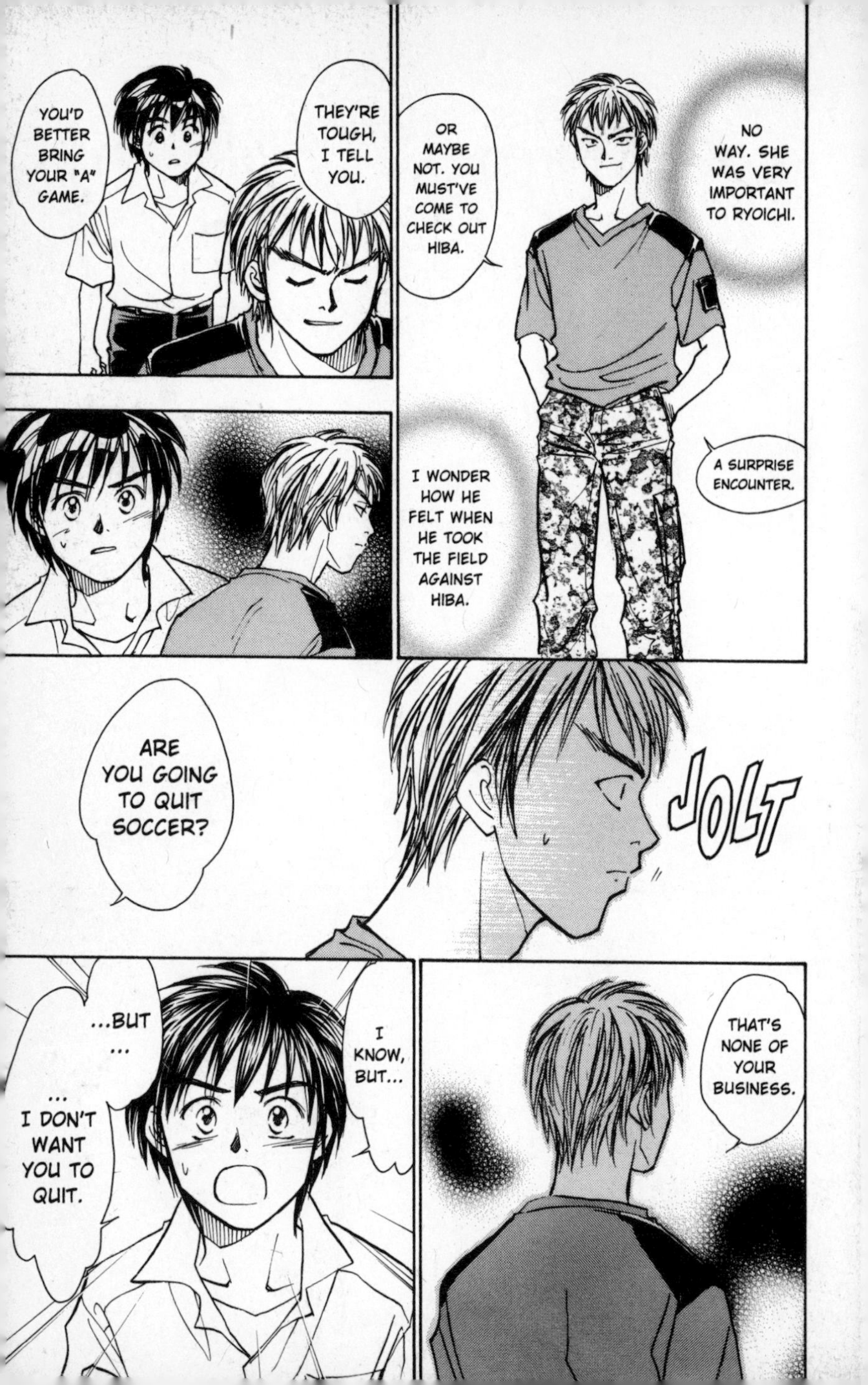
NO WAY. SHE WAS VERY IMPORTANT TO RYOICHI.
OR MAYBE NOT. YOU MUST'VE COME TO CHECK OUT HIBA.
A SURPRISE ENCOUNTER.
I WONDER HOW HE FELT WHEN HE TOOK THE FIELD AGAINST HIBA.
THEY'RE TOUGH, I TELL YOU.
YOU'D BETTER BRING YOUR "A" GAME.
JOLT
ARE YOU GOING TO QUIT SOCCER?
THAT'S NONE OF YOUR BUSINESS.
I KNOW, BUT...
...BUT ...
... I DON'T WANT YOU TO QUIT.

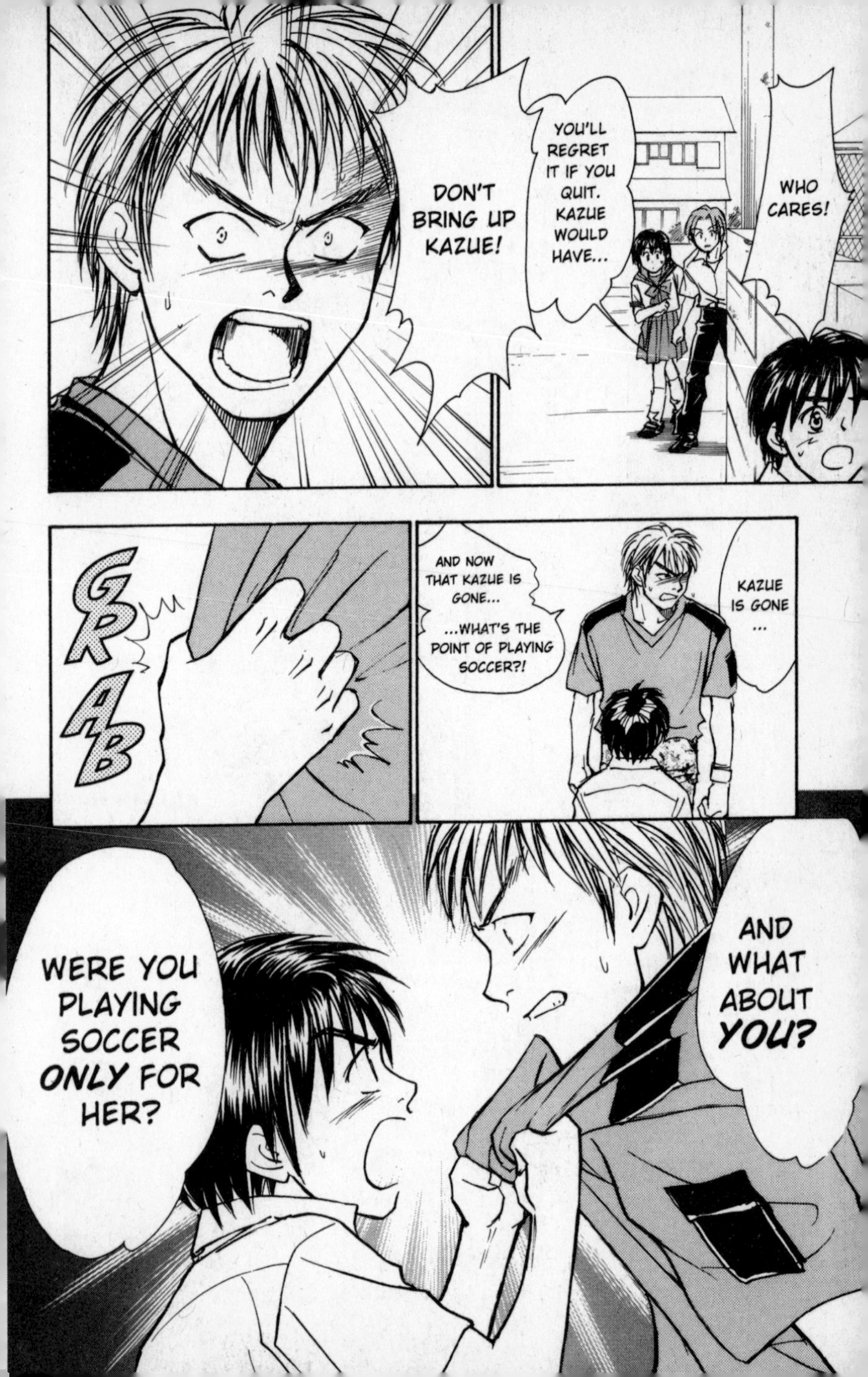
WHO CARES!
YOU'LL REGRET IT IF YOU QUIT. KAZUE WOULD HAVE...
DON'T BRING UP KAZUE!
KAZUE IS GONE ...
AND NOW THAT KAZUE IS GONE...
...WHAT'S THE POINT OF PLAYING SOCCER?!
GRAB
AND WHAT ABOUT YOU?
WERE YOU PLAYING SOCCER ONLY FOR HER?

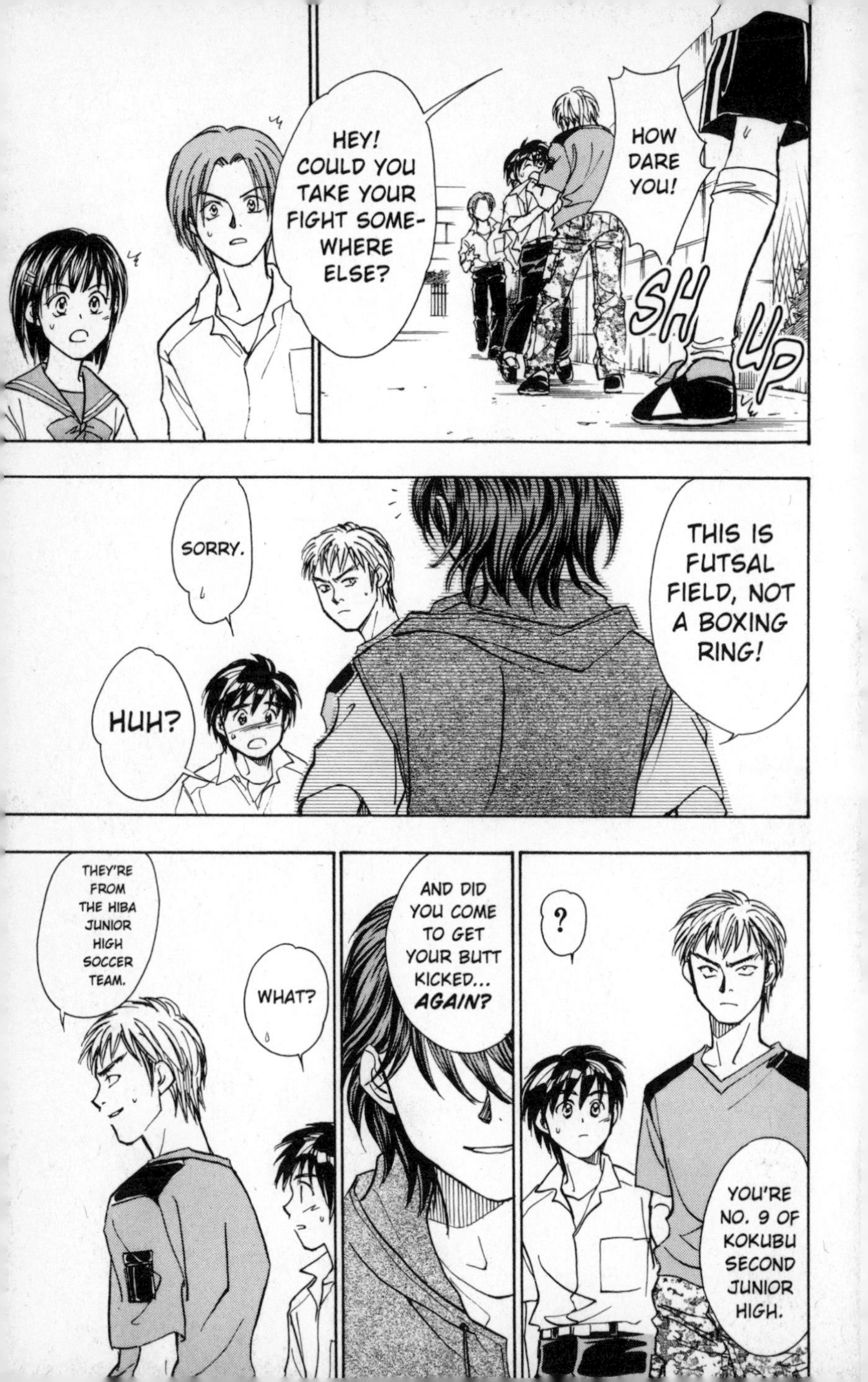
HOW DARE YOU!
SH UP
HEY! COULD YOU TAKE YOUR FIGHT SOME-WHERE ELSE?
THIS IS FUTSAL FIELD, NOT A BOXING RING!
SORRY.
HUH?
?
YOU'RE NO. 9 OF KOKUBU SECOND JUNIOR HIGH.
AND DID YOU COME TO GET YOUR BUTT KICKED... AGAIN?
WHAT?
THEY'RE FROM THE HIBA JUNIOR HIGH SOCCER TEAM.

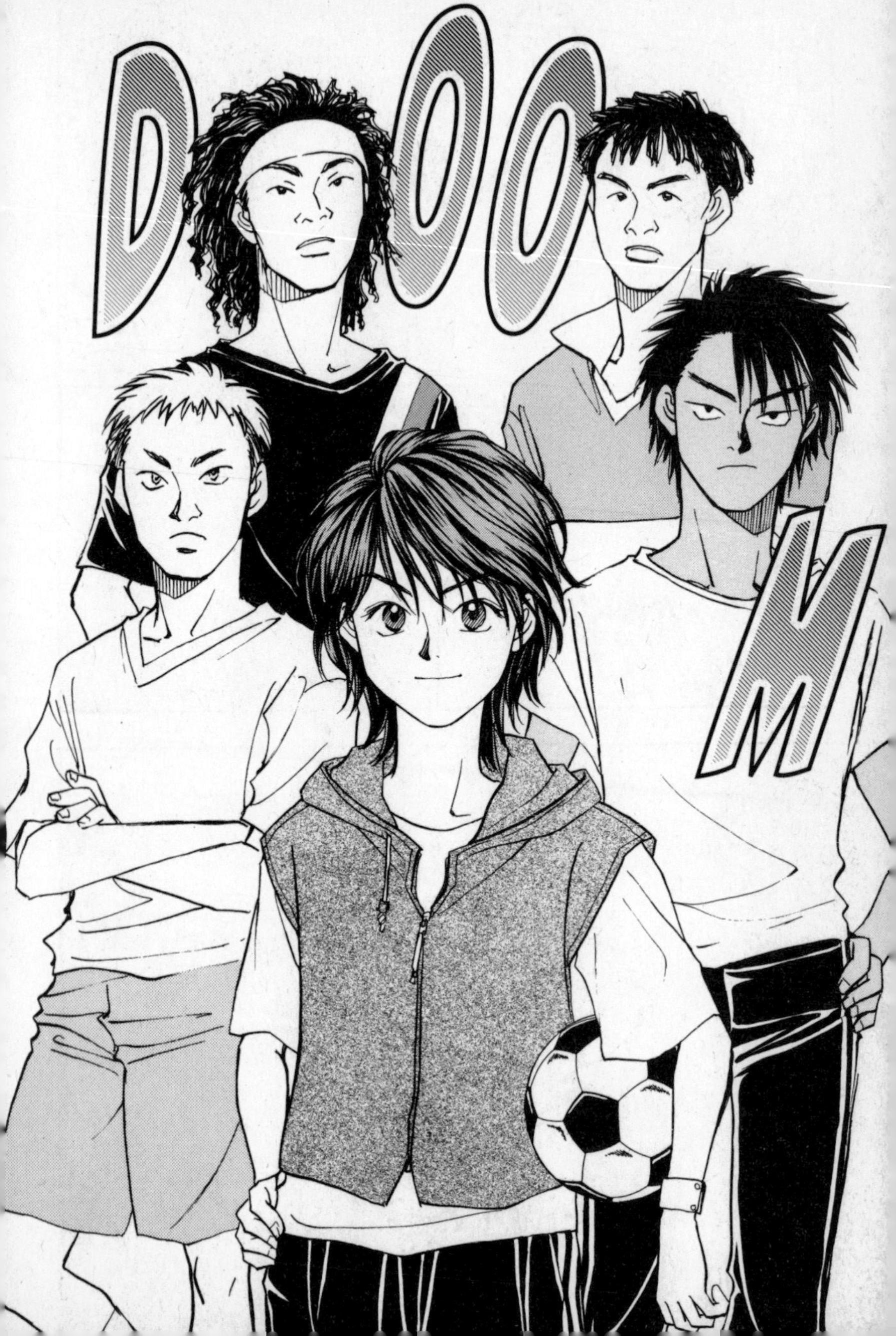
DOOOM

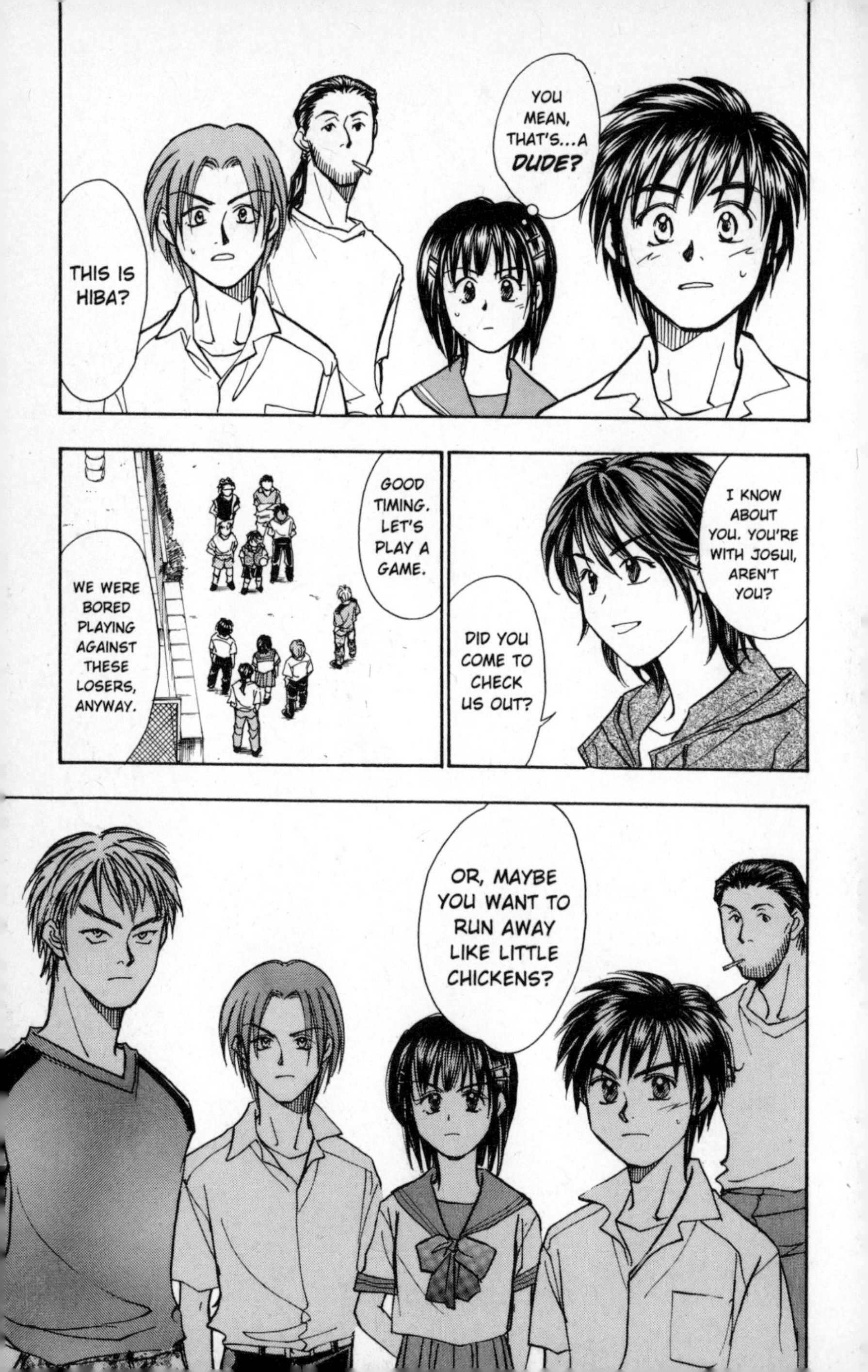
YOU MEAN, THAT'S...A **DUDE?**
THIS IS HIBA?
I KNOW ABOUT YOU. YOU'RE WITH JOSUI, AREN'T YOU?
DID YOU COME TO CHECK US OUT?
GOOD TIMING. LET'S PLAY A GAME.
WE WERE BORED PLAYING AGAINST THESE LOSERS, ANYWAY.
OR, MAYBE YOU WANT TO RUN AWAY LIKE LITTLE CHICKENS?

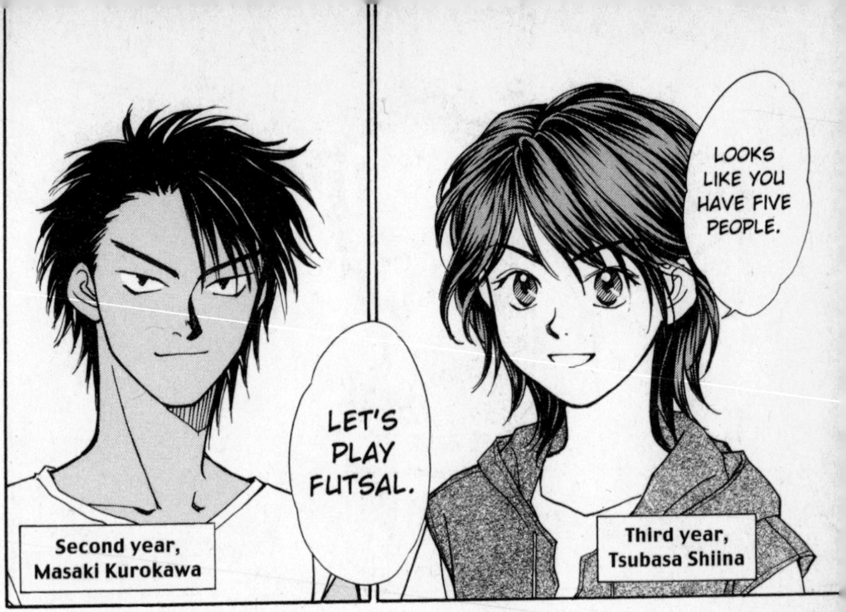
LOOKS LIKE YOU HAVE FIVE PEOPLE.
Third year, Tsubasa Shiina
LET'S PLAY FUTSAL.
Second year, Masaki Kurokawa

We Do? How Will It End?

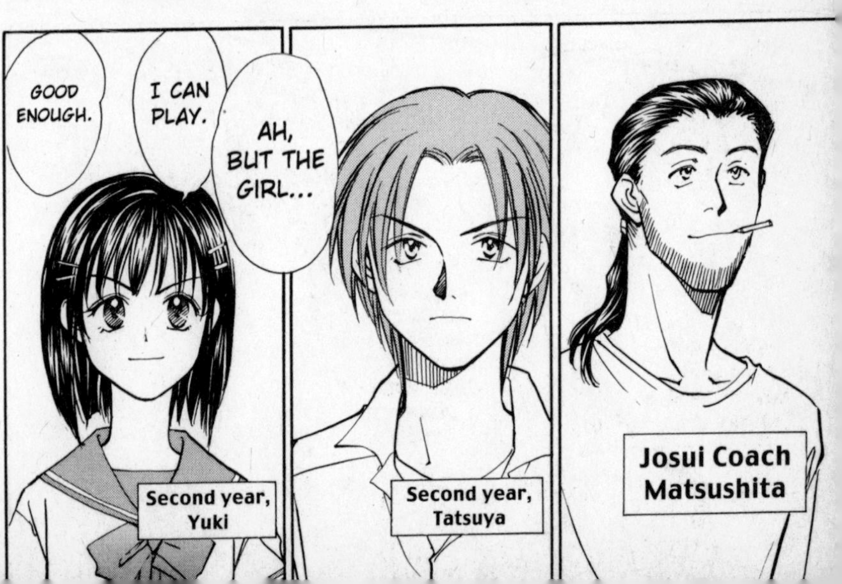
Josui Coach Matsushita
AH, BUT THE GIRL...
Second year, Tatsuya
I CAN PLAY.
GOOD ENOUGH.
Second year, Yuki

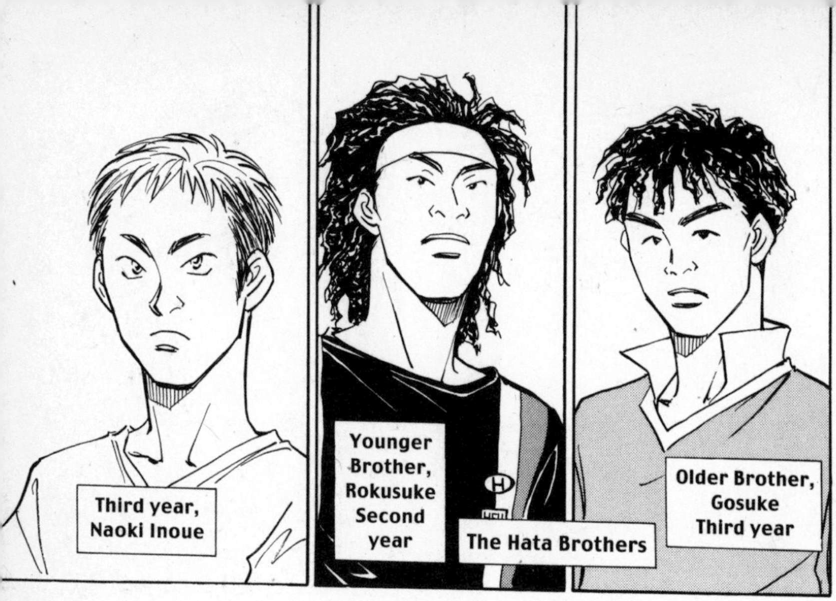
Older Brother, Gosuke Third year
The Hata Brothers
Younger Brother, Rokusuke Second year
Third year, Naoki Inoue

STAGE.82 What Should

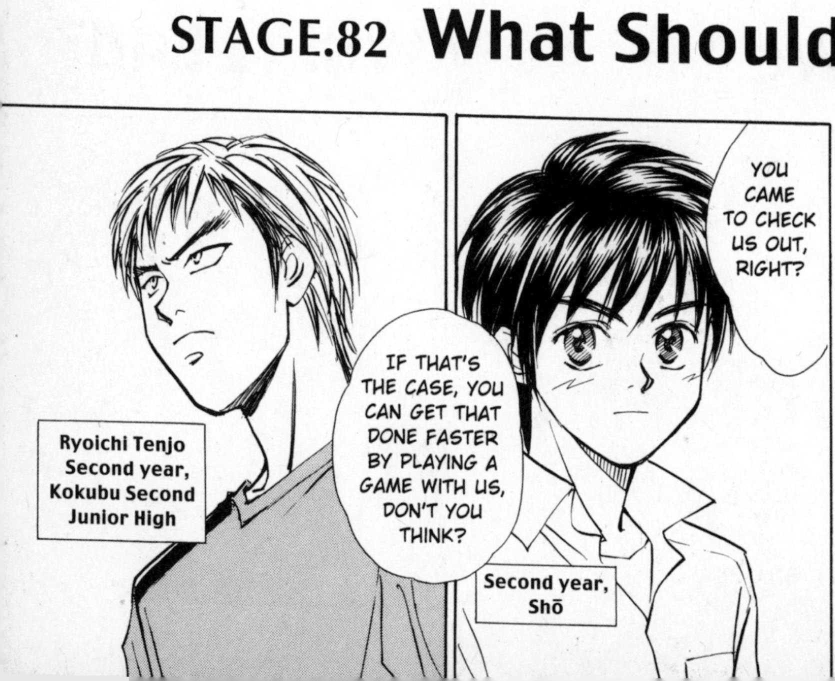
YOU CAME TO CHECK US OUT, RIGHT?
IF THAT'S THE CASE, YOU CAN GET THAT DONE FASTER BY PLAYING A GAME WITH US, DON'T YOU THINK?
Second year, Shō
Ryoichi Tenjo Second year, Kokubu Second Junior High

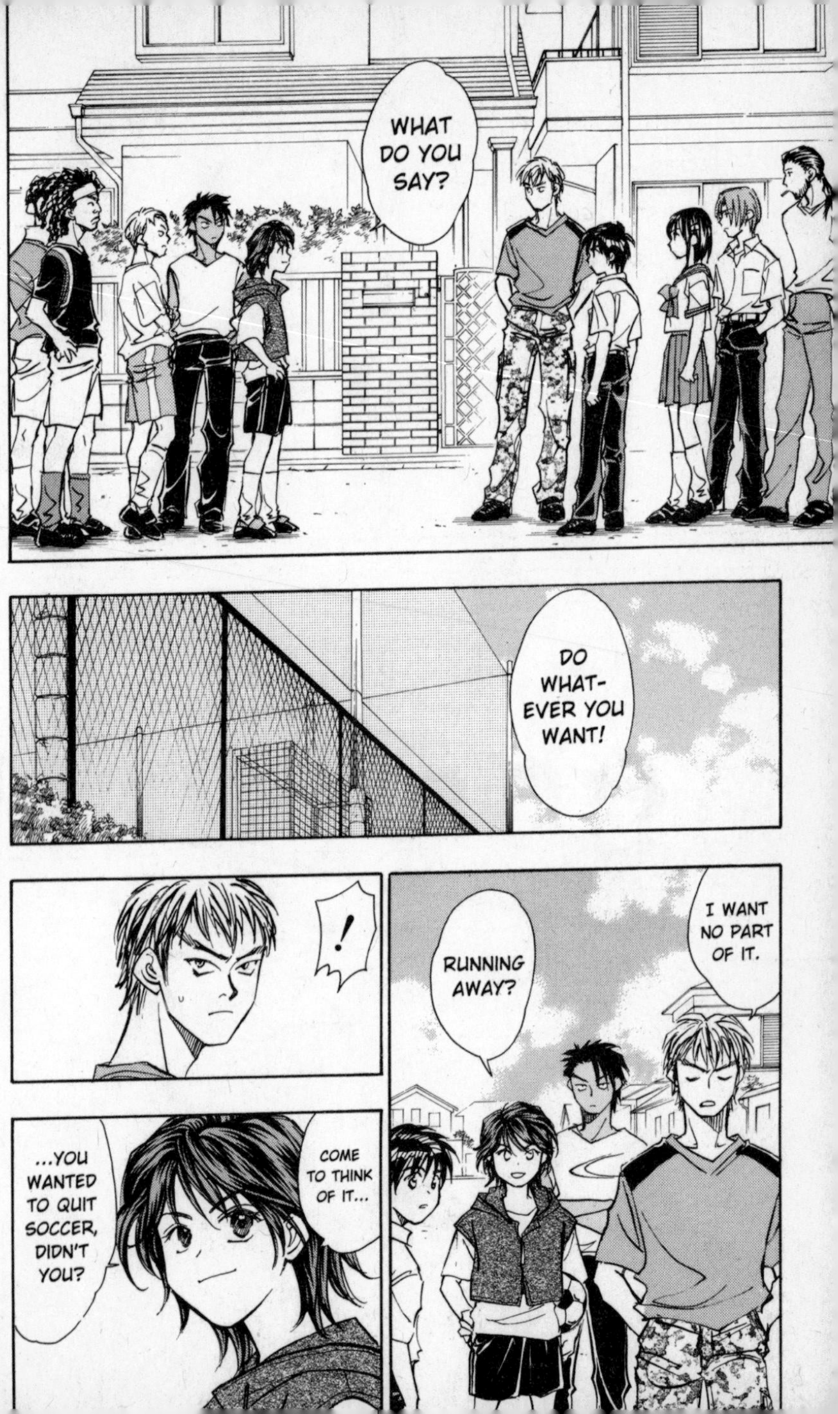
WHAT DO YOU SAY?
DO WHAT-EVER YOU WANT!
I WANT NO PART OF IT.
RUNNING AWAY?
!
COME TO THINK OF IT...
...YOU WANTED TO QUIT SOCCER, DIDN'T YOU?

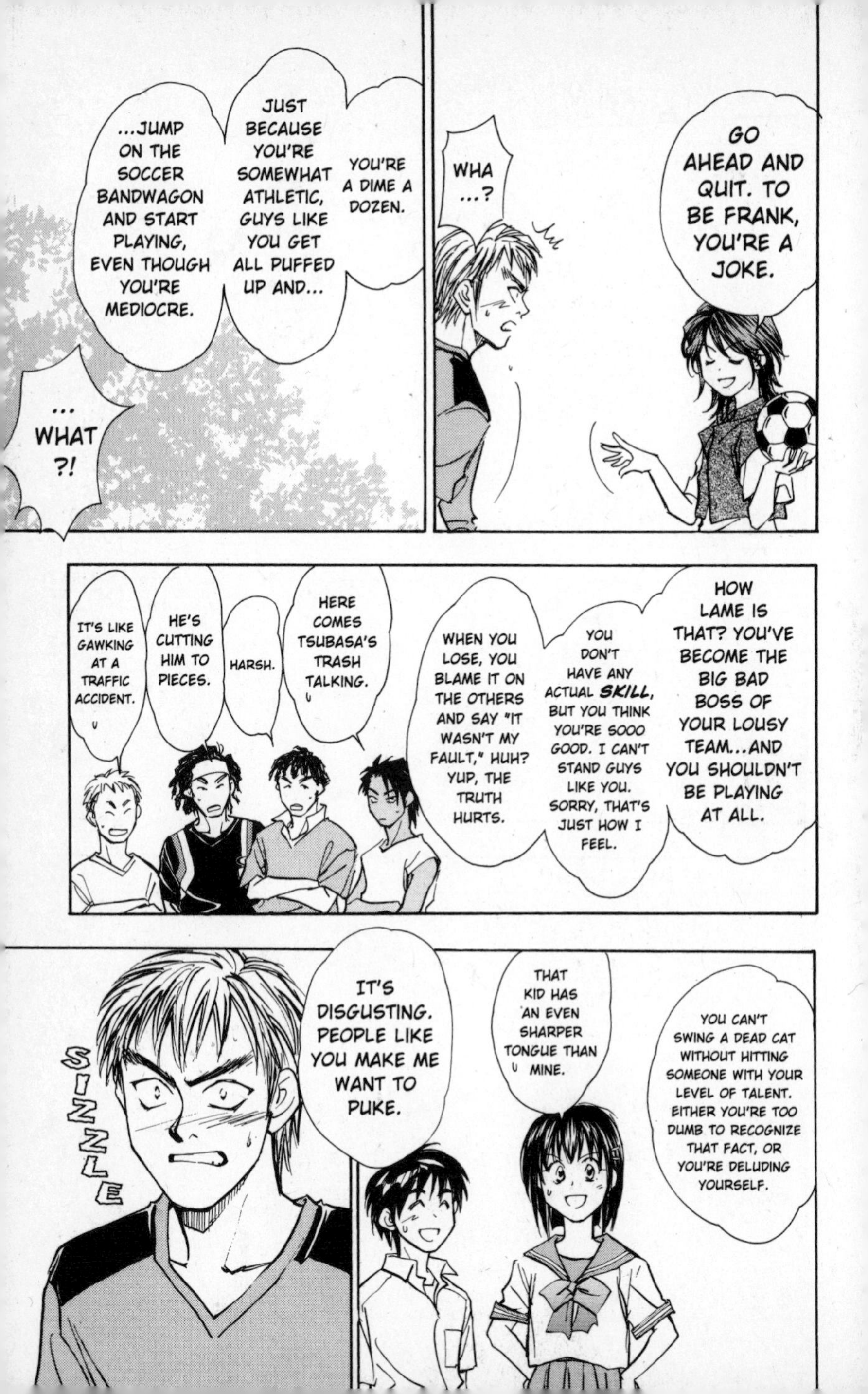
GO AHEAD AND QUIT. TO BE FRANK, YOU'RE A JOKE.
WHA ...?
YOU'RE A DIME A DOZEN.
JUST BECAUSE YOU'RE SOMEWHAT ATHLETIC, GUYS LIKE YOU GET ALL PUFFED UP AND...
...JUMP ON THE SOCCER BANDWAGON AND START PLAYING, EVEN THOUGH YOU'RE MEDIOCRE.
... WHAT?!
HOW LAME IS THAT? YOU'VE BECOME THE BIG BAD BOSS OF YOUR LOUSY TEAM...AND YOU SHOULDN'T BE PLAYING AT ALL.
YOU DON'T HAVE ANY ACTUAL SKILL, BUT YOU THINK YOU'RE SOOO GOOD. I CAN'T STAND GUYS LIKE YOU. SORRY, THAT'S JUST HOW I FEEL.
WHEN YOU LOSE, YOU BLAME IT ON THE OTHERS AND SAY "IT WASN'T MY FAULT," HUH? YUP, THE TRUTH HURTS.
HERE COMES TSUBASA'S TRASH TALKING.
HARSH.
HE'S CUTTING HIM TO PIECES.
IT'S LIKE GAWKING AT A TRAFFIC ACCIDENT.
YOU CAN'T SWING A DEAD CAT WITHOUT HITTING SOMEONE WITH YOUR LEVEL OF TALENT. EITHER YOU'RE TOO DUMB TO RECOGNIZE THAT FACT, OR YOU'RE DELUDING YOURSELF.
THAT KID HAS AN EVEN SHARPER TONGUE THAN MINE.
IT'S DISGUSTING. PEOPLE LIKE YOU MAKE ME WANT TO PUKE.
SIZZLE

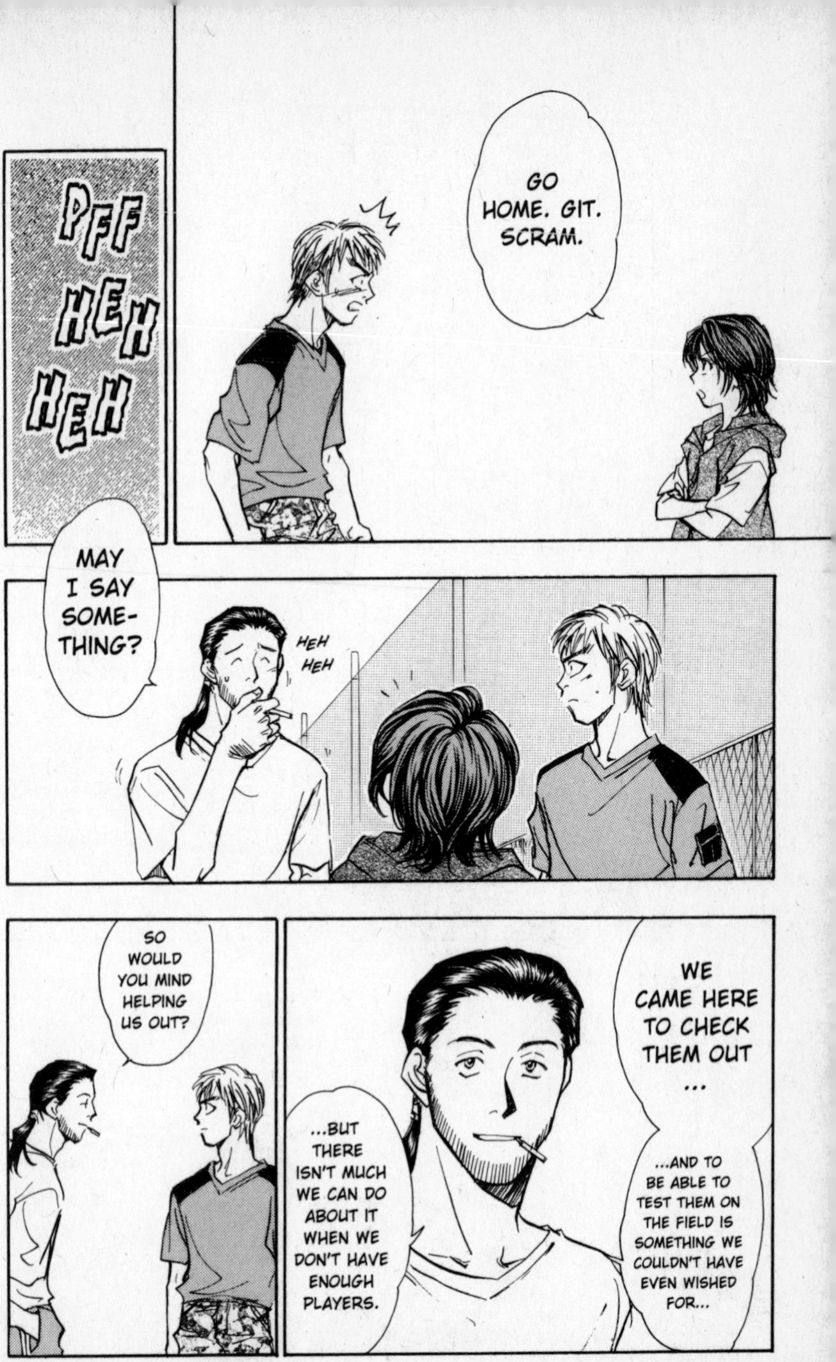
GO HOME. GIT. SCRAM.
PFF HEH HEH
MAY I SAY SOME- THING?
HEH HEH
WE CAME HERE TO CHECK THEM OUT ...
...BUT THERE ISN'T MUCH WE CAN DO ABOUT IT WHEN WE DON'T HAVE ENOUGH PLAYERS.
...AND TO BE ABLE TO TEST THEM ON THE FIELD IS SOMETHING WE COULDN'T HAVE EVEN WISHED FOR...
SO WOULD YOU MIND HELPING US OUT?

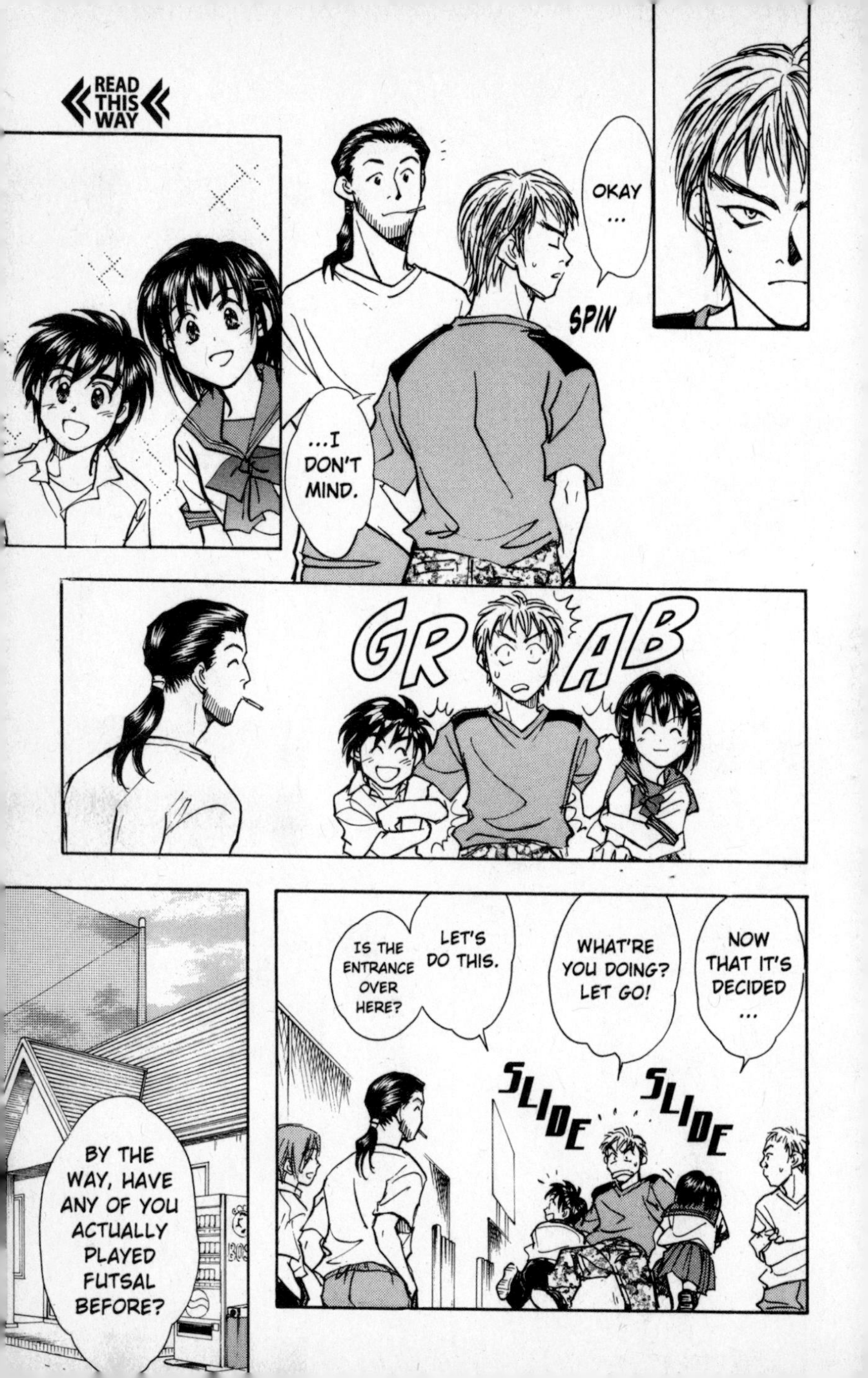
READ THIS WAY
OKAY ...
SPIN
...I DON'T MIND.
GRAB
NOW THAT IT'S DECIDED ...
WHAT'RE YOU DOING? LET GO!
SLIDE
SLIDE
LET'S DO THIS.
IS THE ENTRANCE OVER HERE?
BY THE WAY, HAVE ANY OF YOU ACTUALLY PLAYED FUTSAL BEFORE?

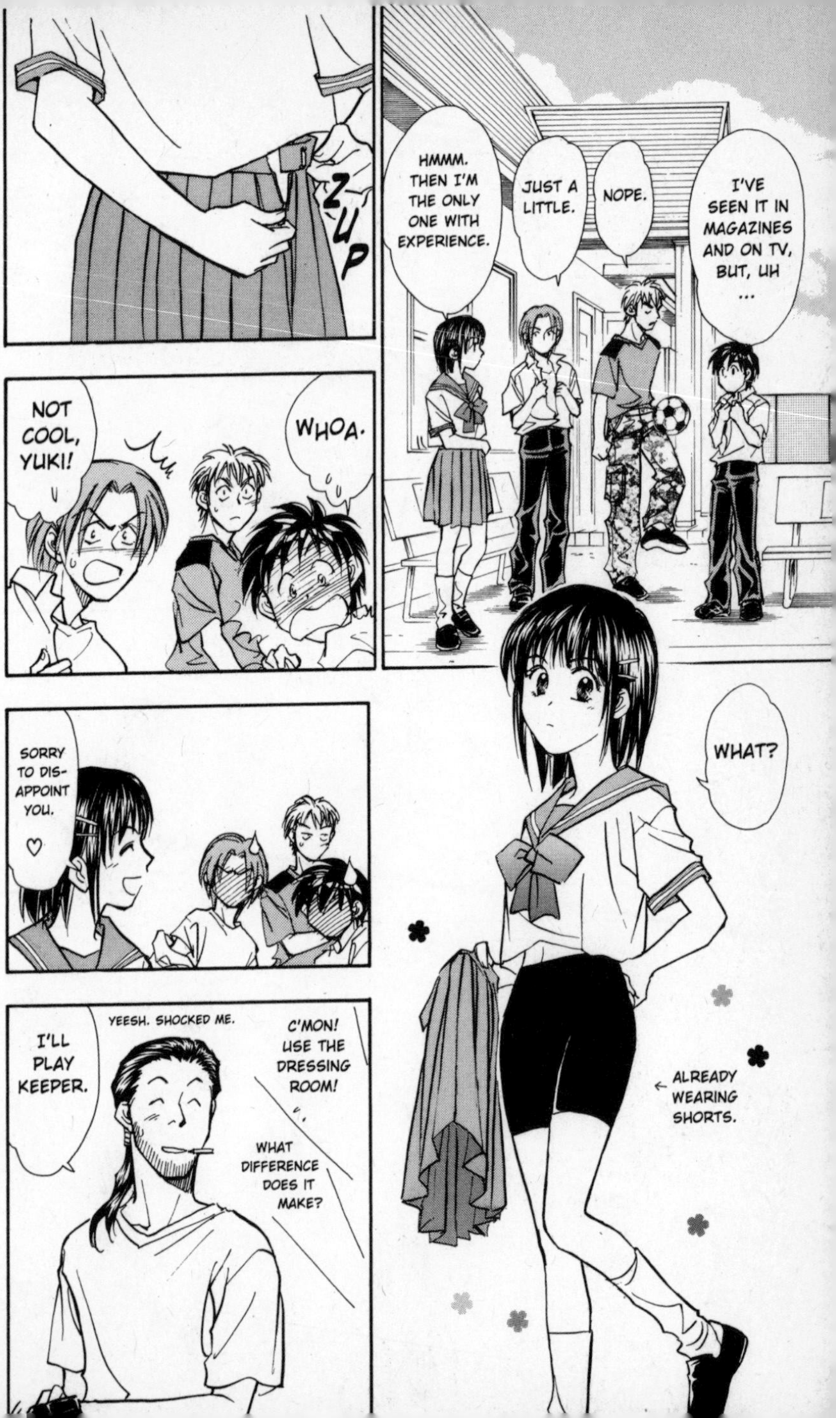
I'VE SEEN IT IN MAGAZINES AND ON TV, BUT, UH ...
NOPE.
JUST A LITTLE.
HMMM. THEN I'M THE ONLY ONE WITH EXPERIENCE.
ZUP
WHOA.
NOT COOL, YUKI!
WHAT?
ALREADY WEARING SHORTS.
SORRY TO DIS-APPOINT YOU. ♡
C'MON! USE THE DRESSING ROOM!
YEESH. SHOCKED ME.
WHAT DIFFERENCE DOES IT MAKE?
I'LL PLAY KEEPER.

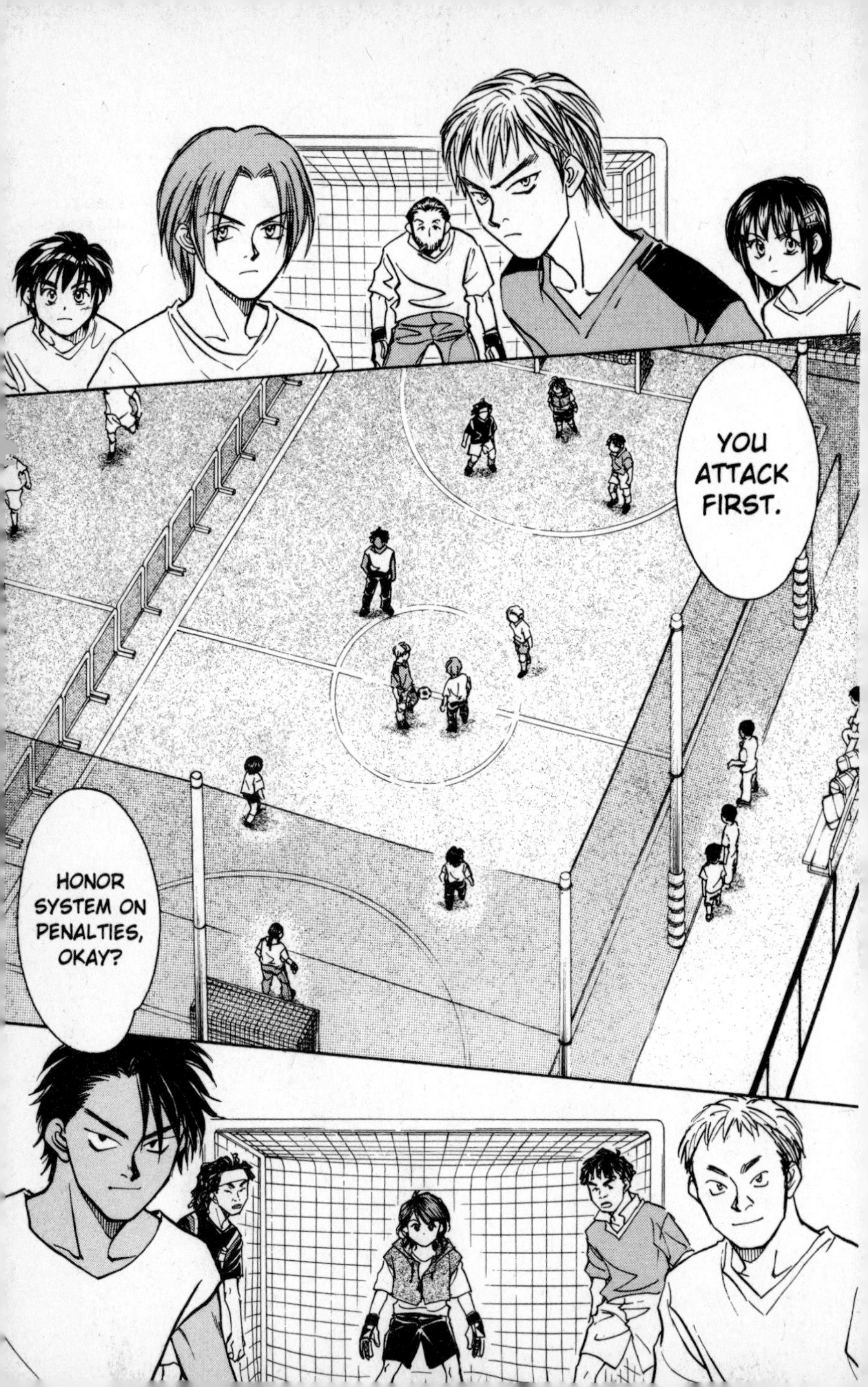
YOU ATTACK FIRST.
HONOR SYSTEM ON PENALTIES, OKAY?

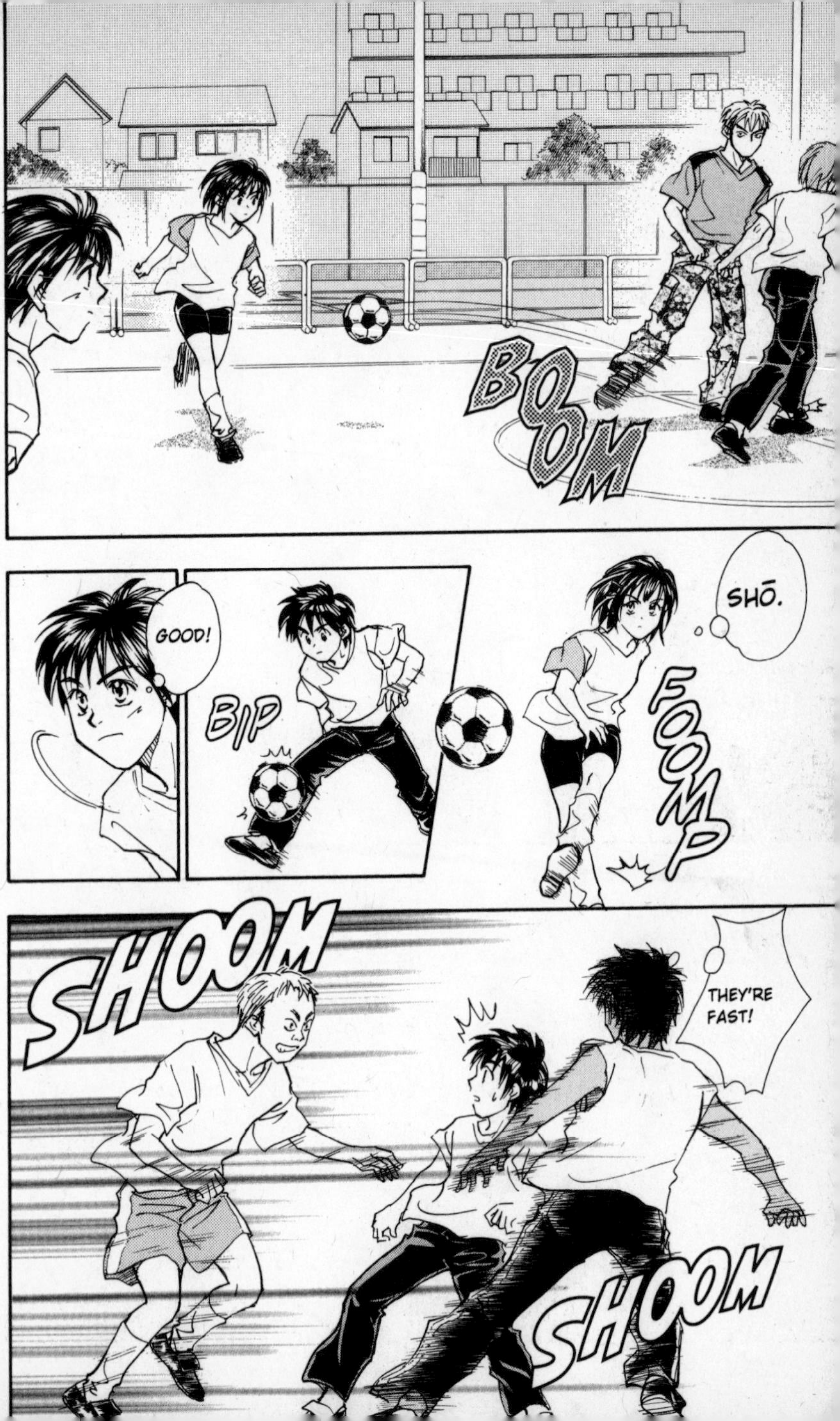
BOOM
SHŌ.
FOOMP
BIP
GOOD!
THEY'RE FAST!
SHOOM
SHOOM

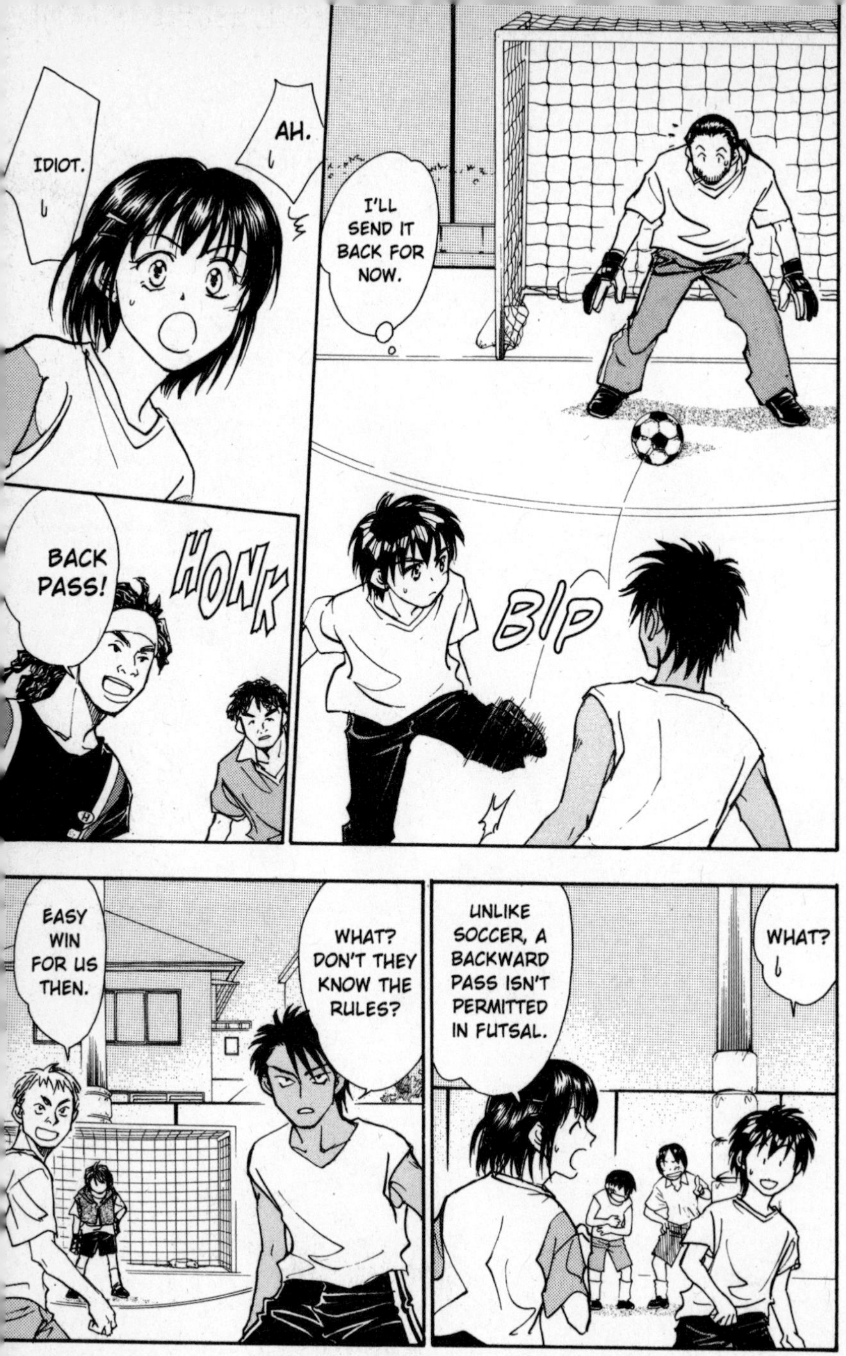
I'LL SEND IT BACK FOR NOW.
BIP
AH.
IDIOT.
HONK
BACK PASS!
WHAT?
UNLIKE SOCCER, A BACKWARD PASS ISN'T PERMITTED IN FUTSAL.
WHAT? DON'T THEY KNOW THE RULES?
EASY WIN FOR US THEN.

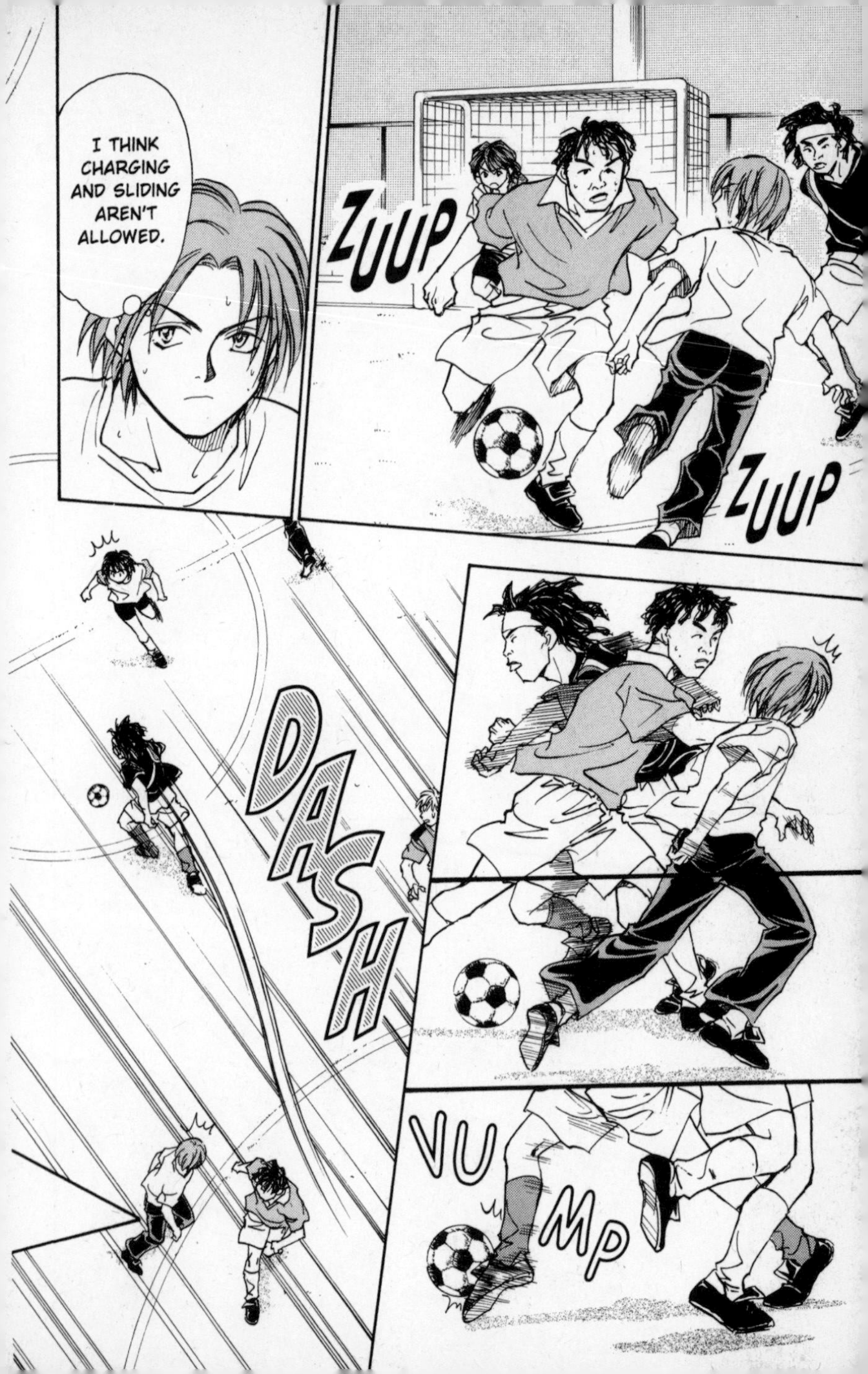
ZUUP
ZUUP
I THINK CHARGING AND SLIDING AREN'T ALLOWED.
VU MP
DASH

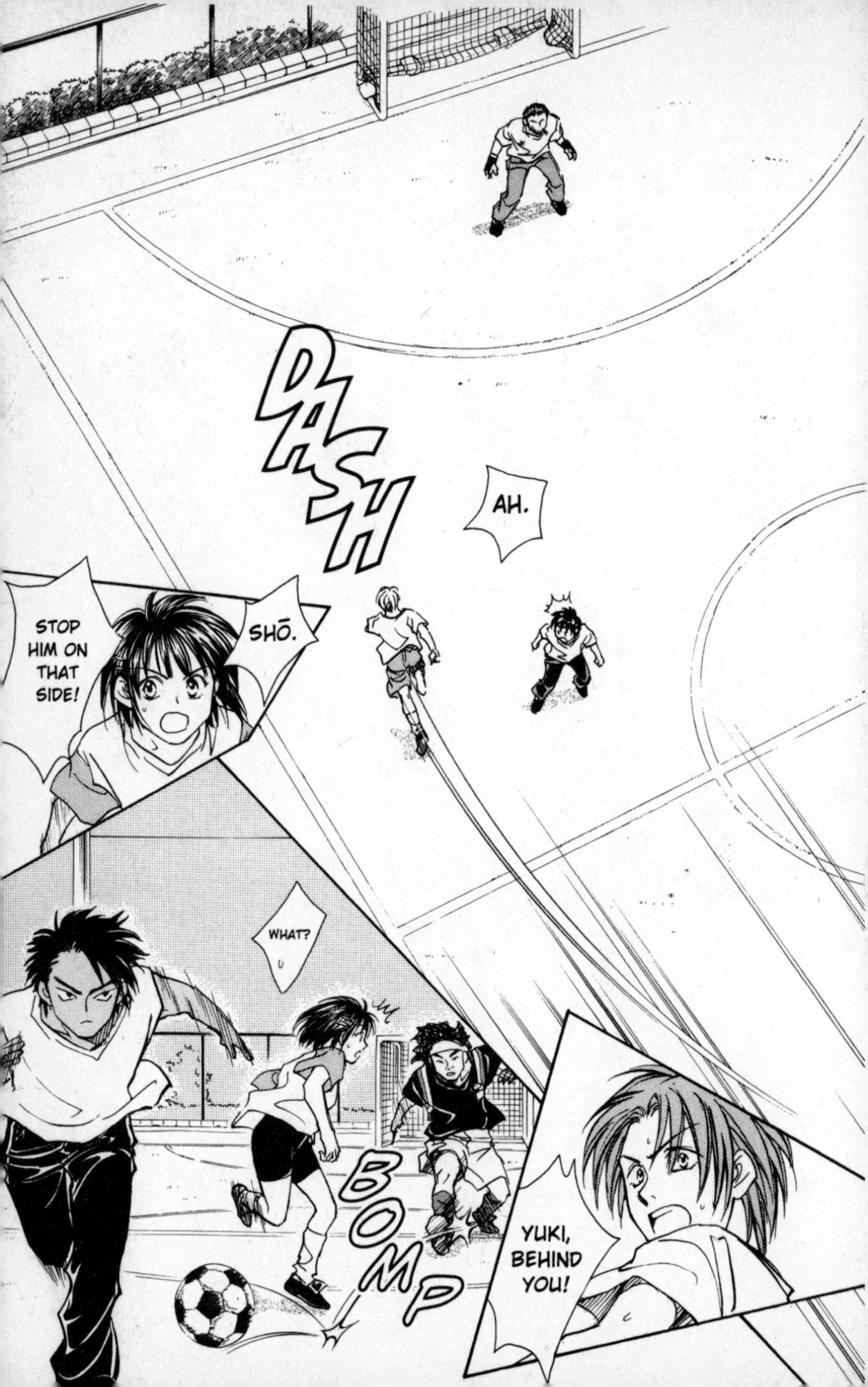
DASH
AH.
SHŌ.
STOP HIM ON THAT SIDE!
YUKI, BEHIND YOU!
WHAT?
BOMP

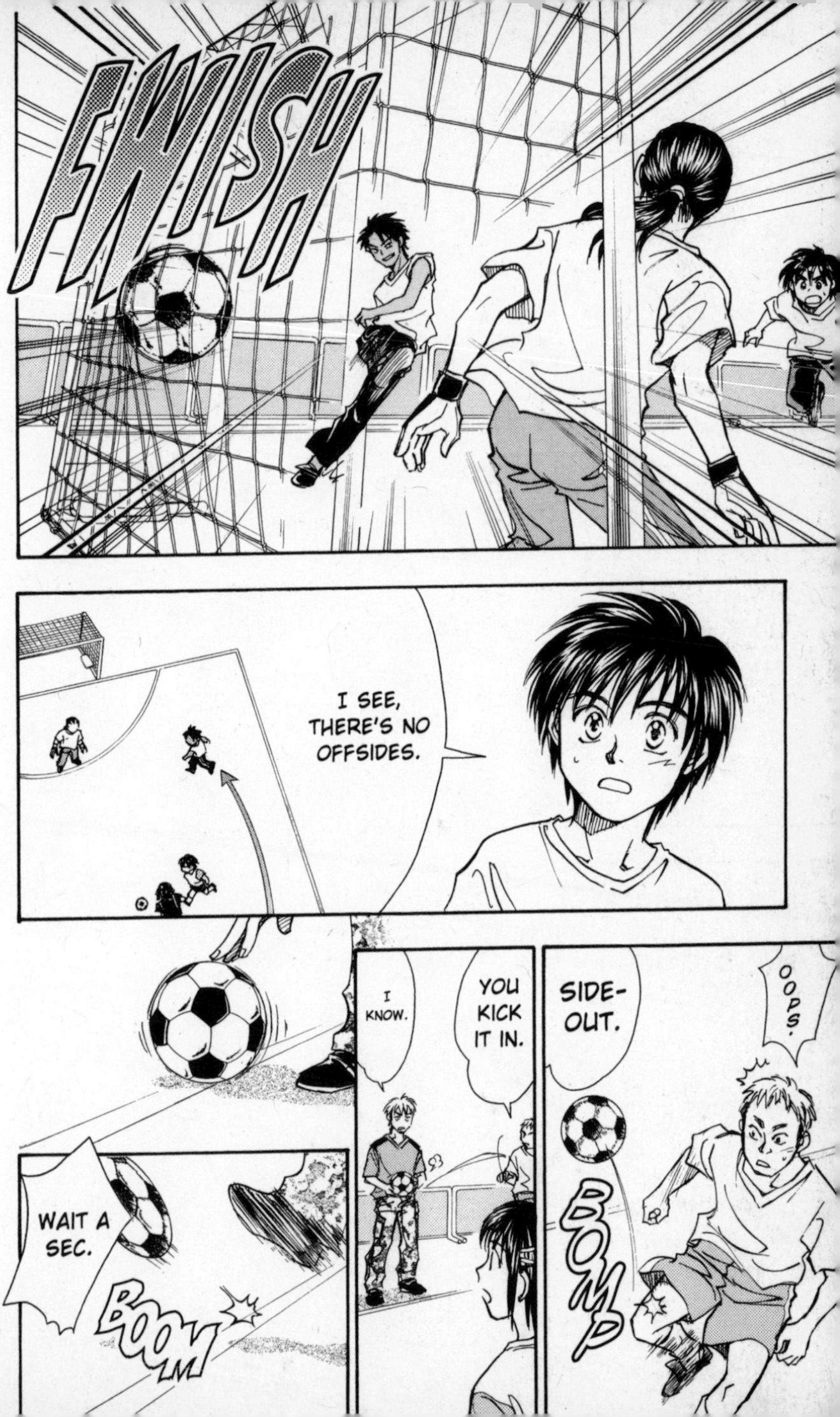
FWISH
I SEE, THERE'S NO OFFSIDES.
OOPS.
SIDE-OUT.
BOMP
YOU KICK IT IN.
I KNOW.
WAIT A SEC.
BOOM

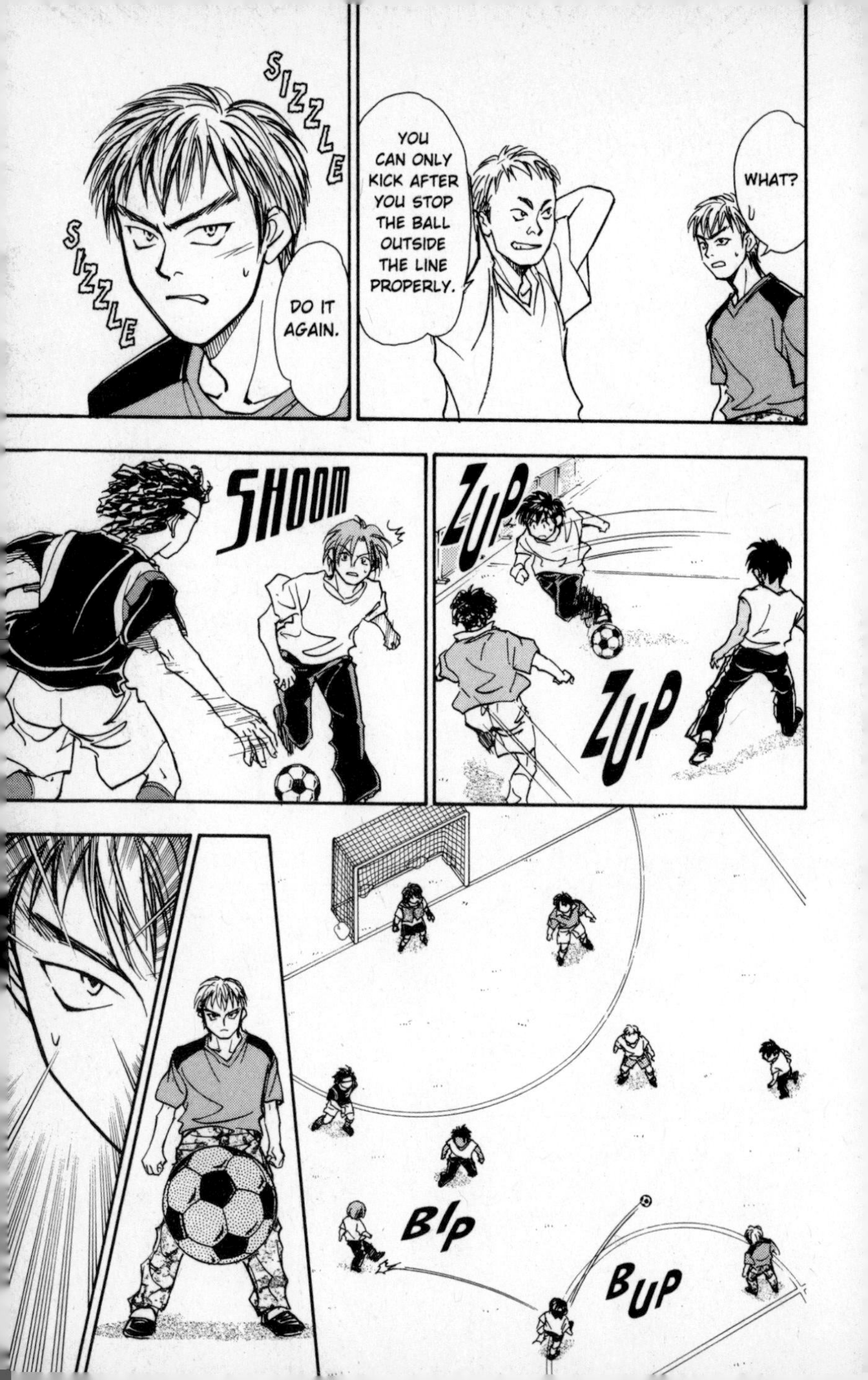
WHAT?
YOU CAN ONLY KICK AFTER YOU STOP THE BALL OUTSIDE THE LINE PROPERLY.
SIZZLE
SIZZLE
DO IT AGAIN.
ZUP
ZUP
SHOOM
BIP
BUP

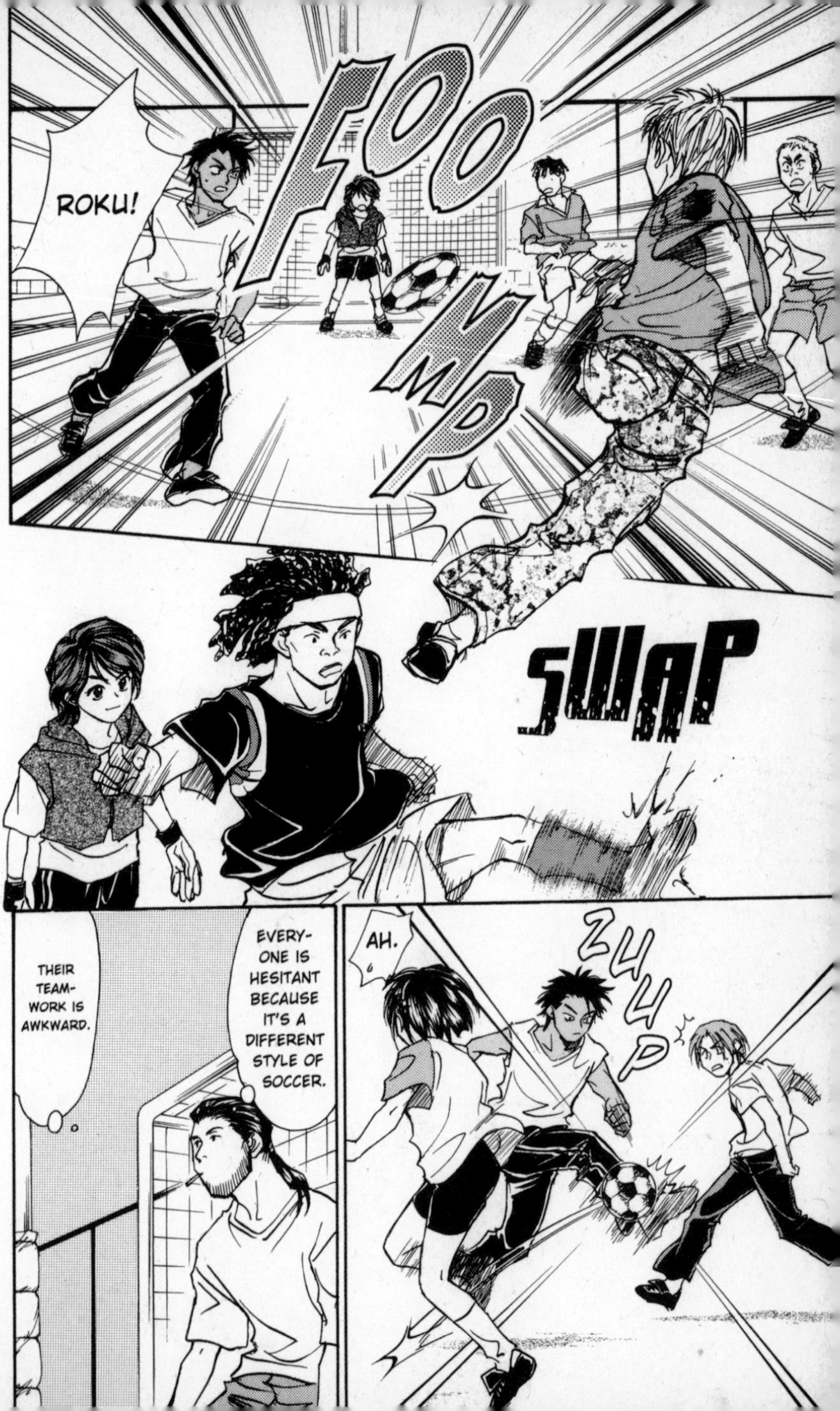
FOOOMP
ROKU!
SWAP
ZUUP
AH.
EVERY-ONE IS HESITANT BECAUSE IT'S A DIFFERENT STYLE OF SOCCER.
THEIR TEAM-WORK IS AWKWARD.

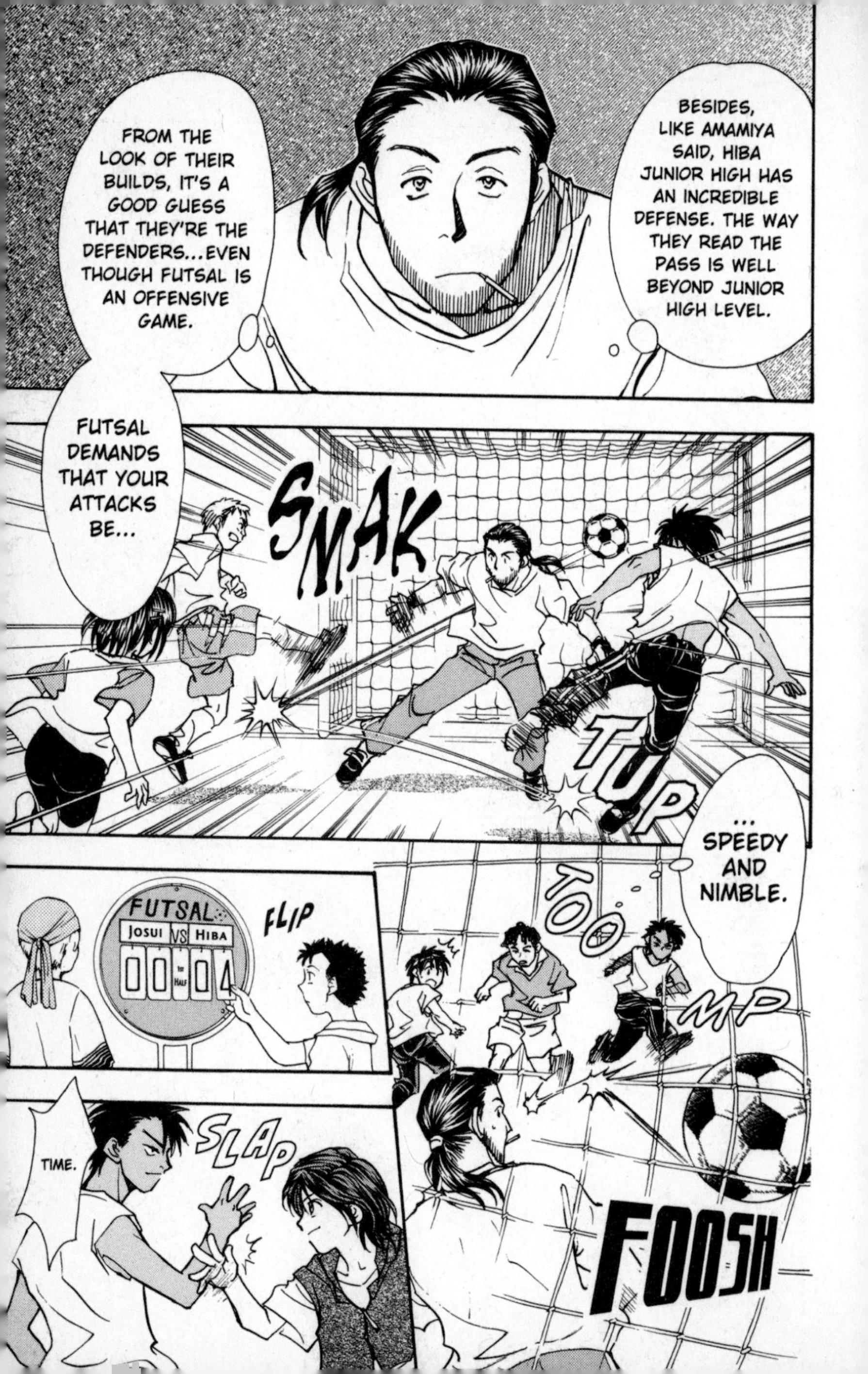
BESIDES, LIKE AMAMIYA SAID, HIBA JUNIOR HIGH HAS AN INCREDIBLE DEFENSE. THE WAY THEY READ THE PASS IS WELL BEYOND JUNIOR HIGH LEVEL.
FROM THE LOOK OF THEIR BUILDS, IT'S A GOOD GUESS THAT THEY'RE THE DEFENDERS...EVEN THOUGH FUTSAL IS AN OFFENSIVE GAME.
TUP
SNAK
FUTSAL DEMANDS THAT YOUR ATTACKS BE...
... SPEEDY AND NIMBLE.
TOOMP
FOOSH
FLIP
FUTSAL
JOSUI VS HIBA
00 1st HALF 04
SLAP
TIME.

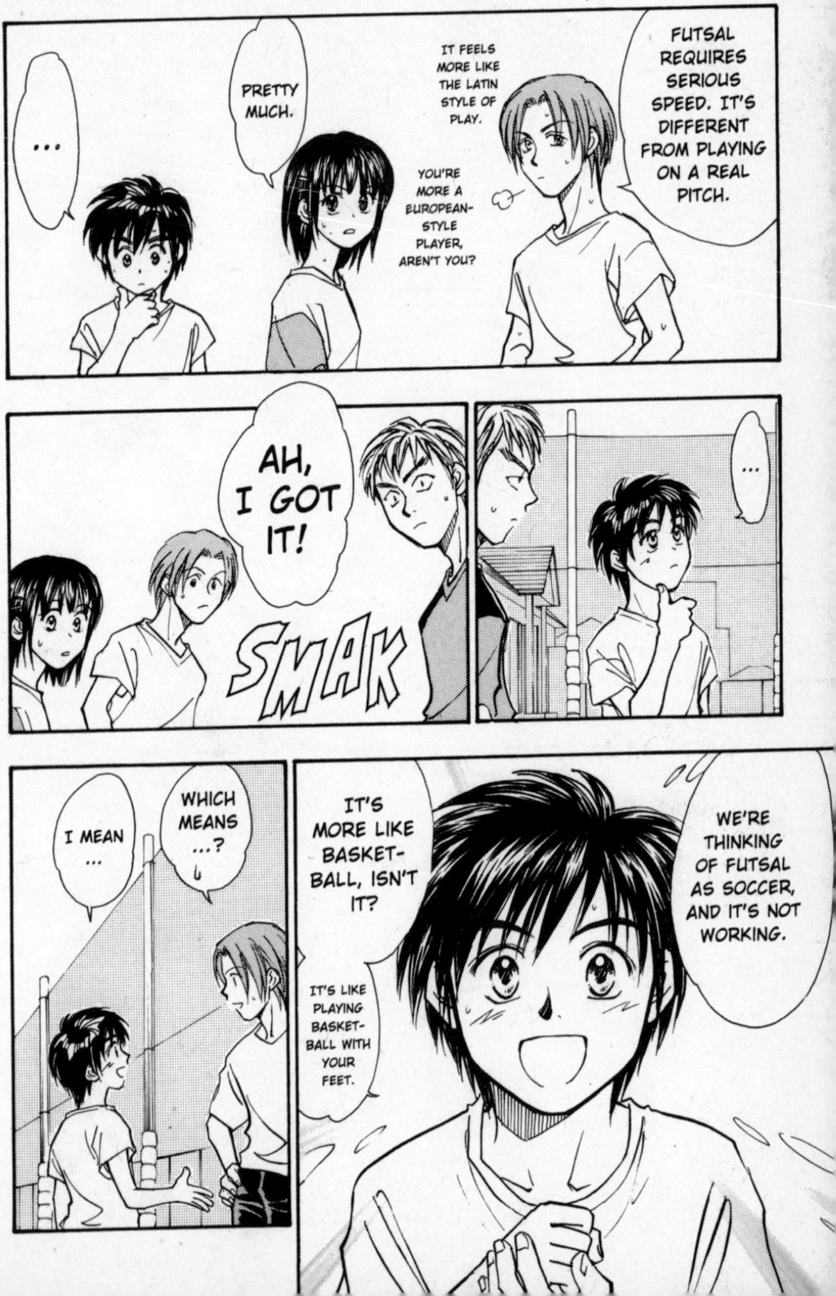
FUTSAL REQUIRES SERIOUS SPEED. IT'S DIFFERENT FROM PLAYING ON A REAL PITCH.
IT FEELS MORE LIKE THE LATIN STYLE OF PLAY.
YOU'RE MORE A EUROPEAN-STYLE PLAYER, AREN'T YOU?
PRETTY MUCH.
...
...
AH, I GOT IT!
SMAK
WE'RE THINKING OF FUTSAL AS SOCCER, AND IT'S NOT WORKING.
IT'S MORE LIKE BASKET-BALL, ISN'T IT?
IT'S LIKE PLAYING BASKET-BALL WITH YOUR FEET.
WHICH MEANS ...?
I MEAN ...

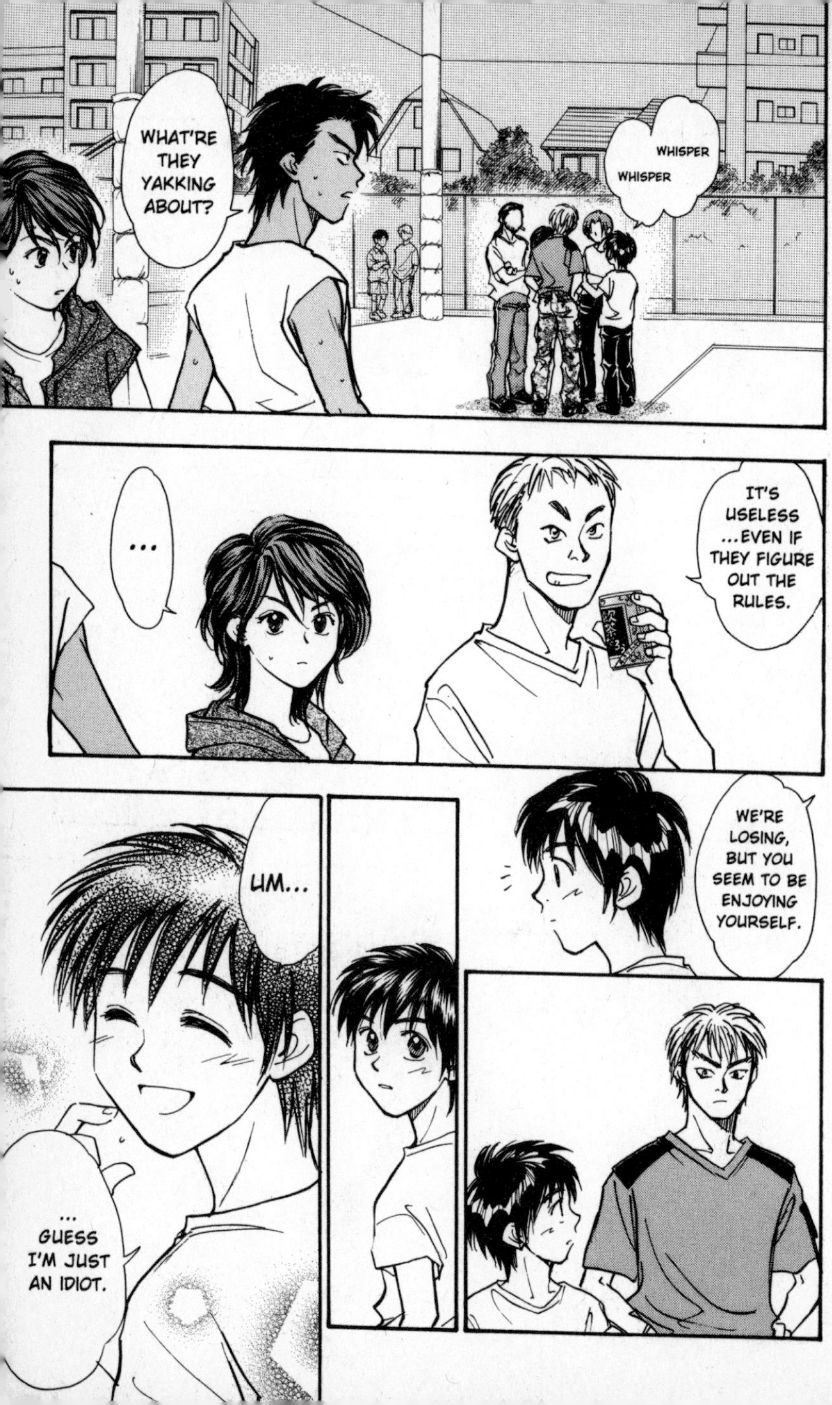
WHISPER WHISPER
WHAT'RE THEY YAKKING ABOUT?
IT'S USELESS ...EVEN IF THEY FIGURE OUT THE RULES.
...
WE'RE LOSING, BUT YOU SEEM TO BE ENJOYING YOURSELF.
UM...
... GUESS I'M JUST AN IDIOT.

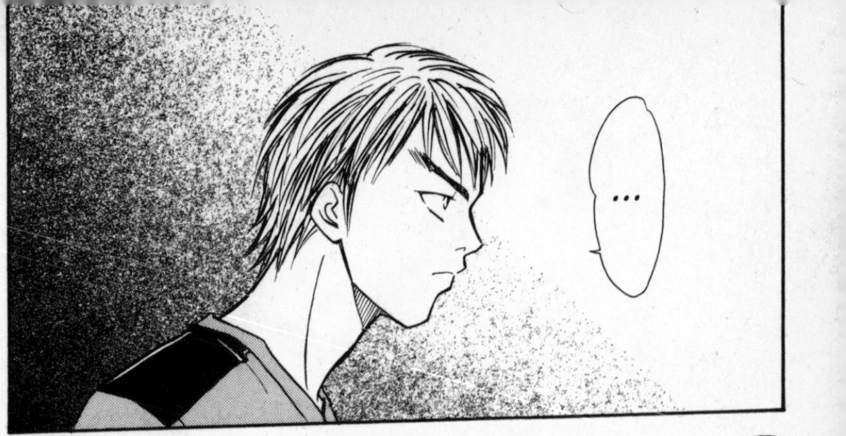
...

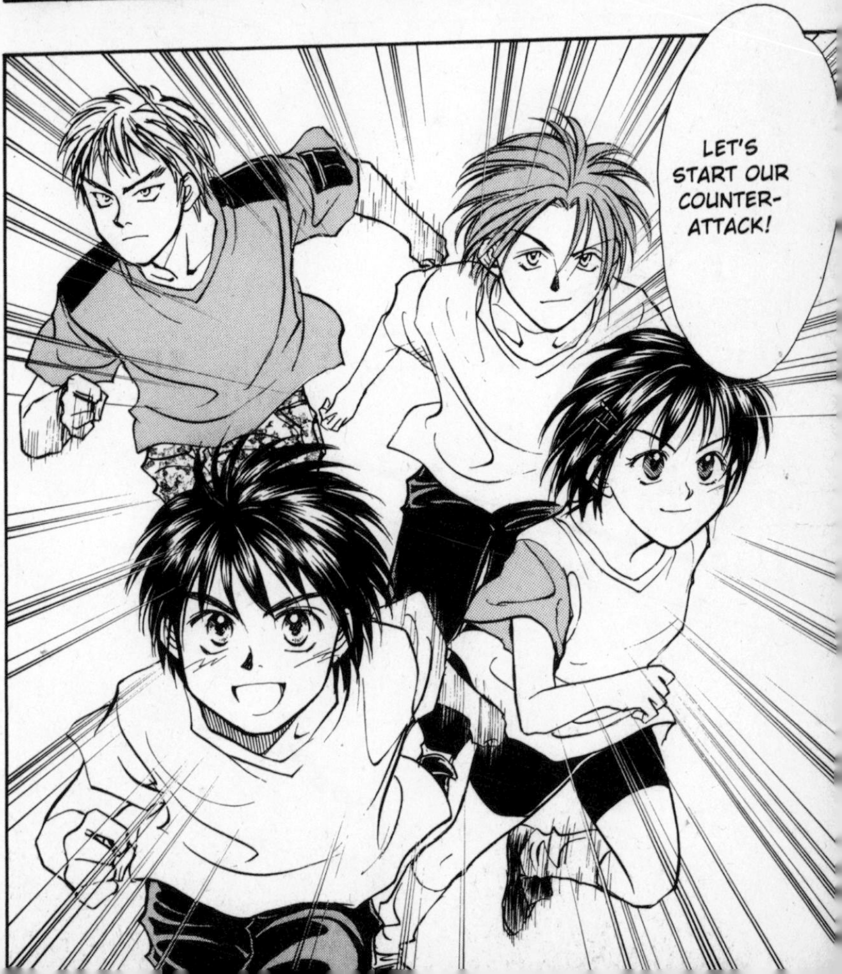
LET'S START OUR COUNTER-ATTACK!

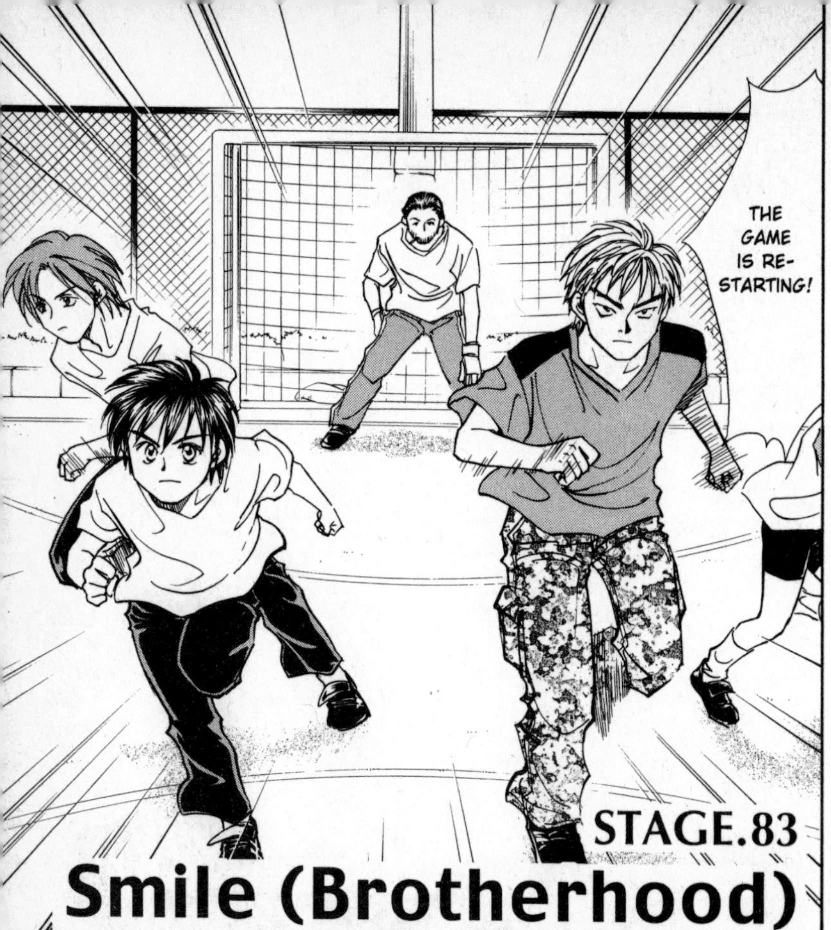
THE GAME IS RE-STARTING!
STAGE.83
Smile (Brotherhood)

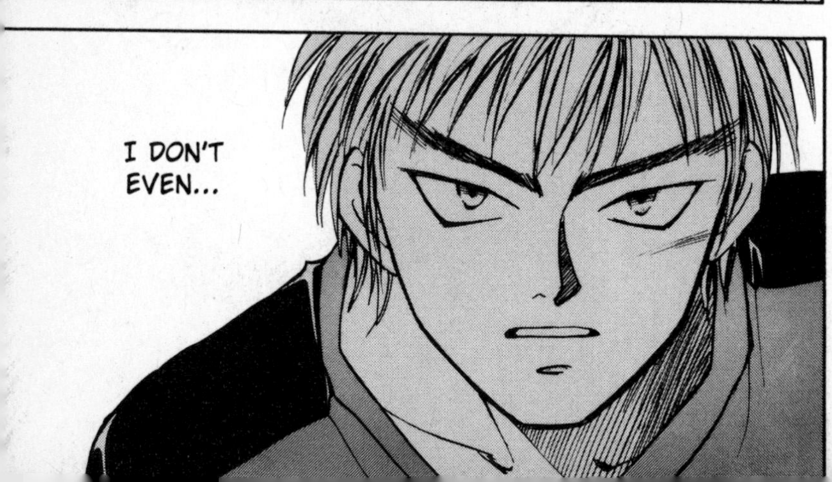
I DON'T EVEN...

...WANT TO PLAY SOCCER, BUT...

...WHY...

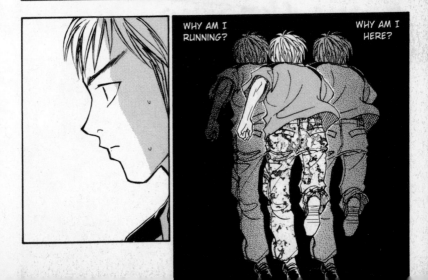

WHY AM I RUNNING?

WHY AM I HERE?

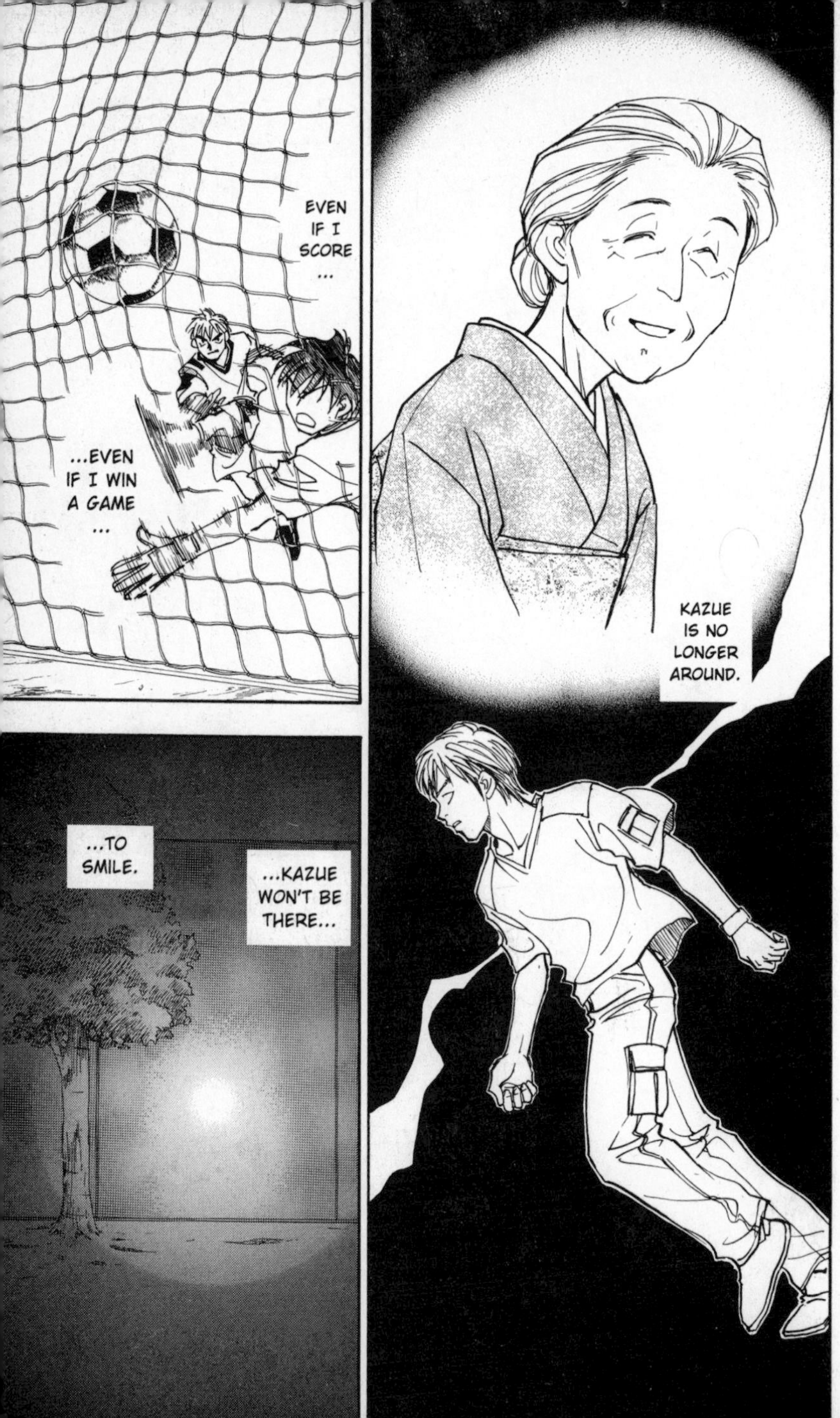
KAZUE IS NO LONGER AROUND.
EVEN IF I SCORE ...
...EVEN IF I WIN A GAME ...
...KAZUE WON'T BE THERE...
...TO SMILE.

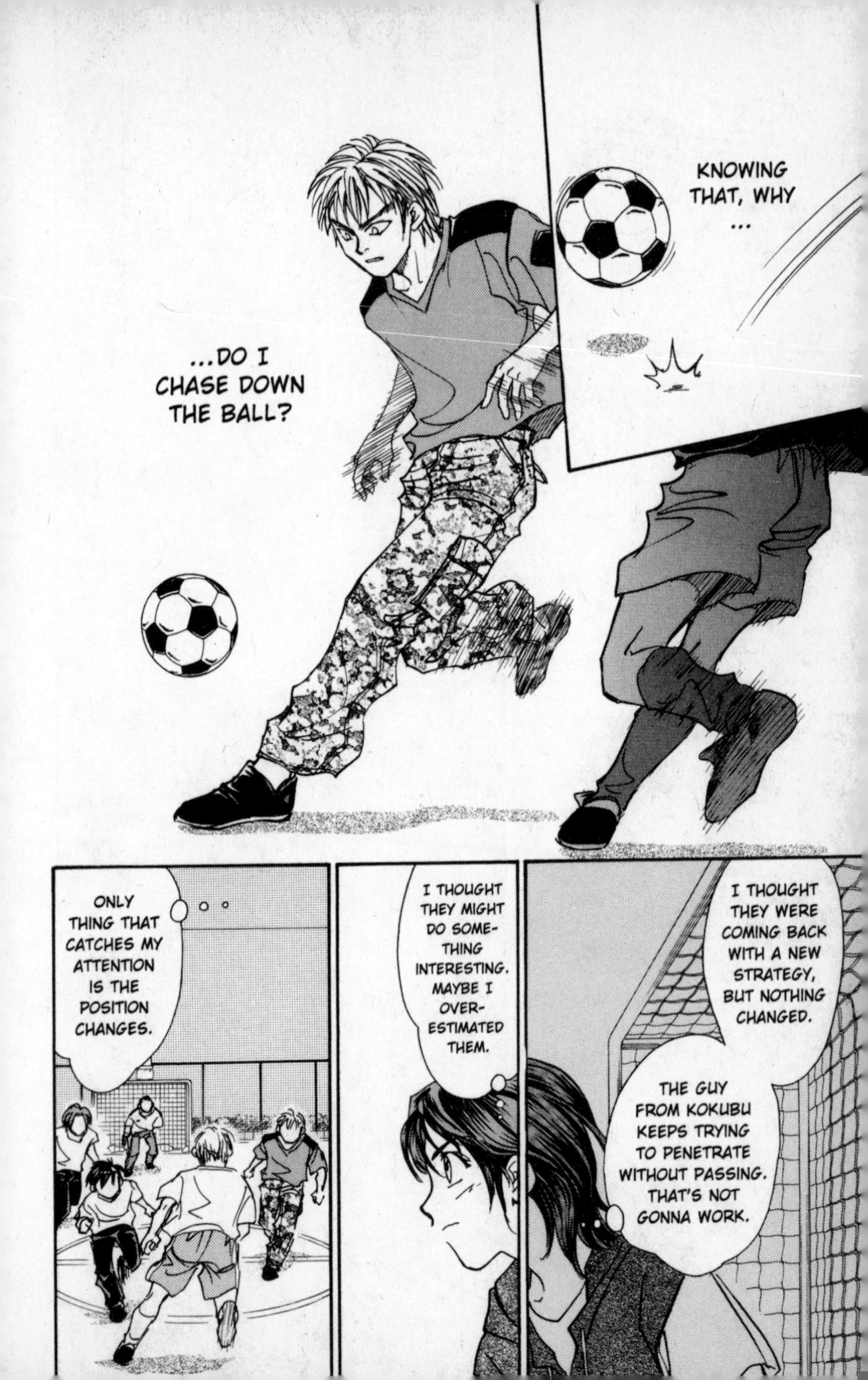
KNOWING THAT, WHY ...
...DO I CHASE DOWN THE BALL?
I THOUGHT THEY WERE COMING BACK WITH A NEW STRATEGY, BUT NOTHING CHANGED.
THE GUY FROM KOKUBU KEEPS TRYING TO PENETRATE WITHOUT PASSING. THAT'S NOT GONNA WORK.
I THOUGHT THEY MIGHT DO SOMETHING INTERESTING. MAYBE I OVERESTIMATED THEM.
ONLY THING THAT CATCHES MY ATTENTION IS THE POSITION CHANGES.

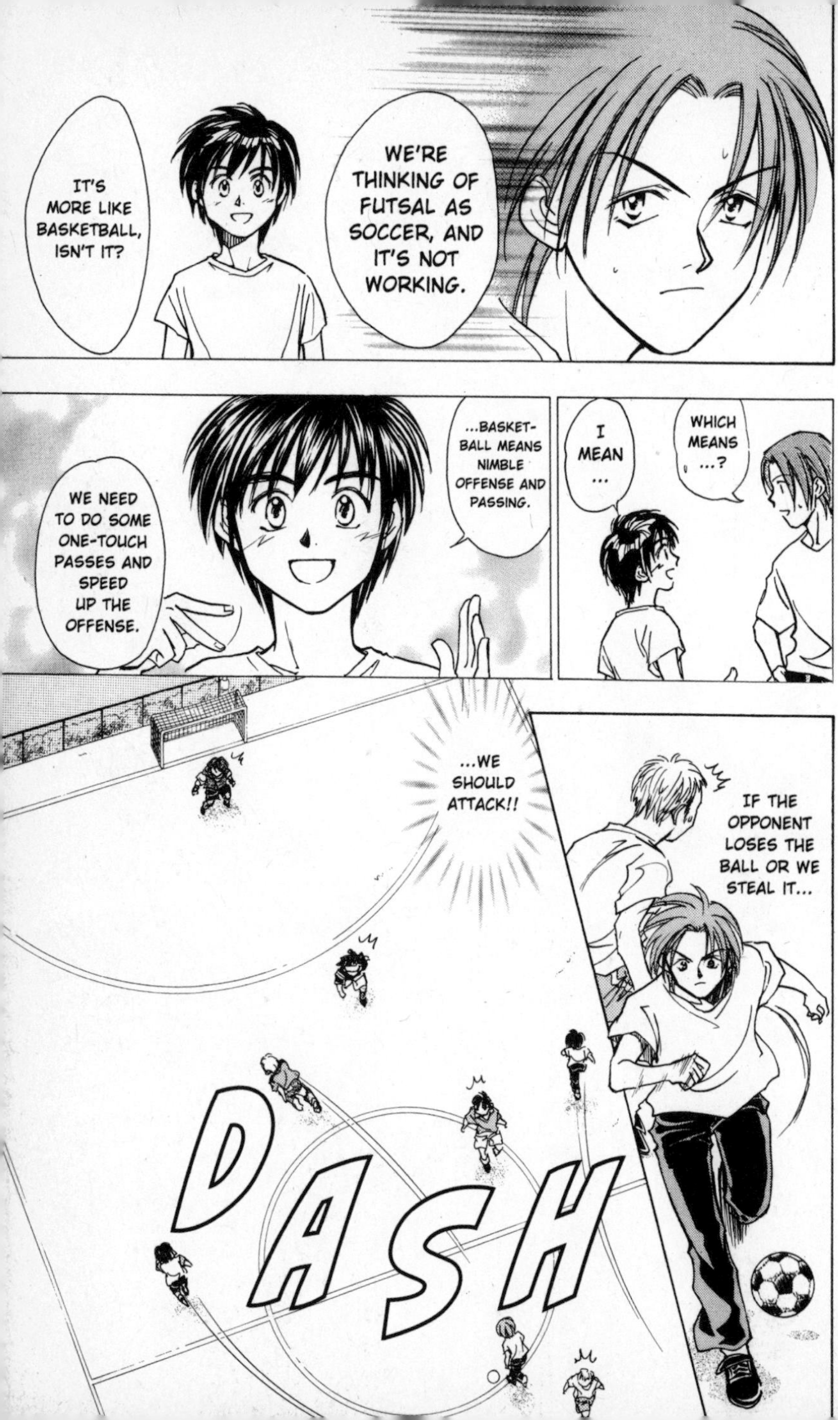
WE'RE THINKING OF FUTSAL AS SOCCER, AND IT'S NOT WORKING.
IT'S MORE LIKE BASKETBALL, ISN'T IT?
WHICH MEANS ...?
I MEAN ...
...BASKET-BALL MEANS NIMBLE OFFENSE AND PASSING.
WE NEED TO DO SOME ONE-TOUCH PASSES AND SPEED UP THE OFFENSE.
IF THE OPPONENT LOSES THE BALL OR WE STEAL IT...
...WE SHOULD ATTACK!!
DASH

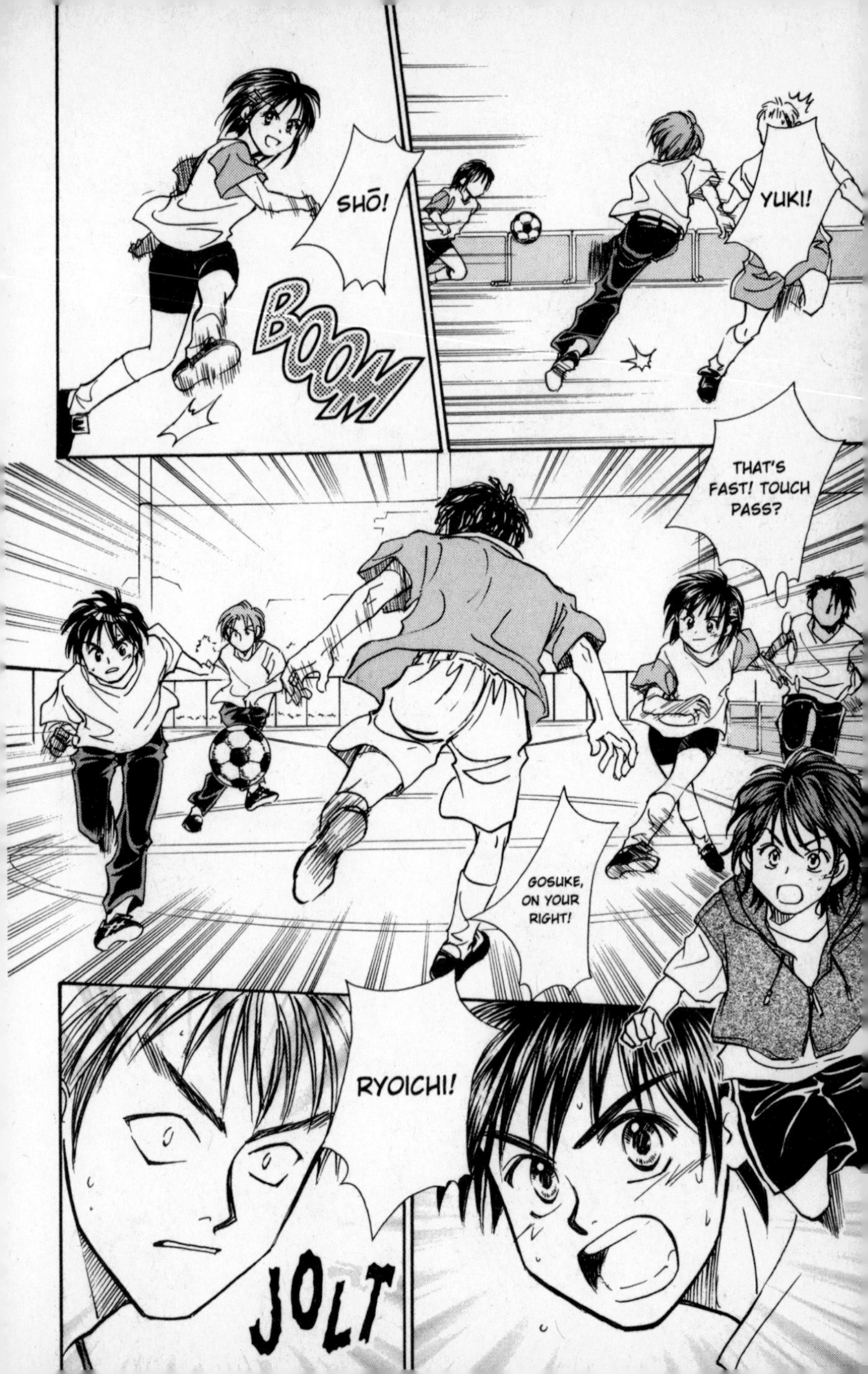
YUKI!
SHŌ!
BOOM
THAT'S FAST! TOUCH PASS?
GOSUKE, ON YOUR RIGHT!
RYOICHI!
JOLT

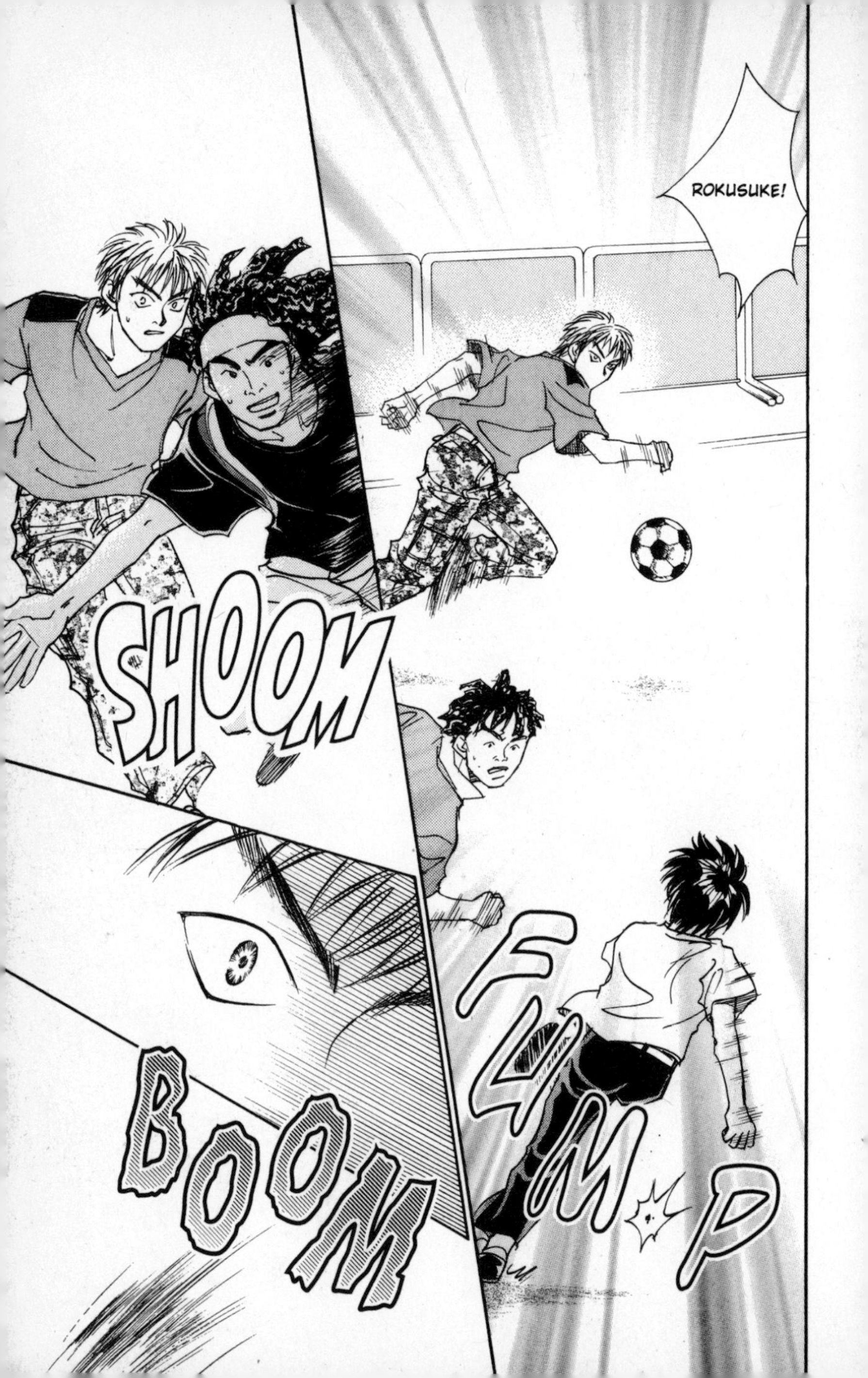
ROKUSUKE!
FUMP
SHOOM
BOOM

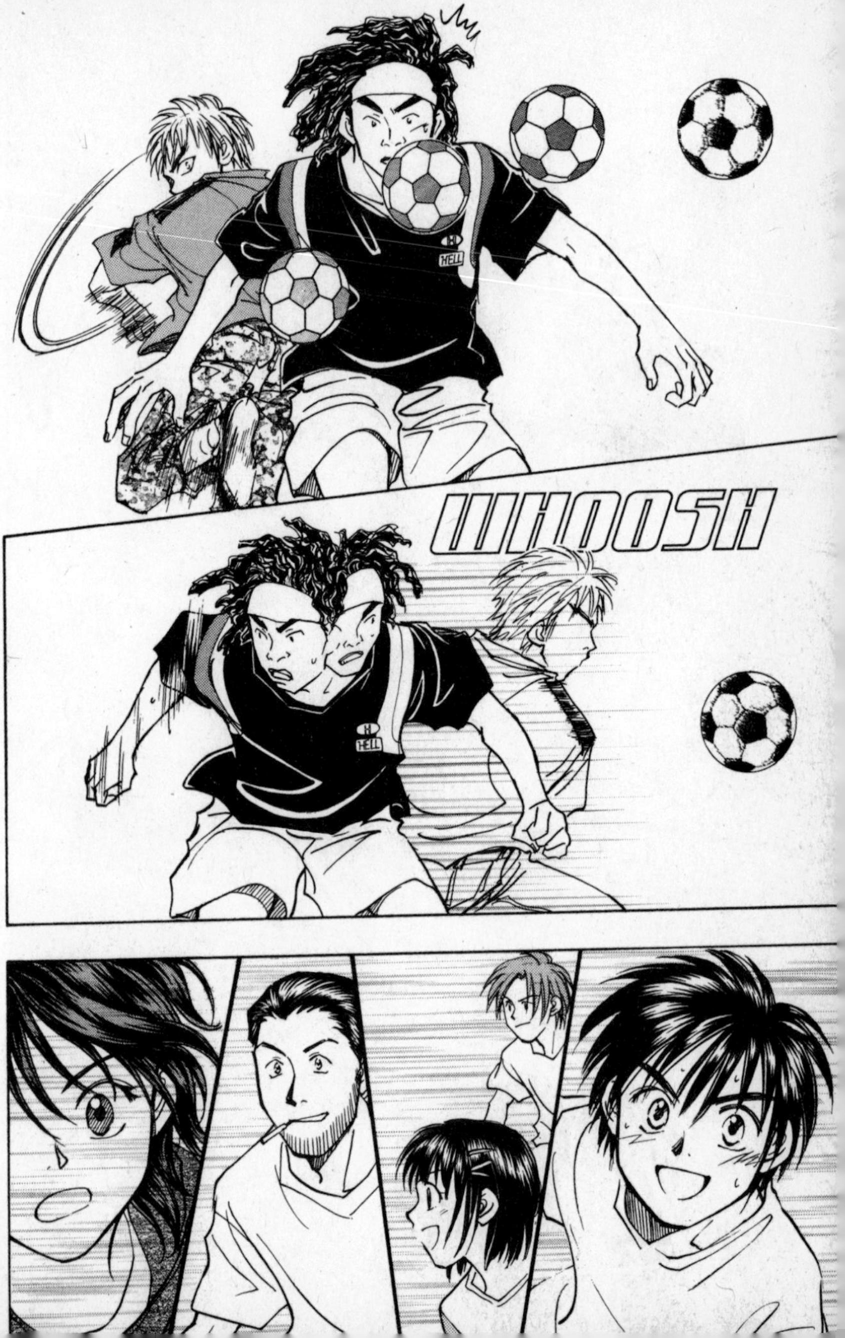
HELL
WHOOSH
HELL

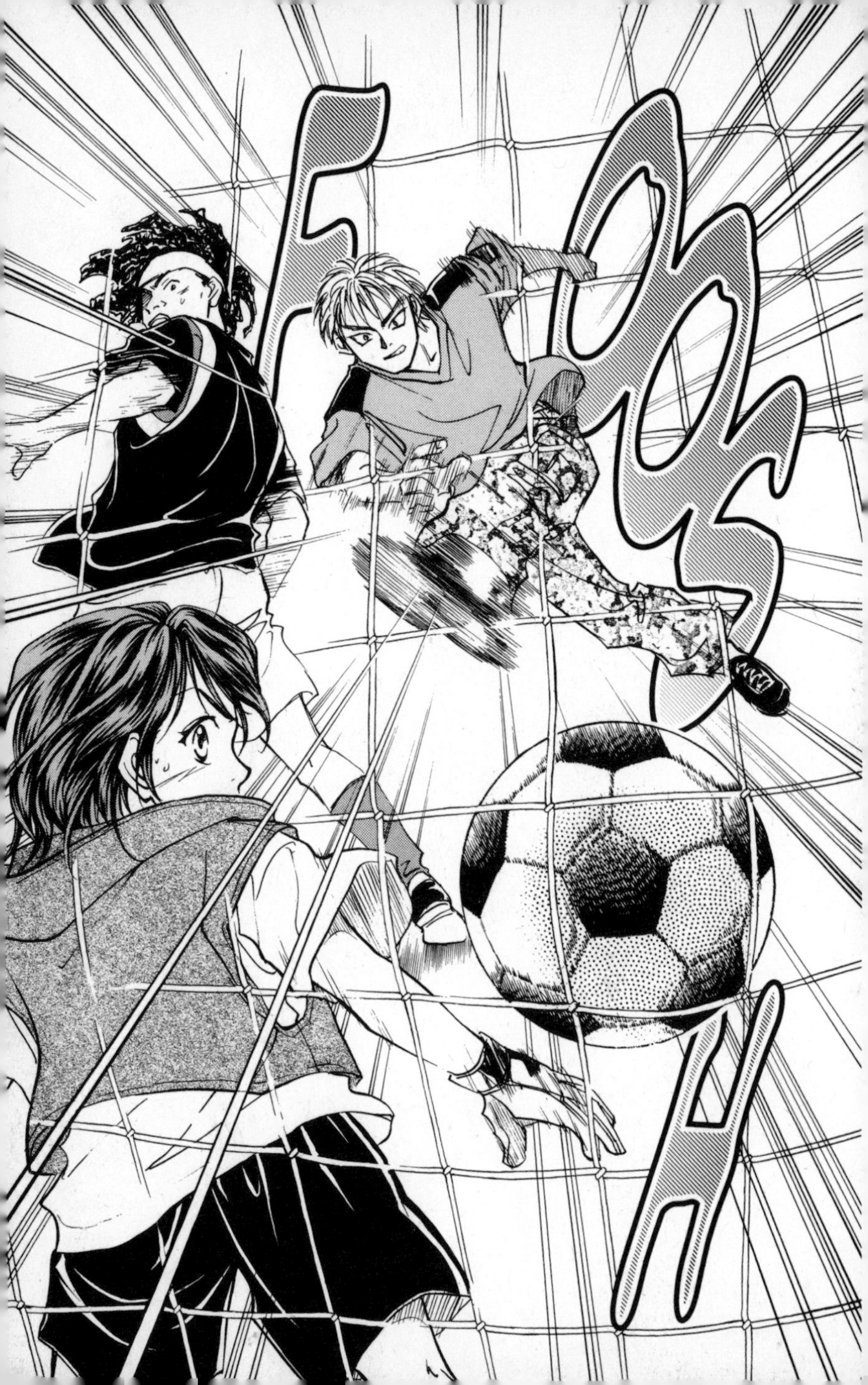
FOOSH

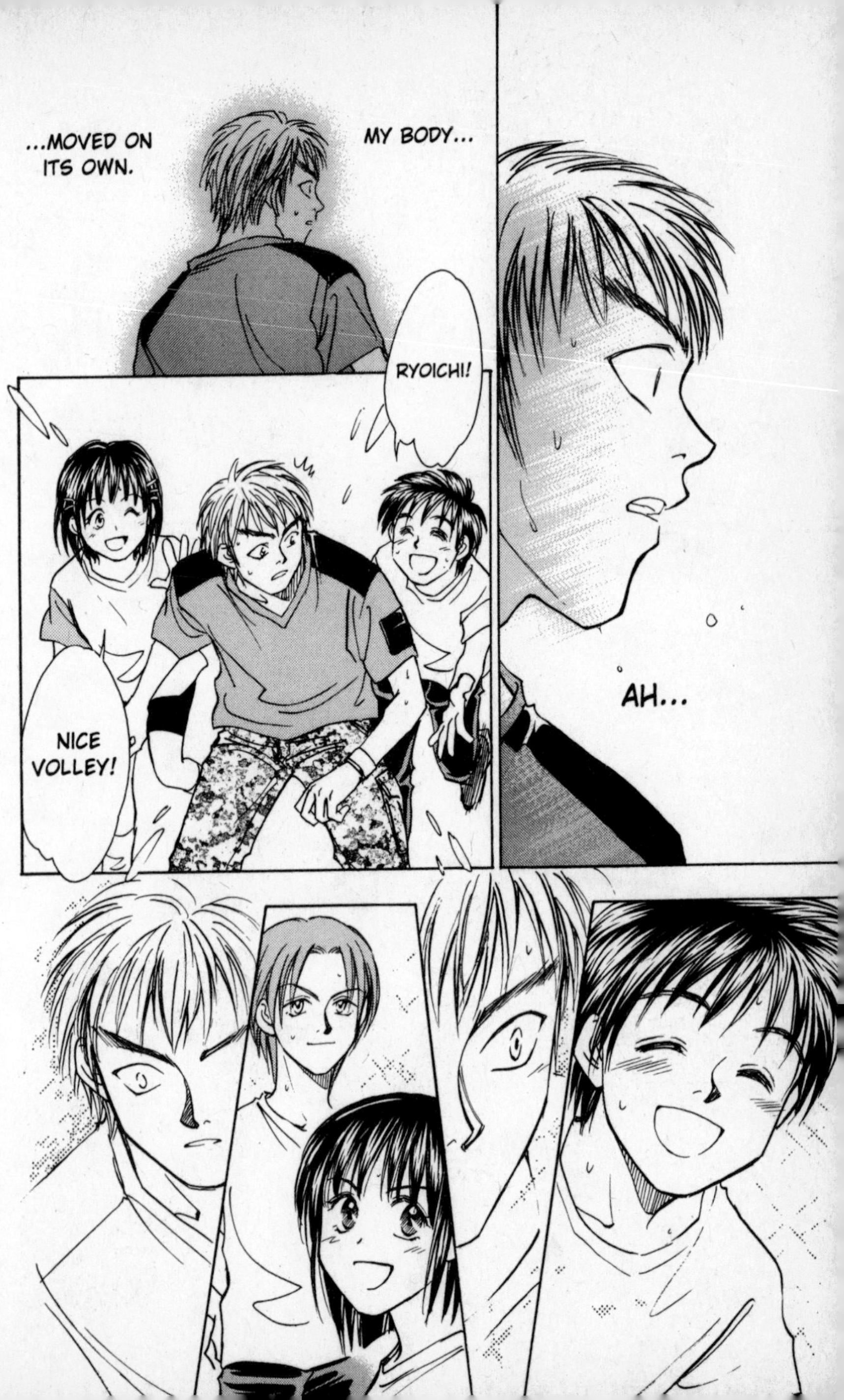
AH...
MY BODY...
...MOVED ON ITS OWN.
RYOICHI!
NICE VOLLEY!

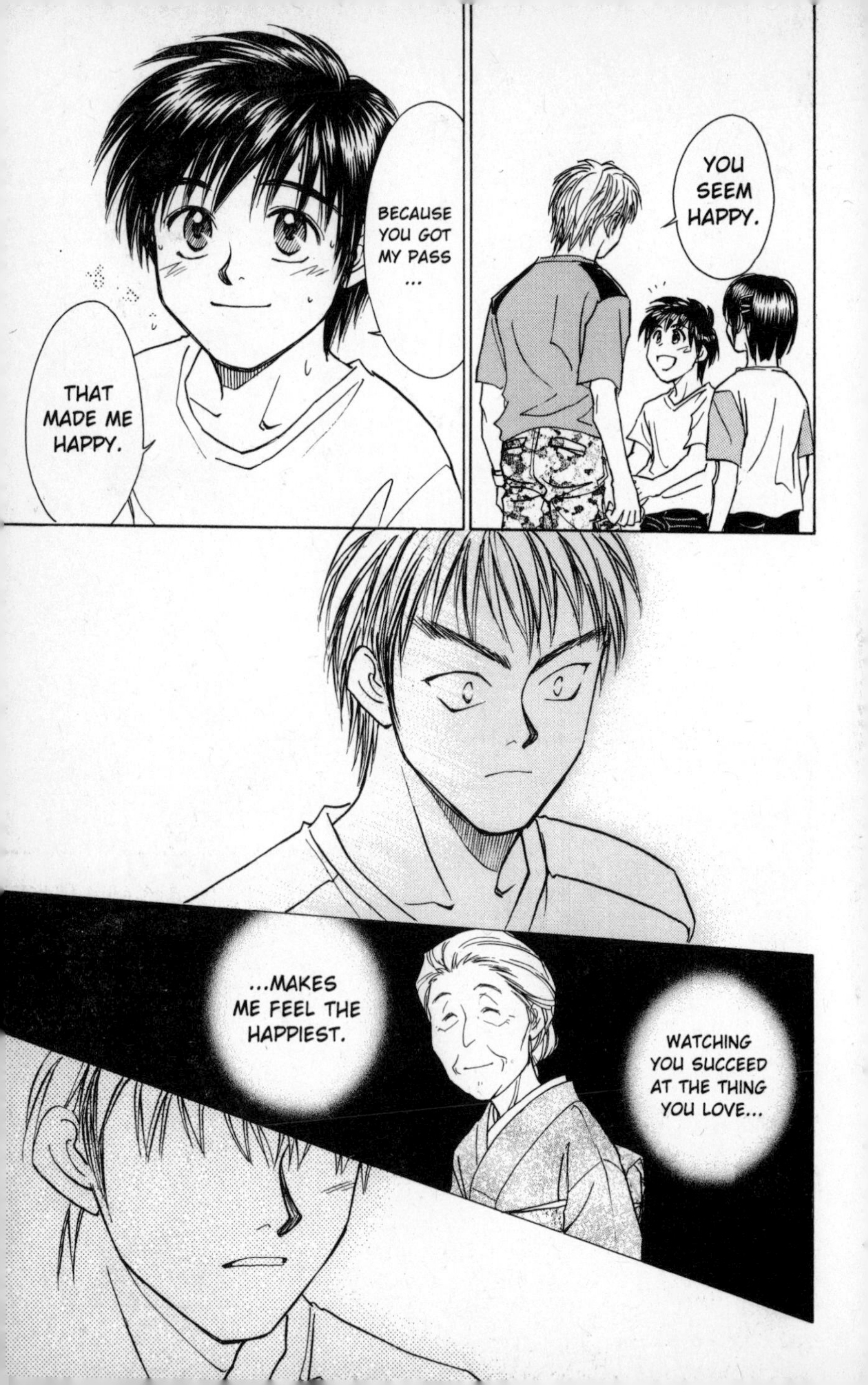
YOU SEEM HAPPY.
BECAUSE YOU GOT MY PASS ...
THAT MADE ME HAPPY.
WATCHING YOU SUCCEED AT THE THING YOU LOVE...
...MAKES ME FEEL THE HAPPIEST.

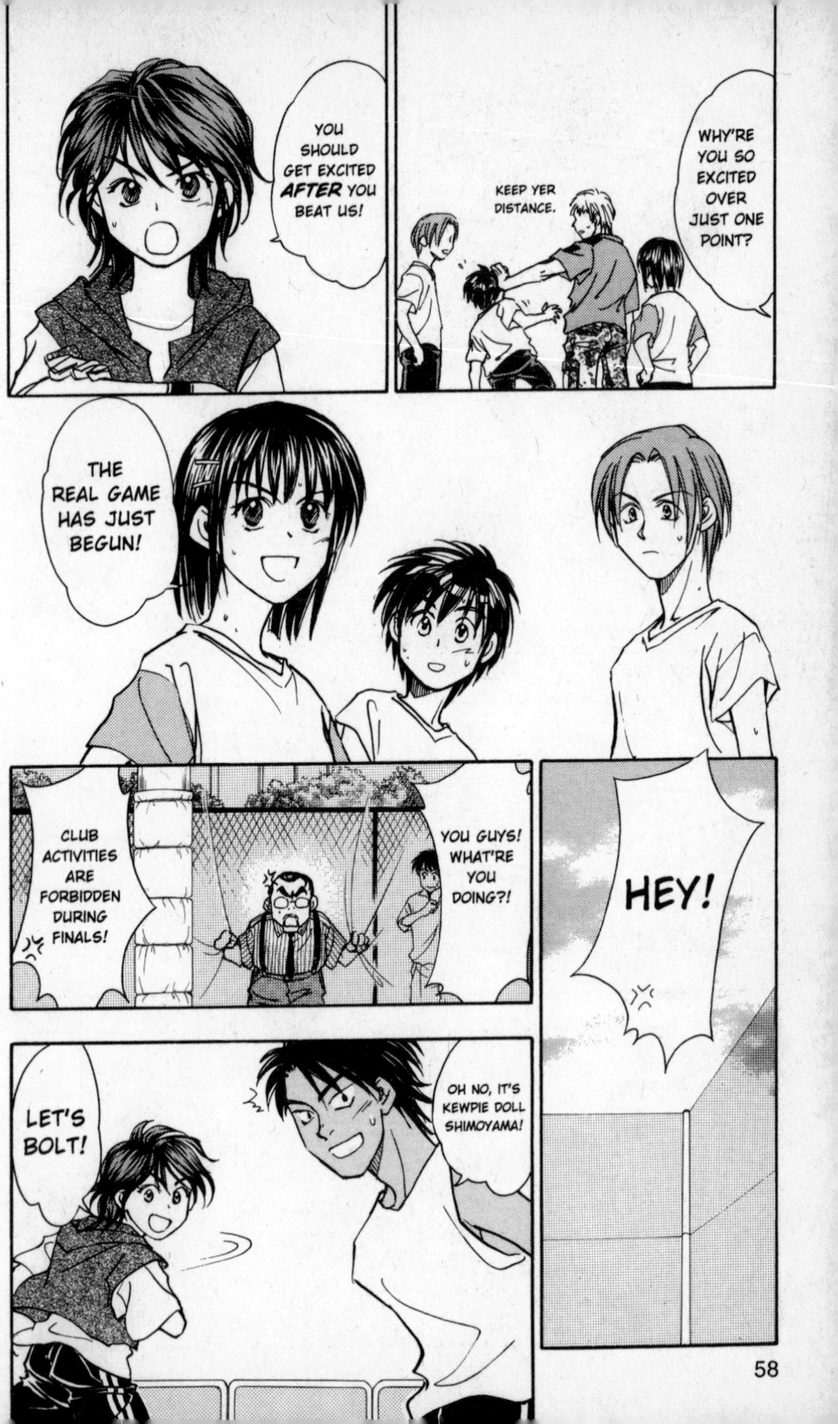

WHY'RE YOU SO EXCITED OVER JUST ONE POINT?
KEEP YER DISTANCE.
YOU SHOULD GET EXCITED **AFTER** YOU BEAT US!
THE REAL GAME HAS JUST BEGUN!
HEY!
YOU GUYS! WHAT'RE YOU DOING?!
CLUB ACTIVITIES ARE FORBIDDEN DURING FINALS!
OH NO, IT'S KEWPIE DOLL SHIMOYAMA!
LET'S BOLT!

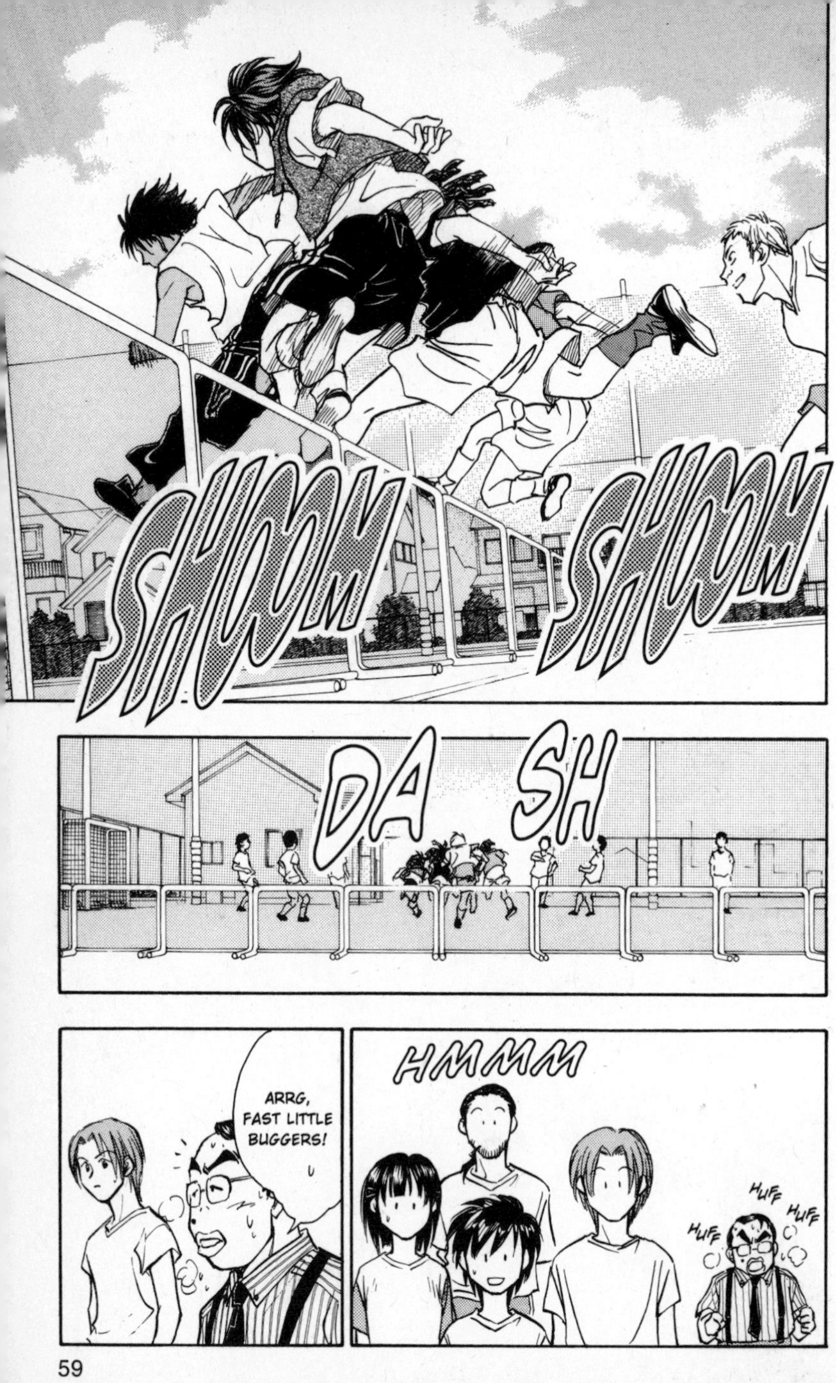
SHOOM
SHOOM
DASH
HMMMM
HUFF
HUFF
HUFF
ARRG, FAST LITTLE BUGGERS!

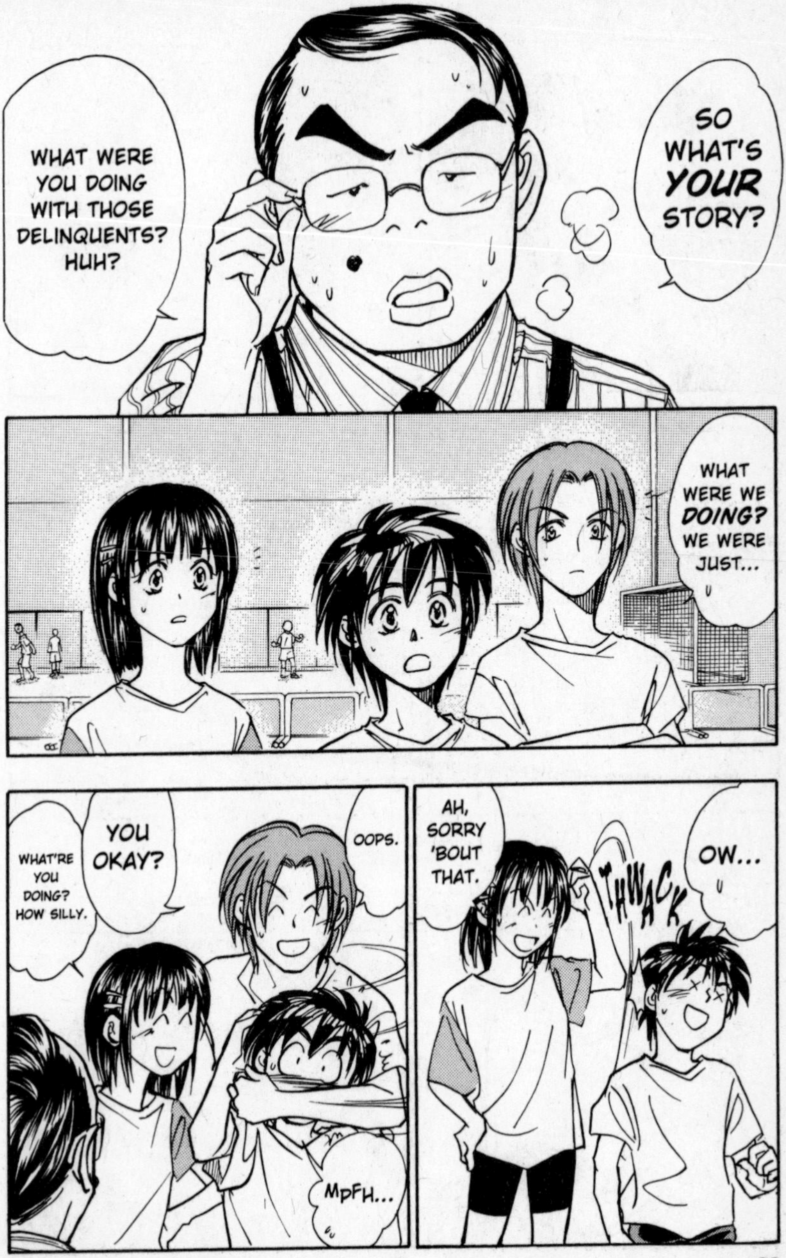
SO WHAT'S ***YOUR*** STORY?
WHAT WERE YOU DOING WITH THOSE DELINQUENTS? HUH?
WHAT WERE WE ***DOING?*** WE WERE JUST...
OW...
THWACK
AH, SORRY 'BOUT THAT.
OOPS.
YOU OKAY?
WHAT'RE YOU DOING? HOW SILLY.
MPFH...

READ THIS WAY

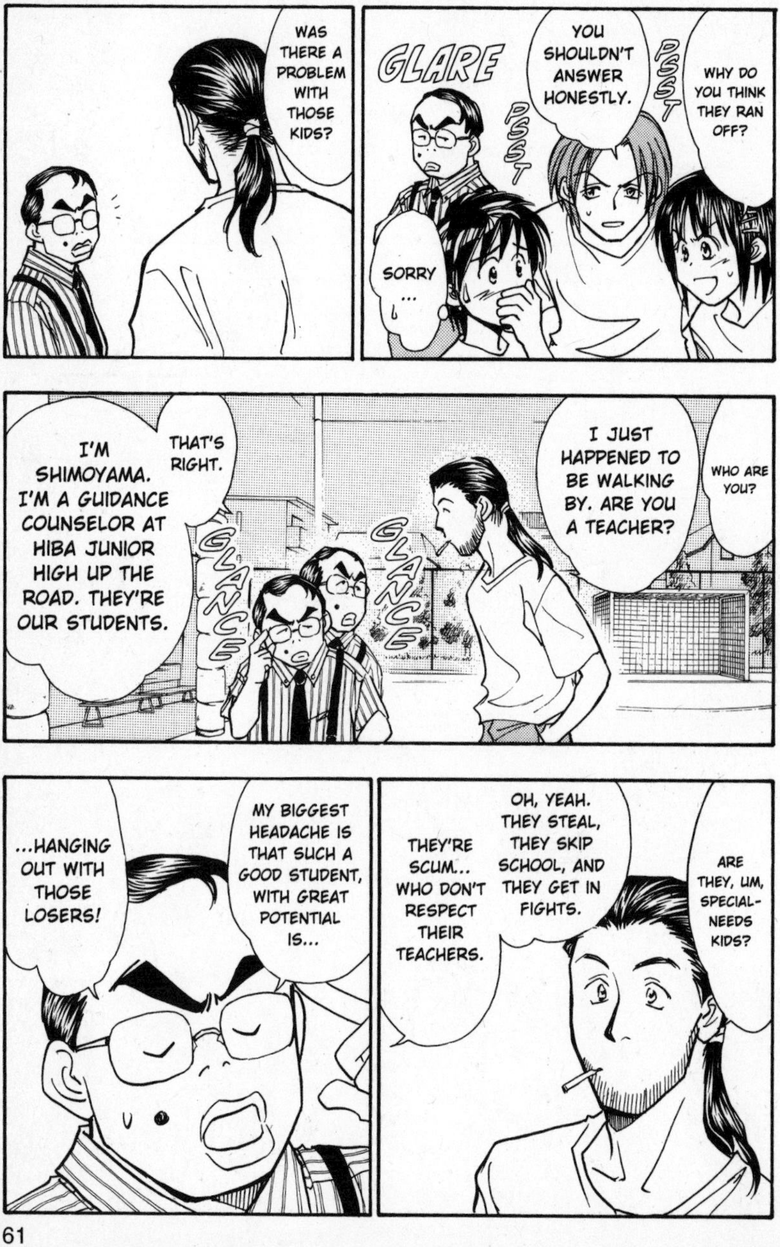

WHY DO YOU THINK THEY RAN OFF?
PSST
YOU SHOULDN'T ANSWER HONESTLY.
PSST
GLARE
SORRY...
WAS THERE A PROBLEM WITH THOSE KIDS?
WHO ARE YOU?
I JUST HAPPENED TO BE WALKING BY. ARE YOU A TEACHER?
GLANCE
GLANCE
THAT'S RIGHT.
I'M SHIMOYAMA. I'M A GUIDANCE COUNSELOR AT HIBA JUNIOR HIGH UP THE ROAD. THEY'RE OUR STUDENTS.
ARE THEY, UM, SPECIAL-NEEDS KIDS?
OH, YEAH. THEY STEAL, THEY SKIP SCHOOL, AND THEY GET IN FIGHTS.
THEY'RE SCUM... WHO DON'T RESPECT THEIR TEACHERS.
MY BIGGEST HEADACHE IS THAT SUCH A GOOD STUDENT, WITH GREAT POTENTIAL IS...
...HANGING OUT WITH THOSE LOSERS!

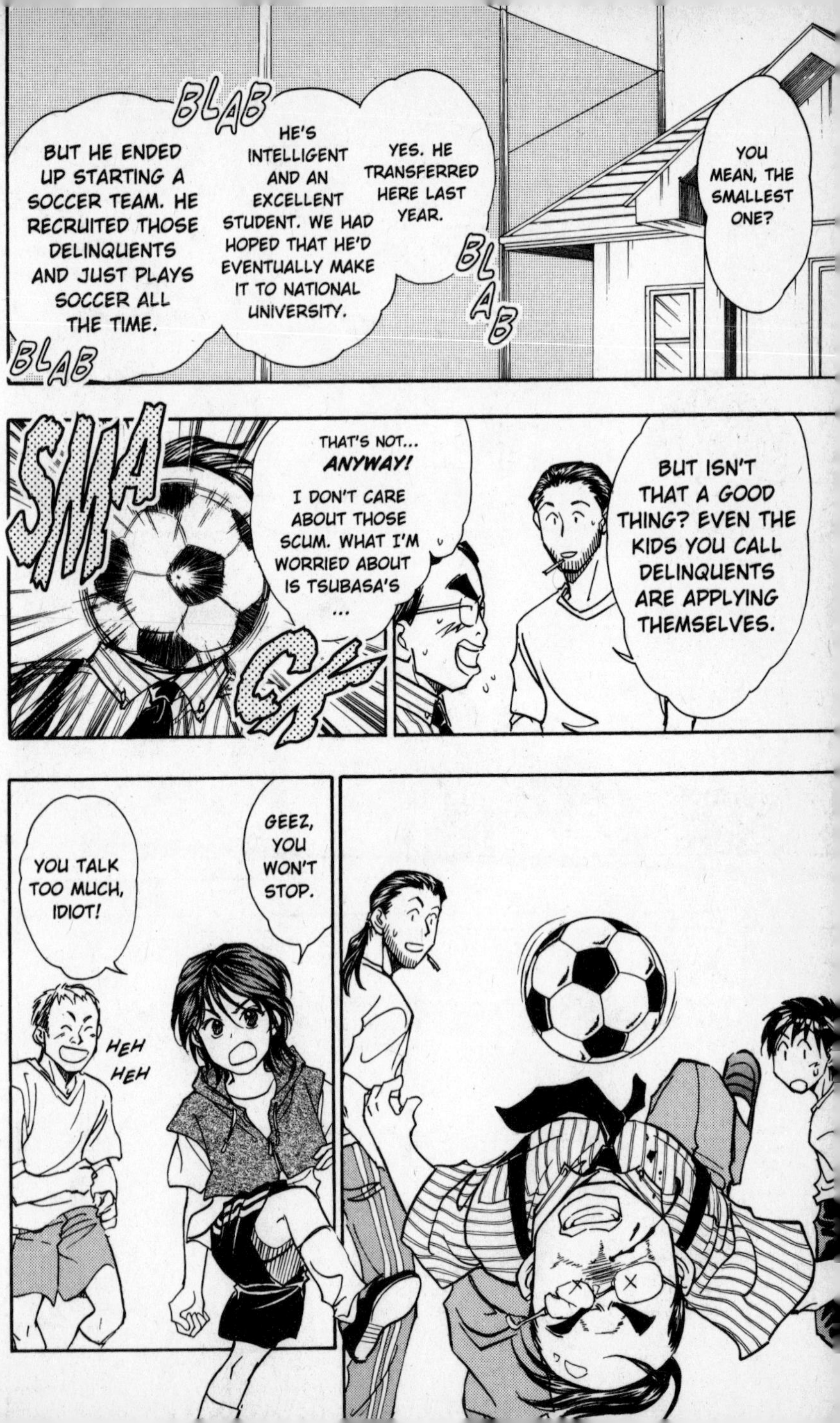
YOU MEAN, THE SMALLEST ONE?
BLAB
YES. HE TRANSFERRED HERE LAST YEAR.
BLAB
HE'S INTELLIGENT AND AN EXCELLENT STUDENT. WE HAD HOPED THAT HE'D EVENTUALLY MAKE IT TO NATIONAL UNIVERSITY.
BUT HE ENDED UP STARTING A SOCCER TEAM. HE RECRUITED THOSE DELINQUENTS AND JUST PLAYS SOCCER ALL THE TIME.
BLAB
BUT ISN'T THAT A GOOD THING? EVEN THE KIDS YOU CALL DELINQUENTS ARE APPLYING THEMSELVES.
THAT'S NOT... ANYWAY!
I DON'T CARE ABOUT THOSE SCUM. WHAT I'M WORRIED ABOUT IS TSUBASA'S ...
SMA
CK
GEEZ, YOU WON'T STOP.
YOU TALK TOO MUCH, IDIOT!
HEH HEH

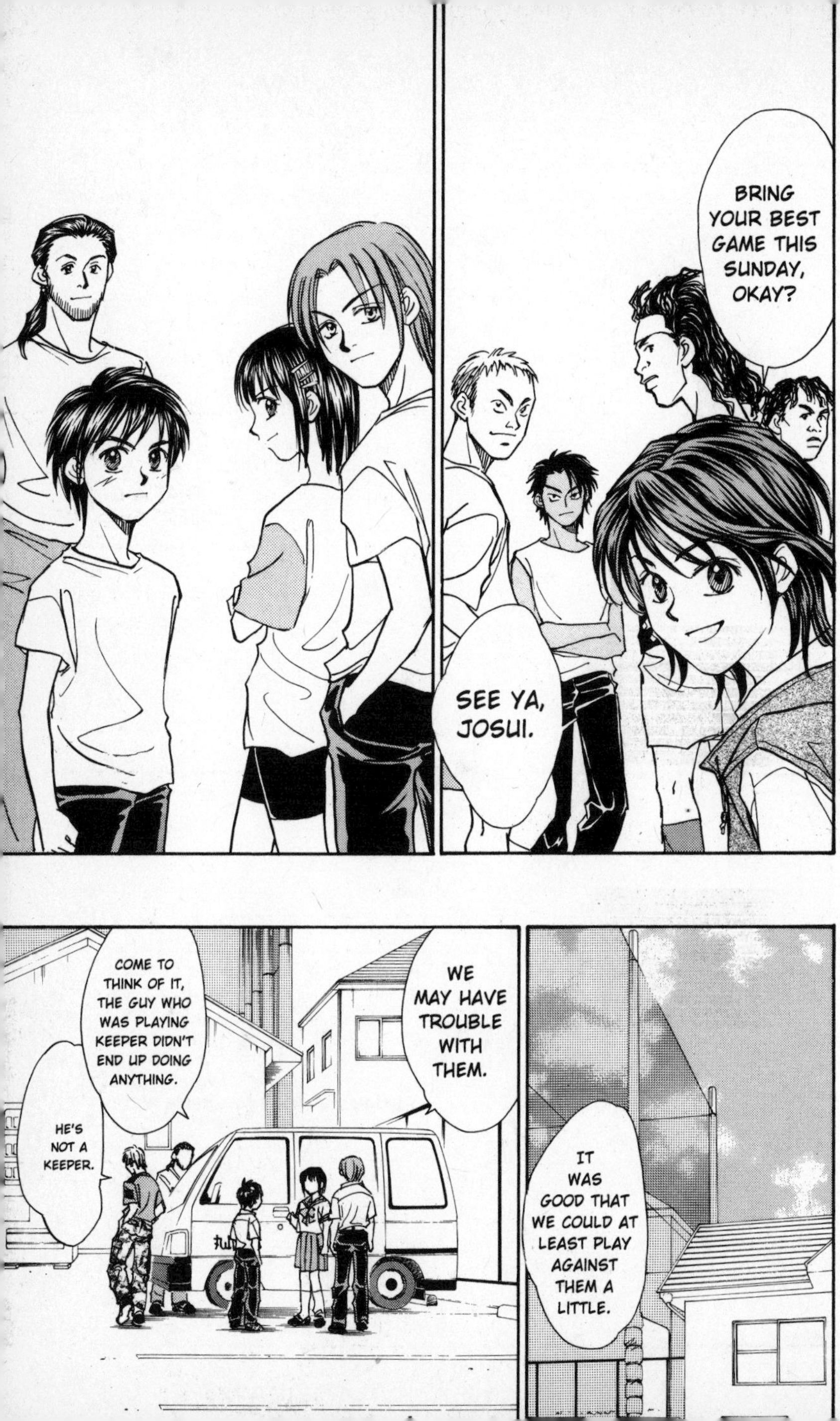
BRING YOUR BEST GAME THIS SUNDAY, OKAY?
SEE YA, JOSUI.
IT WAS GOOD THAT WE COULD AT LEAST PLAY AGAINST THEM A LITTLE.
WE MAY HAVE TROUBLE WITH THEM.
COME TO THINK OF IT, THE GUY WHO WAS PLAYING KEEPER DIDN'T END UP DOING ANYTHING.
HE'S NOT A KEEPER.

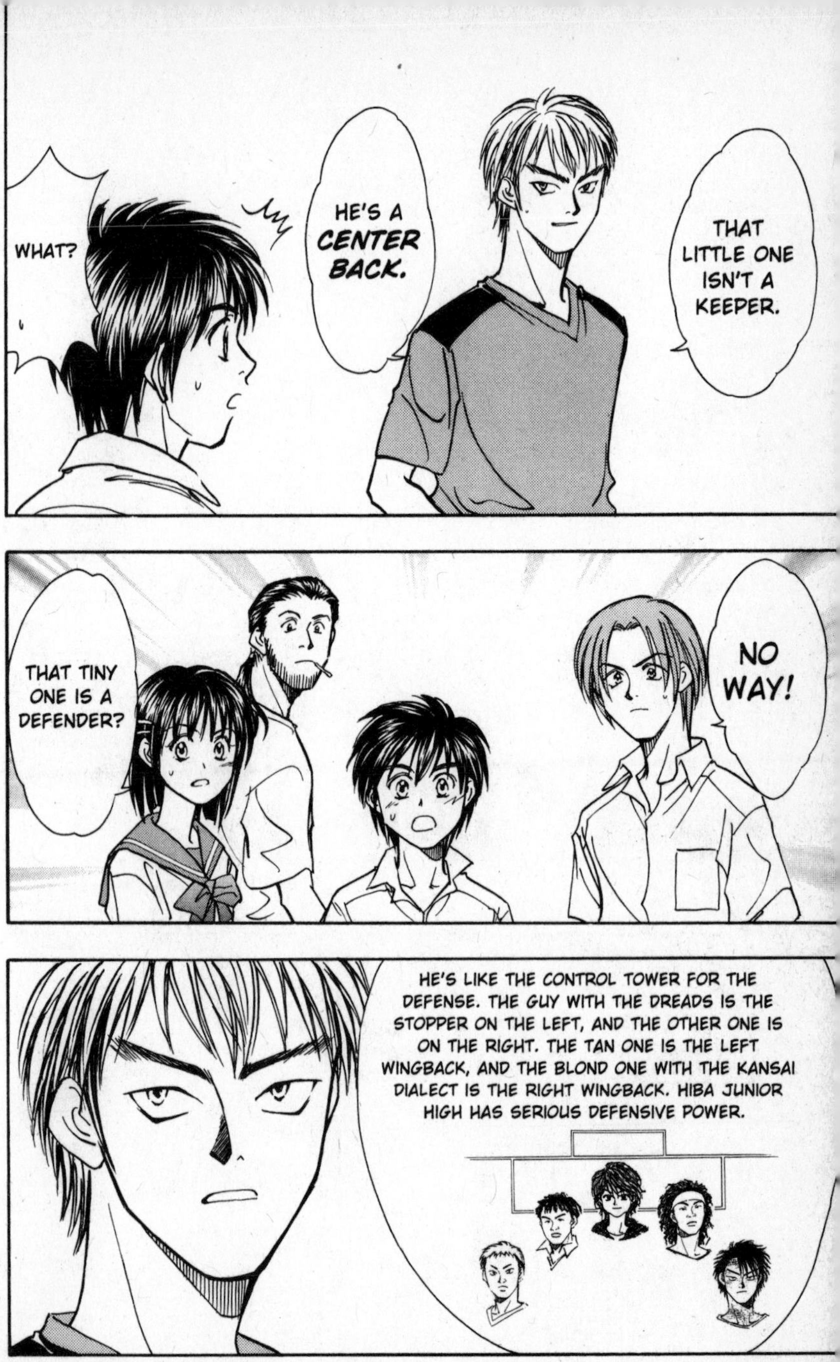
THAT LITTLE ONE ISN'T A KEEPER.
HE'S A CENTER BACK.
WHAT?
NO WAY!
THAT TINY ONE IS A DEFENDER?
HE'S LIKE THE CONTROL TOWER FOR THE DEFENSE. THE GUY WITH THE DREADS IS THE STOPPER ON THE LEFT, AND THE OTHER ONE IS ON THE RIGHT. THE TAN ONE IS THE LEFT WINGBACK, AND THE BLOND ONE WITH THE KANSAI DIALECT IS THE RIGHT WINGBACK. HIBA JUNIOR HIGH HAS SERIOUS DEFENSIVE POWER.

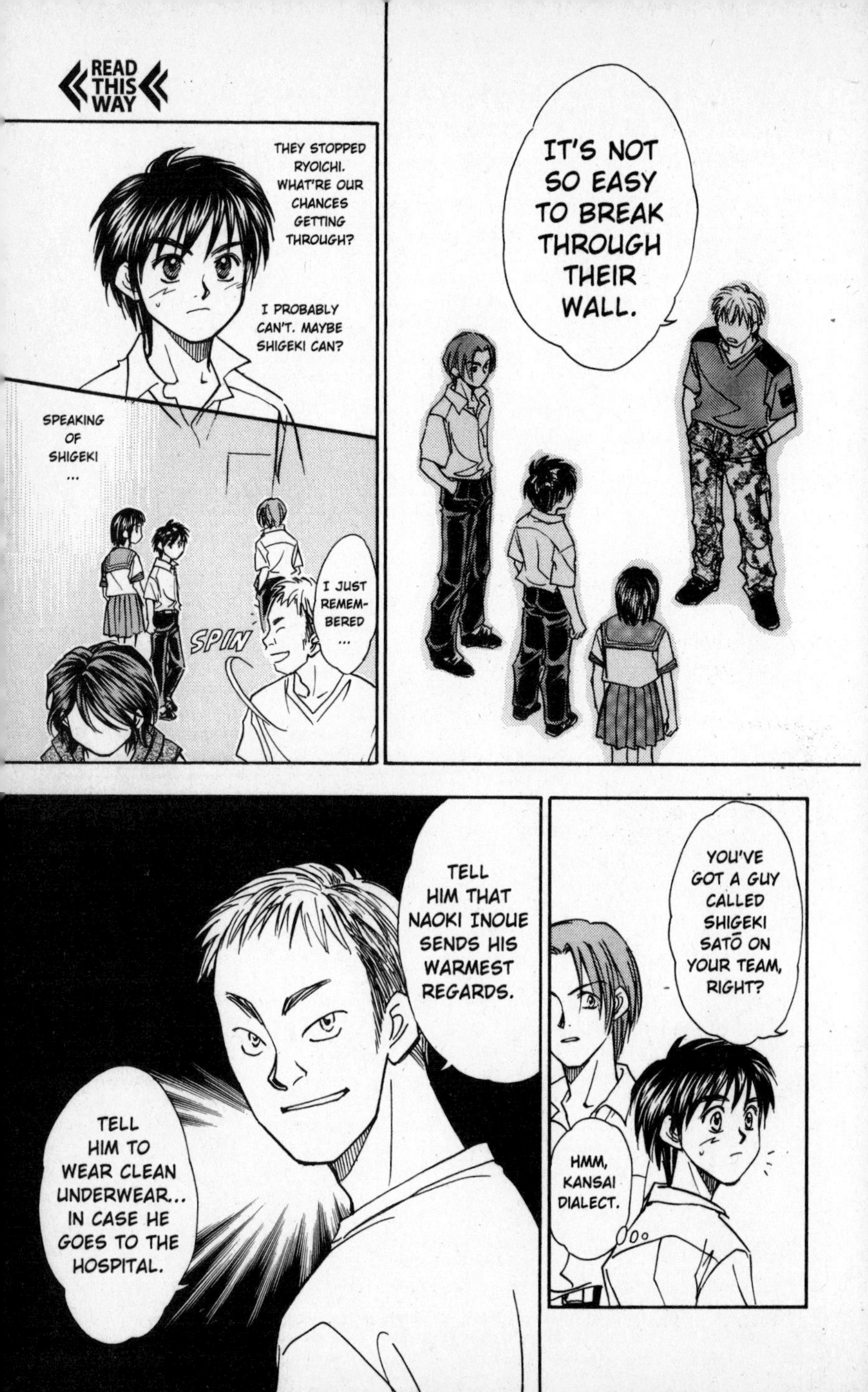
READ THIS WAY
IT'S NOT SO EASY TO BREAK THROUGH THEIR WALL.
THEY STOPPED RYOICHI. WHAT'RE OUR CHANCES GETTING THROUGH?
I PROBABLY CAN'T. MAYBE SHIGEKI CAN?
SPEAKING OF SHIGEKI ...
I JUST REMEMBERED ...
SPIN
YOU'VE GOT A GUY CALLED SHIGEKI SATŌ ON YOUR TEAM, RIGHT?
HMM, KANSAI DIALECT.
TELL HIM THAT NAOKI INOUE SENDS HIS WARMEST REGARDS.
TELL HIM TO WEAR CLEAN UNDERWEAR... IN CASE HE GOES TO THE HOSPITAL.

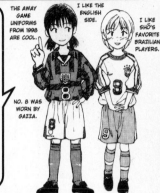

Now You Know: All About Futsal

LET ME EXPLAIN A LITTLE BIT MORE ABOUT FUTSAL. THERE ARE ONLY FIVE PLAYERS -- AS OPPOSED TO 11 -- AND THE SIZE OF THE COURT IS ABOUT A THIRD THE SIZE OF A SOCCER PITCH (WHICH MAKES IT ABOUT THE SAME SIZE AS A TENNIS COURT). AS A RESULT, FUTSAL IS A MUCH MORE ACCESSIBLE SPORT. IF YOU'RE AT SCHOOL, IT'S PERFECT TO PLAY DURING A LUNCH BREAK. IF YOU HAVE A SERIOUS INTEREST IN THE SPORT, THERE ARE ALSO COURTS SPECIFICALLY BUILT FOR FUTSAL. YOU'LL HAVE TO PAY A FEE TO USE THEM, THOUGH. YOU MIGHT BE ABLE TO FIND ONE CLOSE BY. AND, IF YOU'RE GOING TO PLAY, TRY TO LOOK COOL. WEAR A UNIFORM.

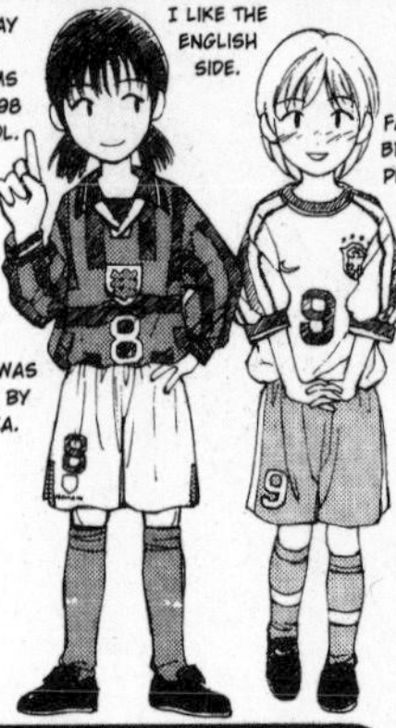
I LIKE SHŌ'S FAVORITE BRAZILIAN PLAYERS.
I LIKE THE ENGLISH SIDE.
THE AWAY GAME UNIFORMS FROM 1998 ARE COOL.
NO. 8 WAS WORN BY GAZZA.

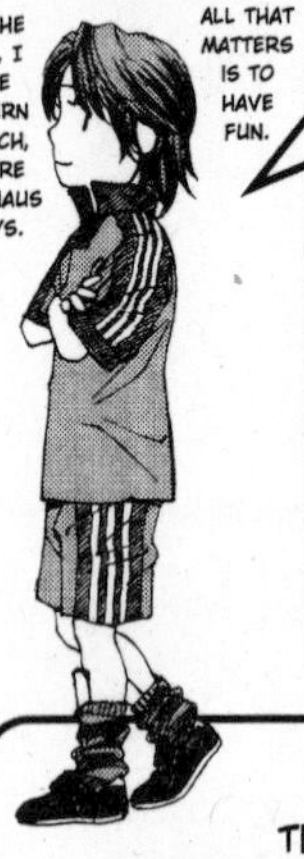
ALL THAT MATTERS IS TO HAVE FUN.
BY THE WAY, I LIKE BAYERN MUNICH, WHERE MÄTTHAUS PLAYS.

IF YOU FEEL LIKE TRYING IT OUT, DO IT RIGHT AWAY. IT DOESN'T MATTER EVEN IF YOU'RE INEXPERIENCED OR A GIRL. IN REALITY, MOST FUTSAL TEAMS HAVE BOTH INEXPERIENCED AND EXPERIENCED PLAYERS. IT'S NOT UNUSUAL FOR A TEAM TO HAVE FEMALE PLAYERS, EITHER. BASICALLY, WHAT'S IMPORTANT IS YOUR DRIVE TO PLAY THE GAME. OF COURSE, IF YOU RUN A LOT, IT'LL EXHAUST YOU, AND YOU MIGHT MAKE MISTAKES AND BECOME A BURDEN TO YOUR TEAMMATES. WHEN YOU GET TIRED, YOU CAN ALWAYS HAVE SOMEONE ELSE TAKE YOUR SPOT. IT'S NATURAL FOR AN INEXPERIENCED PLAYER TO BE LOUSY AT HANDLING THE BALL, SO DON'T WORRY ABOUT THAT. THE EMBARRASSMENT IS NOTHING COMPARED WITH THE JOY YOU GET FROM TAKING A SHOT ON GOAL. SCORING FEELS GREAT!

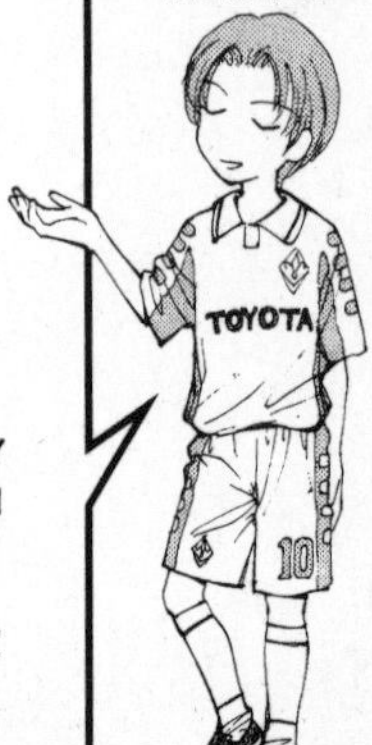
FUTSAL IS A DIFFERENT ANIMAL FROM SOCCER.
YOU'RE NOT ALLOWED TO MAKE A RUI COSTA-STYLE THROUGH PASS.

I LEARNED A LITTLE BIT ABOUT FUTSAL THIS TIME. A WHILE BACK, I HEARD THAT A NUMBER OF BRAZILIAN PLAYERS, LIKE RONALDO AND EDMUNDO, STARTED WITH FUTSAL AND I TOTALLY BELIEVE IT. BRAZILIAN PLAYERS OFTEN USE FLASHY EVASION TECHNIQUES WHEN THEY'RE FACED WITH A NUMERICAL MISMATCH (TWO VS. ONE OR THREE VS. ONE), LIKE DRIBBLING THROUGH A TIGHT SPOT OR USING INTERESTING FEINTS. I MEAN, THOSE TYPES OF TECHNIQUES MIGHT BE SOMETHING THEY LEARNED PLAYING FUTSAL. THAT MAKES ME WANT TO PLAY FUTSAL MORE OFTEN. AND, TO TELL YOU THE TRUTH, I REGRET LOSING AGAINST THE GUYS FROM HIBA THE OTHER DAY. I'M COMPELLED TO PRACTICE SO THAT I CAN TAKE MY REVENGE.

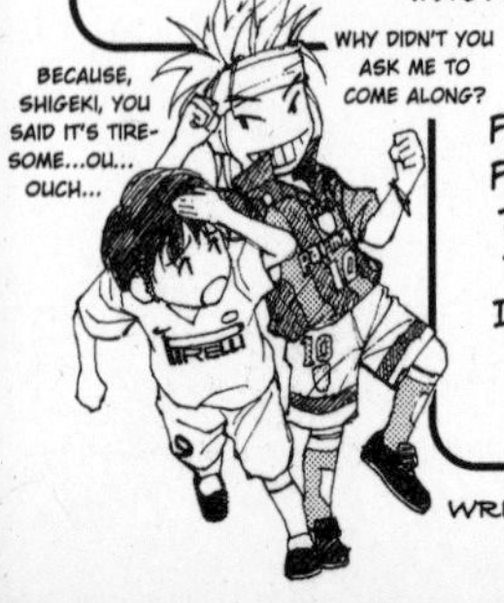
WHY DIDN'T YOU ASK ME TO COME ALONG?
BECAUSE, SHIGEKI, YOU SAID IT'S TIRE-SOME...OU... OUCH...

WRITTEN by ASSISTANT N (SOCCER MANIAC)

WRITING • ILLUSTRATION / ASSISTANT N THANKS ♡

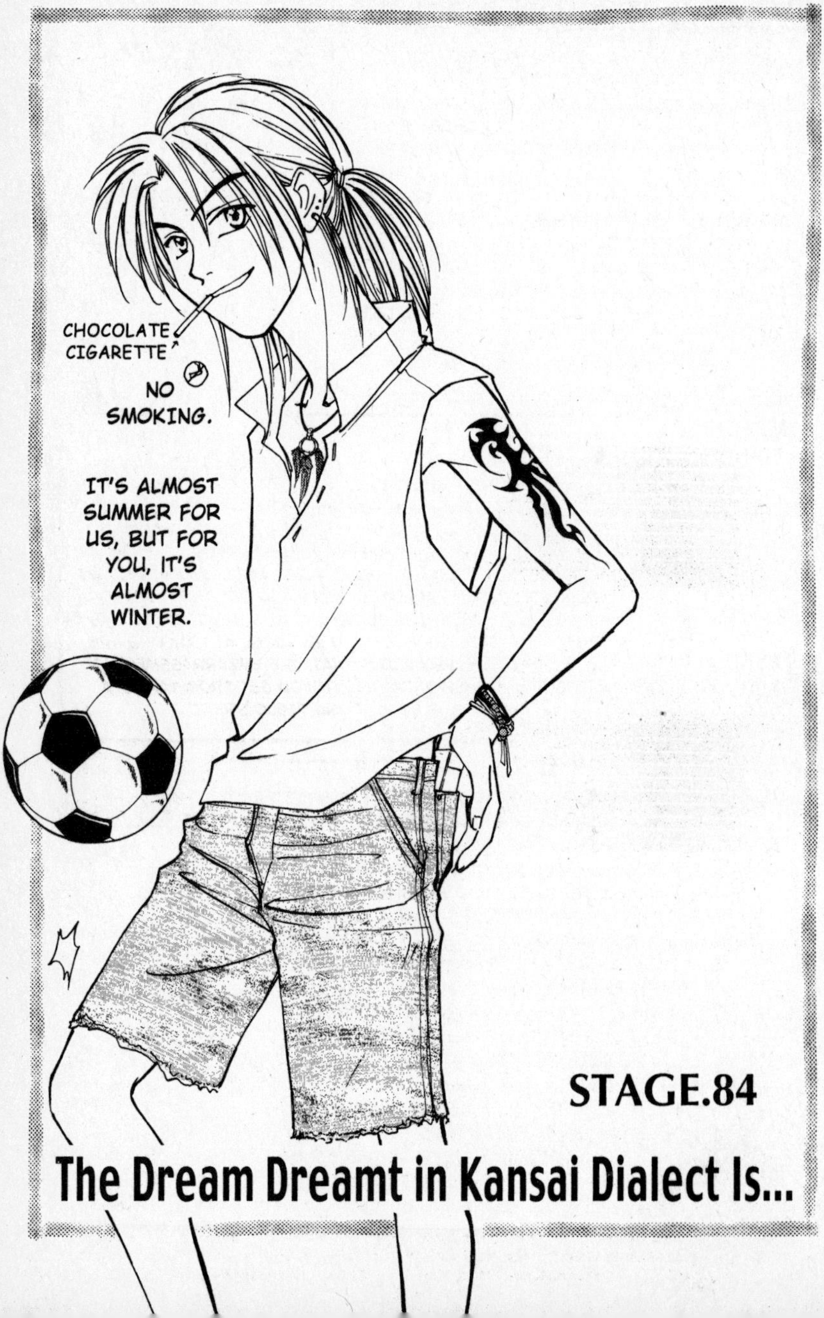
CHOCOLATE CIGARETTE
NO SMOKING.
IT'S ALMOST SUMMER FOR US, BUT FOR YOU, IT'S ALMOST WINTER.

STAGE.84

The Dream Dreamt in Kansai Dialect Is...

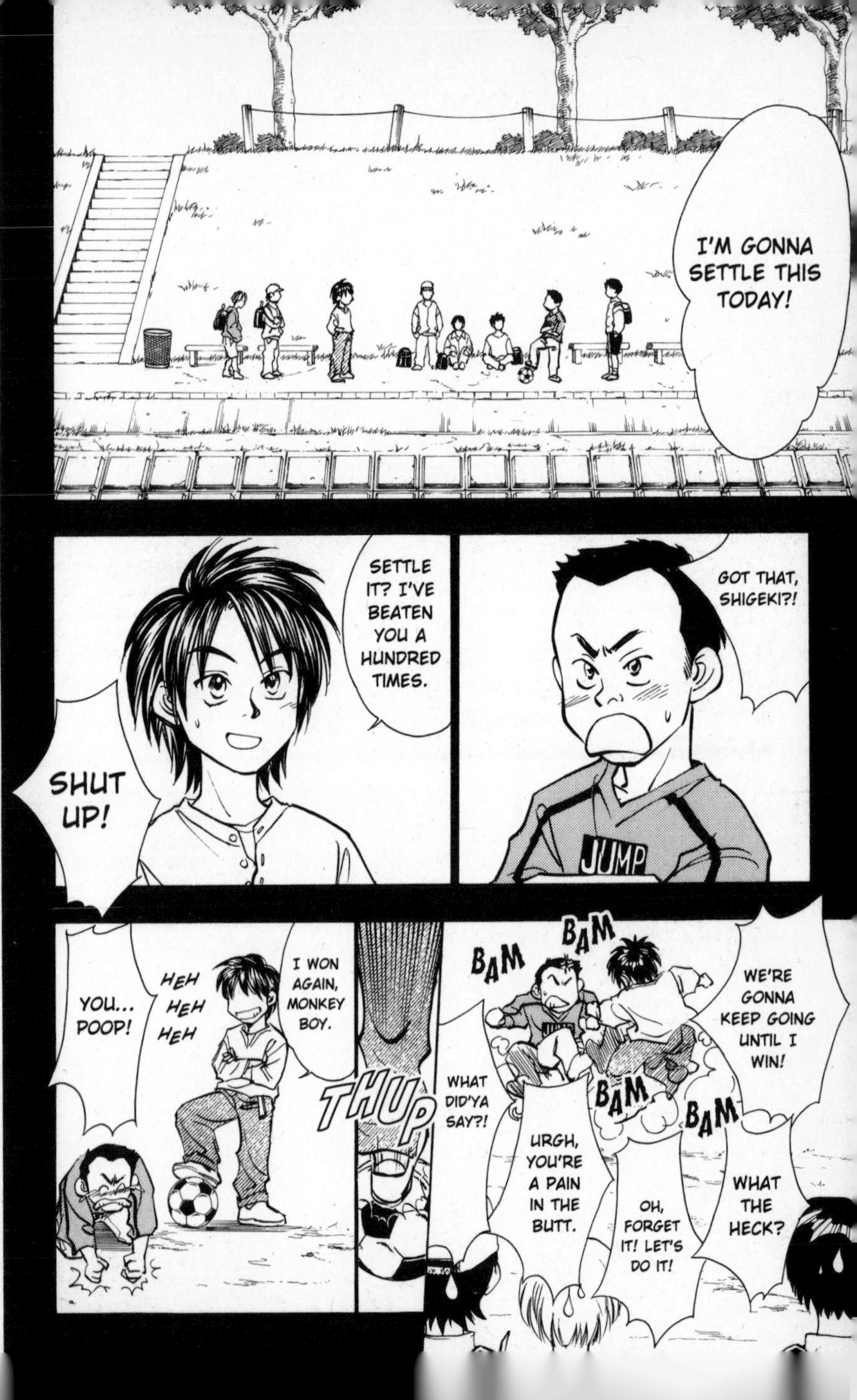
I'M GONNA SETTLE THIS TODAY!
GOT THAT, SHIGEKI?!
JUMP
SETTLE IT? I'VE BEATEN YOU A HUNDRED TIMES.
SHUT UP!
BAM
BAM
WE'RE GONNA KEEP GOING UNTIL I WIN!
BAM
BAM
WHAT DID'YA SAY?!
WHAT THE HECK?
OH, FORGET IT! LET'S DO IT!
URGH, YOU'RE A PAIN IN THE BUTT.
THUP
I WON AGAIN, MONKEY BOY.
HEH HEH HEH
YOU... POOP!

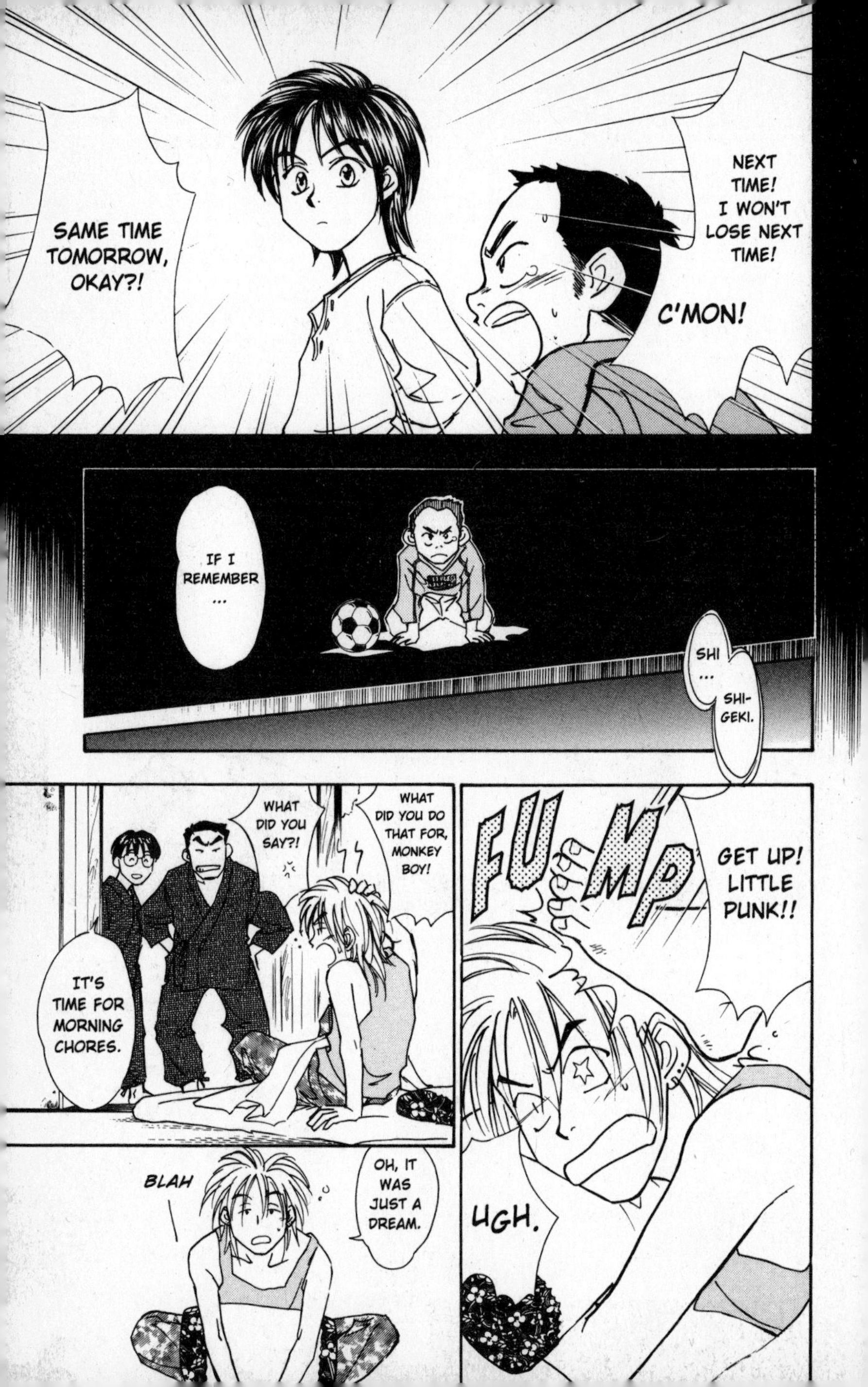
NEXT TIME! I WON'T LOSE NEXT TIME!
C'MON!
SAME TIME TOMORROW, OKAY?!
IF I REMEMBER ...
SHI ... SHI-GEKI.
GET UP! LITTLE PUNK!!
FUMP
UGH.
WHAT DID YOU DO THAT FOR, MONKEY BOY!
WHAT DID YOU SAY?!
IT'S TIME FOR MORNING CHORES.
OH, IT WAS JUST A DREAM.
BLAH

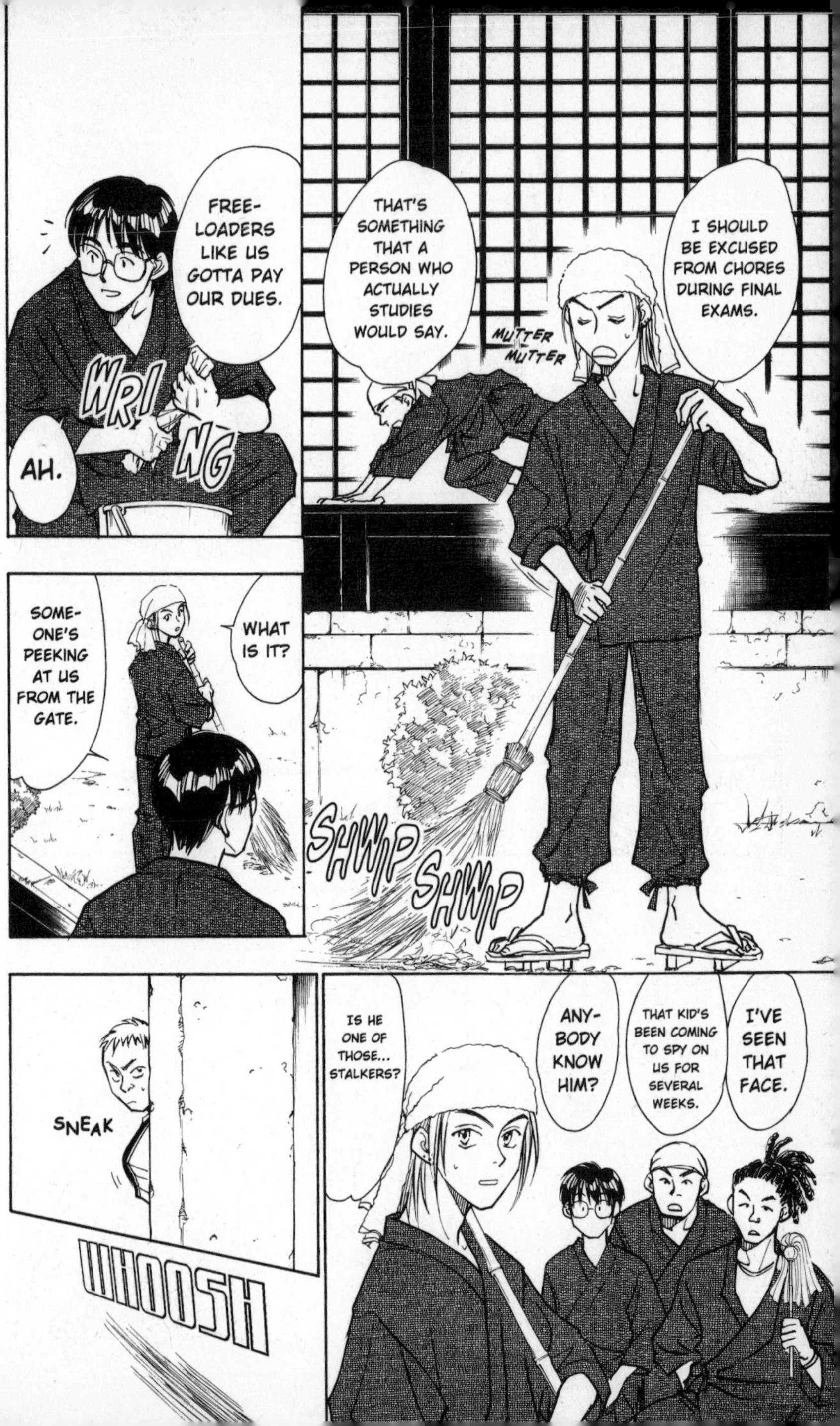
I SHOULD BE EXCUSED FROM CHORES DURING FINAL EXAMS.
MUTTER MUTTER
THAT'S SOMETHING THAT A PERSON WHO ACTUALLY STUDIES WOULD SAY.
SHWIP SHWIP
FREE-LOADERS LIKE US GOTTA PAY OUR DUES.
WRING
AH.
WHAT IS IT?
SOME-ONE'S PEEKING AT US FROM THE GATE.
I'VE SEEN THAT FACE.
THAT KID'S BEEN COMING TO SPY ON US FOR SEVERAL WEEKS.
ANY-BODY KNOW HIM?
IS HE ONE OF THOSE... STALKERS?
SNEAK
WHOOSH

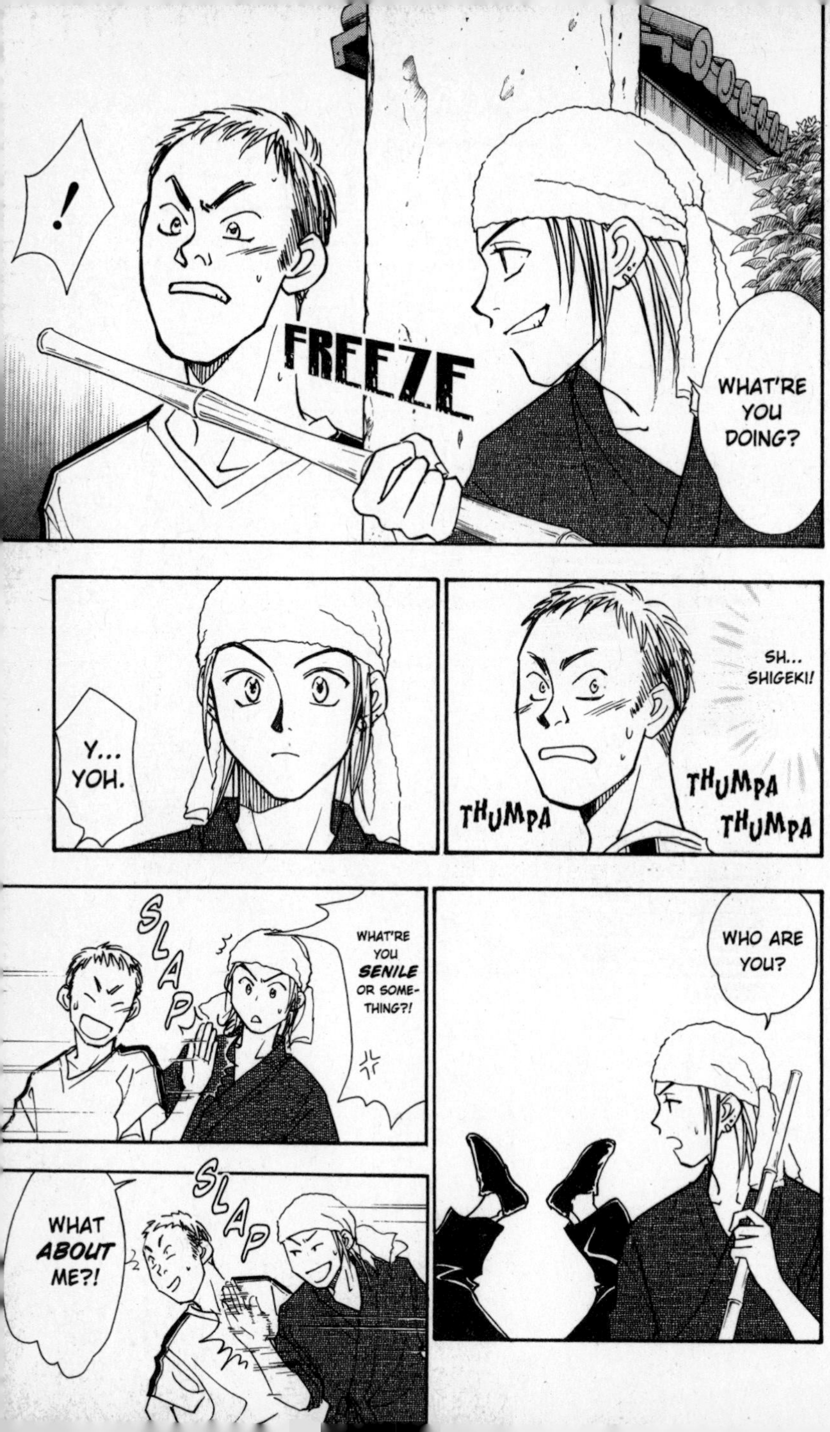
WHAT'RE YOU DOING?
FREEZE
!
SH... SHIGEKI!
THUMPA THUMPA
THUMPA
Y... YOH.
WHO ARE YOU?
SLAP
WHAT'RE YOU SENILE OR SOMETHING?!
SLAP
WHAT ABOUT ME?!

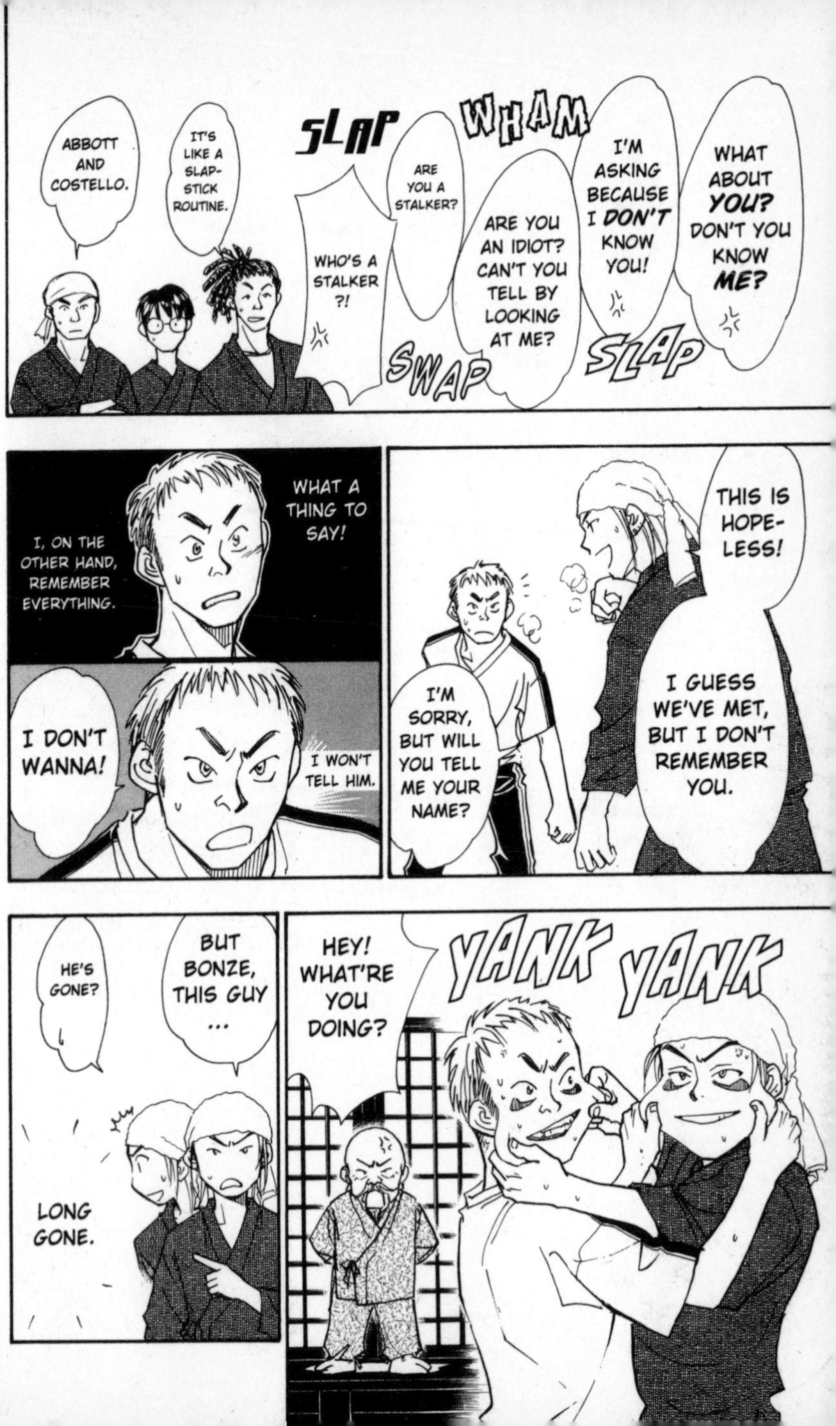
WHAM
WHAT ABOUT YOU? DON'T YOU KNOW ME?
SLAP
I'M ASKING BECAUSE I DON'T KNOW YOU!
ARE YOU AN IDIOT? CAN'T YOU TELL BY LOOKING AT ME?
SWAP
ARE YOU A STALKER?
SLAP
WHO'S A STALKER ?!
IT'S LIKE A SLAP-STICK ROUTINE.
ABBOTT AND COSTELLO.
THIS IS HOPE-LESS!
I GUESS WE'VE MET, BUT I DON'T REMEMBER YOU.
I'M SORRY, BUT WILL YOU TELL ME YOUR NAME?
WHAT A THING TO SAY!
I, ON THE OTHER HAND, REMEMBER EVERYTHING.
I WON'T TELL HIM.
I DON'T WANNA!
YANK YANK
HEY! WHAT'RE YOU DOING?
BUT BONZE, THIS GUY ...
HE'S GONE?
LONG GONE.

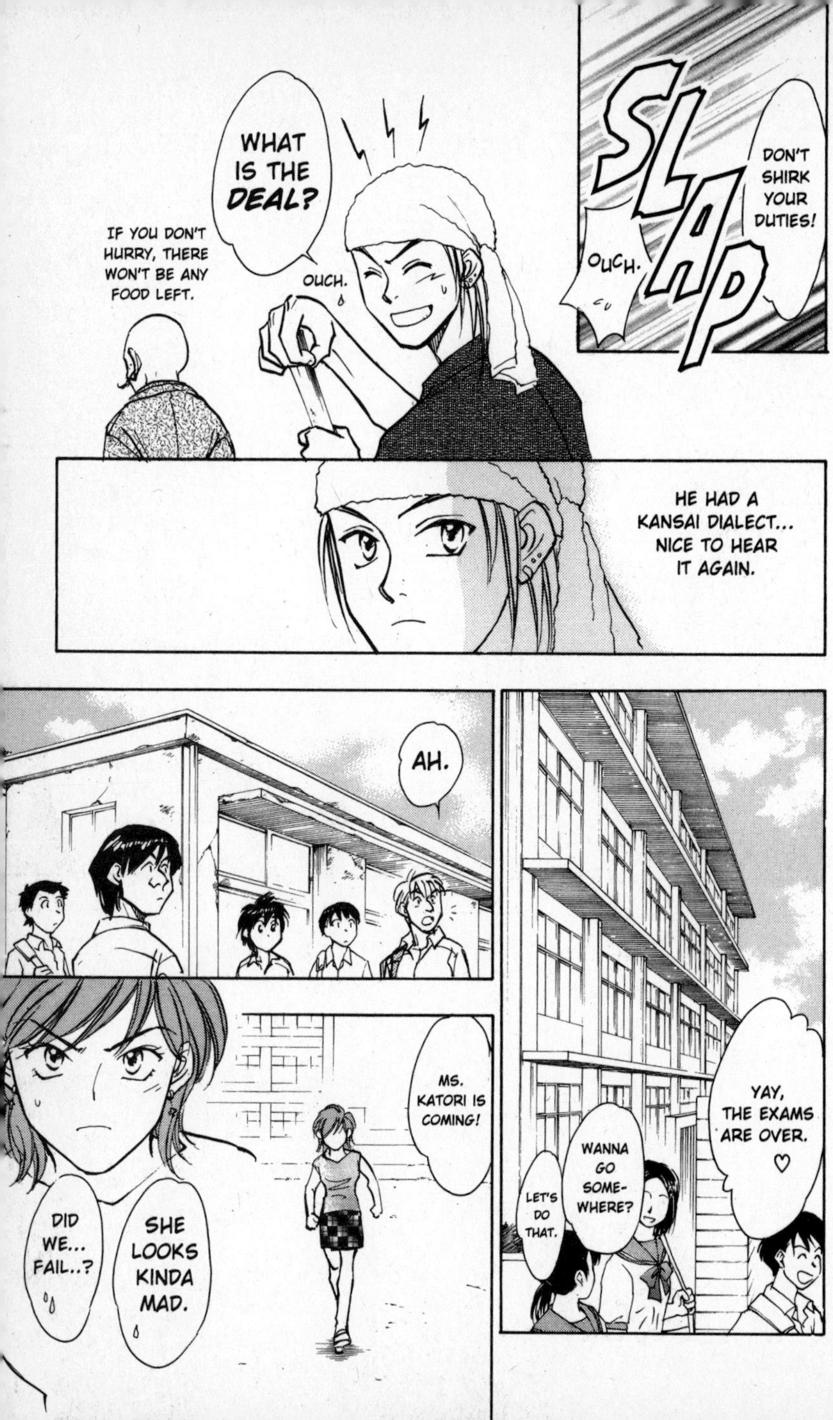
DON'T SHIRK YOUR DUTIES!
SLAP
OUCH.
WHAT IS THE DEAL?
OUCH.
IF YOU DON'T HURRY, THERE WON'T BE ANY FOOD LEFT.
HE HAD A KANSAI DIALECT... NICE TO HEAR IT AGAIN.
YAY, THE EXAMS ARE OVER. ♡
WANNA GO SOME-WHERE?
LET'S DO THAT.
AH.
MS. KATORI IS COMING!
SHE LOOKS KINDA MAD.
DID WE... FAIL..?

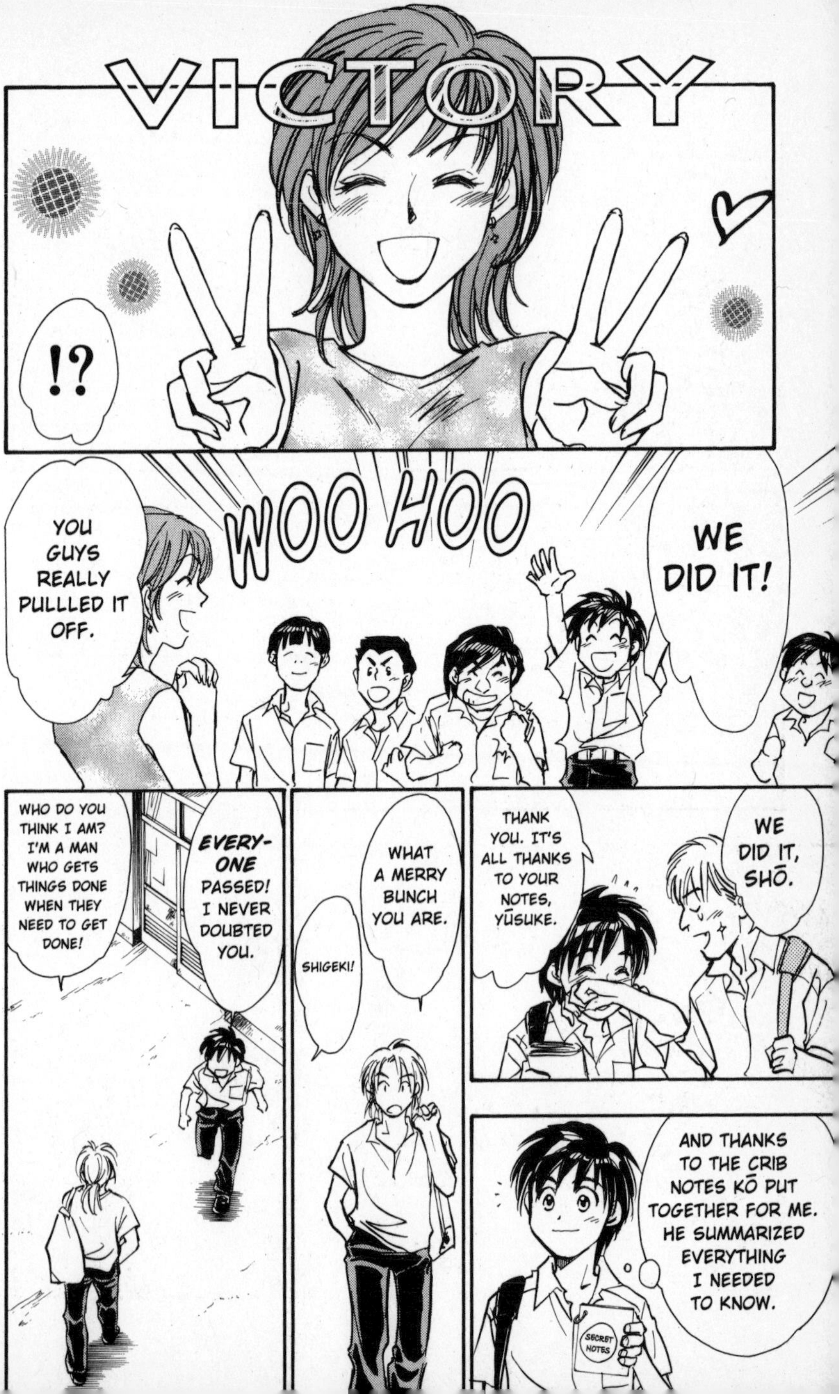
VICTORY
!?
WE DID IT!
WOO HOO
YOU GUYS REALLY PULLLED IT OFF.
WE DID IT, SHŌ.
THANK YOU. IT'S ALL THANKS TO YOUR NOTES, YŪSUKE.
AND THANKS TO THE CRIB NOTES KŌ PUT TOGETHER FOR ME. HE SUMMARIZED EVERYTHING I NEEDED TO KNOW.
SECRET NOTES
WHAT A MERRY BUNCH YOU ARE.
SHIGEKI!
EVERY-ONE PASSED! I NEVER DOUBTED YOU.
WHO DO YOU THINK I AM? I'M A MAN WHO GETS THINGS DONE WHEN THEY NEED TO GET DONE!

READ THIS WAY

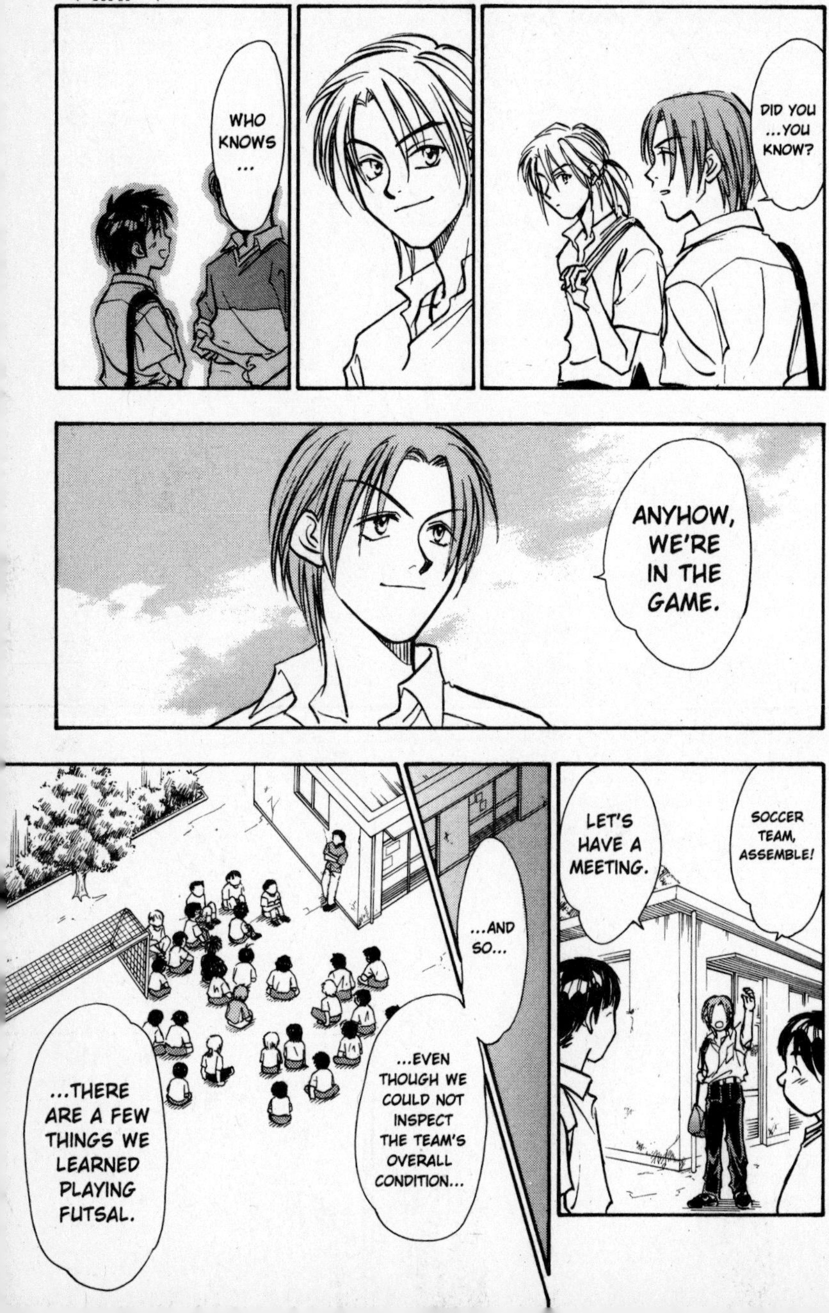
DID YOU ...YOU KNOW?
WHO KNOWS ...
ANYHOW, WE'RE IN THE GAME.
SOCCER TEAM, ASSEMBLE!
LET'S HAVE A MEETING.
...AND SO...
...EVEN THOUGH WE COULD NOT INSPECT THE TEAM'S OVERALL CONDITION...
...THERE ARE A FEW THINGS WE LEARNED PLAYING FUTSAL.

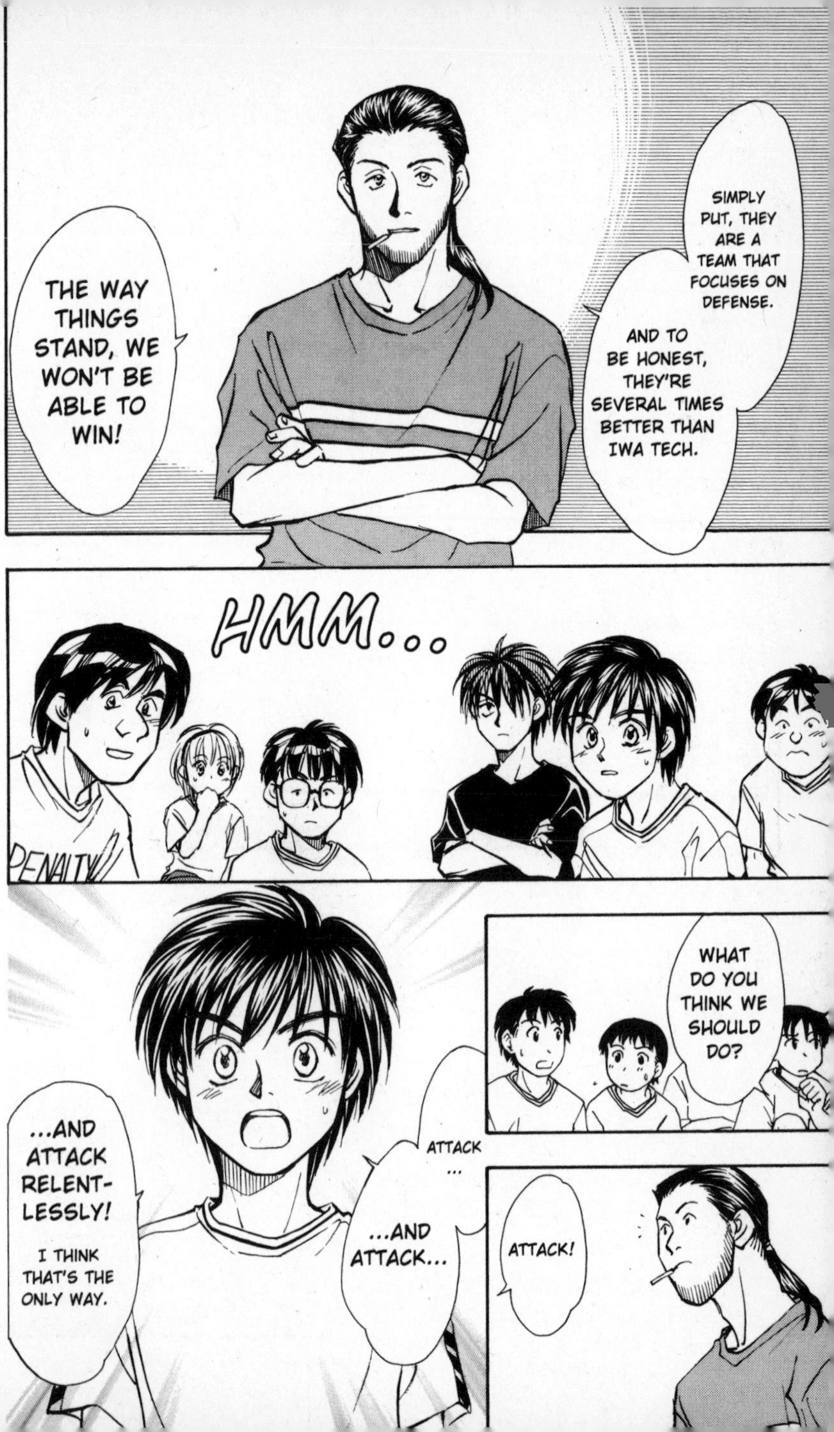
SIMPLY PUT, THEY ARE A TEAM THAT FOCUSES ON DEFENSE.
AND TO BE HONEST, THEY'RE SEVERAL TIMES BETTER THAN IWA TECH.
THE WAY THINGS STAND, WE WON'T BE ABLE TO WIN!
HMM...
WHAT DO YOU THINK WE SHOULD DO?
ATTACK!
ATTACK ...
...AND ATTACK...
...AND ATTACK RELENT-LESSLY!
I THINK THAT'S THE ONLY WAY.
PENALTY

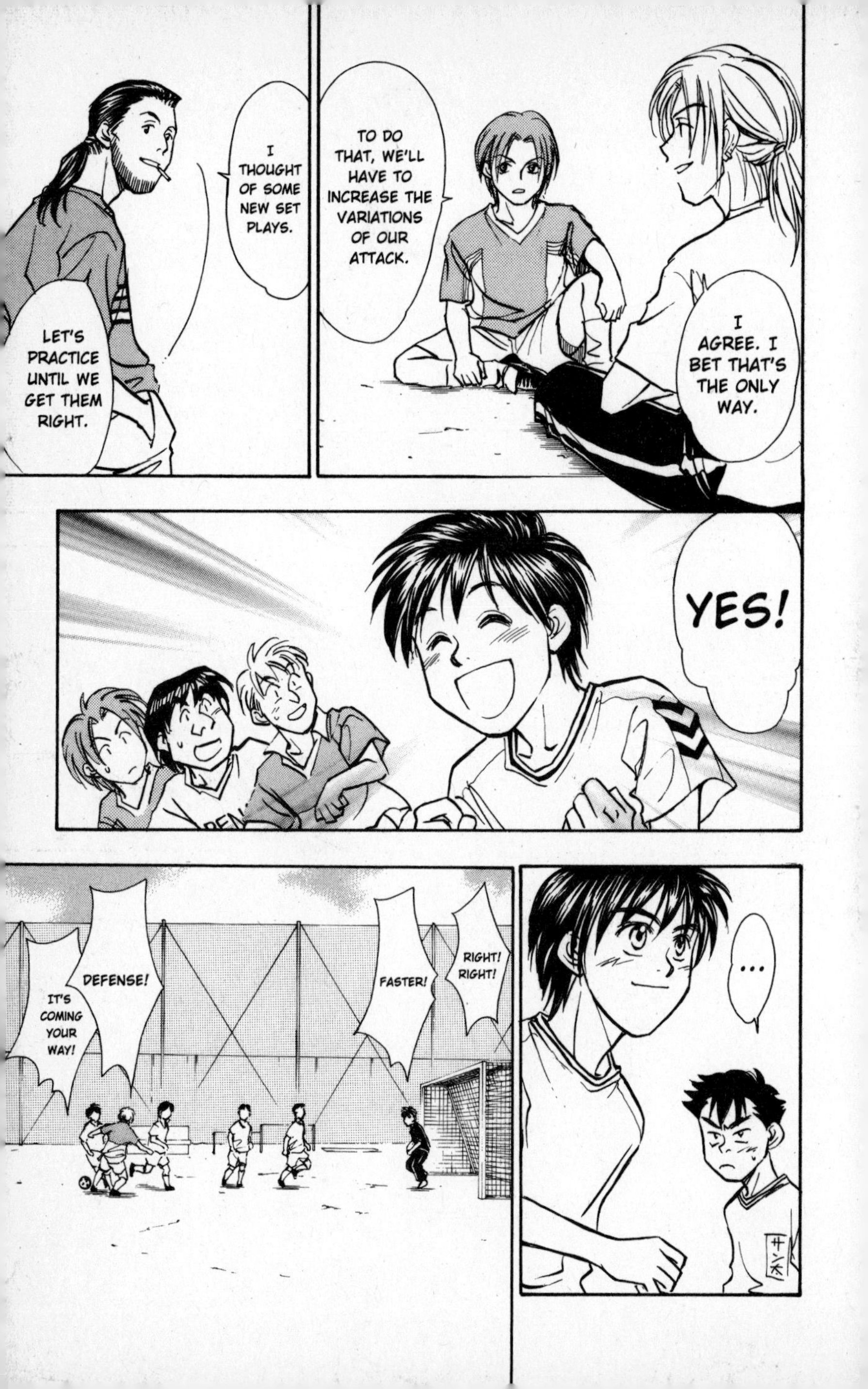
TO DO THAT, WE'LL HAVE TO INCREASE THE VARIATIONS OF OUR ATTACK.
I AGREE. I BET THAT'S THE ONLY WAY.
I THOUGHT OF SOME NEW SET PLAYS.
LET'S PRACTICE UNTIL WE GET THEM RIGHT.
YES!
...
RIGHT! RIGHT!
FASTER!
DEFENSE!
IT'S COMING YOUR WAY!

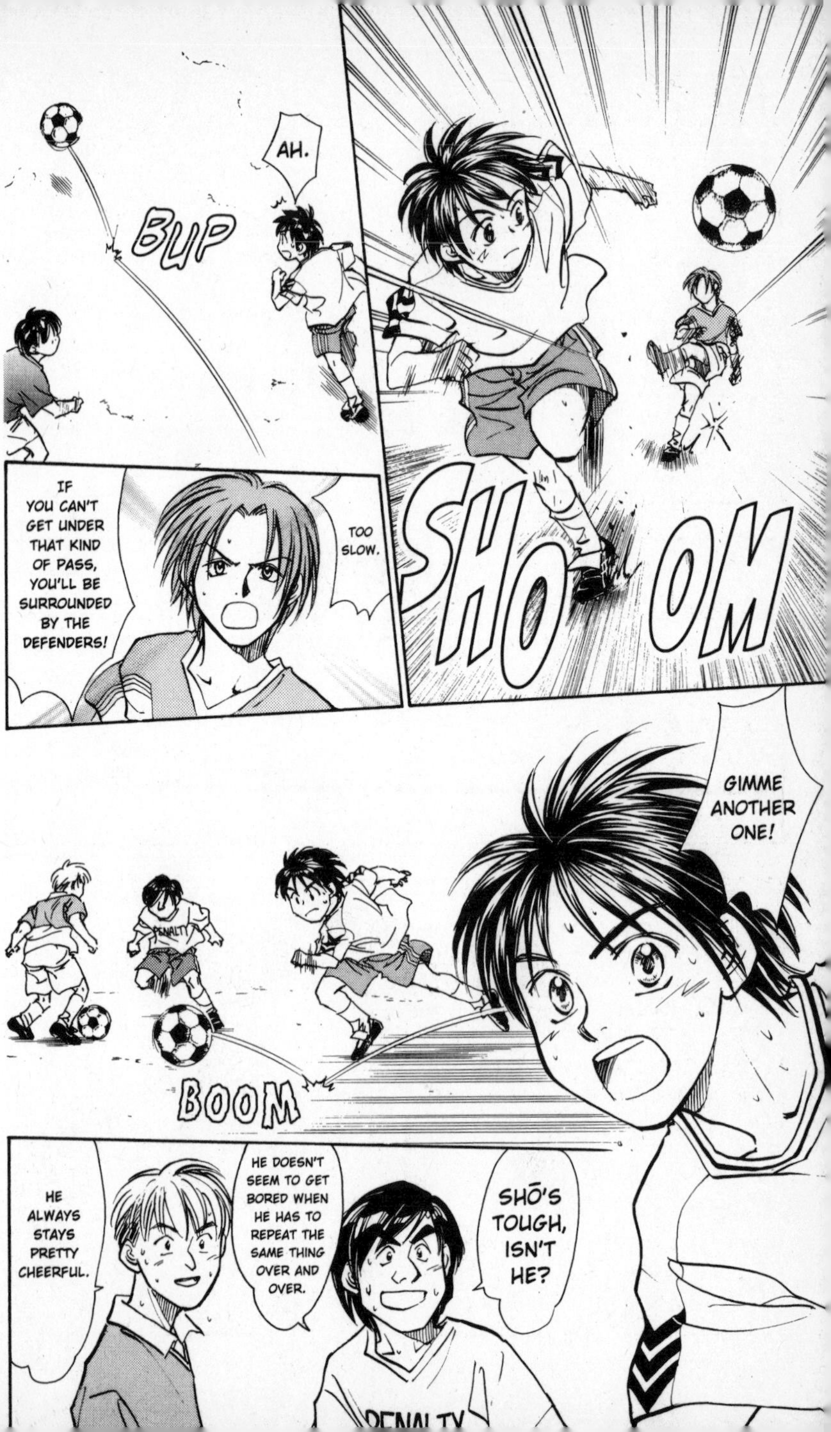
SHOOM
AH.
BUP
TOO SLOW.
IF YOU CAN'T GET UNDER THAT KIND OF PASS, YOU'LL BE SURROUNDED BY THE DEFENDERS!
GIMME ANOTHER ONE!
BOOM
SHŌ'S TOUGH, ISN'T HE?
HE DOESN'T SEEM TO GET BORED WHEN HE HAS TO REPEAT THE SAME THING OVER AND OVER.
HE ALWAYS STAYS PRETTY CHEERFUL.

READ THIS WAY

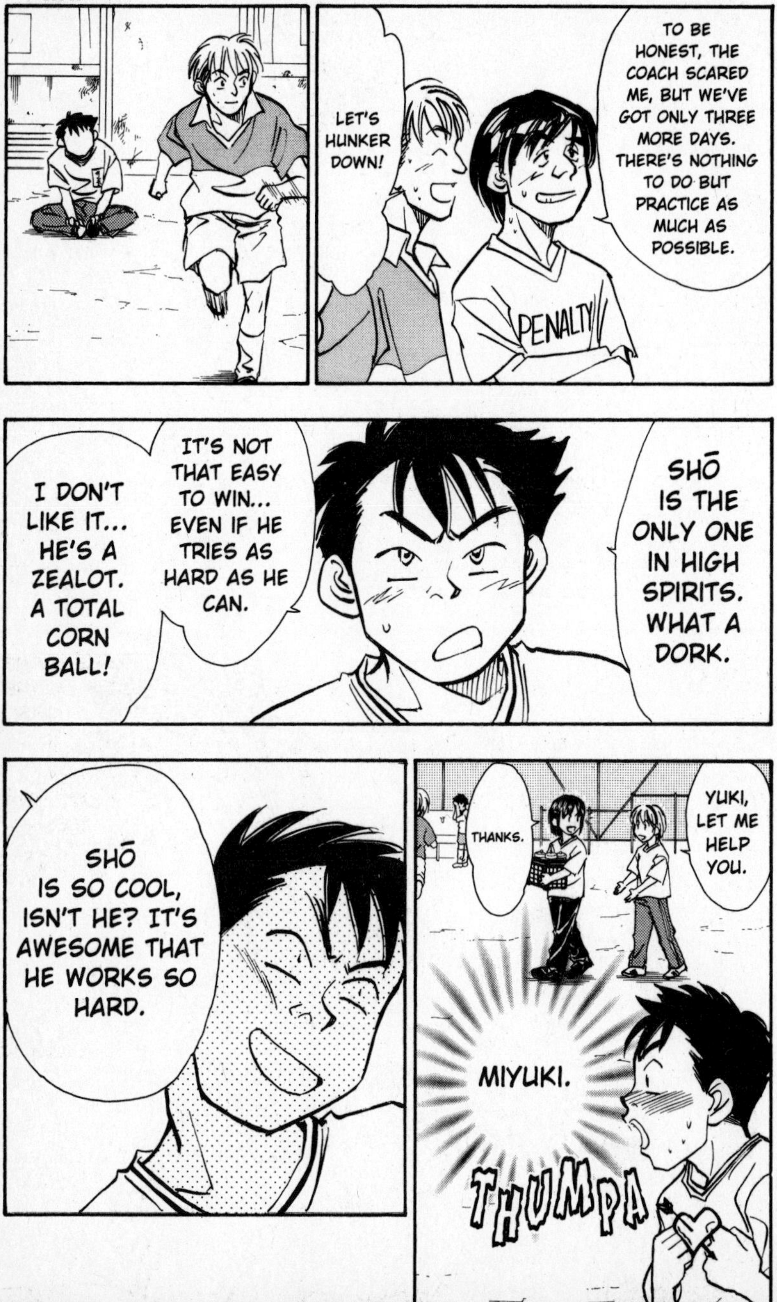

TO BE HONEST, THE COACH SCARED ME, BUT WE'VE GOT ONLY THREE MORE DAYS. THERE'S NOTHING TO DO BUT PRACTICE AS MUCH AS POSSIBLE.
LET'S HUNKER DOWN!
PENALTY
SHŌ IS THE ONLY ONE IN HIGH SPIRITS. WHAT A DORK.
IT'S NOT THAT EASY TO WIN... EVEN IF HE TRIES AS HARD AS HE CAN.
I DON'T LIKE IT... HE'S A ZEALOT. A TOTAL CORN BALL!
YUKI, LET ME HELP YOU.
THANKS.
MIYUKI.
THUMPA
SHŌ IS SO COOL, ISN'T HE? IT'S AWESOME THAT HE WORKS SO HARD.

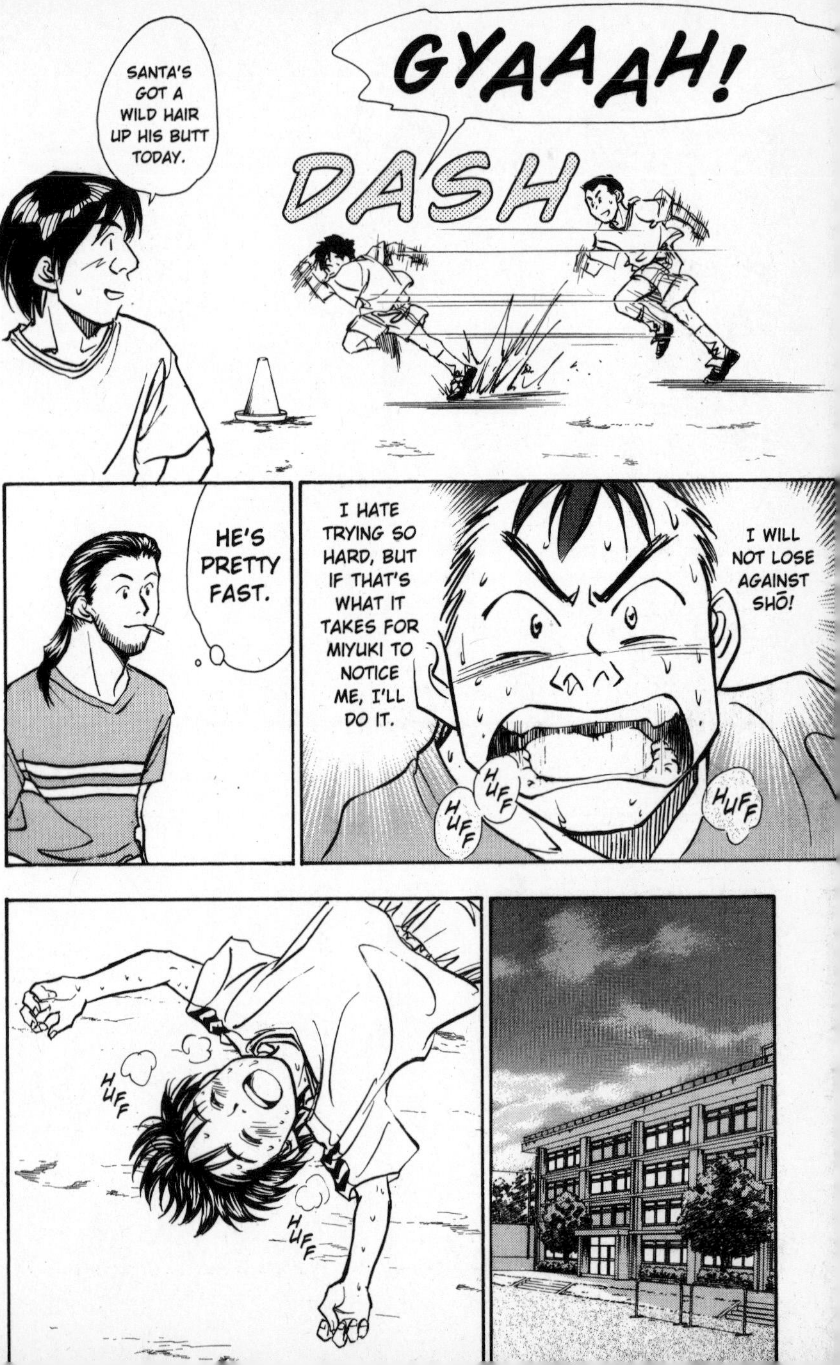
GYAAAH!
DASH
SANTA'S GOT A WILD HAIR UP HIS BUTT TODAY.
I WILL NOT LOSE AGAINST SHŌ!
I HATE TRYING SO HARD, BUT IF THAT'S WHAT IT TAKES FOR MIYUKI TO NOTICE ME, I'LL DO IT.
HUFF
HUFF
HUFF
HE'S PRETTY FAST.
HUFF
HUFF

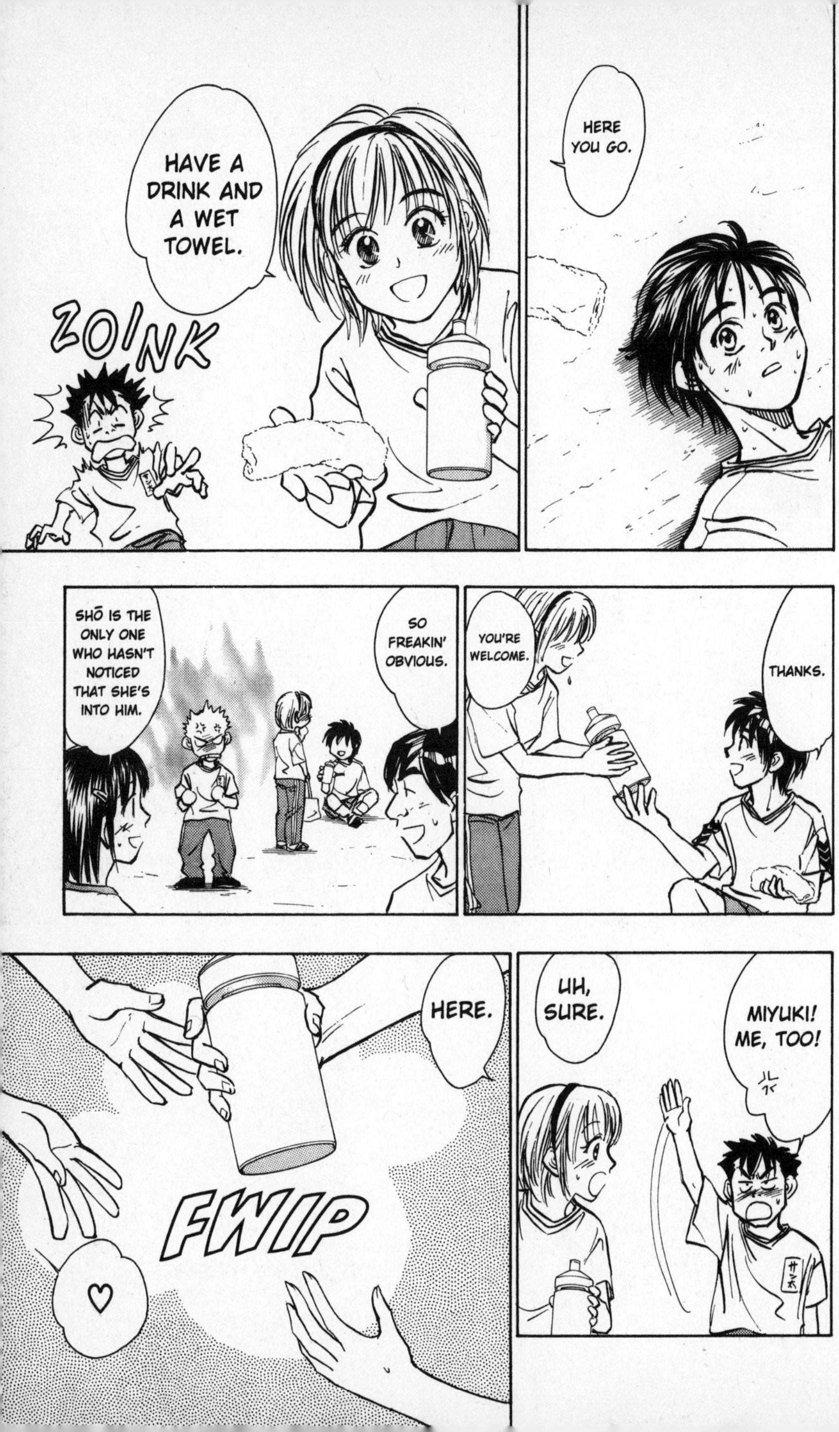
HERE YOU GO.
HAVE A DRINK AND A WET TOWEL.
ZOINK
THANKS.
YOU'RE WELCOME.
SO FREAKIN' OBVIOUS.
SHŌ IS THE ONLY ONE WHO HASN'T NOTICED THAT SHE'S INTO HIM.
MIYUKI! ME, TOO!
UH, SURE.
HERE.
FWIP
♥

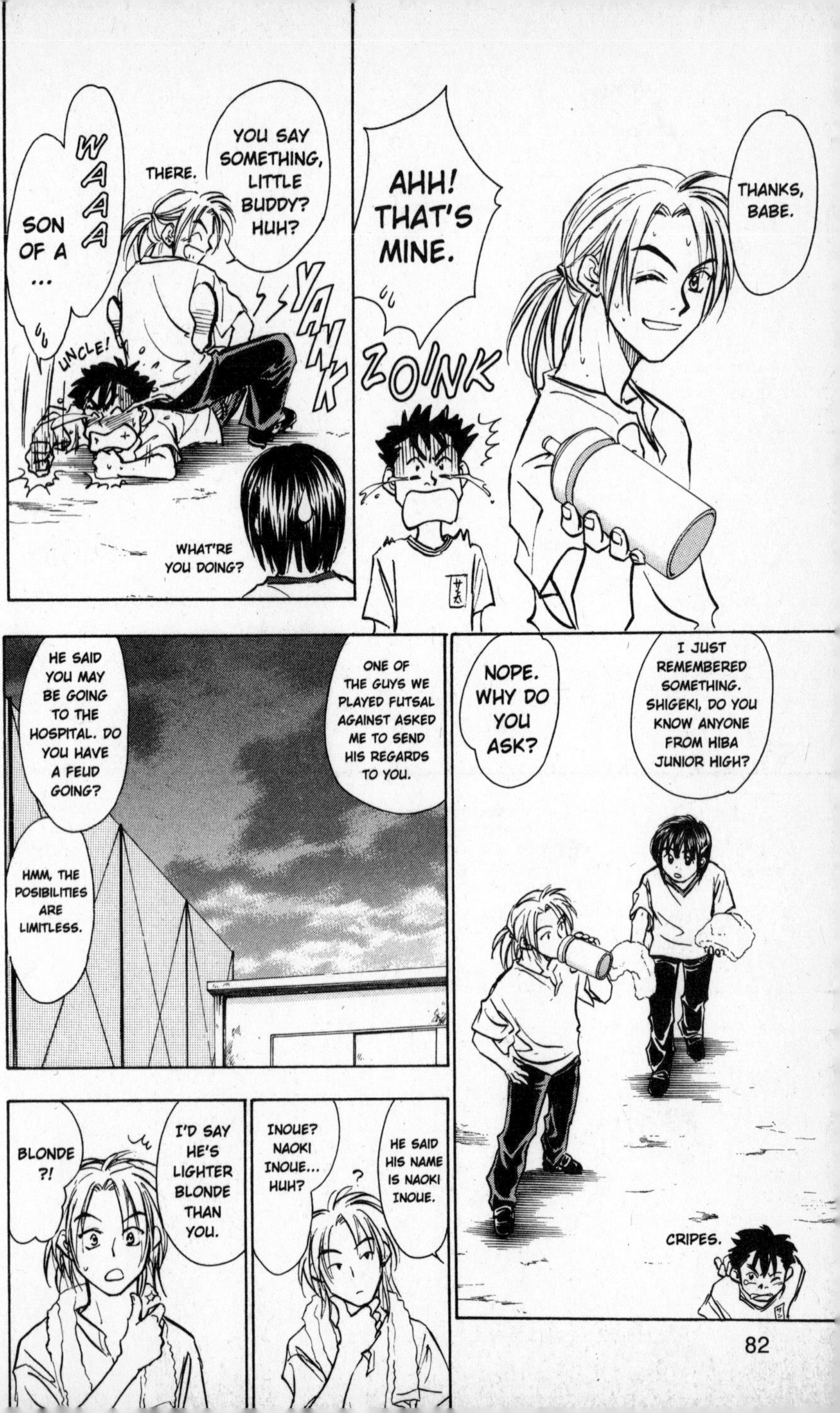
THANKS, BABE.
AHH! THAT'S MINE.
ZOINK
YOU SAY SOMETHING, LITTLE BUDDY? HUH?
YANK
THERE.
WAAAA
SON OF A ...
UNCLE!
WHAT'RE YOU DOING?
I JUST REMEMBERED SOMETHING. SHIGEKI, DO YOU KNOW ANYONE FROM HIBA JUNIOR HIGH?
NOPE. WHY DO YOU ASK?
CRIPES.
ONE OF THE GUYS WE PLAYED FUTSAL AGAINST ASKED ME TO SEND HIS REGARDS TO YOU.
HE SAID YOU MAY BE GOING TO THE HOSPITAL. DO YOU HAVE A FEUD GOING?
HMM, THE POSIBILITIES ARE LIMITLESS.
HE SAID HIS NAME IS NAOKI INOUE.
INOUE? NAOKI INOUE... HUH?
I'D SAY HE'S LIGHTER BLONDE THAN YOU.
BLONDE ?!

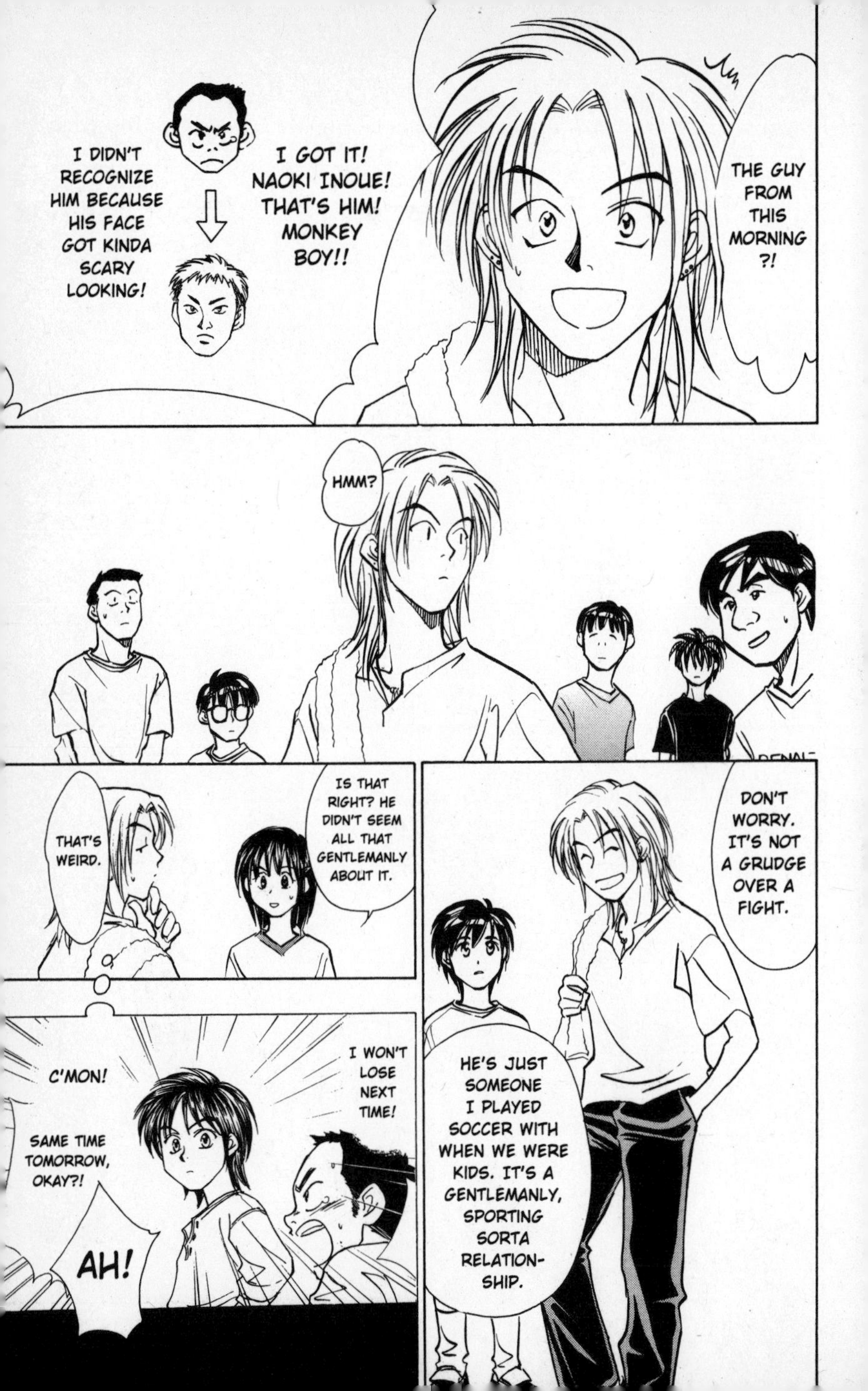
THE GUY FROM THIS MORNING?!
I GOT IT! NAOKI INOUE! THAT'S HIM! MONKEY BOY!!
I DIDN'T RECOGNIZE HIM BECAUSE HIS FACE GOT KINDA SCARY LOOKING!
HMM?
DON'T WORRY. IT'S NOT A GRUDGE OVER A FIGHT.
HE'S JUST SOMEONE I PLAYED SOCCER WITH WHEN WE WERE KIDS. IT'S A GENTLEMANLY, SPORTING SORTA RELATION-SHIP.
IS THAT RIGHT? HE DIDN'T SEEM ALL THAT GENTLEMANLY ABOUT IT.
THAT'S WEIRD.
I WON'T LOSE NEXT TIME!
C'MON!
SAME TIME TOMORROW, OKAY?!
AH!

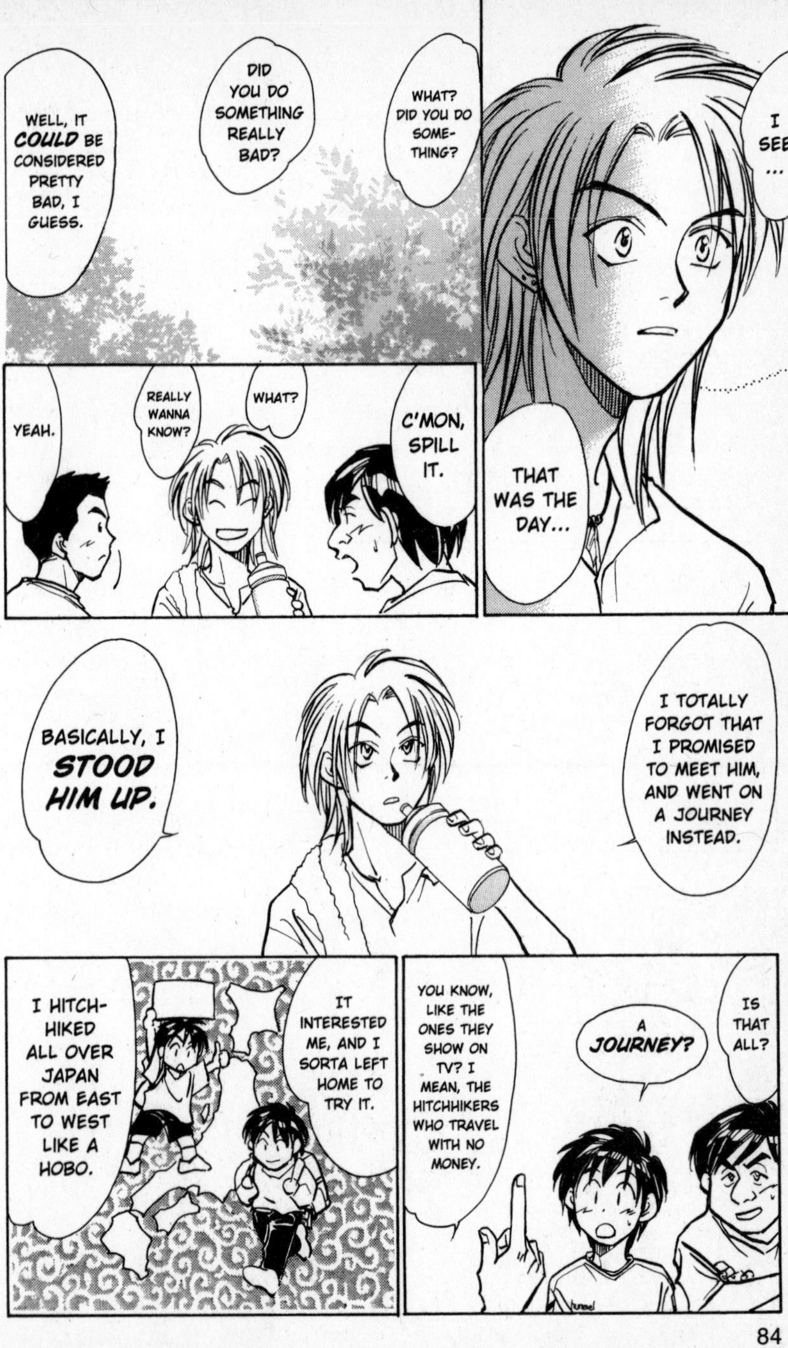
I SEE ...
THAT WAS THE DAY...
WHAT? DID YOU DO SOME-THING?
DID YOU DO SOMETHING REALLY BAD?
WELL, IT **COULD** BE CONSIDERED PRETTY BAD, I GUESS.
C'MON, SPILL IT.
WHAT?
REALLY WANNA KNOW?
YEAH.
I TOTALLY FORGOT THAT I PROMISED TO MEET HIM, AND WENT ON A JOURNEY INSTEAD.
BASICALLY, I **STOOD HIM UP.**
IS THAT ALL?
A **JOURNEY?**
YOU KNOW, LIKE THE ONES THEY SHOW ON TV? I MEAN, THE HITCHHIKERS WHO TRAVEL WITH NO MONEY.
IT INTERESTED ME, AND I SORTA LEFT HOME TO TRY IT.
I HITCH-HIKED ALL OVER JAPAN FROM EAST TO WEST LIKE A HOBO.

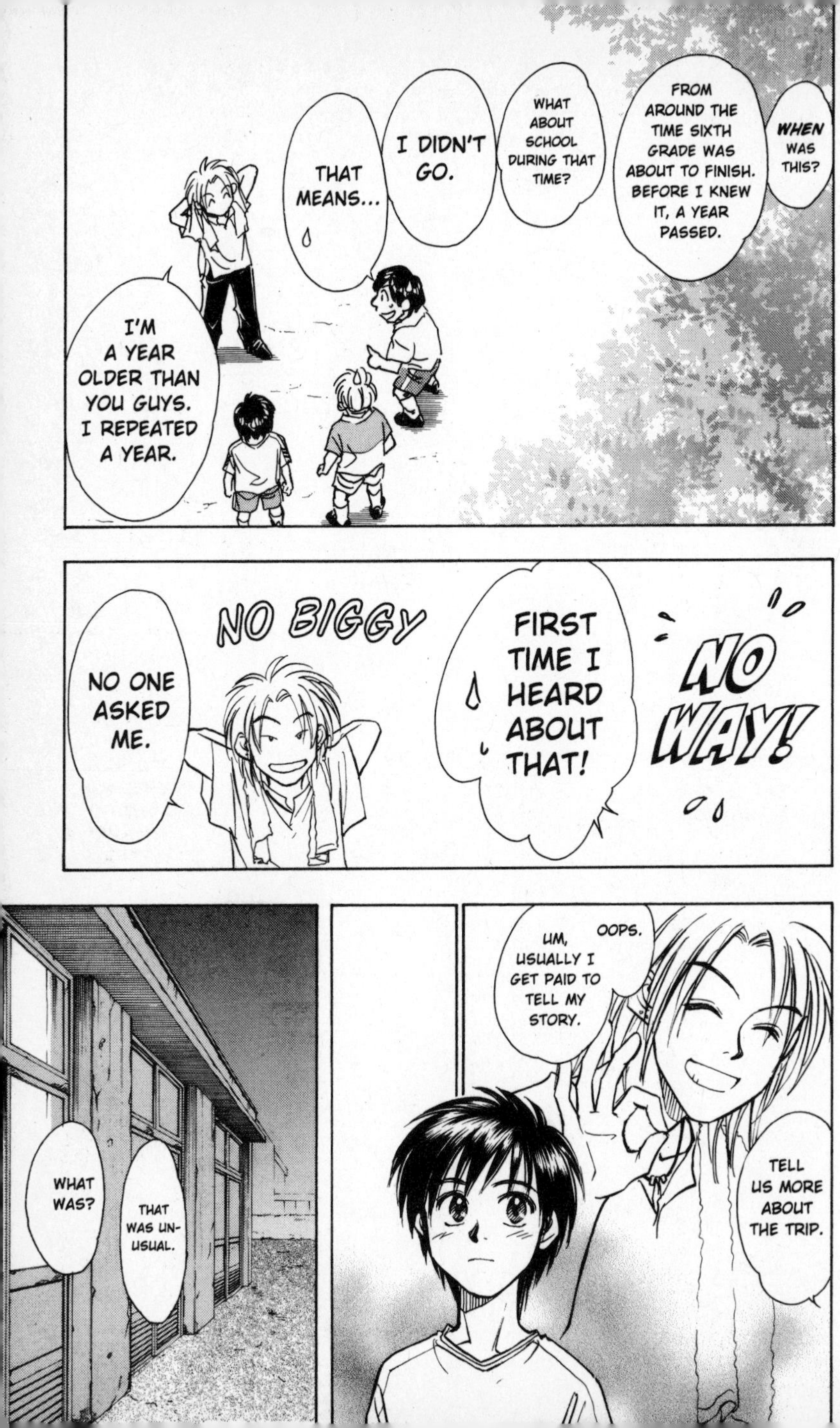
WHEN WAS THIS?
FROM AROUND THE TIME SIXTH GRADE WAS ABOUT TO FINISH. BEFORE I KNEW IT, A YEAR PASSED.
WHAT ABOUT SCHOOL DURING THAT TIME?
I DIDN'T GO.
THAT MEANS...
I'M A YEAR OLDER THAN YOU GUYS. I REPEATED A YEAR.
NO WAY!
FIRST TIME I HEARD ABOUT THAT!
NO BIGGY
NO ONE ASKED ME.
OOPS.
UM, USUALLY I GET PAID TO TELL MY STORY.
TELL US MORE ABOUT THE TRIP.
THAT WAS UN-USUAL.
WHAT WAS?

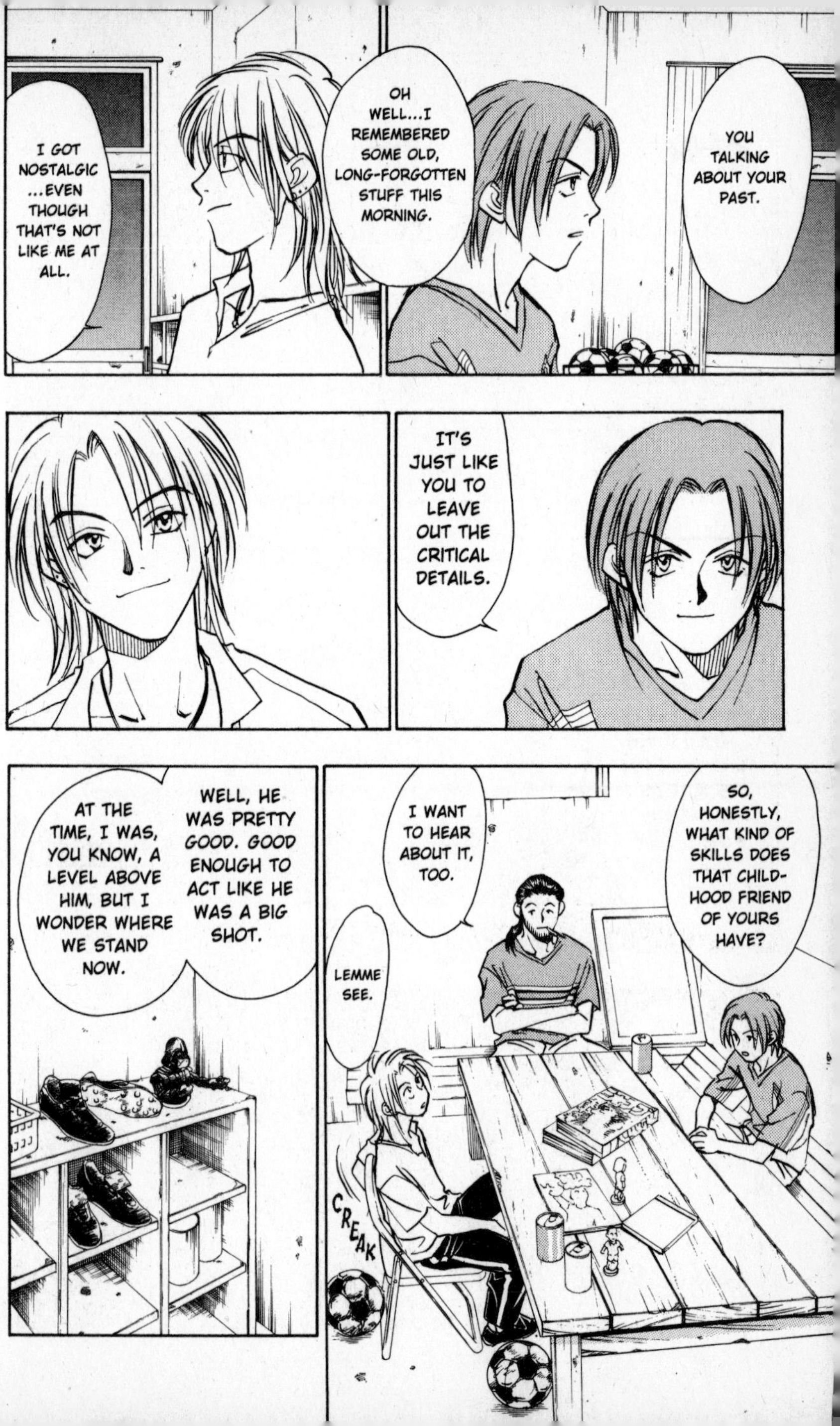
YOU TALKING ABOUT YOUR PAST.
OH WELL...I REMEMBERED SOME OLD, LONG-FORGOTTEN STUFF THIS MORNING.
I GOT NOSTALGIC ...EVEN THOUGH THAT'S NOT LIKE ME AT ALL.
IT'S JUST LIKE YOU TO LEAVE OUT THE CRITICAL DETAILS.
SO, HONESTLY, WHAT KIND OF SKILLS DOES THAT CHILD-HOOD FRIEND OF YOURS HAVE?
I WANT TO HEAR ABOUT IT, TOO.
LEMME SEE.
CREAK
WELL, HE WAS PRETTY GOOD. GOOD ENOUGH TO ACT LIKE HE WAS A BIG SHOT.
AT THE TIME, I WAS, YOU KNOW, A LEVEL ABOVE HIM, BUT I WONDER WHERE WE STAND NOW.

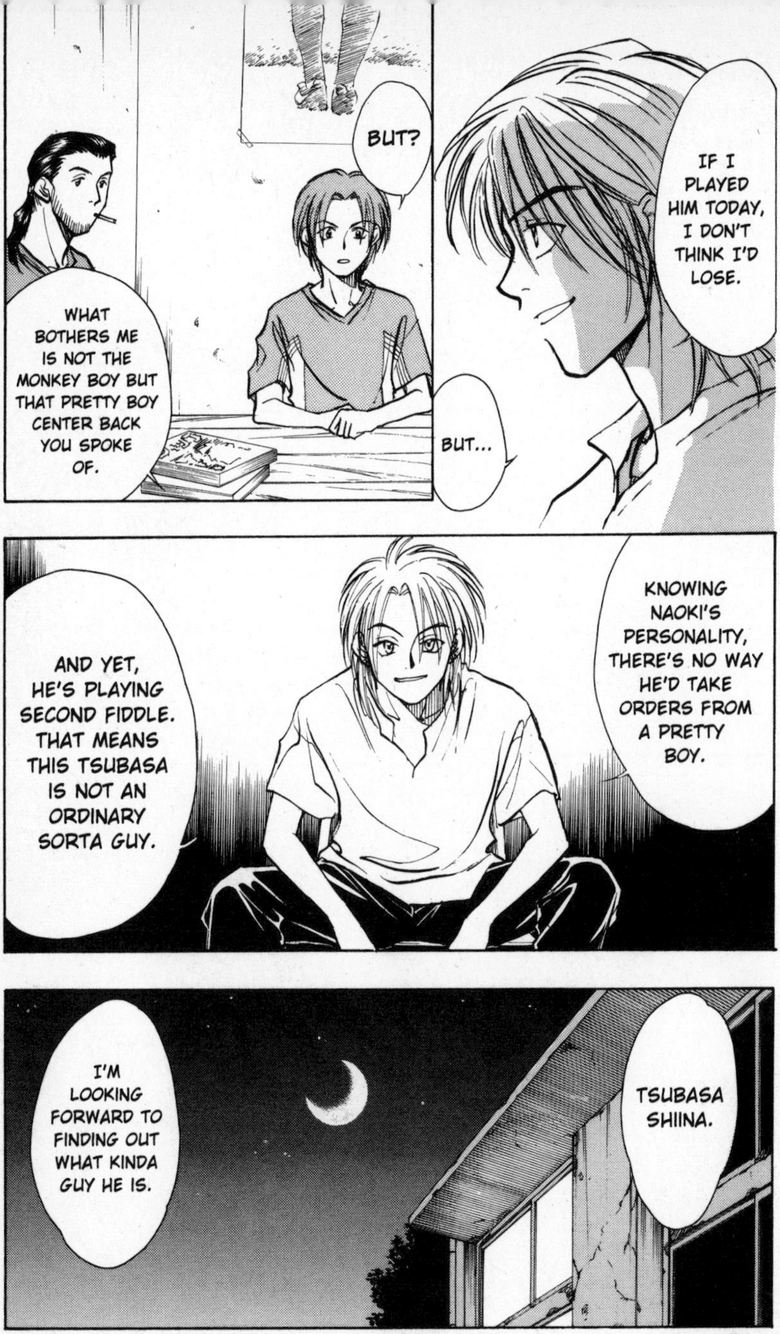
IF I PLAYED HIM TODAY, I DON'T THINK I'D LOSE.
BUT...
BUT?
WHAT BOTHERS ME IS NOT THE MONKEY BOY BUT THAT PRETTY BOY CENTER BACK YOU SPOKE OF.
KNOWING NAOKI'S PERSONALITY, THERE'S NO WAY HE'D TAKE ORDERS FROM A PRETTY BOY.
AND YET, HE'S PLAYING SECOND FIDDLE. THAT MEANS THIS TSUBASA IS NOT AN ORDINARY SORTA GUY.
TSUBASA SHIINA.
I'M LOOKING FORWARD TO FINDING OUT WHAT KINDA GUY HE IS.

WHISTLE! THEATRE !!

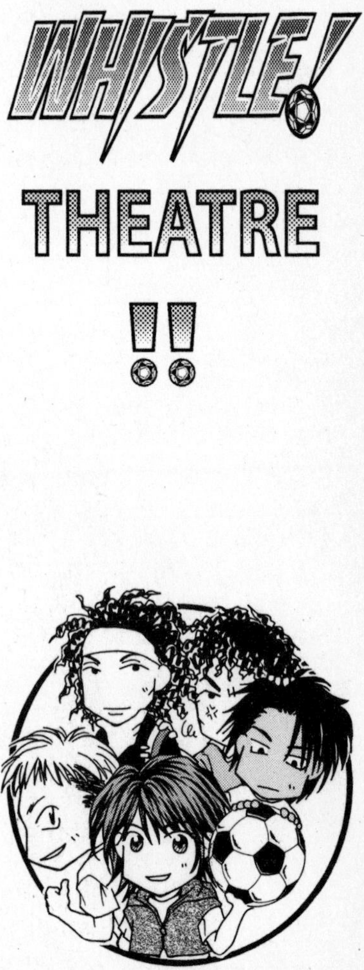

MANGA BY SEKI, ASSISTANT S

I'm always with you...

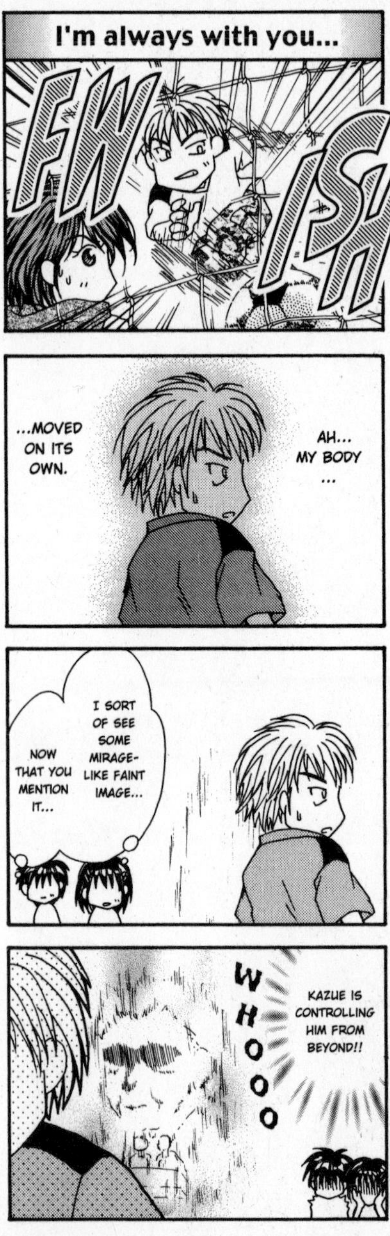
FWISH
AH... MY BODY ...
...MOVED ON ITS OWN.
I SORT OF SEE SOME MIRAGE-LIKE FAINT IMAGE...
NOW THAT YOU MENTION IT...
KAZUE IS CONTROLLING HIM FROM BEYOND!!
WHOOOO

STAGE.85

A Wing Descends

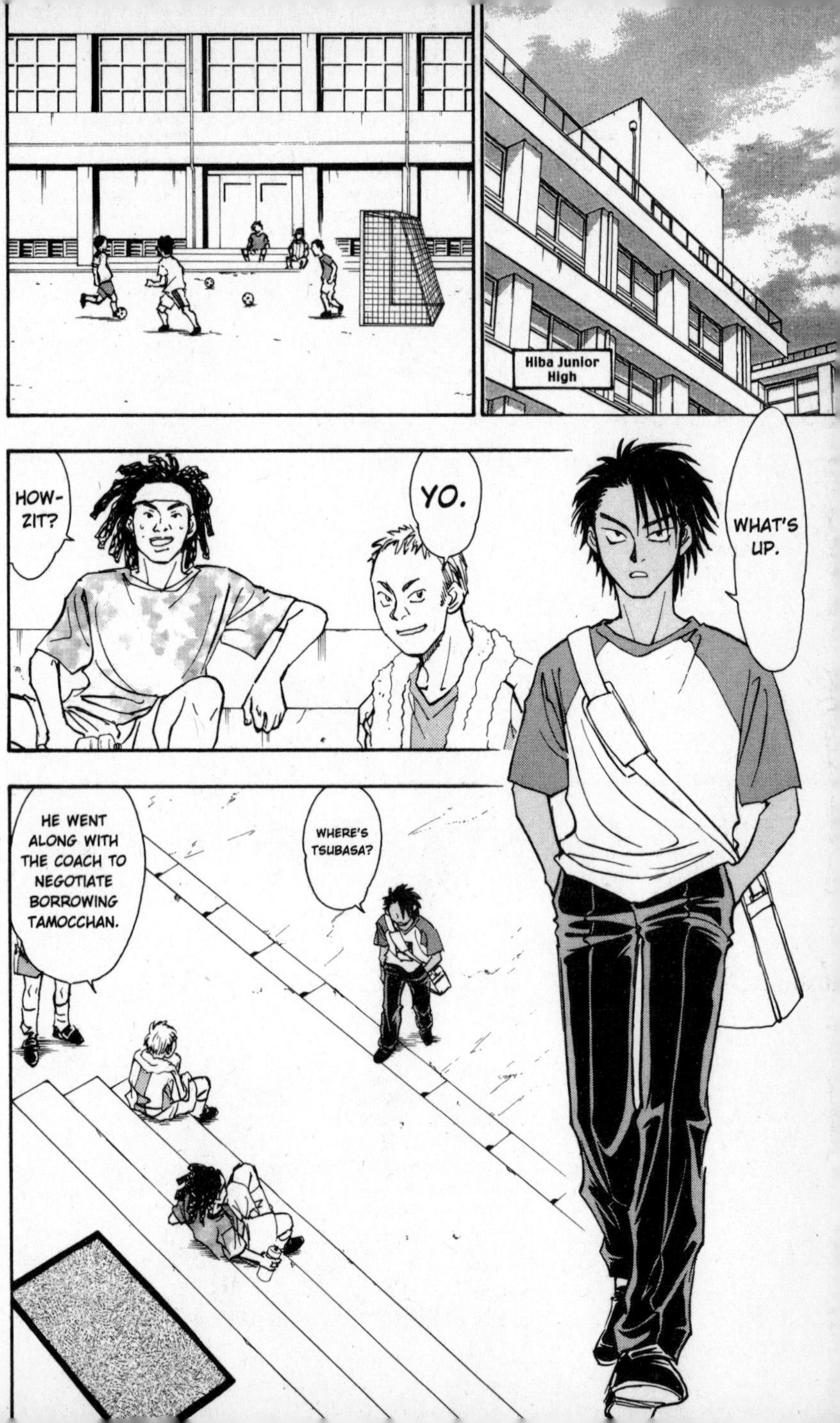
Hiba Junior High
WHAT'S UP.
YO.
HOW-ZIT?
WHERE'S TSUBASA?
HE WENT ALONG WITH THE COACH TO NEGOTIATE BORROWING TAMOCCHAN.

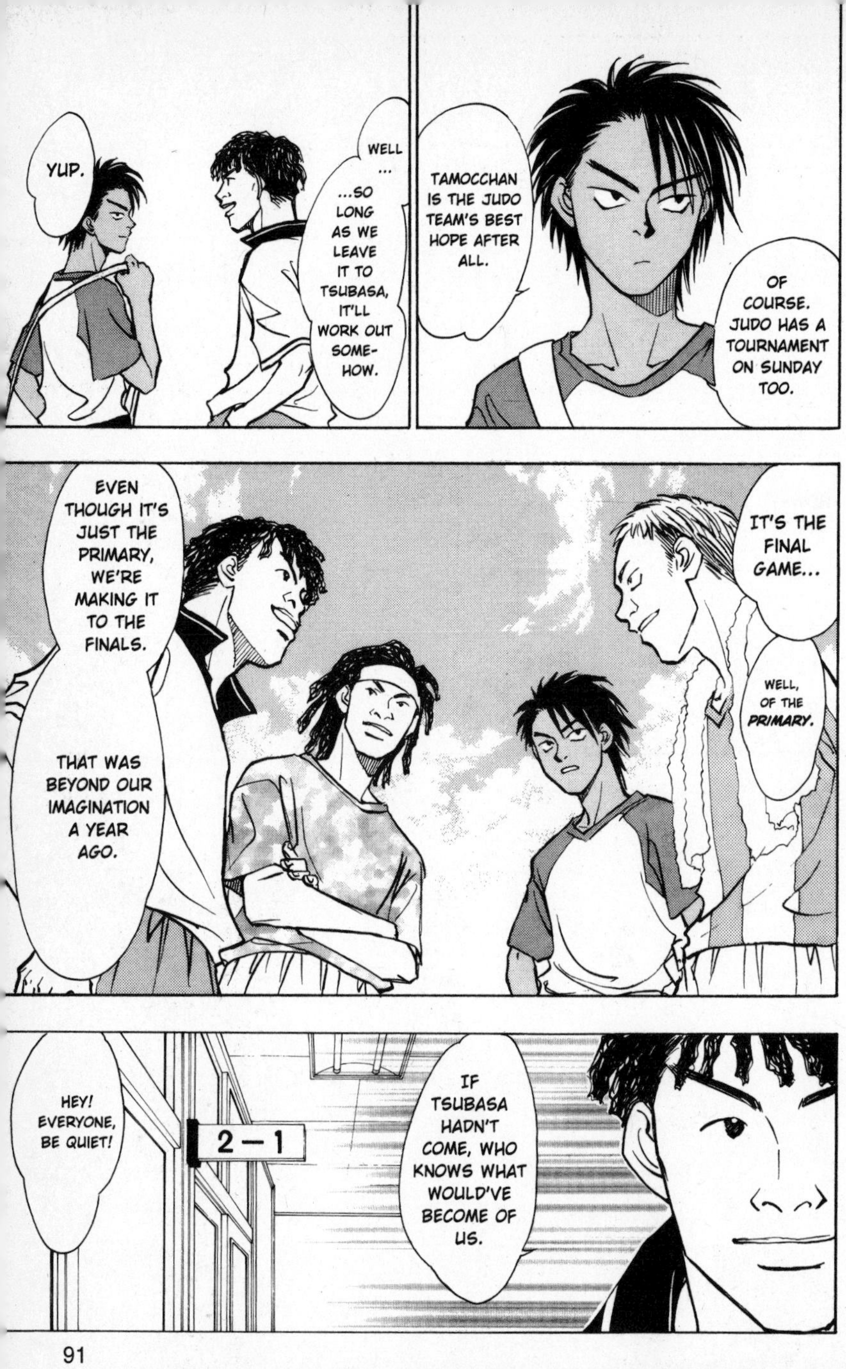
TAMOCCHAN IS THE JUDO TEAM'S BEST HOPE AFTER ALL.
OF COURSE. JUDO HAS A TOURNAMENT ON SUNDAY TOO.
WELL ...
...SO LONG AS WE LEAVE IT TO TSUBASA, IT'LL WORK OUT SOME-HOW.
YUP.
IT'S THE FINAL GAME...
WELL, OF THE ***PRIMARY.***
EVEN THOUGH IT'S JUST THE PRIMARY, WE'RE MAKING IT TO THE FINALS.
THAT WAS BEYOND OUR IMAGINATION A YEAR AGO.
IF TSUBASA HADN'T COME, WHO KNOWS WHAT WOULD'VE BECOME OF US.
2—1
HEY! EVERYONE, BE QUIET!

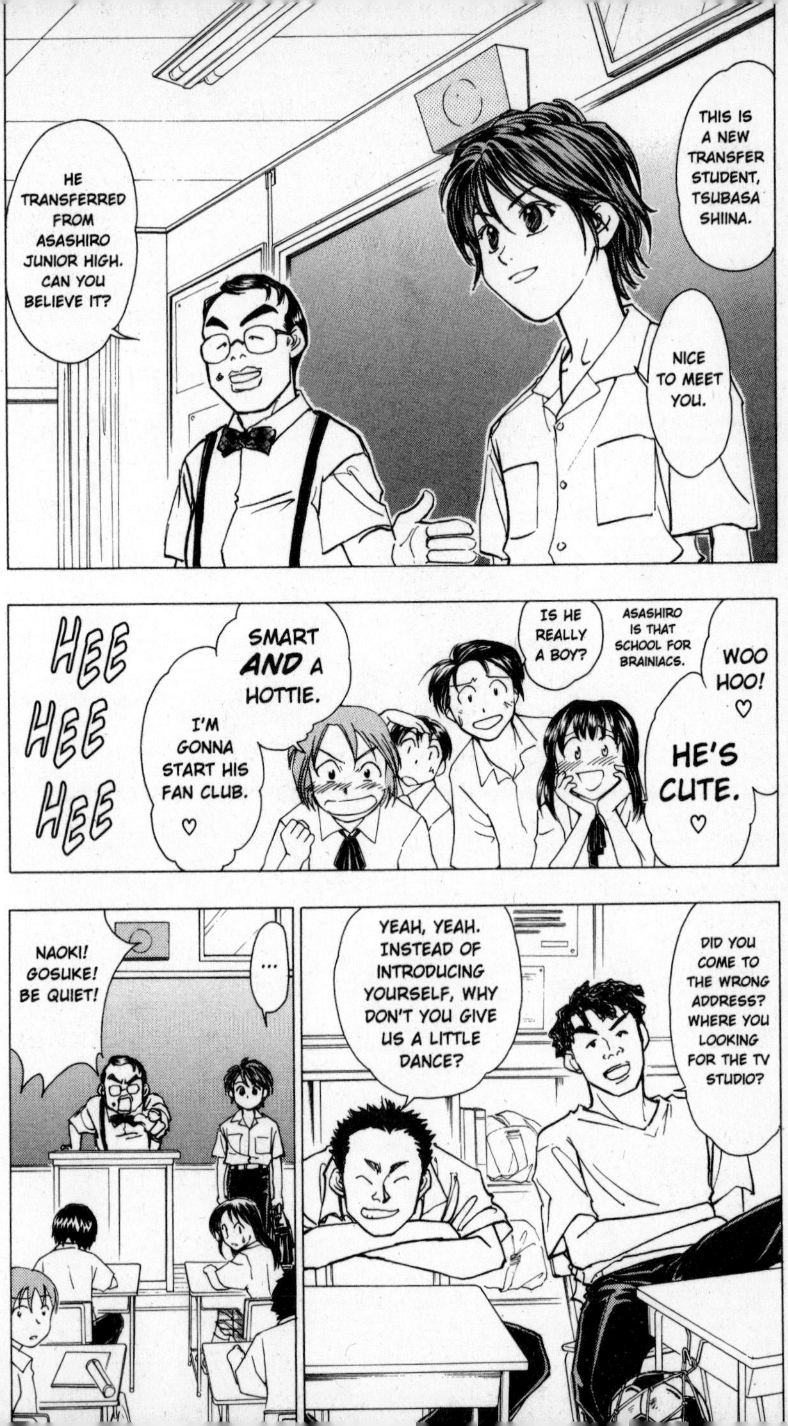

THIS IS A NEW TRANSFER STUDENT, TSUBASA SHIINA.
HE TRANSFERRED FROM ASASHIRO JUNIOR HIGH. CAN YOU BELIEVE IT?
NICE TO MEET YOU.
WOO HOO! ♡
HE'S CUTE. ♡
ASASHIRO IS THAT SCHOOL FOR BRAINIACS.
IS HE REALLY A BOY?
SMART AND A HOTTIE.
I'M GONNA START HIS FAN CLUB. ♡
HEE HEE HEE
DID YOU COME TO THE WRONG ADDRESS? WHERE YOU LOOKING FOR THE TV STUDIO?
YEAH, YEAH. INSTEAD OF INTRODUCING YOURSELF, WHY DON'T YOU GIVE US A LITTLE DANCE?
...
NAOKI! GOSUKE! BE QUIET!

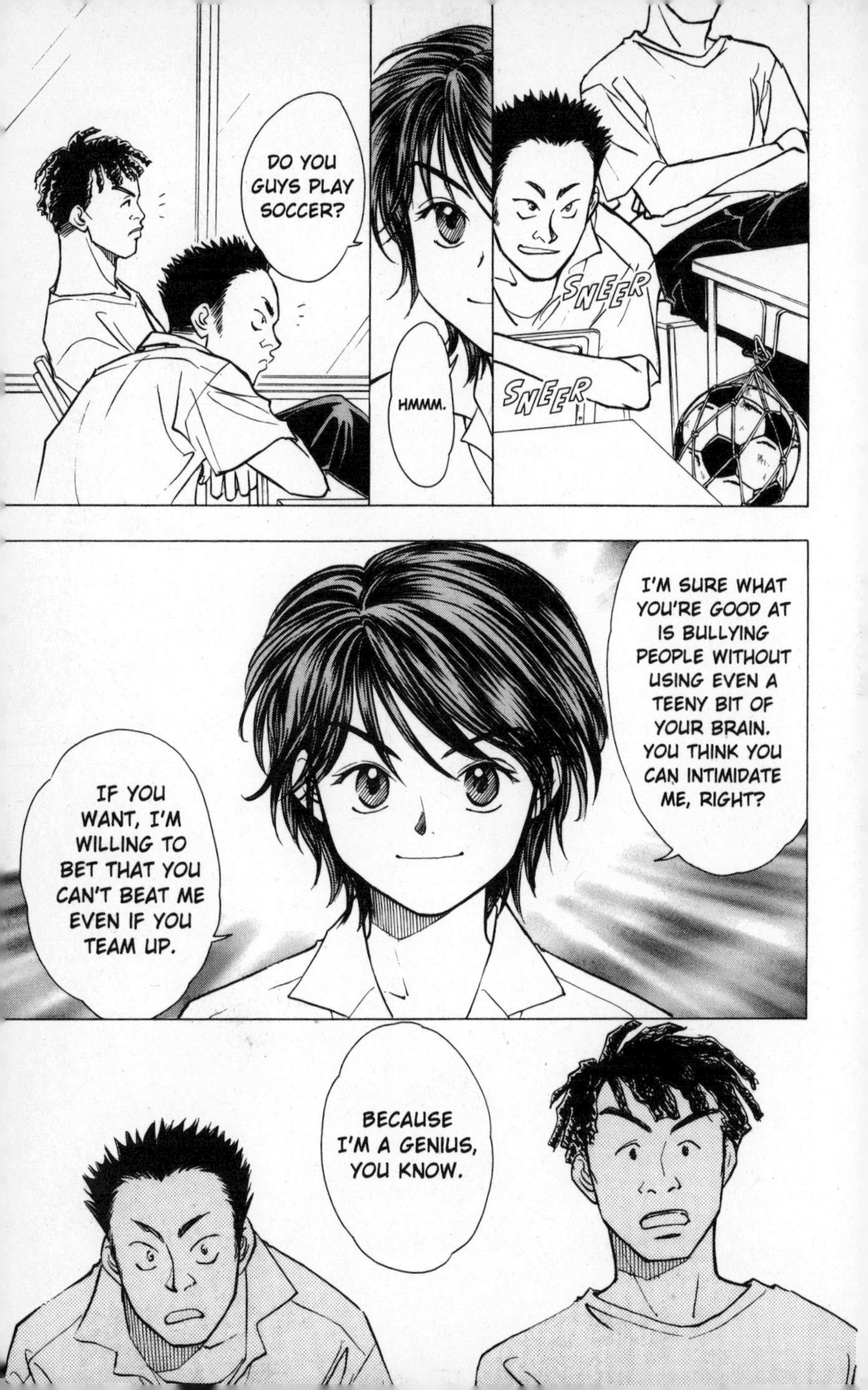
SNEER
SNEER
HMMM.
DO YOU GUYS PLAY SOCCER?
I'M SURE WHAT YOU'RE GOOD AT IS BULLYING PEOPLE WITHOUT USING EVEN A TEENY BIT OF YOUR BRAIN. YOU THINK YOU CAN INTIMIDATE ME, RIGHT?
IF YOU WANT, I'M WILLING TO BET THAT YOU CAN'T BEAT ME EVEN IF YOU TEAM UP.
BECAUSE I'M A GENIUS, YOU KNOW.

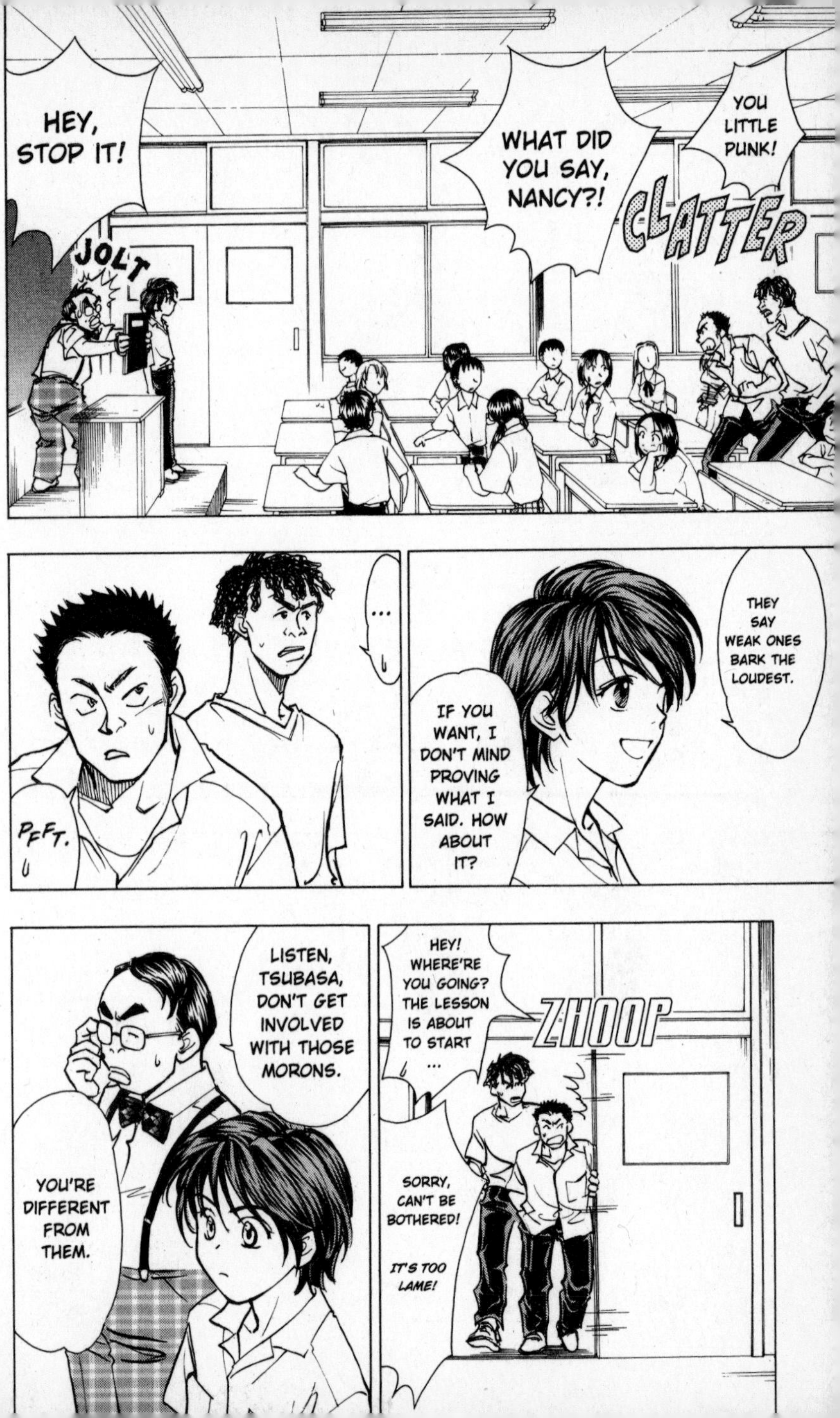
YOU LITTLE PUNK!
CLATTER
WHAT DID YOU SAY, NANCY?!
HEY, STOP IT!
JOLT
THEY SAY WEAK ONES BARK THE LOUDEST.
IF YOU WANT, I DON'T MIND PROVING WHAT I SAID. HOW ABOUT IT?
...
PFFT.
ZHOOP
HEY! WHERE'RE YOU GOING? THE LESSON IS ABOUT TO START ...
SORRY, CAN'T BE BOTHERED!
IT'S TOO LAME!
LISTEN, TSUBASA, DON'T GET INVOLVED WITH THOSE MORONS.
YOU'RE DIFFERENT FROM THEM.

READ THIS WAY

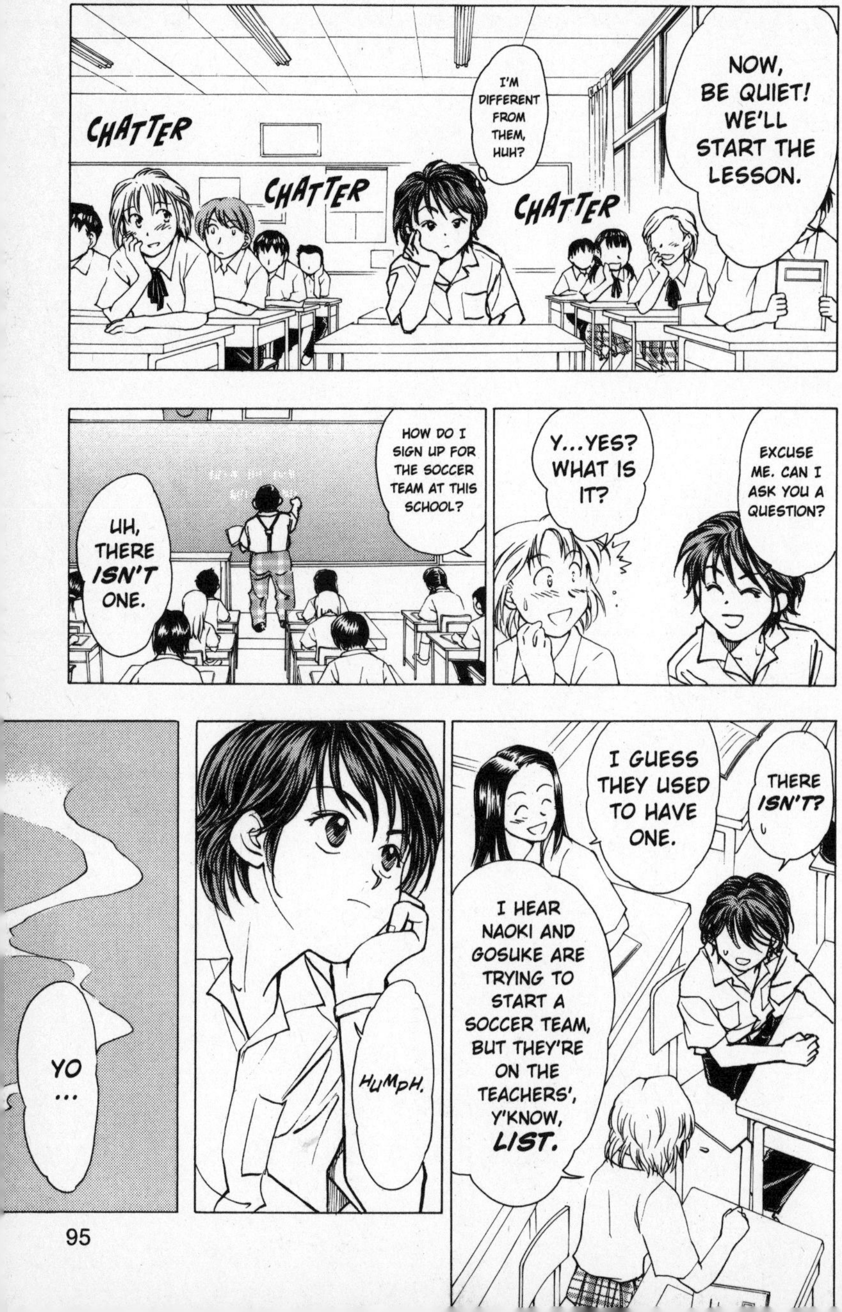

NOW, BE QUIET! WE'LL START THE LESSON.
CHATTER
I'M DIFFERENT FROM THEM, HUH?
CHATTER
CHATTER
EXCUSE ME. CAN I ASK YOU A QUESTION?
Y...YES? WHAT IS IT?
HOW DO I SIGN UP FOR THE SOCCER TEAM AT THIS SCHOOL?
UH, THERE *ISN'T* ONE.
THERE *ISN'T*?
I GUESS THEY USED TO HAVE ONE.
I HEAR NAOKI AND GOSUKE ARE TRYING TO START A SOCCER TEAM, BUT THEY'RE ON THE TEACHERS', Y'KNOW, **LIST**.
HUMPH.
YO ...

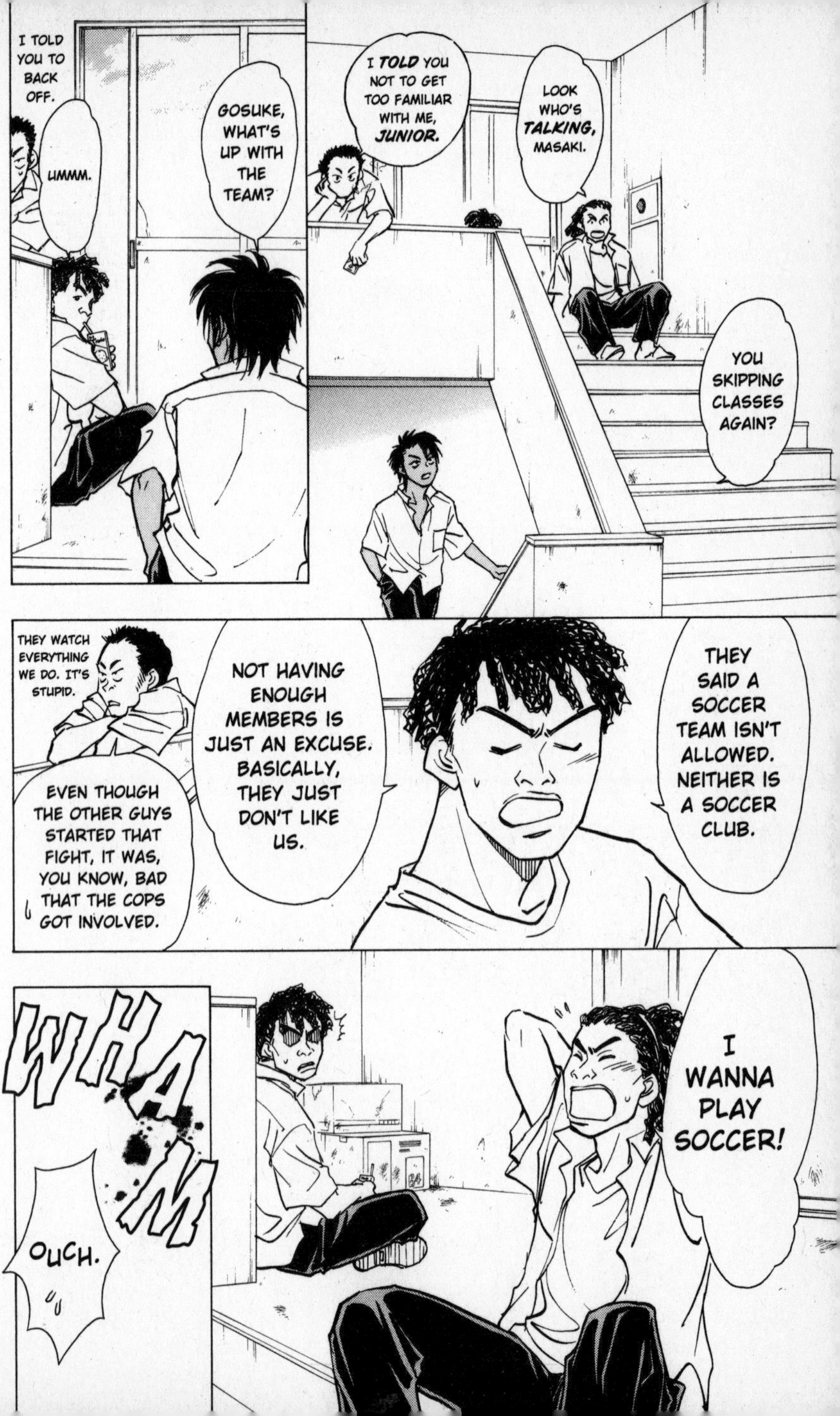
I TOLD YOU NOT TO GET TOO FAMILIAR WITH ME, JUNIOR.
LOOK WHO'S TALKING, MASAKI.
YOU SKIPPING CLASSES AGAIN?
GOSUKE, WHAT'S UP WITH THE TEAM?
UMMM.
I TOLD YOU TO BACK OFF.
THEY SAID A SOCCER TEAM ISN'T ALLOWED. NEITHER IS A SOCCER CLUB.
NOT HAVING ENOUGH MEMBERS IS JUST AN EXCUSE. BASICALLY, THEY JUST DON'T LIKE US.
THEY WATCH EVERYTHING WE DO. IT'S STUPID.
EVEN THOUGH THE OTHER GUYS STARTED THAT FIGHT, IT WAS, YOU KNOW, BAD THAT THE COPS GOT INVOLVED.
I WANNA PLAY SOCCER!
WHAM
OUCH.

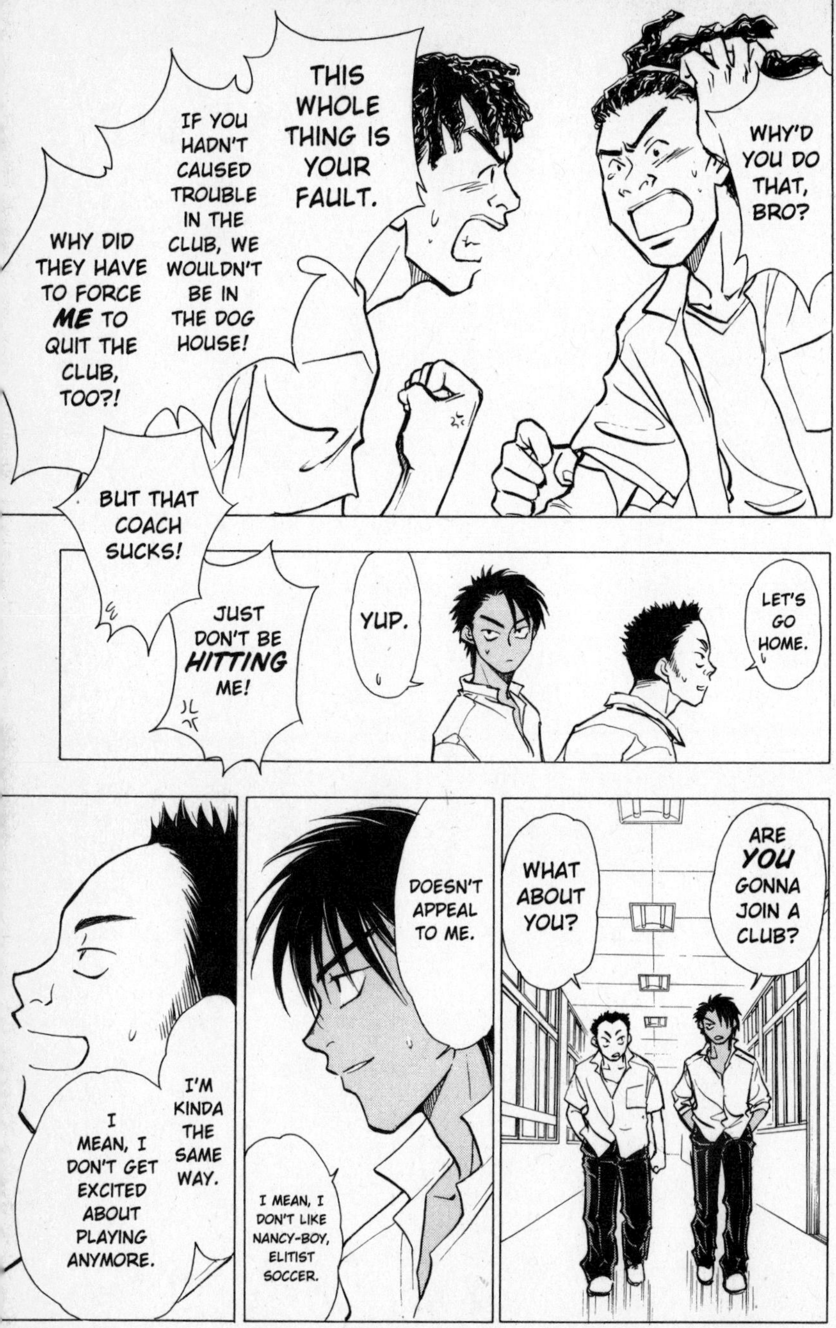
WHY'D YOU DO THAT, BRO?
THIS WHOLE THING IS YOUR FAULT.
IF YOU HADN'T CAUSED TROUBLE IN THE CLUB, WE WOULDN'T BE IN THE DOG HOUSE!
WHY DID THEY HAVE TO FORCE ME TO QUIT THE CLUB, TOO?!
BUT THAT COACH SUCKS!
JUST DON'T BE HITTING ME!
LET'S GO HOME.
YUP.
ARE YOU GONNA JOIN A CLUB?
WHAT ABOUT YOU?
DOESN'T APPEAL TO ME.
I MEAN, I DON'T LIKE NANCY-BOY, ELITIST SOCCER.
I'M KINDA THE SAME WAY.
I MEAN, I DON'T GET EXCITED ABOUT PLAYING ANYMORE.

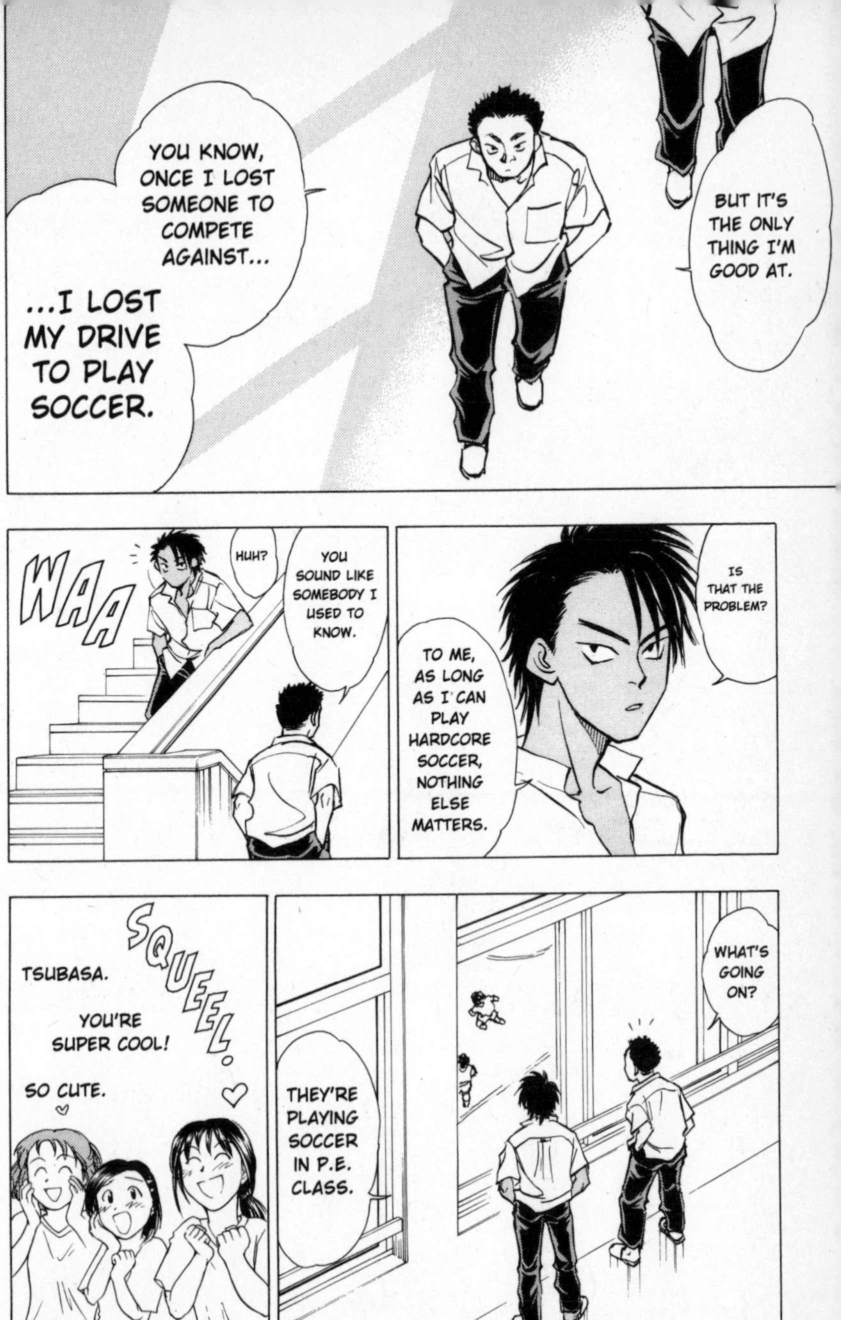
BUT IT'S THE ONLY THING I'M GOOD AT.
YOU KNOW, ONCE I LOST SOMEONE TO COMPETE AGAINST...
...I LOST MY DRIVE TO PLAY SOCCER.
IS THAT THE PROBLEM?
TO ME, AS LONG AS I CAN PLAY HARDCORE SOCCER, NOTHING ELSE MATTERS.
YOU SOUND LIKE SOMEBODY I USED TO KNOW.
HUH?
WAA
WHAT'S GOING ON?
THEY'RE PLAYING SOCCER IN P.E. CLASS.
SQUEEL
TSUBASA.
YOU'RE SUPER COOL!
SO CUTE.

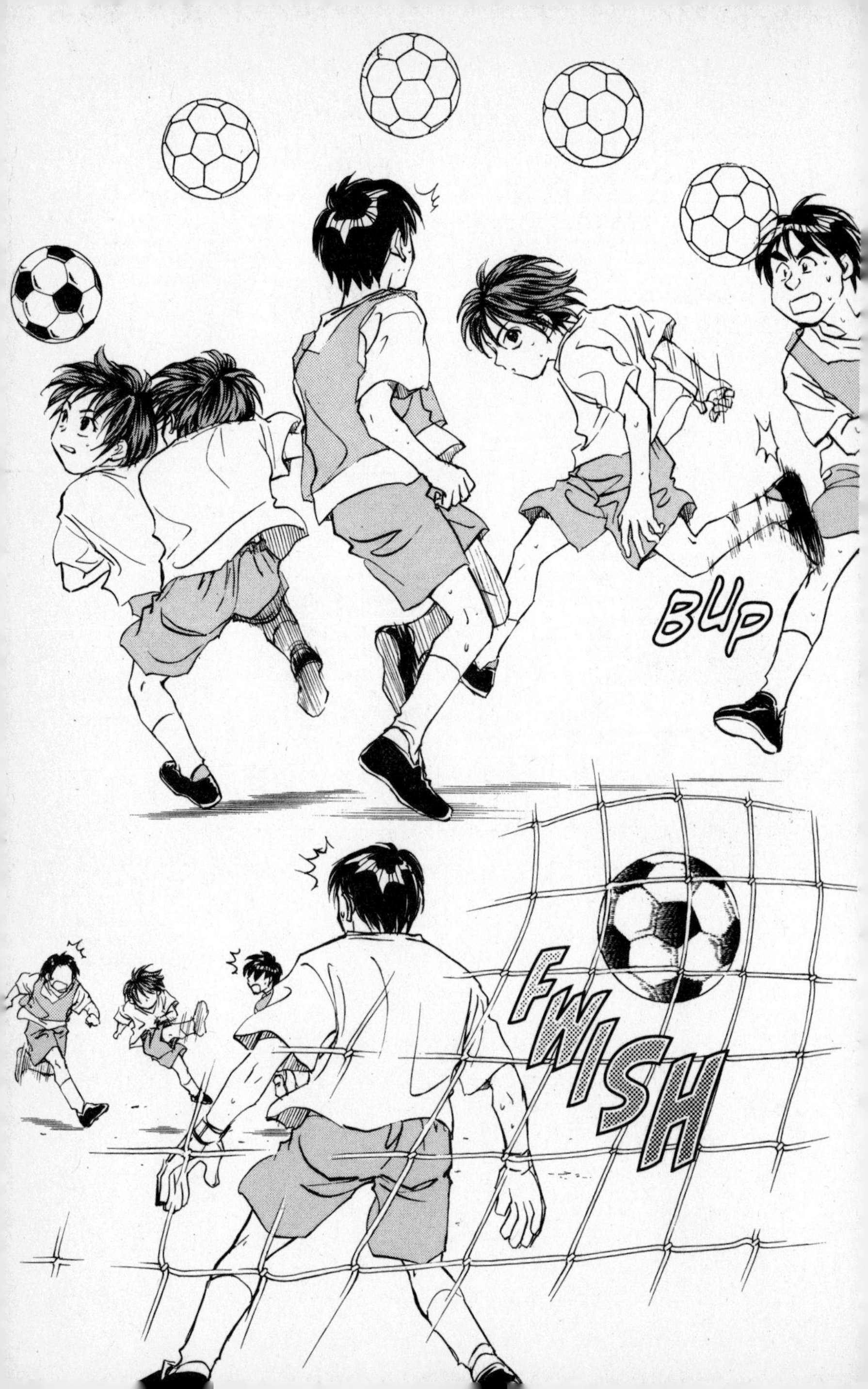
BUP
FWISH

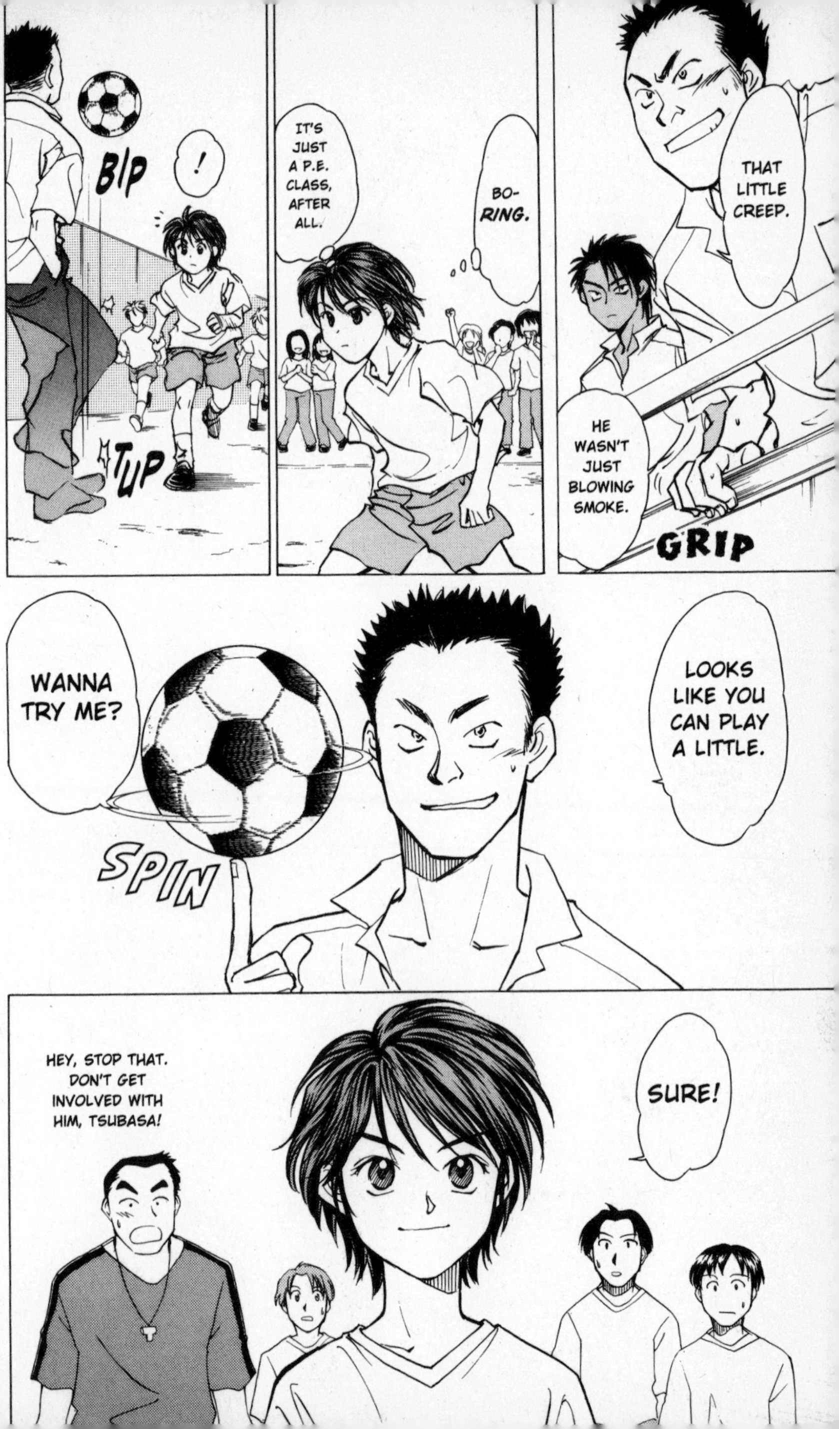
THAT LITTLE CREEP.
HE WASN'T JUST BLOWING SMOKE.
GRIP
BO-RING.
IT'S JUST A P.E. CLASS, AFTER ALL.
!
BIP
TUP
LOOKS LIKE YOU CAN PLAY A LITTLE.
WANNA TRY ME?
SPIN
SURE!
HEY, STOP THAT. DON'T GET INVOLVED WITH HIM, TSUBASA!

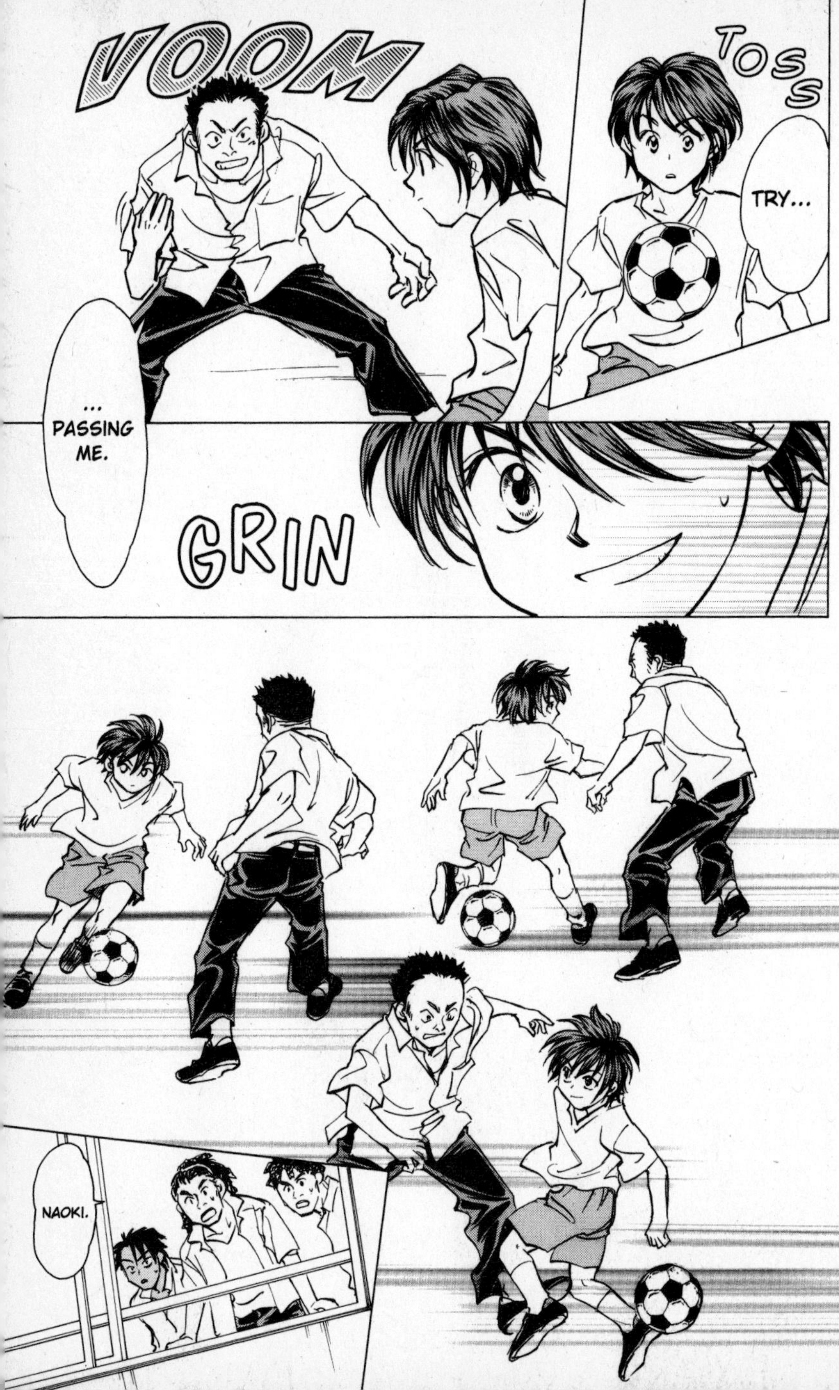
TOSS
TRY...
VOOM
... PASSING ME.
GRIN
NAOKI.

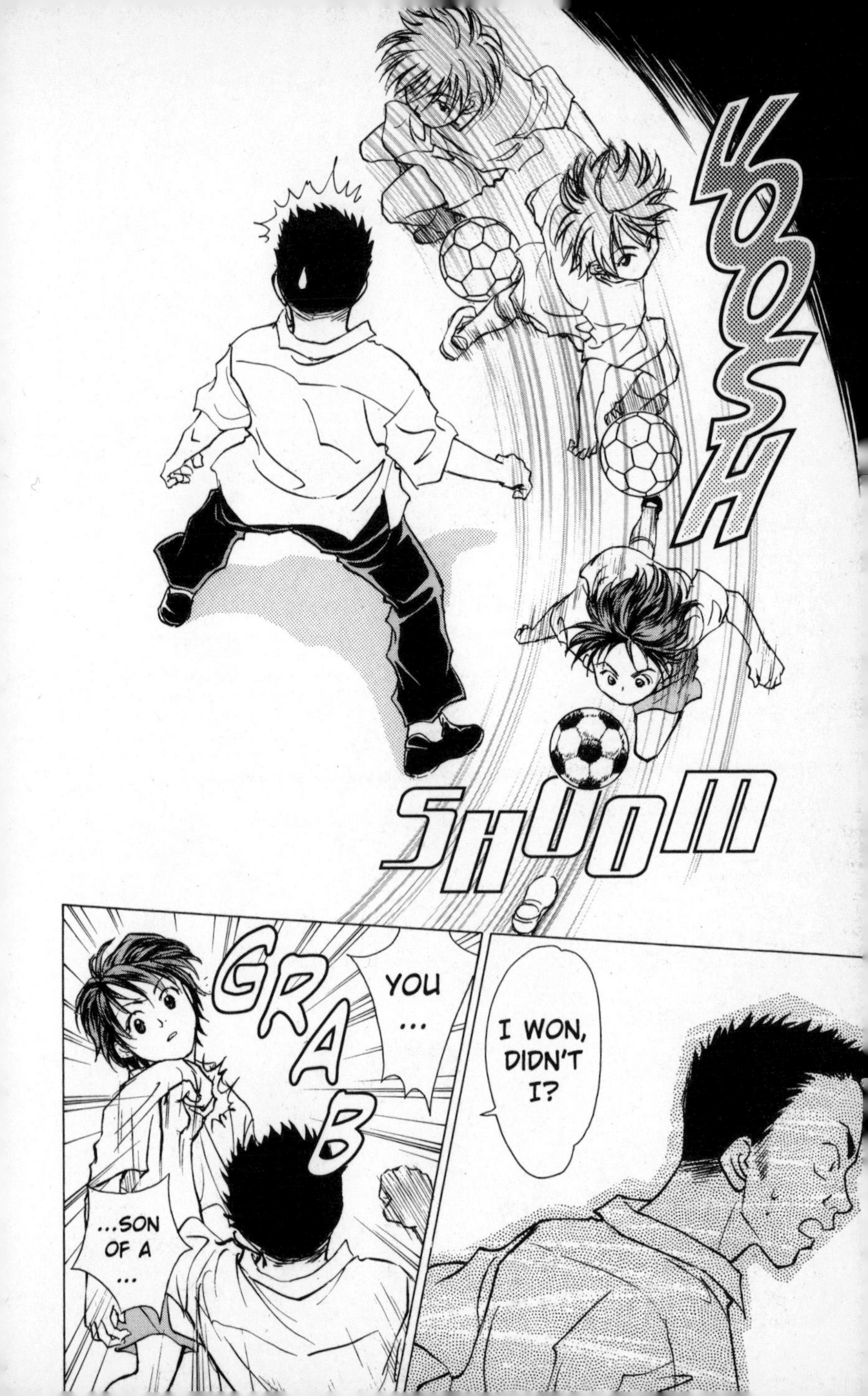
VOOSH
SHOOM
I WON, DIDN'T I?
YOU ...
GRAB
...SON OF A ...

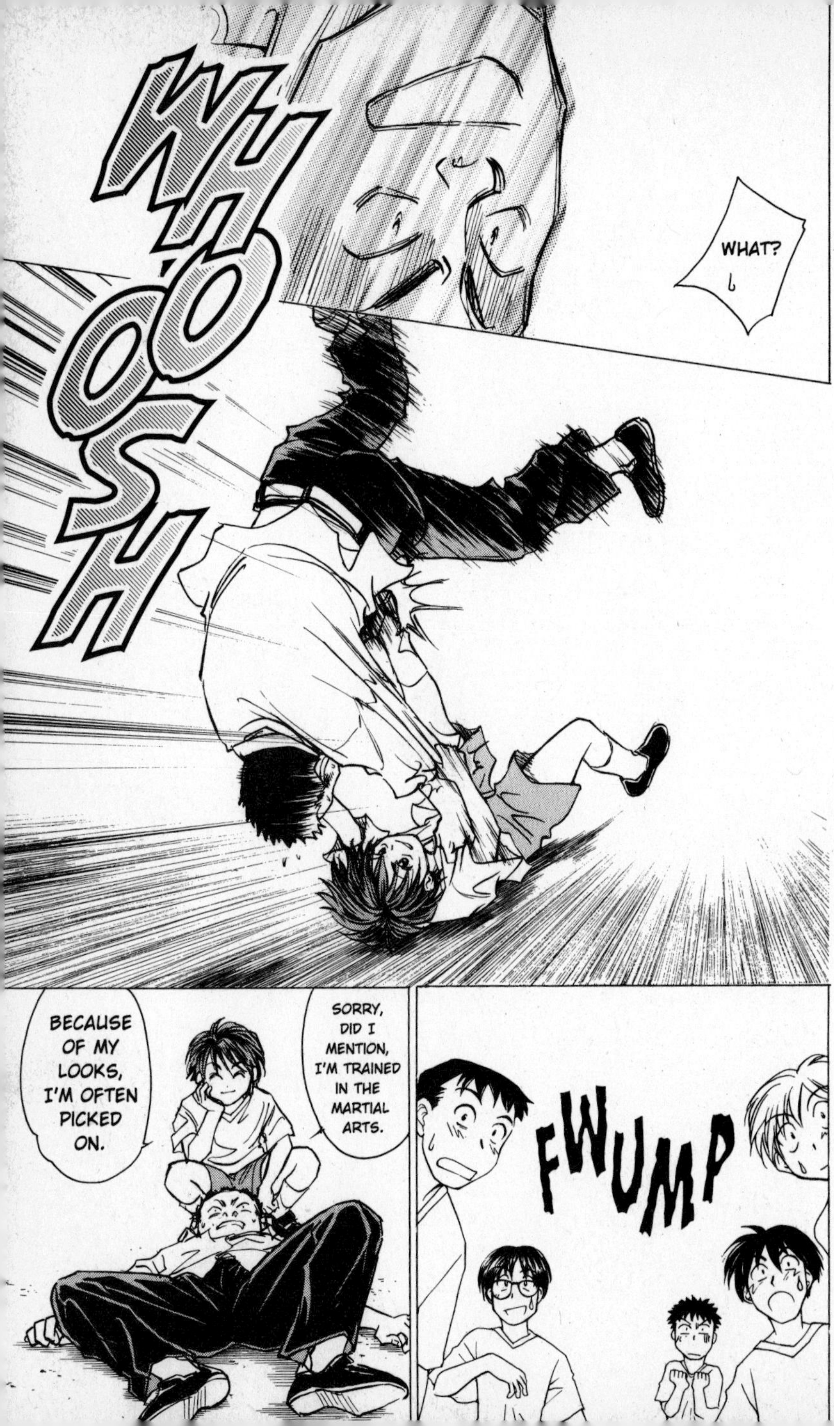
WHAT?
WHOOSH
FWUMP
SORRY, DID I MENTION, I'M TRAINED IN THE MARTIAL ARTS.
BECAUSE OF MY LOOKS, I'M OFTEN PICKED ON.

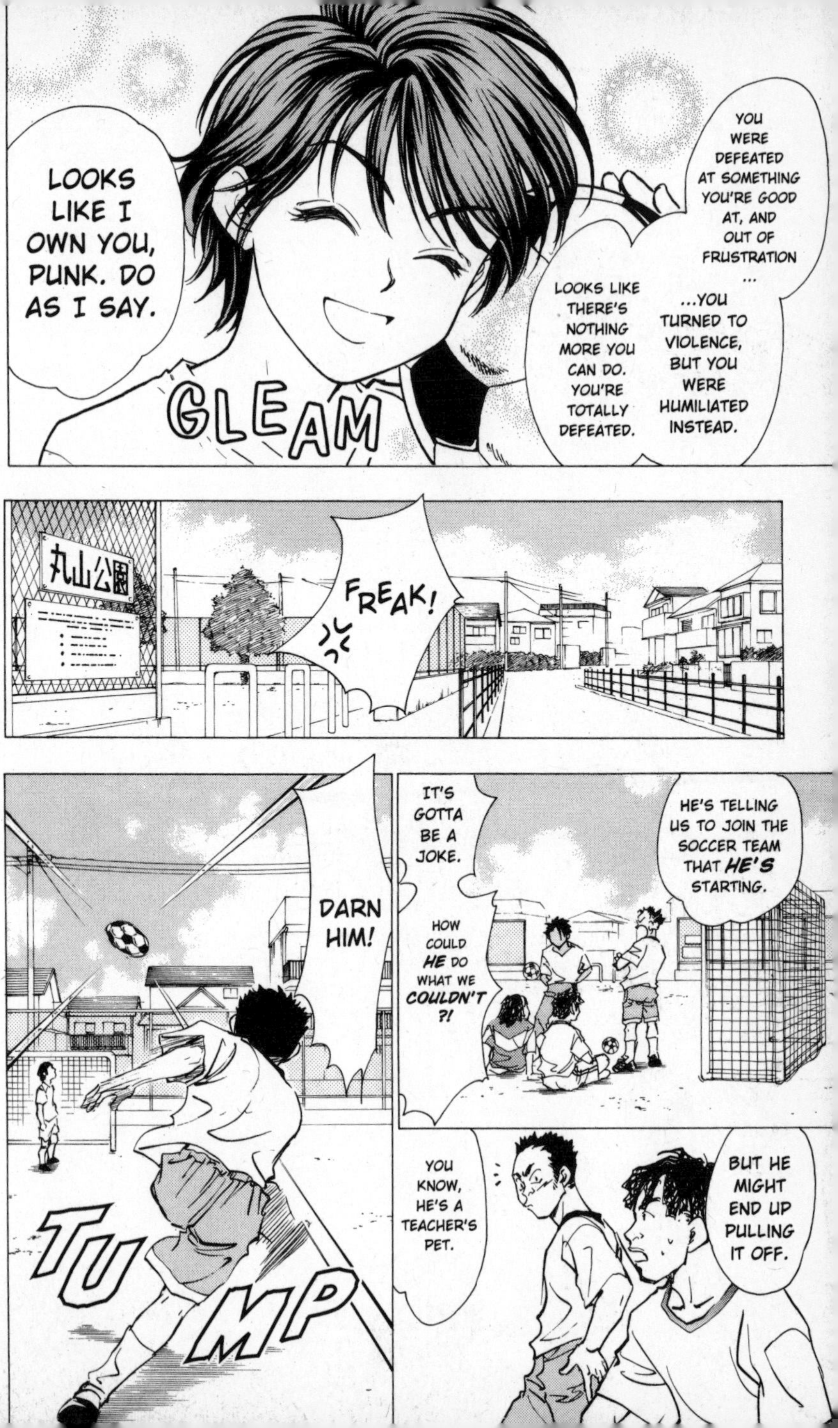
YOU WERE DEFEATED AT SOMETHING YOU'RE GOOD AT, AND OUT OF FRUSTRATION ...
...YOU TURNED TO VIOLENCE, BUT YOU WERE HUMILIATED INSTEAD.
LOOKS LIKE THERE'S NOTHING MORE YOU CAN DO. YOU'RE TOTALLY DEFEATED.
LOOKS LIKE I OWN YOU, PUNK. DO AS I SAY.
GLEAM
丸山公園
FREAK!
HE'S TELLING US TO JOIN THE SOCCER TEAM THAT *HE'S* STARTING.
IT'S GOTTA BE A JOKE.
HOW COULD *HE* DO WHAT WE *COULDN'T* ?!
BUT HE MIGHT END UP PULLING IT OFF.
YOU KNOW, HE'S A TEACHER'S PET.
DARN HIM!
TUMP

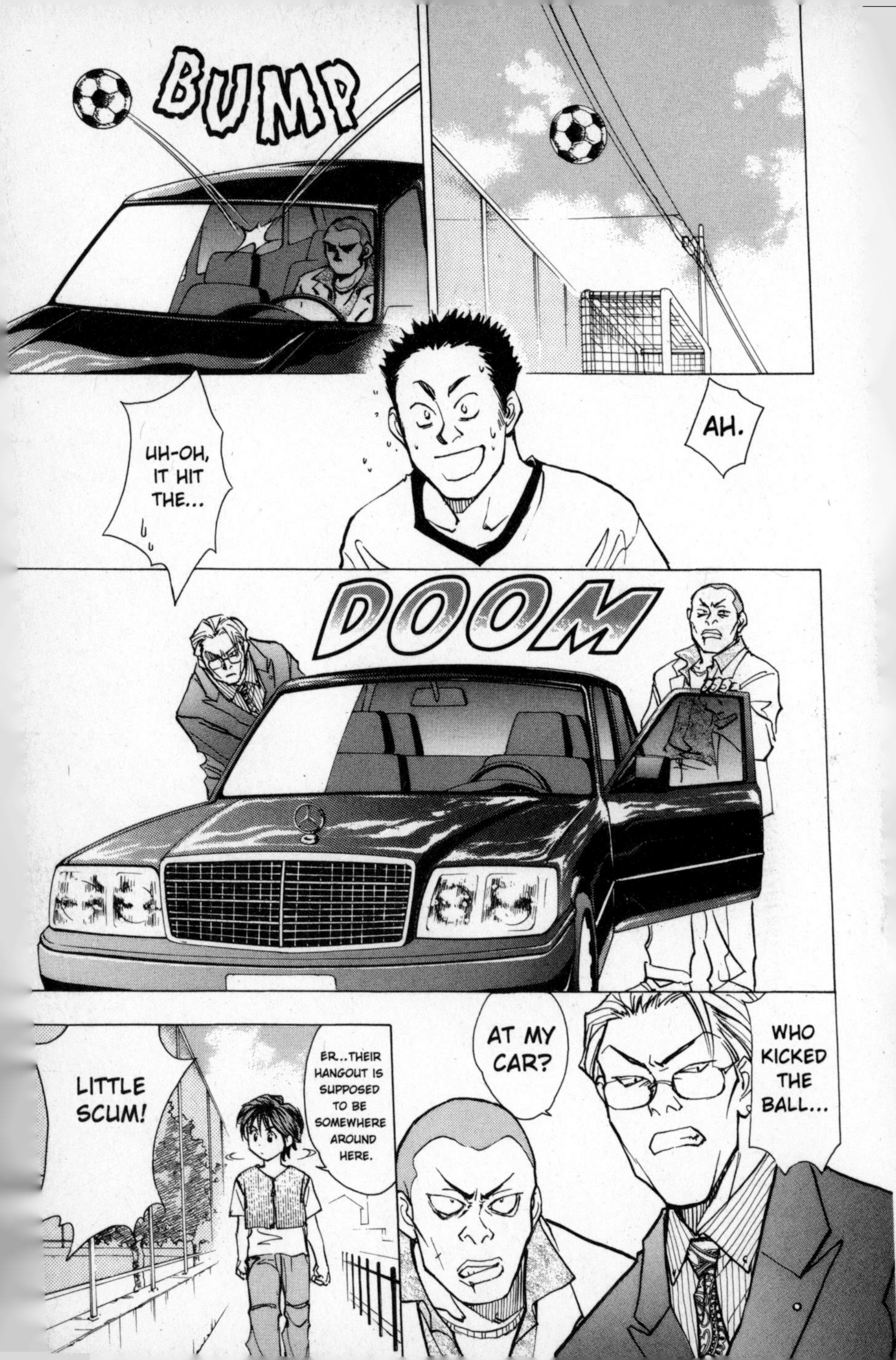
BUMP
AH.
UH-OH, IT HIT THE...
DOOM
WHO KICKED THE BALL...
AT MY CAR?
LITTLE SCUM!
ER...THEIR HANGOUT IS SUPPOSED TO BE SOMEWHERE AROUND HERE.

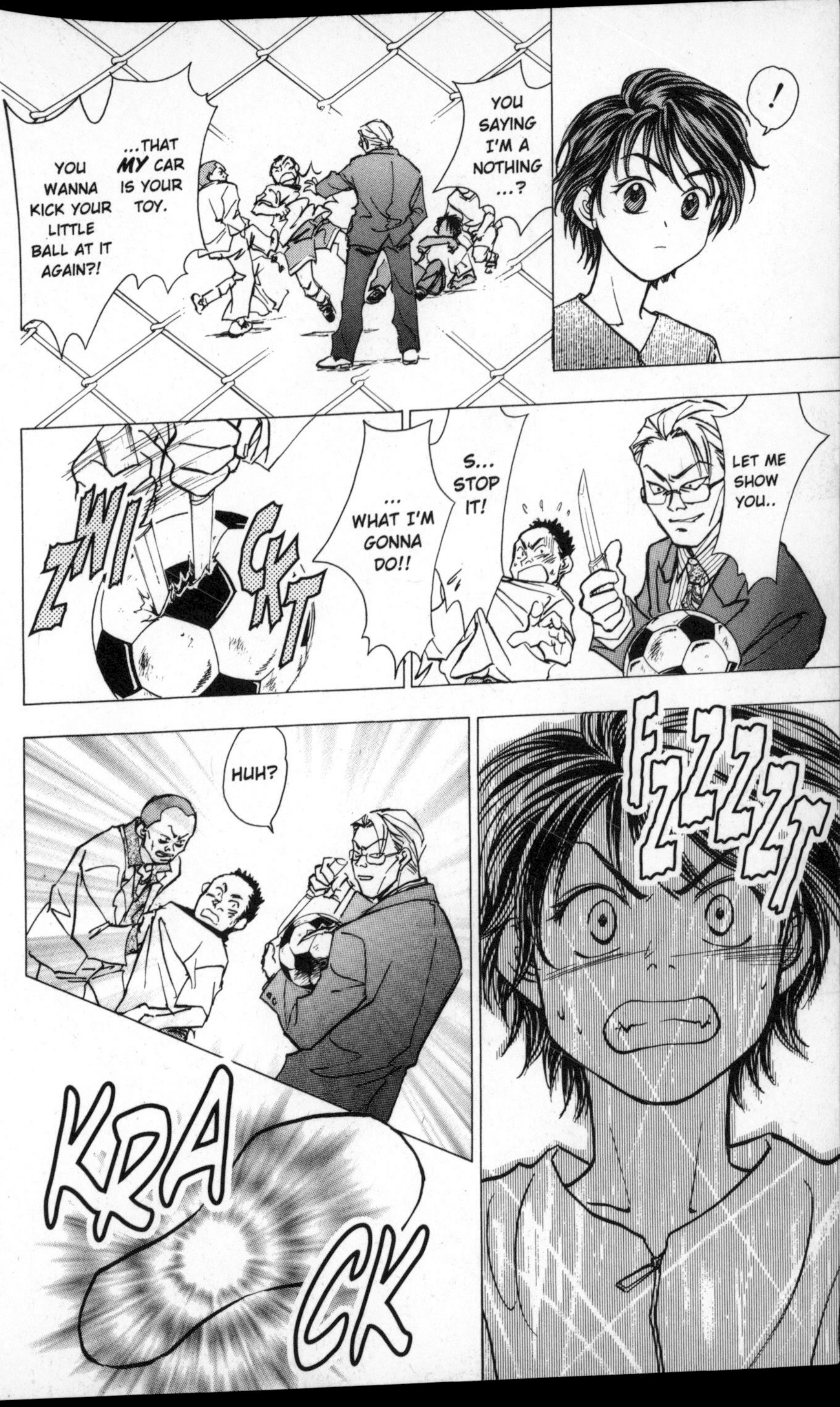
!
YOU SAYING I'M A NOTHING ...?
...THAT **MY** CAR IS YOUR TOY.
YOU WANNA KICK YOUR LITTLE BALL AT IT AGAIN?!
LET ME SHOW YOU..
S... STOP IT!
... WHAT I'M GONNA DO!!
ZWICKT
FZZZZZT
HUH?
KRACK

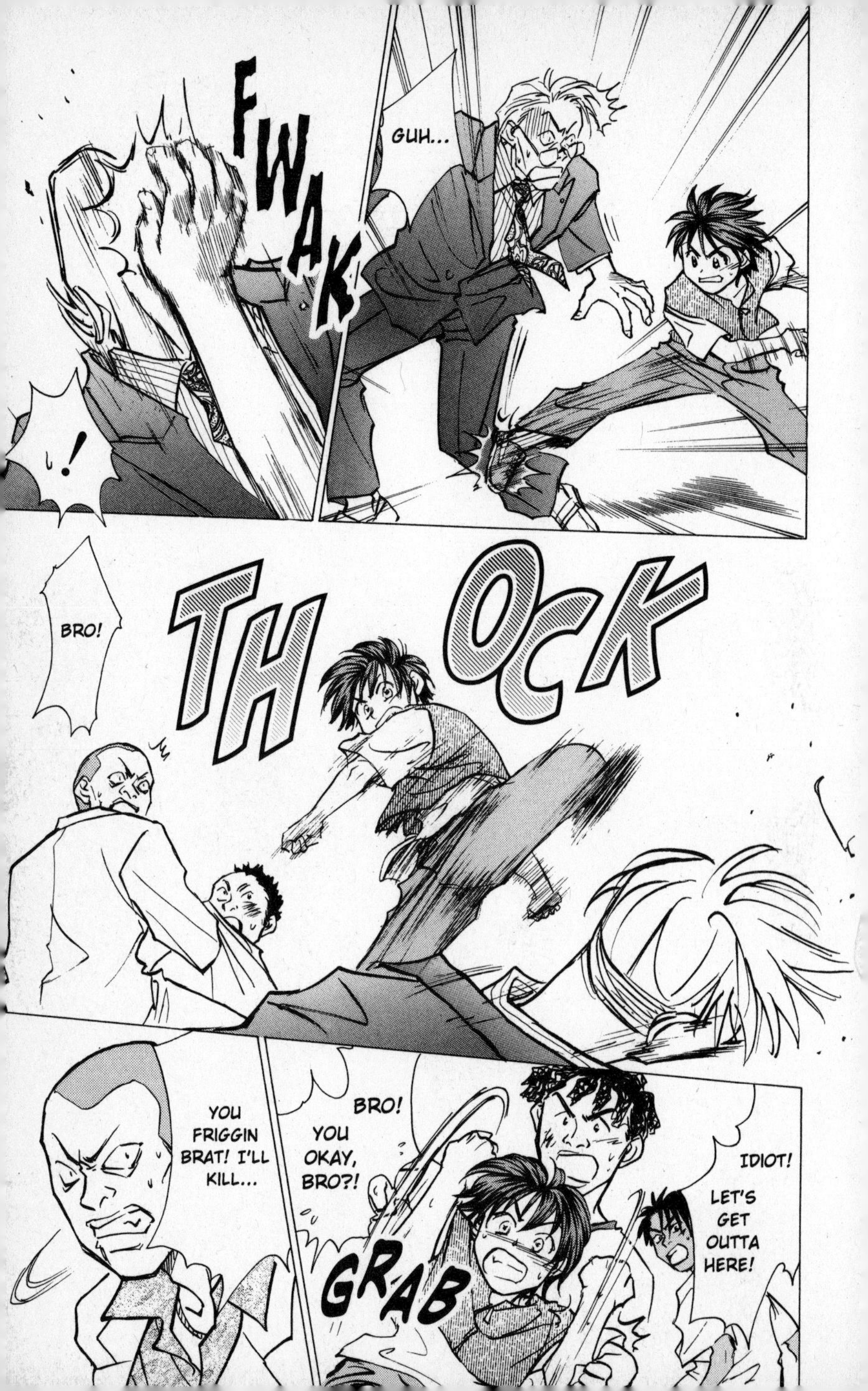
GUH...
FWAK
!
THOCK
BRO!
IDIOT!
LET'S GET OUTTA HERE!
BRO!
YOU OKAY, BRO?!
GRAB
YOU FRIGGIN BRAT! I'LL KILL...

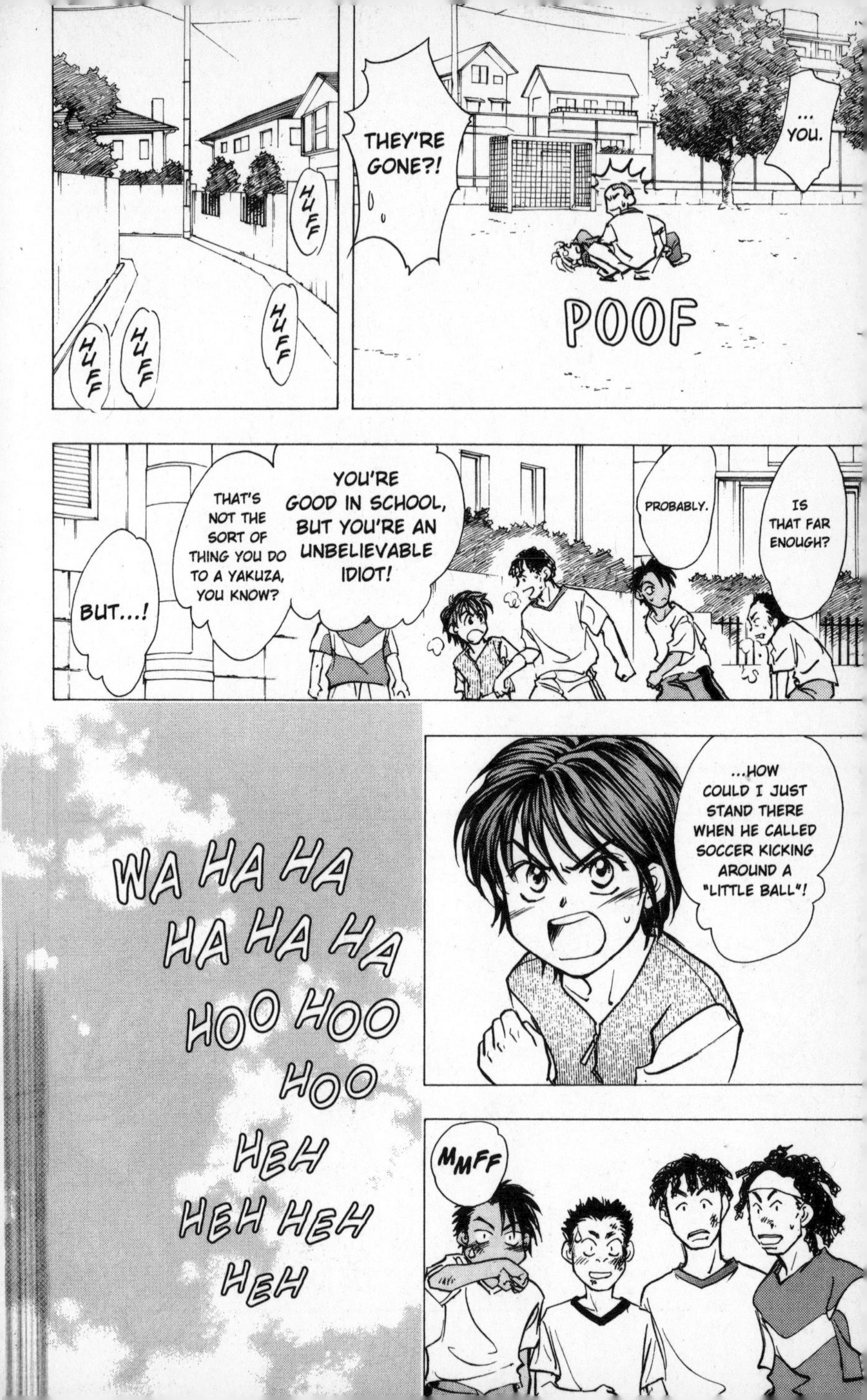
...YOU.
POOF
THEY'RE GONE?!
HUFF
HUFF
HUFF
HUFF
IS THAT FAR ENOUGH?
PROBABLY.
YOU'RE GOOD IN SCHOOL, BUT YOU'RE AN UNBELIEVABLE IDIOT!
THAT'S NOT THE SORT OF THING YOU DO TO A YAKUZA, YOU KNOW?
BUT...!
...HOW COULD I JUST STAND THERE WHEN HE CALLED SOCCER KICKING AROUND A "LITTLE BALL"!
MMFF
WA HA HA HA HA HA HOO HOO HOO HEH HEH HEH HEH

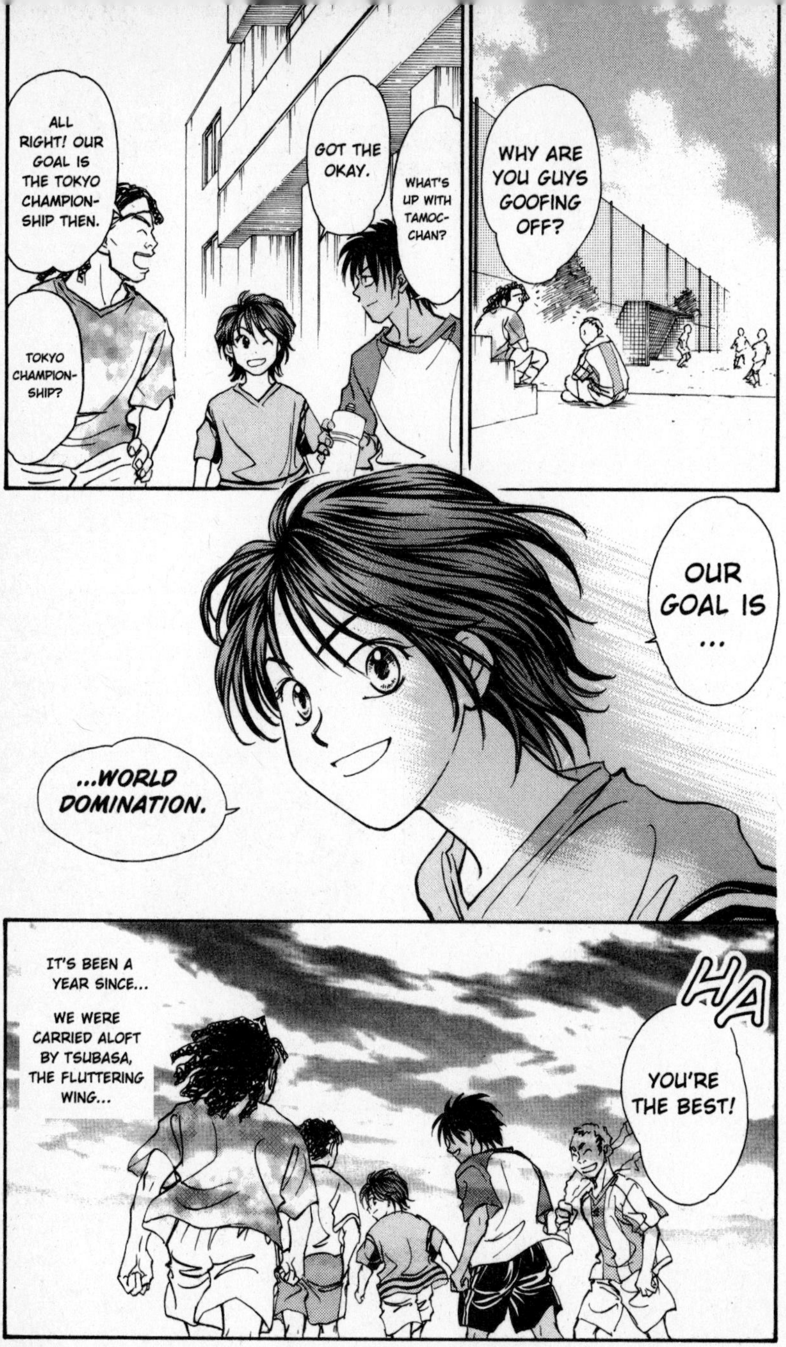
WHY ARE YOU GUYS GOOFING OFF?
WHAT'S UP WITH TAMOC-CHAN?
GOT THE OKAY.
ALL RIGHT! OUR GOAL IS THE TOKYO CHAMPIONSHIP THEN.
TOKYO CHAMPIONSHIP?
OUR GOAL IS ...
...WORLD DOMINATION.
HA
YOU'RE THE BEST!
IT'S BEEN A YEAR SINCE...
WE WERE CARRIED ALOFT BY TSUBASA, THE FLUTTERING WING...

☆ 4-PANEL MANGA INCLUDED IN E-JUMP ☆

A dream at the end of the century?

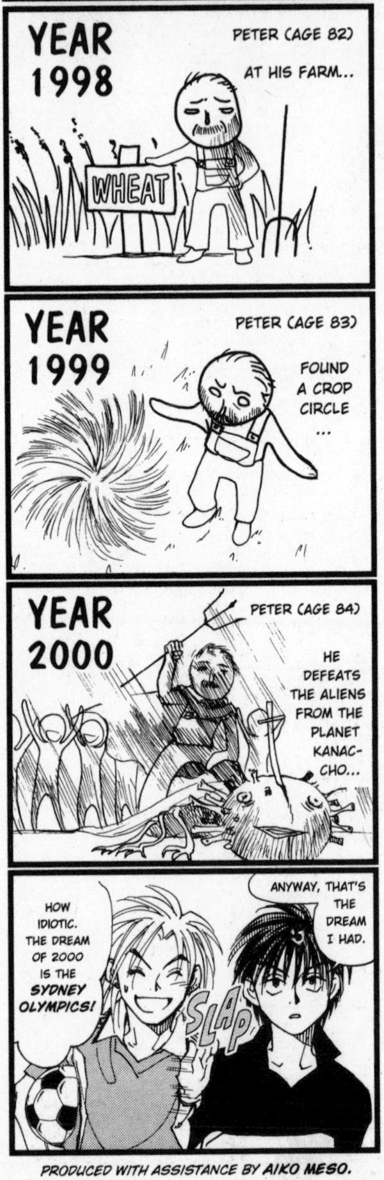
PETER (AGE 82)
AT HIS FARM...
YEAR 1998
WHEAT
PETER (AGE 83)
FOUND A CROP CIRCLE ...
YEAR 1999
PETER (AGE 84)
HE DEFEATS THE ALIENS FROM THE PLANET KANAC-CHO...
YEAR 2000
ANYWAY, THAT'S THE DREAM I HAD.
HOW IDIOTIC. THE DREAM OF 2000 IS THE SYDNEY OLYMPICS!
SLAP

PRODUCED WITH ASSISTANCE BY AIKO MESO.

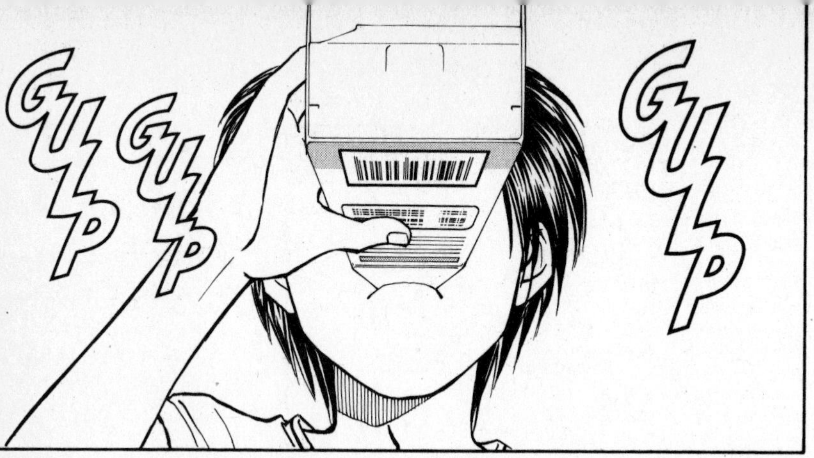
GULP
GULP
GULP

STAGE.86 A Remarkable Game

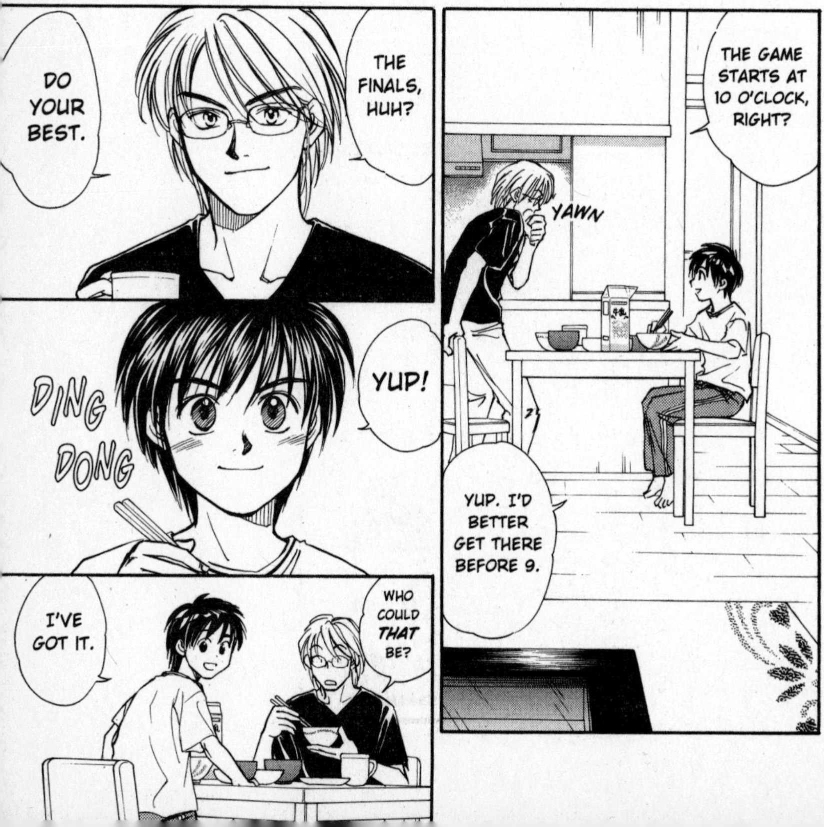
THE GAME STARTS AT 10 O'CLOCK, RIGHT?
YAWN
YUP. I'D BETTER GET THERE BEFORE 9.
THE FINALS, HUH?
DO YOUR BEST.
YUP!
DING DONG
WHO COULD *THAT* BE?
I'VE GOT IT.

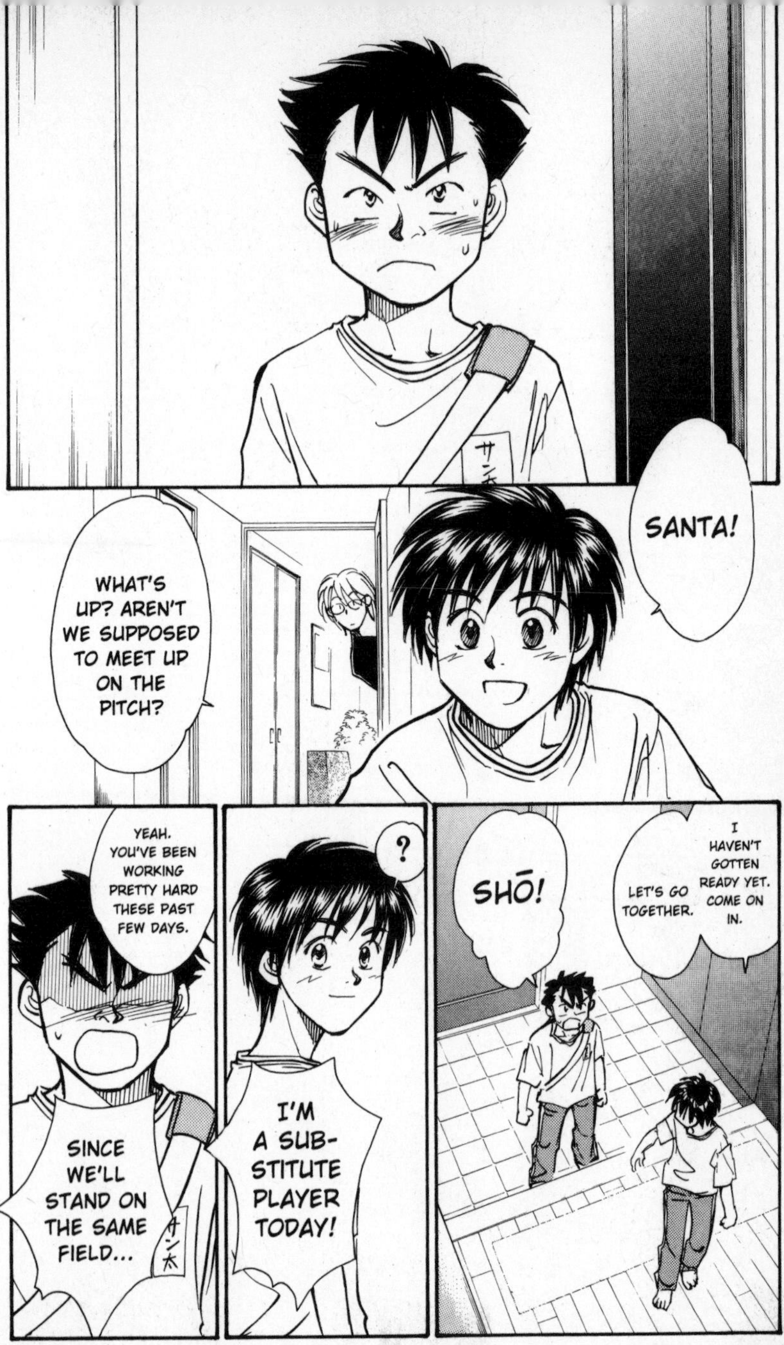
SANTA!
WHAT'S UP? AREN'T WE SUPPOSED TO MEET UP ON THE PITCH?
I HAVEN'T GOTTEN READY YET. COME ON IN.
LET'S GO TOGETHER.
SHŌ!
?
I'M A SUB-STITUTE PLAYER TODAY!
YEAH. YOU'VE BEEN WORKING PRETTY HARD THESE PAST FEW DAYS.
SINCE WE'LL STAND ON THE SAME FIELD...
サン太

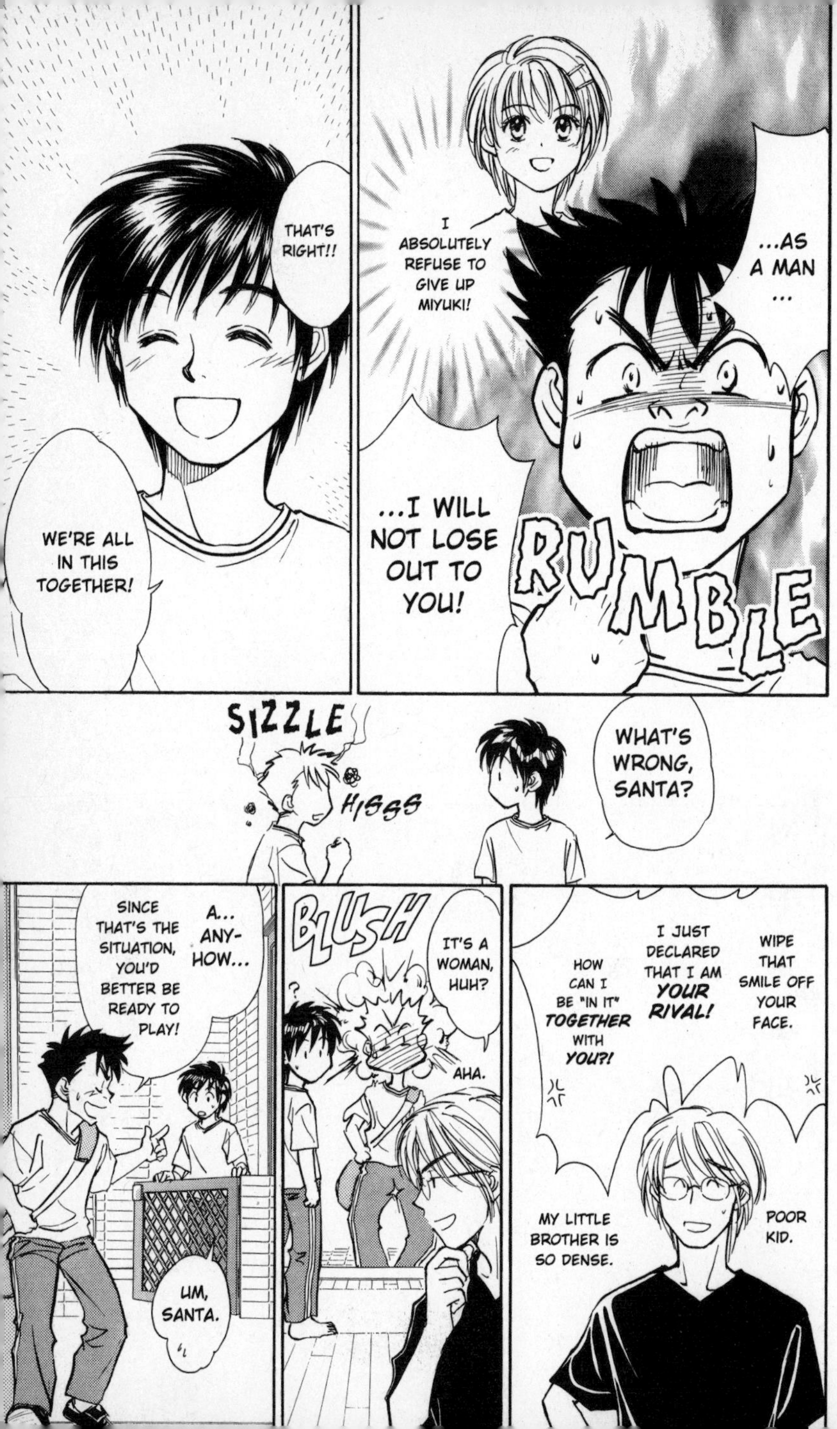
...AS A MAN ...
I ABSOLUTELY REFUSE TO GIVE UP MIYUKI!
...I WILL NOT LOSE OUT TO YOU!
RUMBLE
THAT'S RIGHT!!
WE'RE ALL IN THIS TOGETHER!
WHAT'S WRONG, SANTA?
SIZZLE
HISSS
WIPE THAT SMILE OFF YOUR FACE.
I JUST DECLARED THAT I AM **YOUR RIVAL!**
HOW CAN I BE "IN IT" **TOGETHER** WITH **YOU?!**
POOR KID.
MY LITTLE BROTHER IS SO DENSE.
IT'S A WOMAN, HUH?
BLUSH
AHA.
A... ANY-HOW...
SINCE THAT'S THE SITUATION, YOU'D BETTER BE READY TO PLAY!
UM, SANTA.

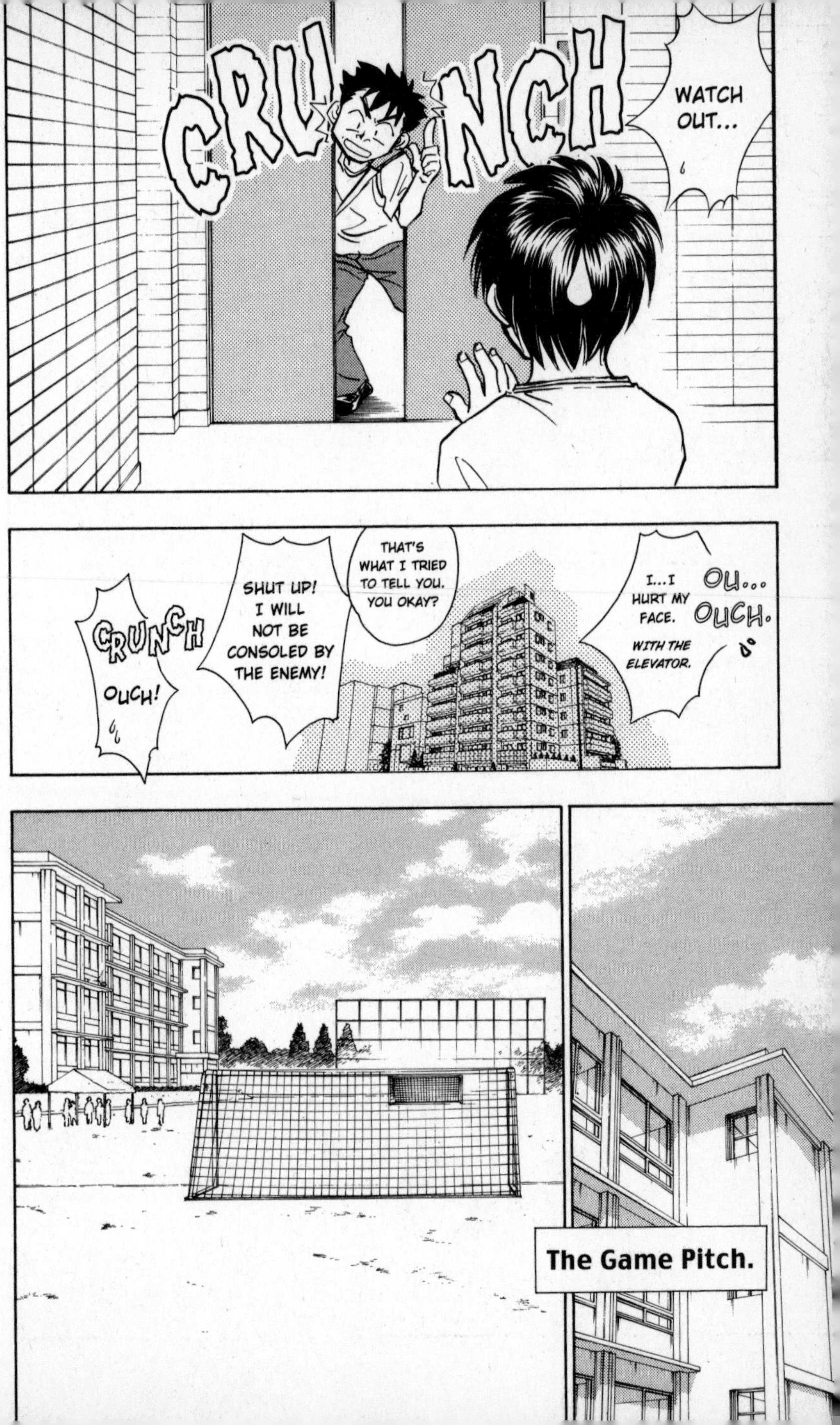
WATCH OUT...
CRUNCH
OU... OUCH.
I...I HURT MY FACE.
WITH THE ELEVATOR.
THAT'S WHAT I TRIED TO TELL YOU. YOU OKAY?
SHUT UP! I WILL NOT BE CONSOLED BY THE ENEMY!
CRUNCH
OUCH!
The Game Pitch.

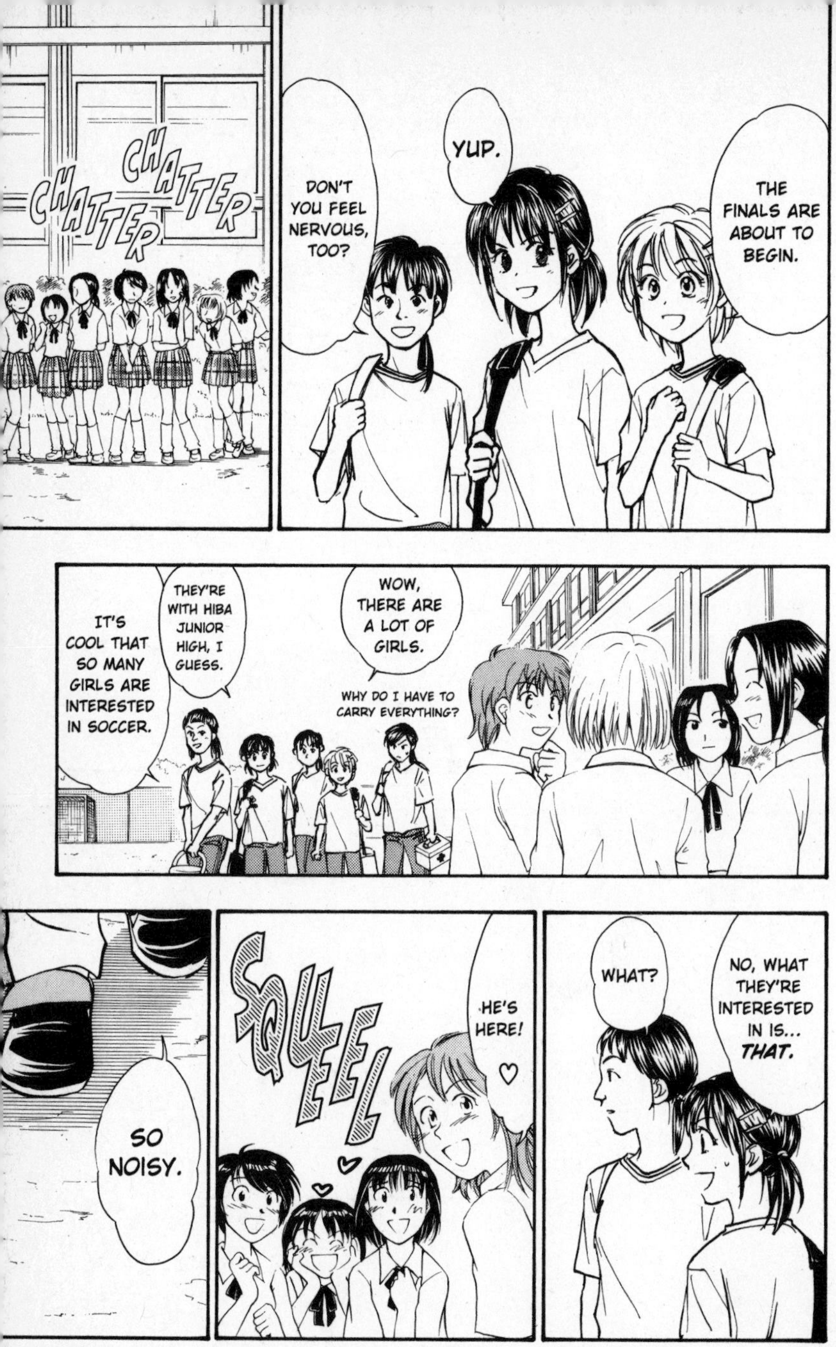
THE FINALS ARE ABOUT TO BEGIN.
YUP.
DON'T YOU FEEL NERVOUS, TOO?
CHATTER CHATTER
WOW, THERE ARE A LOT OF GIRLS.
WHY DO I HAVE TO CARRY EVERYTHING?
THEY'RE WITH HIBA JUNIOR HIGH, I GUESS.
IT'S COOL THAT SO MANY GIRLS ARE INTERESTED IN SOCCER.
NO, WHAT THEY'RE INTERESTED IN IS... *THAT.*
WHAT?
HE'S HERE! ♡
SQUEEL
SO NOISY.

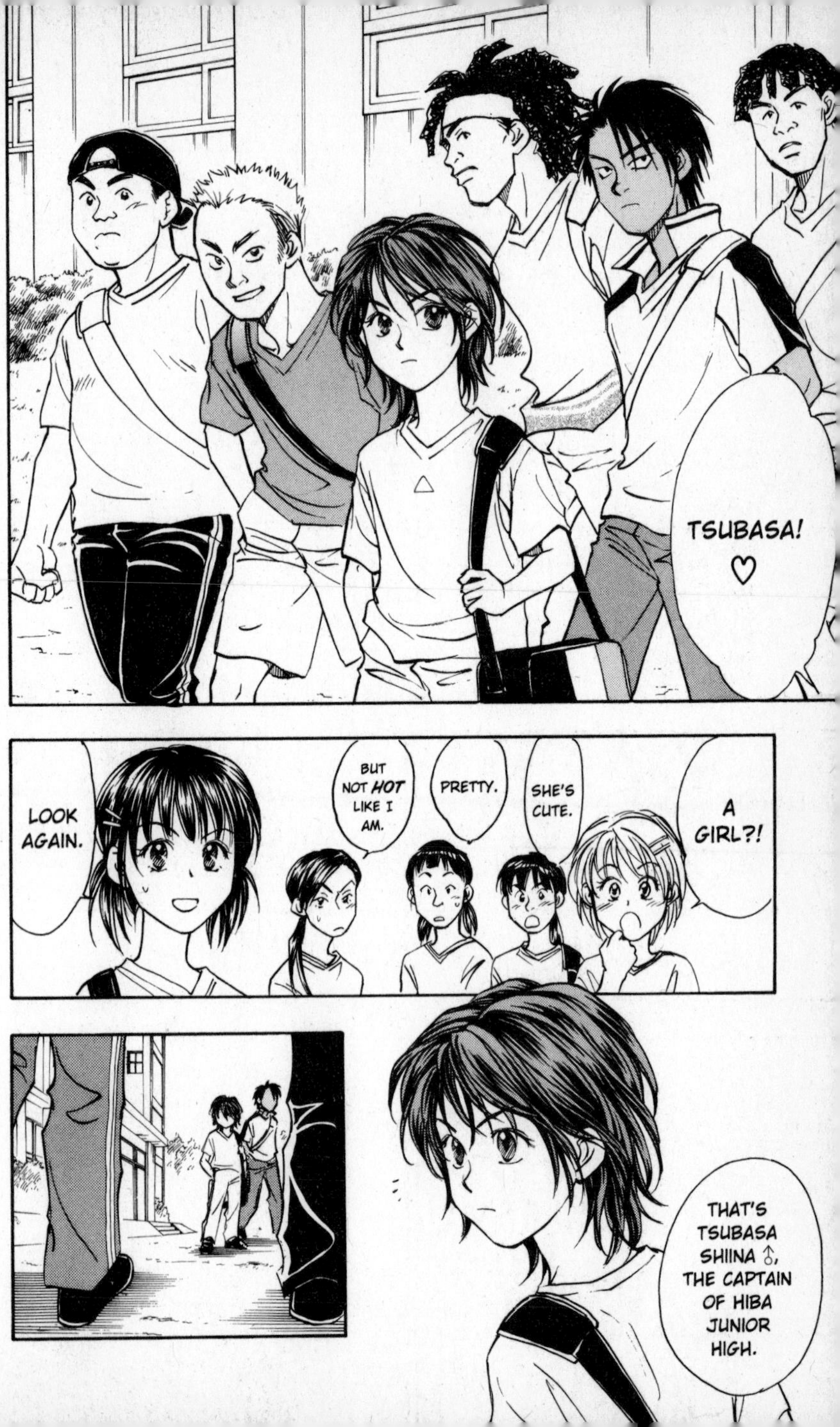
TSUBASA! ♡
A GIRL?!
SHE'S CUTE.
PRETTY.
BUT NOT HOT LIKE I AM.
LOOK AGAIN.
THAT'S TSUBASA SHIINA ♂, THE CAPTAIN OF HIBA JUNIOR HIGH.

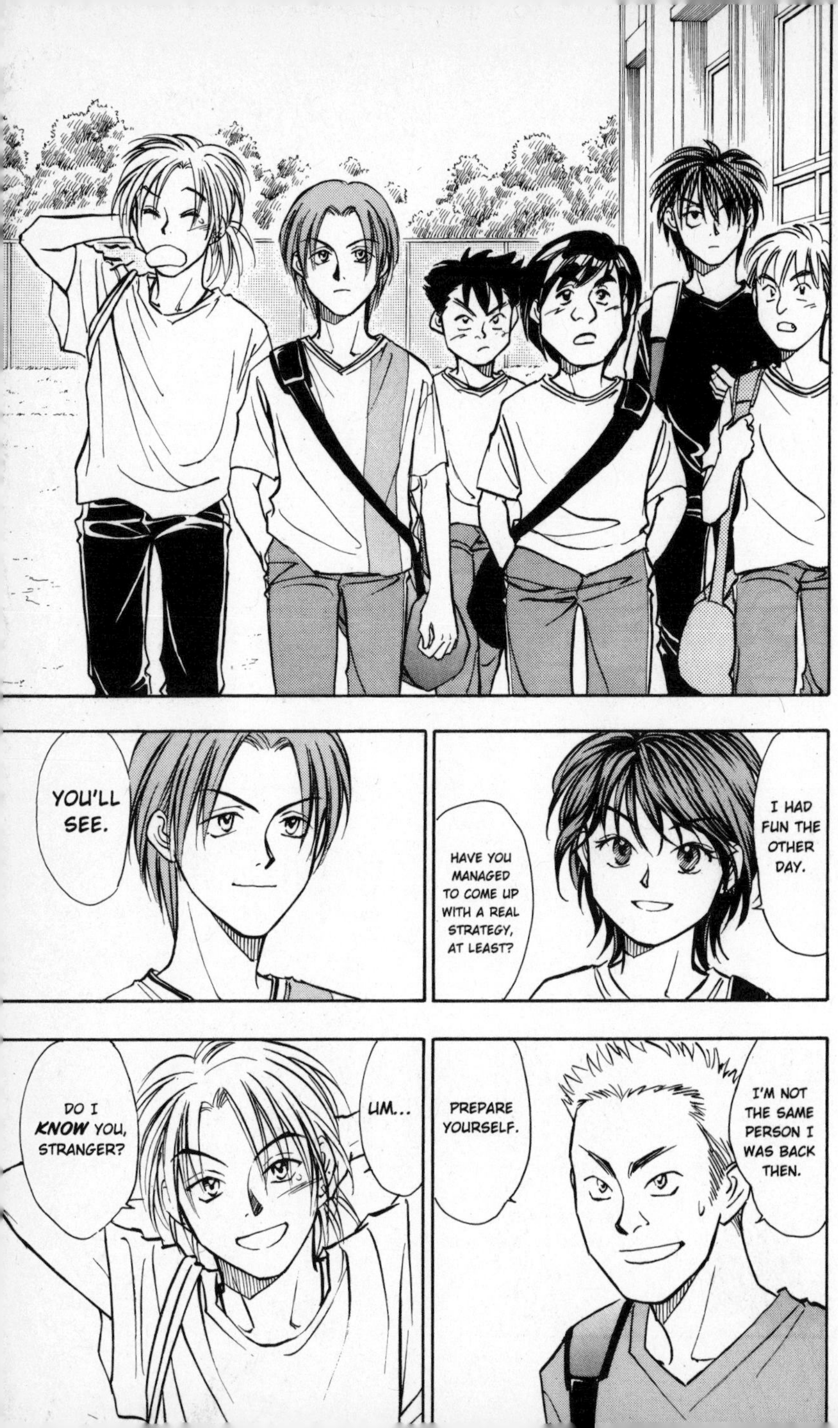
I HAD FUN THE OTHER DAY.
HAVE YOU MANAGED TO COME UP WITH A REAL STRATEGY, AT LEAST?
YOU'LL SEE.
I'M NOT THE SAME PERSON I WAS BACK THEN.
PREPARE YOURSELF.
UM...
DO I *KNOW* YOU, STRANGER?

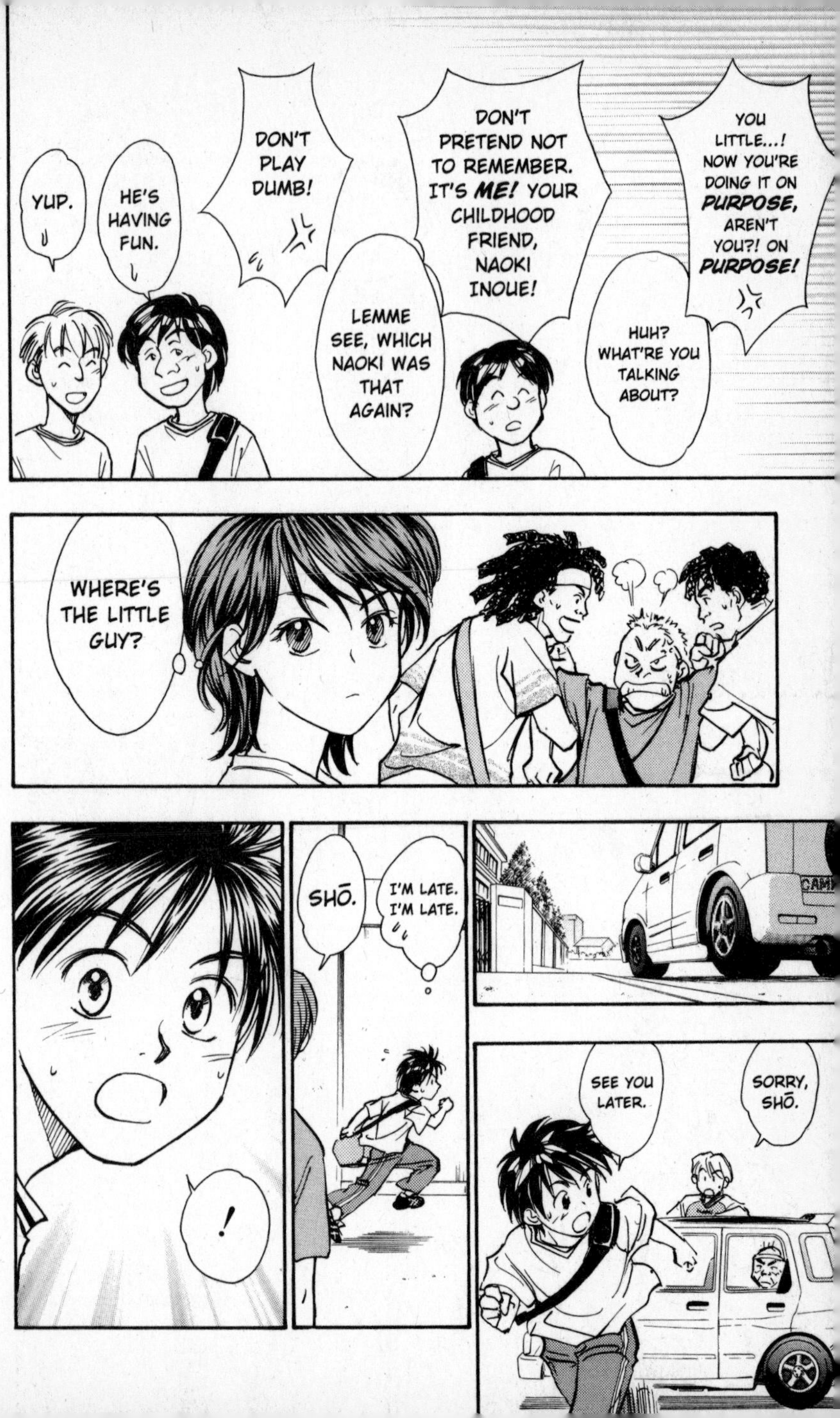
YOU LITTLE...! NOW YOU'RE DOING IT ON PURPOSE, AREN'T YOU?! ON PURPOSE!
HUH? WHAT'RE YOU TALKING ABOUT?
DON'T PRETEND NOT TO REMEMBER. IT'S ME! YOUR CHILDHOOD FRIEND, NAOKI INOUE!
LEMME SEE, WHICH NAOKI WAS THAT AGAIN?
DON'T PLAY DUMB!
HE'S HAVING FUN.
YUP.
WHERE'S THE LITTLE GUY?
SORRY, SHŌ.
SEE YOU LATER.
I'M LATE. I'M LATE.
SHŌ.
!

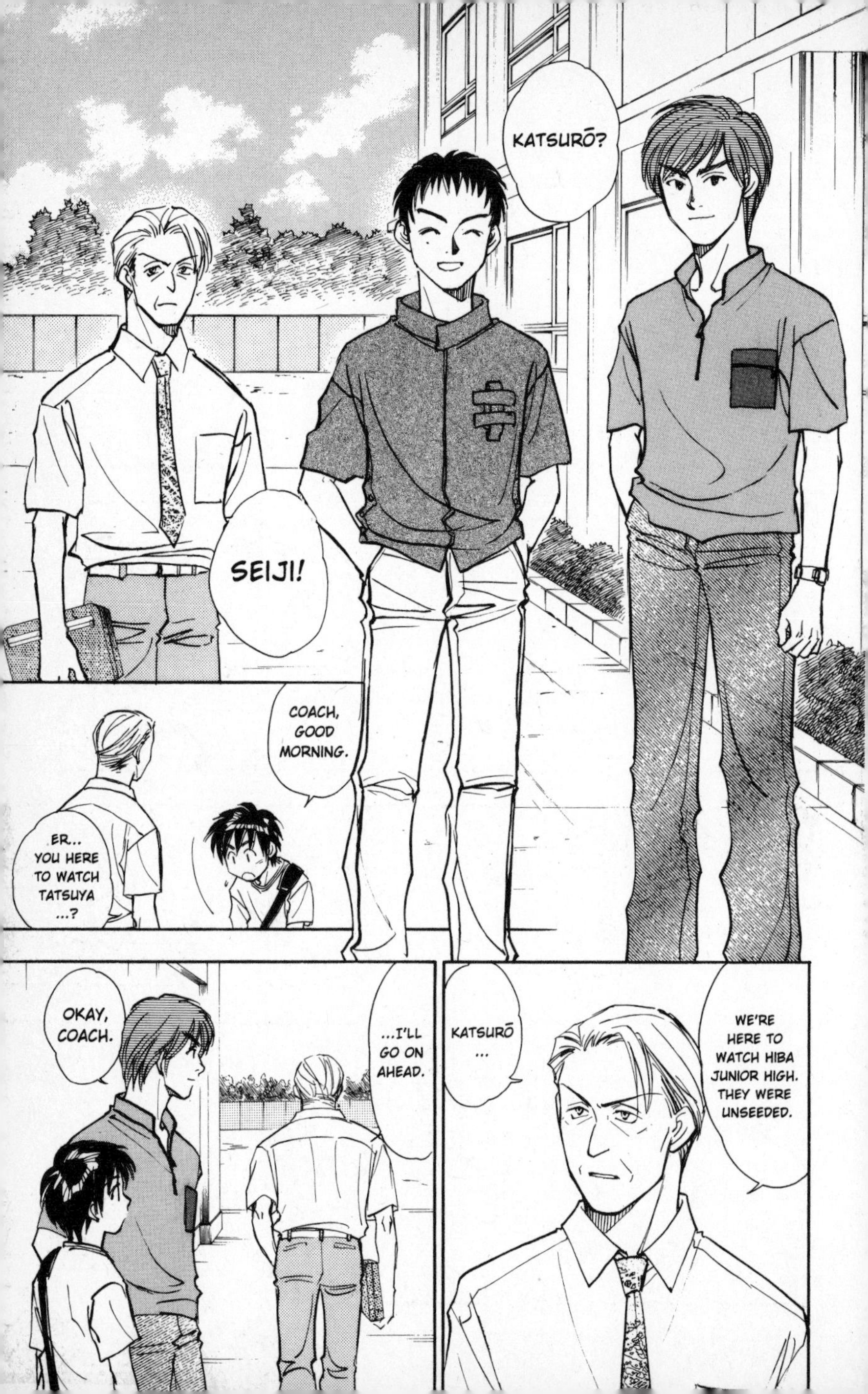
KATSURŌ?
SEIJI!
COACH, GOOD MORNING.
ER... YOU HERE TO WATCH TATSUYA ...?
WE'RE HERE TO WATCH HIBA JUNIOR HIGH. THEY WERE UNSEEDED.
KATSURŌ ...
...I'LL GO ON AHEAD.
OKAY, COACH.

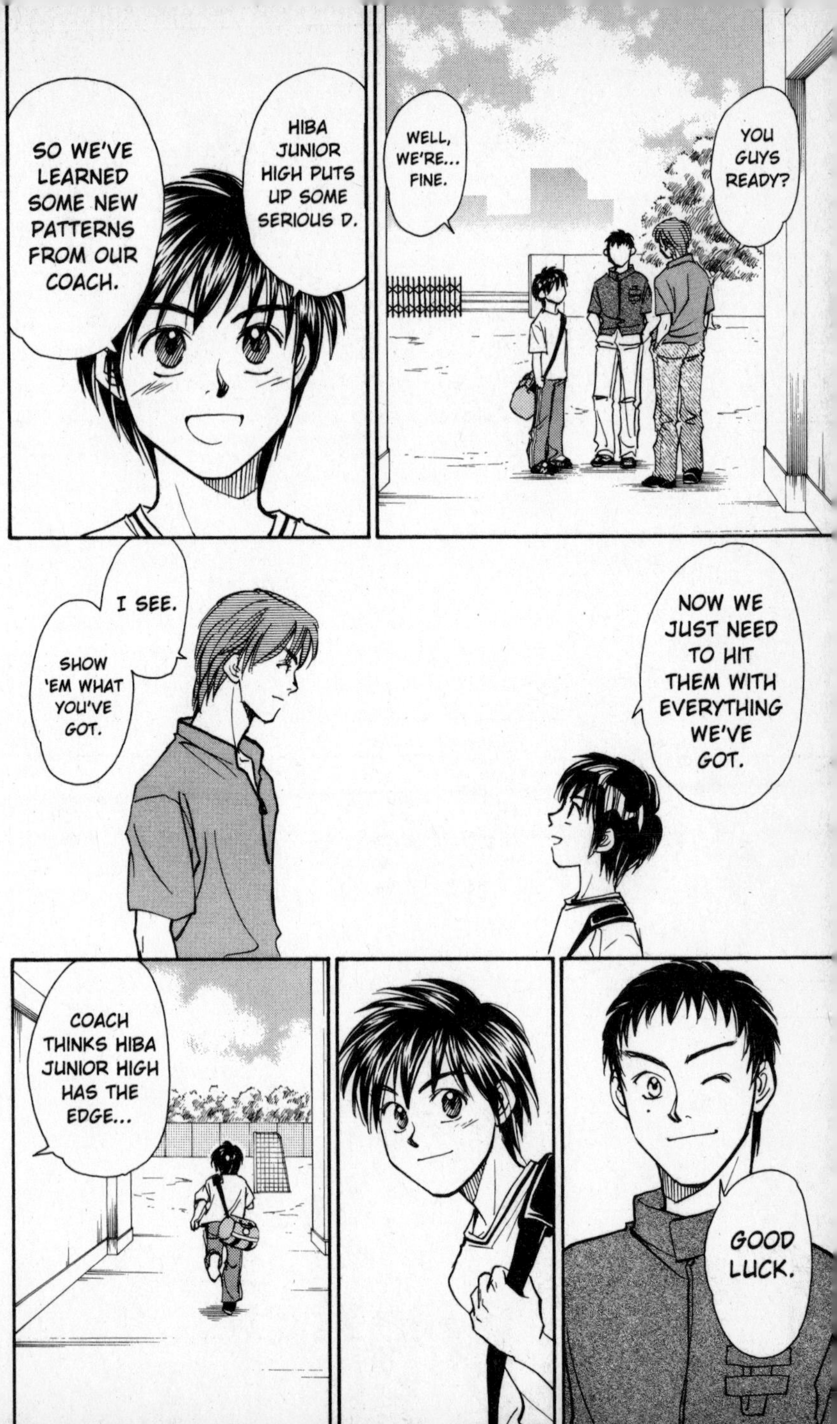
YOU GUYS READY?
WELL, WE'RE... FINE.
HIBA JUNIOR HIGH PUTS UP SOME SERIOUS D.
SO WE'VE LEARNED SOME NEW PATTERNS FROM OUR COACH.
NOW WE JUST NEED TO HIT THEM WITH EVERYTHING WE'VE GOT.
I SEE.
SHOW 'EM WHAT YOU'VE GOT.
GOOD LUCK.
COACH THINKS HIBA JUNIOR HIGH HAS THE EDGE...

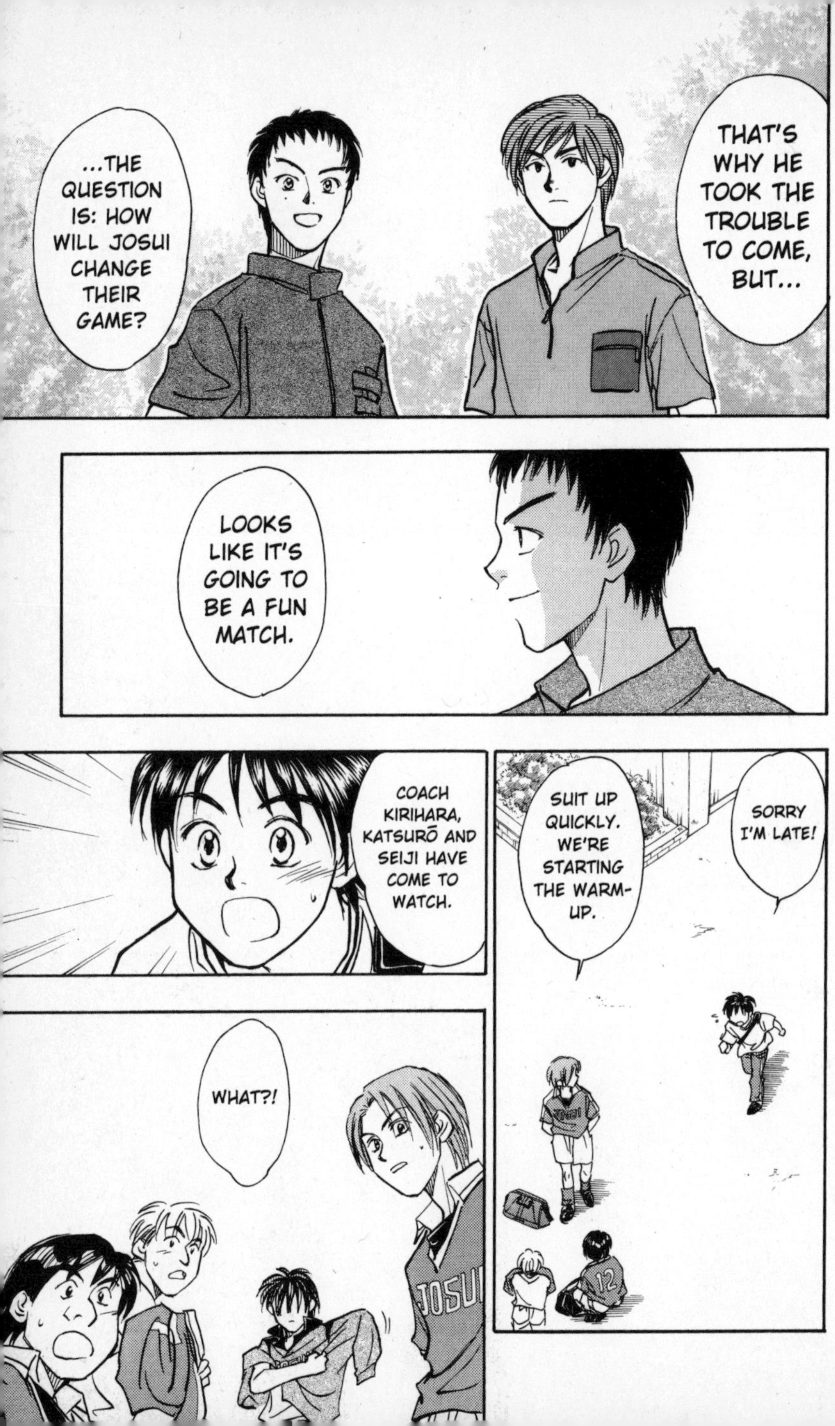
THAT'S WHY HE TOOK THE TROUBLE TO COME, BUT...
...THE QUESTION IS: HOW WILL JOSUI CHANGE THEIR GAME?
LOOKS LIKE IT'S GOING TO BE A FUN MATCH.
SORRY I'M LATE!
SUIT UP QUICKLY. WE'RE STARTING THE WARM-UP.
COACH KIRIHARA, KATSURŌ AND SEIJI HAVE COME TO WATCH.
WHAT?!

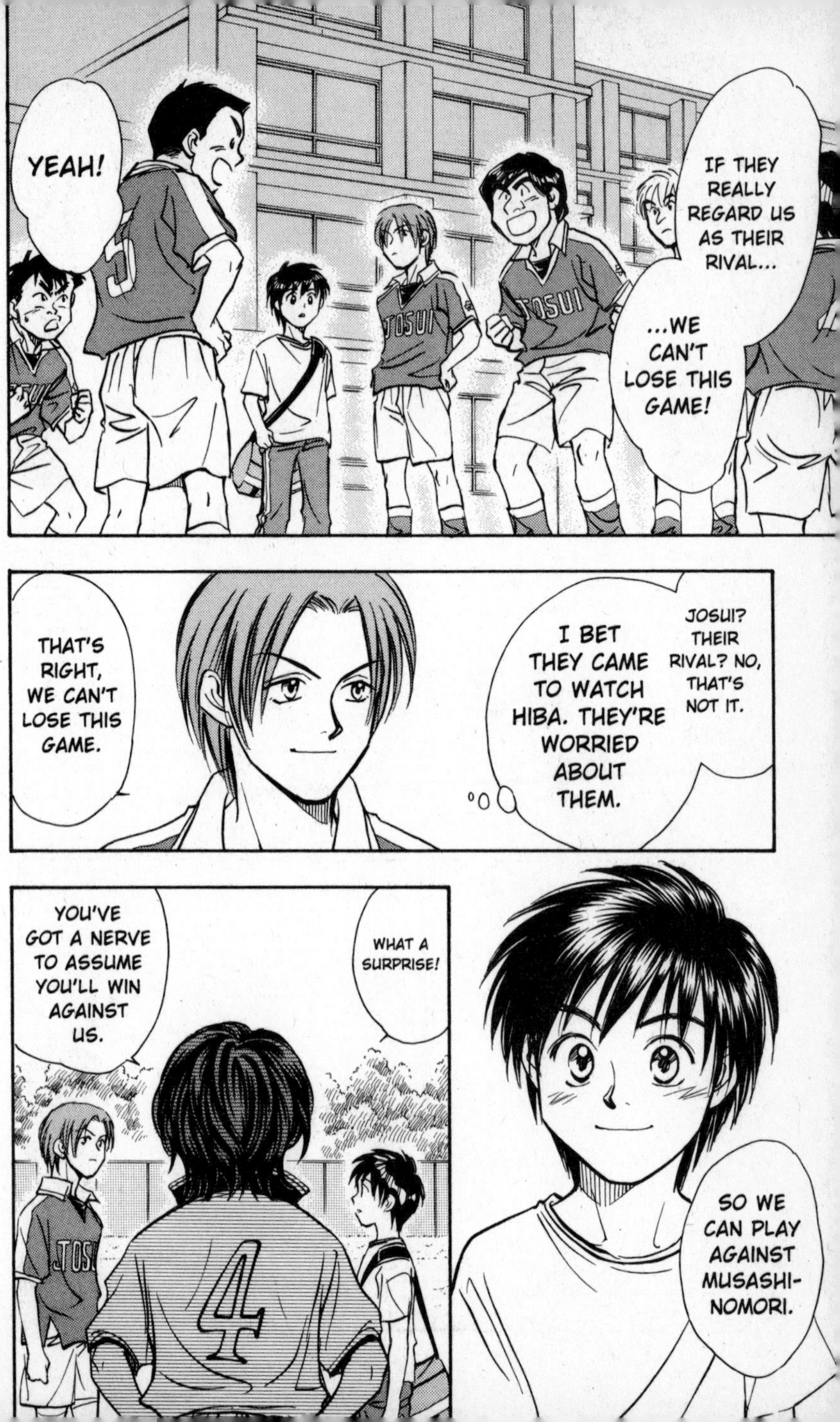
IF THEY REALLY REGARD US AS THEIR RIVAL...
...WE CAN'T LOSE THIS GAME!
YEAH!
JOSUI? THEIR RIVAL? NO, THAT'S NOT IT.
I BET THEY CAME TO WATCH HIBA. THEY'RE WORRIED ABOUT THEM.
THAT'S RIGHT, WE CAN'T LOSE THIS GAME.
SO WE CAN PLAY AGAINST MUSASHI-NOMORI.
WHAT A SURPRISE!
YOU'VE GOT A NERVE TO ASSUME YOU'LL WIN AGAINST US.
JOSUI
JOSUI
JOSUI

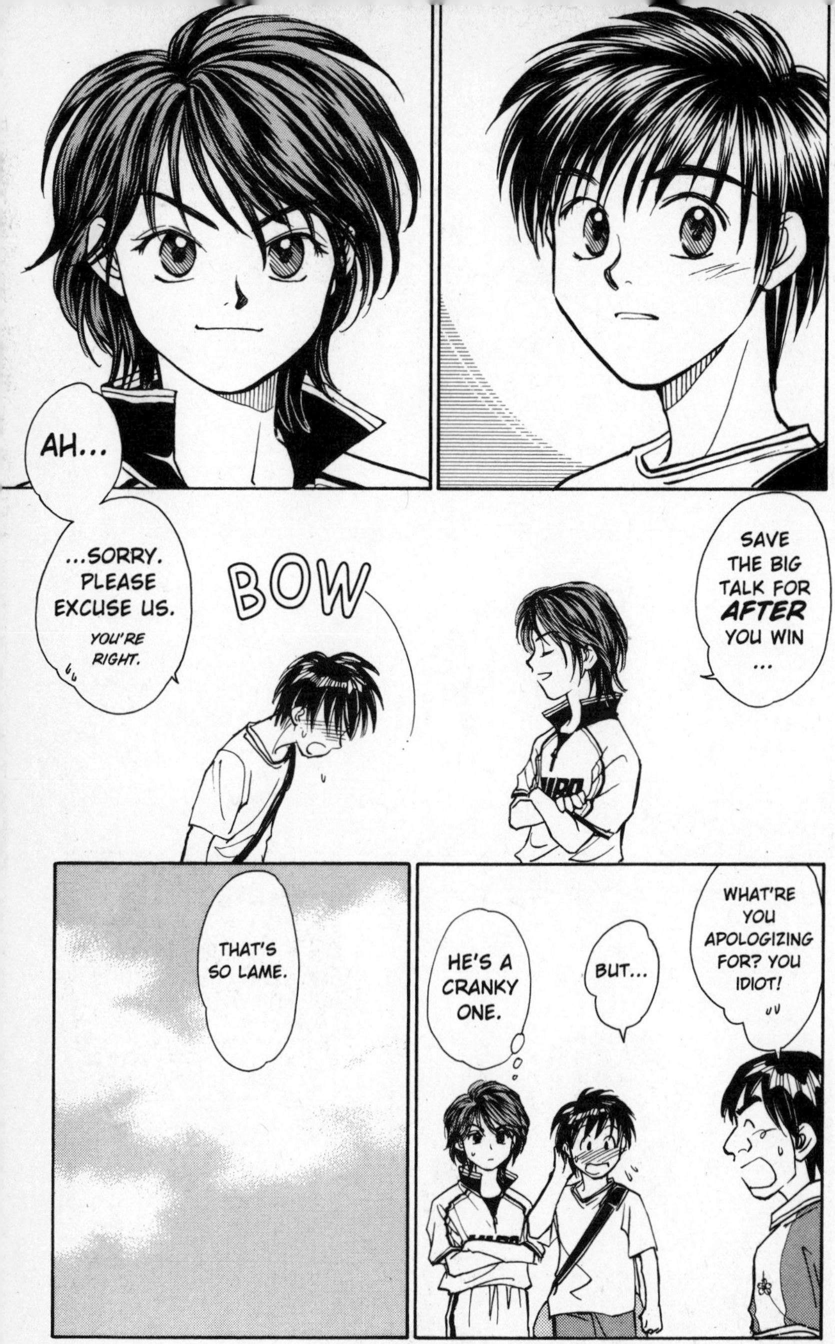
AH...
SAVE THE BIG TALK FOR AFTER YOU WIN...
BOW
...SORRY. PLEASE EXCUSE US.
YOU'RE RIGHT.
WHAT'RE YOU APOLOGIZING FOR? YOU IDIOT!
BUT...
HE'S A CRANKY ONE.
THAT'S SO LAME.

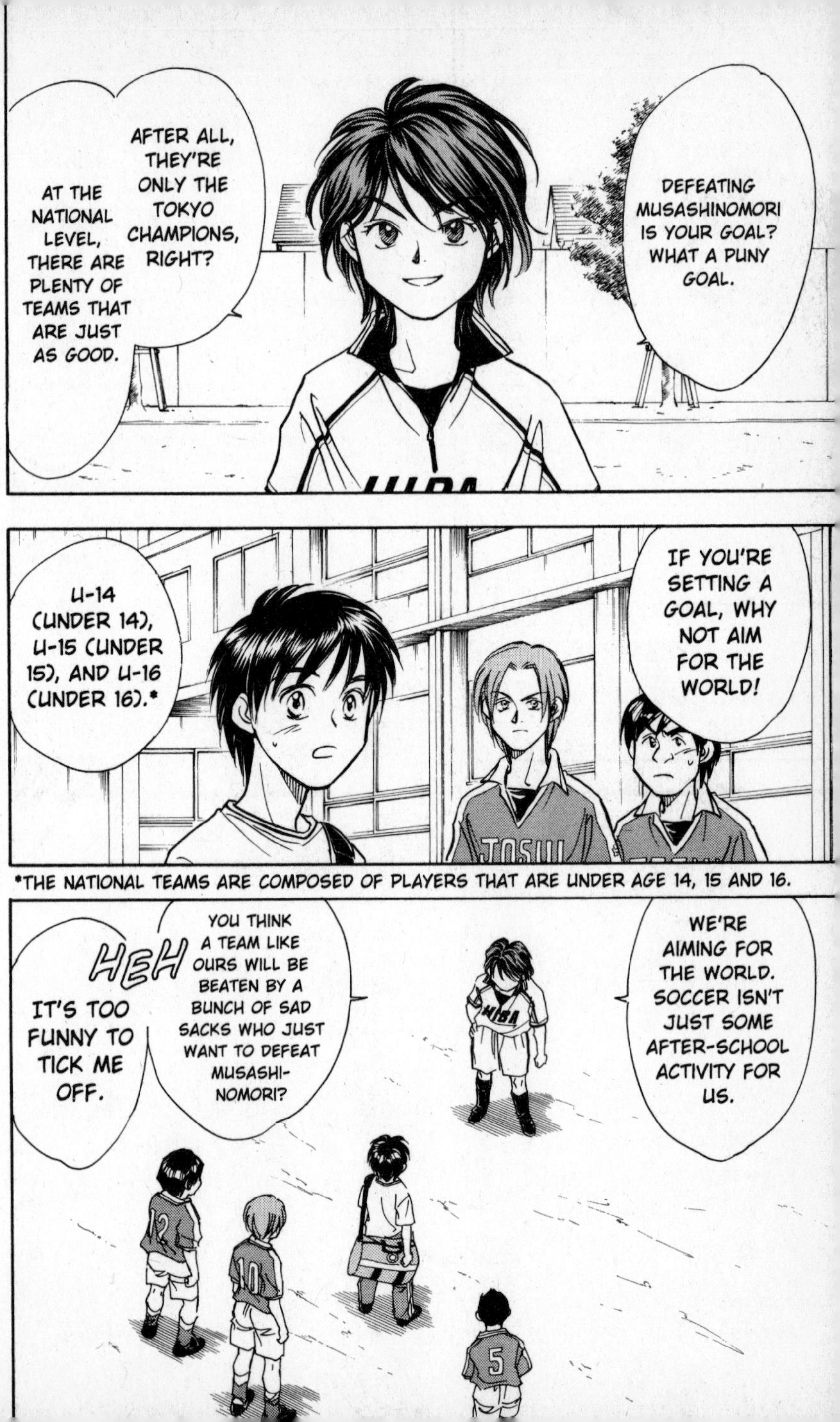
DEFEATING MUSASHINOMORI IS YOUR GOAL? WHAT A PUNY GOAL.
AFTER ALL, THEY'RE ONLY THE TOKYO CHAMPIONS, RIGHT?
AT THE NATIONAL LEVEL, THERE ARE PLENTY OF TEAMS THAT ARE JUST AS GOOD.
IF YOU'RE SETTING A GOAL, WHY NOT AIM FOR THE WORLD!
U-14 (UNDER 14), U-15 (UNDER 15), AND U-16 (UNDER 16).*
WE'RE AIMING FOR THE WORLD. SOCCER ISN'T JUST SOME AFTER-SCHOOL ACTIVITY FOR US.
YOU THINK A TEAM LIKE OURS WILL BE BEATEN BY A BUNCH OF SAD SACKS WHO JUST WANT TO DEFEAT MUSASHI-NOMORI?
HEH
IT'S TOO FUNNY TO TICK ME OFF.

*THE NATIONAL TEAMS ARE COMPOSED OF PLAYERS THAT ARE UNDER AGE 14, 15 AND 16.

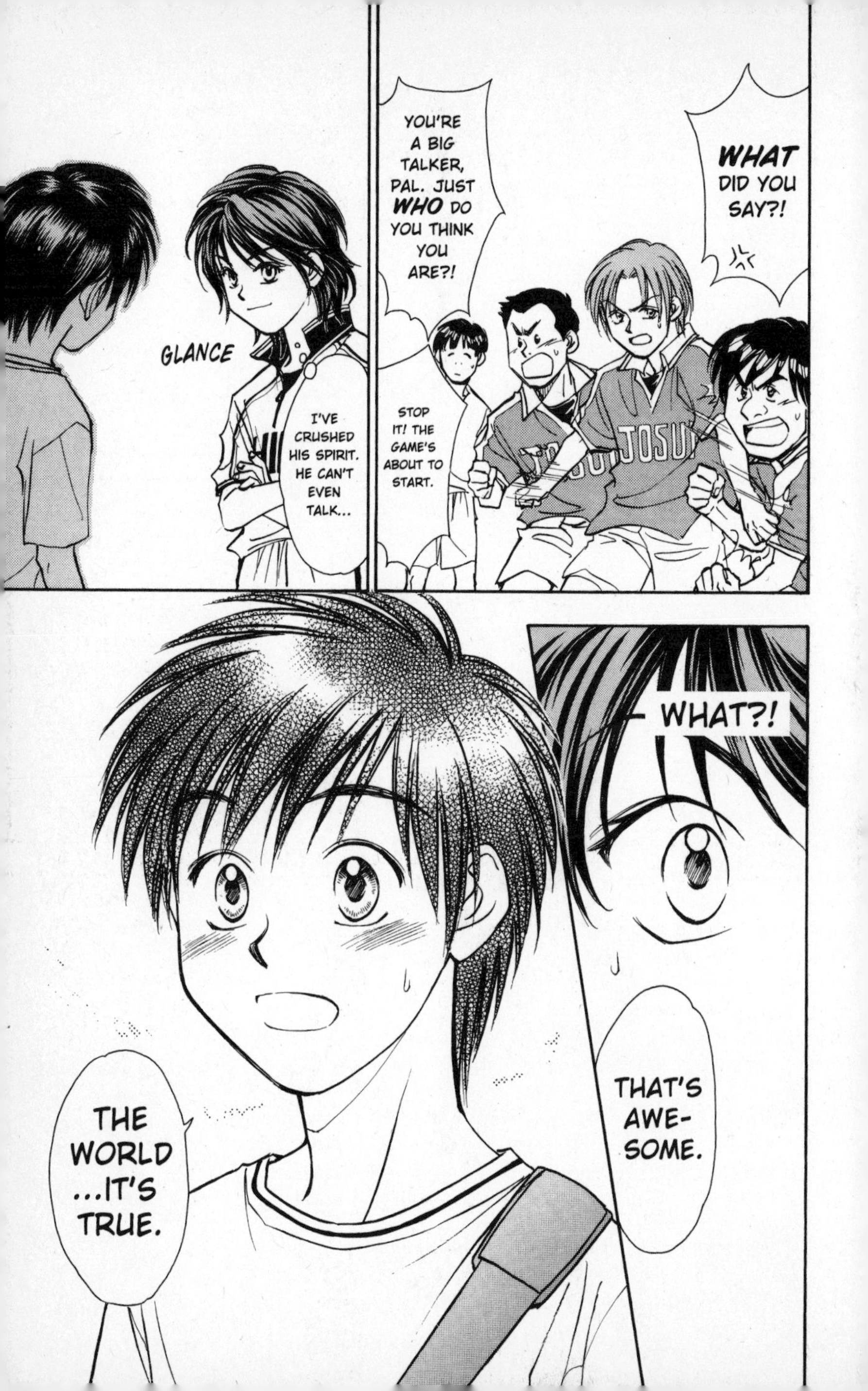
WHAT DID YOU SAY?!
YOU'RE A BIG TALKER, PAL. JUST WHO DO YOU THINK YOU ARE?!
STOP IT! THE GAME'S ABOUT TO START.
JOSUI
GLANCE
I'VE CRUSHED HIS SPIRIT. HE CAN'T EVEN TALK...
WHAT?!
THAT'S AWE-SOME.
THE WORLD ...IT'S TRUE.

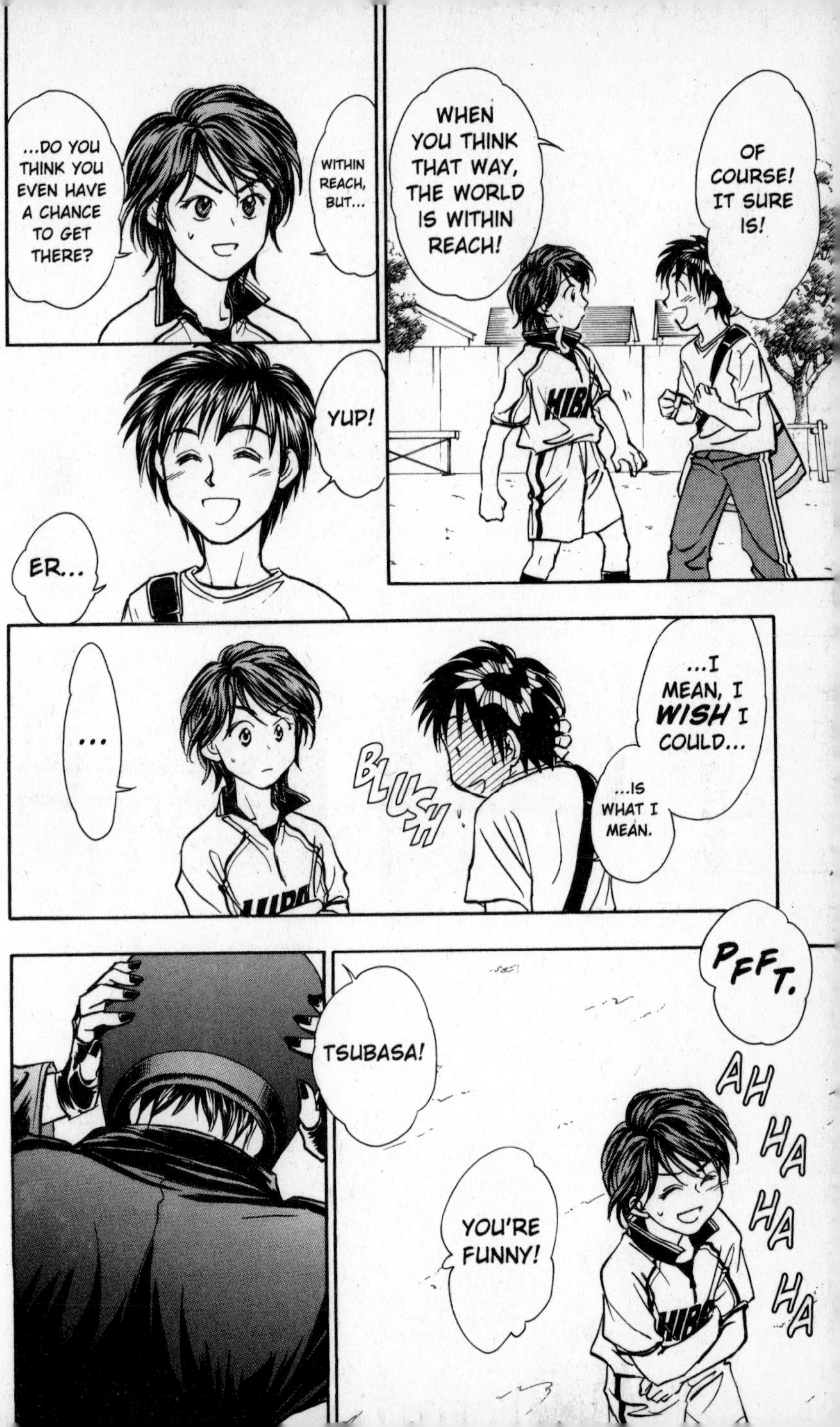
OF COURSE! IT SURE IS!
WHEN YOU THINK THAT WAY, THE WORLD IS WITHIN REACH!
WITHIN REACH, BUT...
...DO YOU THINK YOU EVEN HAVE A CHANCE TO GET THERE?
YUP!
ER...
...I MEAN, I ***WISH*** I COULD...
...IS WHAT I MEAN.
BLUSH
...
PFFT.
AH HA HA HA HA
YOU'RE FUNNY!
TSUBASA!

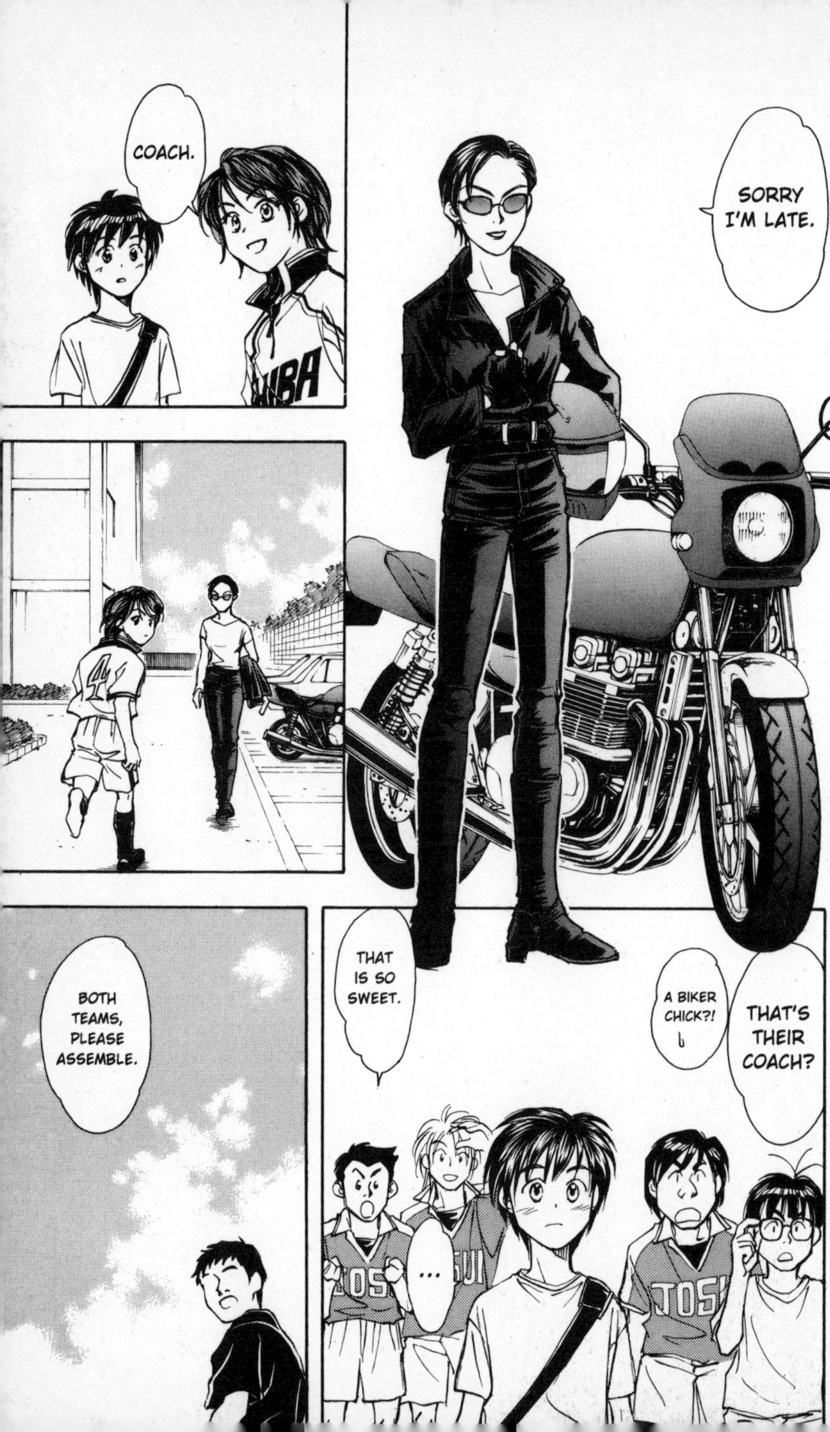
SORRY I'M LATE.
COACH.
THAT'S THEIR COACH?
A BIKER CHICK?!
THAT IS SO SWEET.
...
BOTH TEAMS, PLEASE ASSEMBLE.

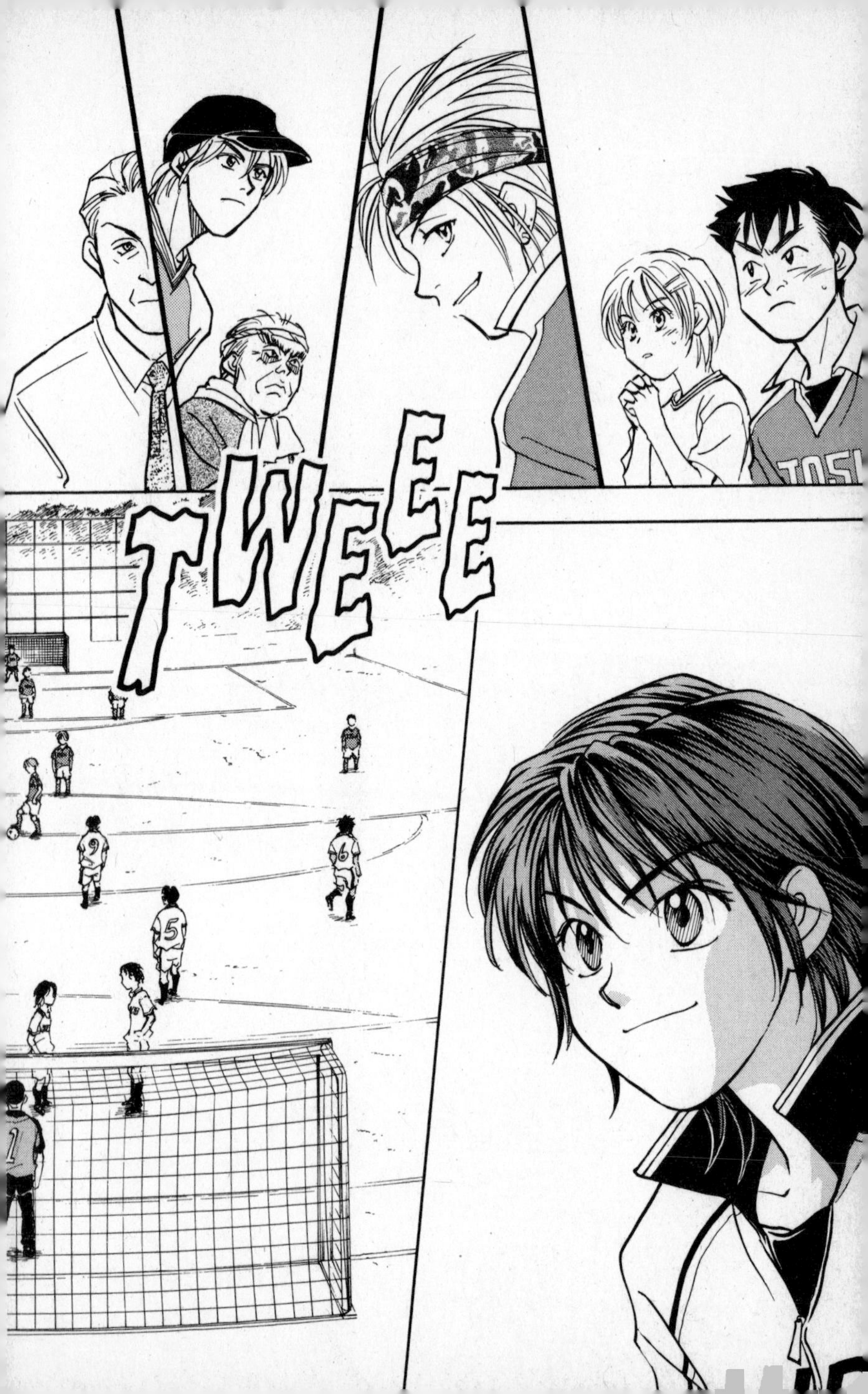
TWEEE

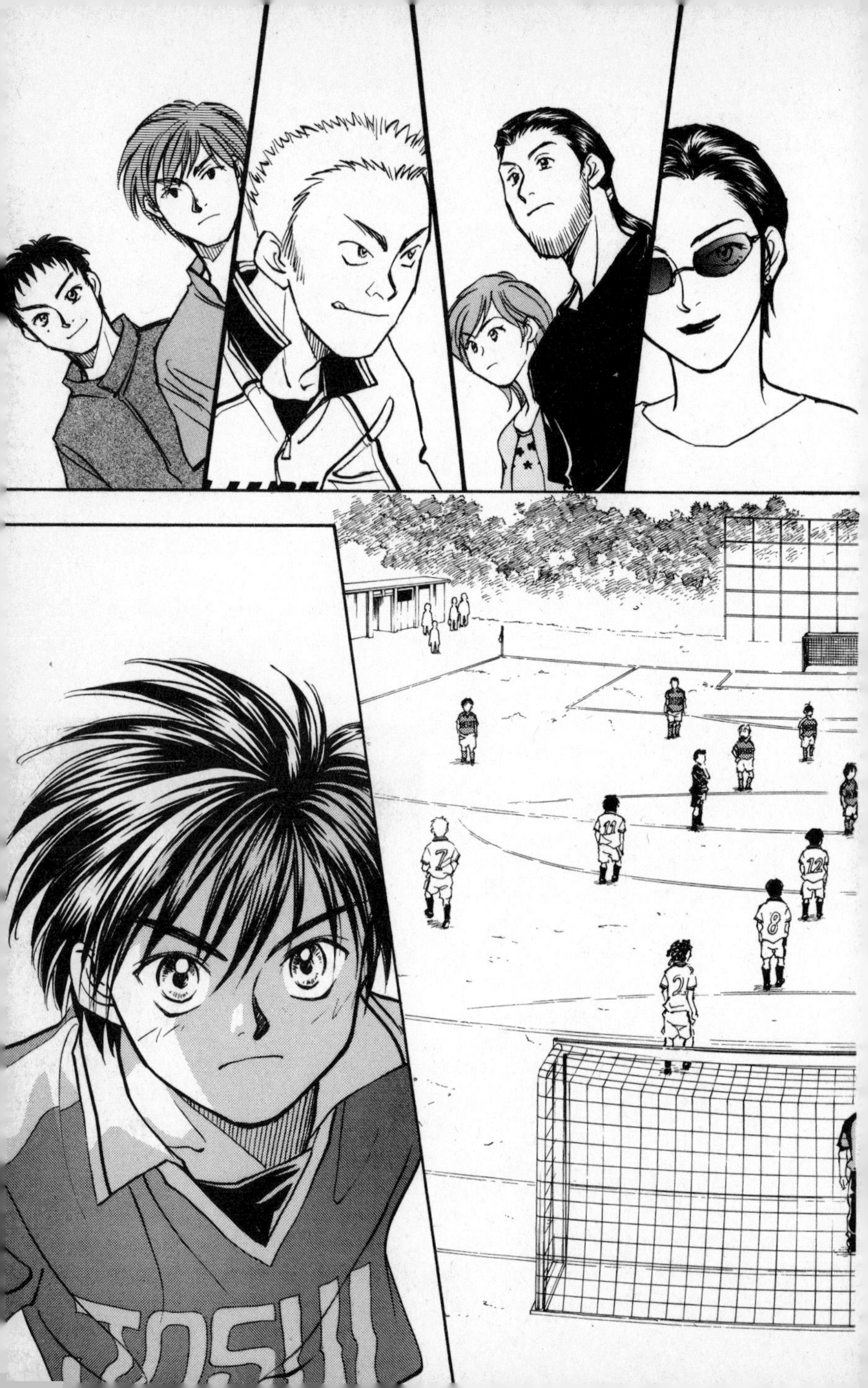

WHISTLE!

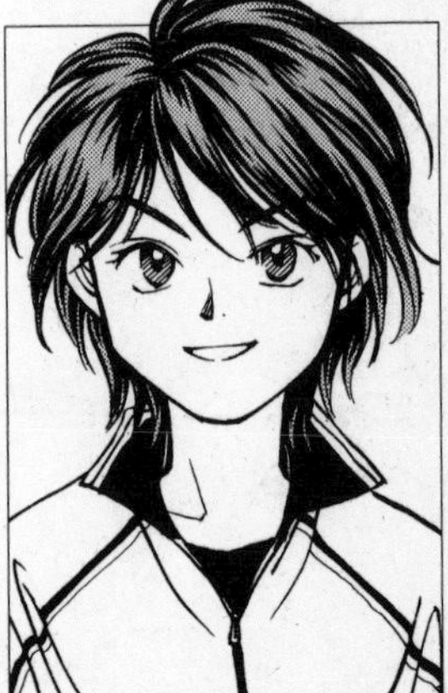

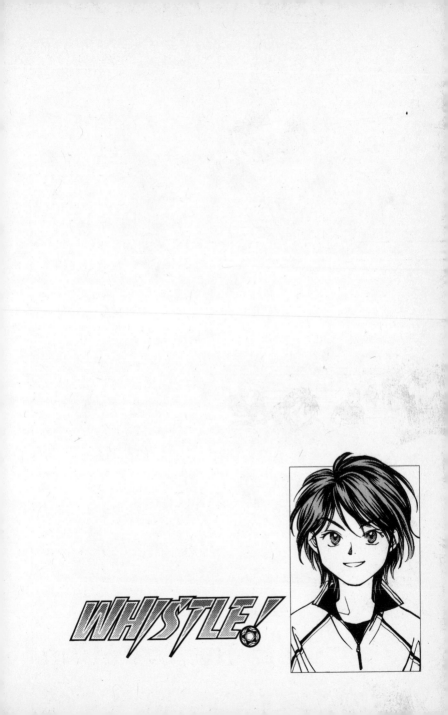

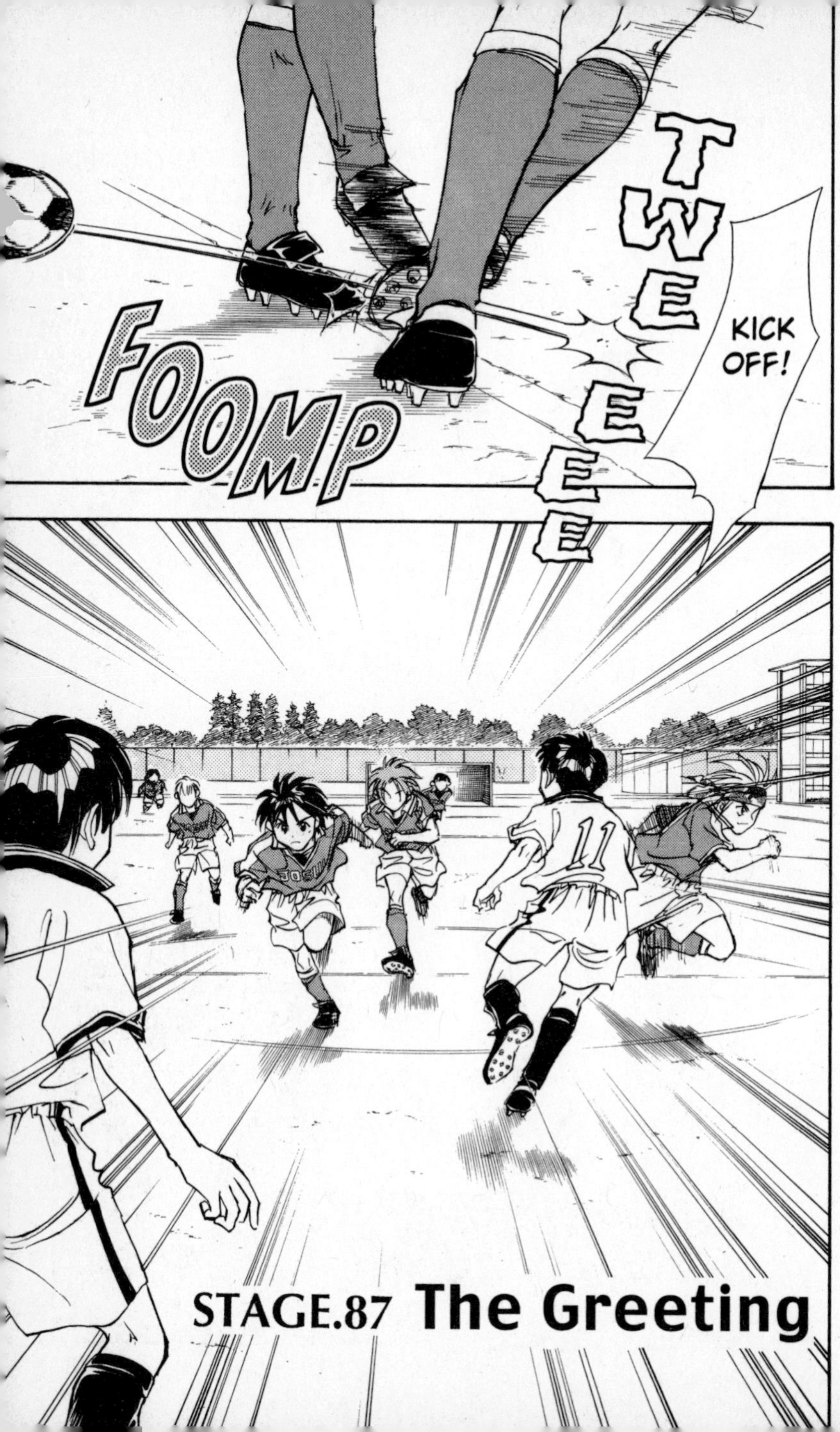
TWEEEEE
KICK OFF!
FOOMP

STAGE.87 The Greeting

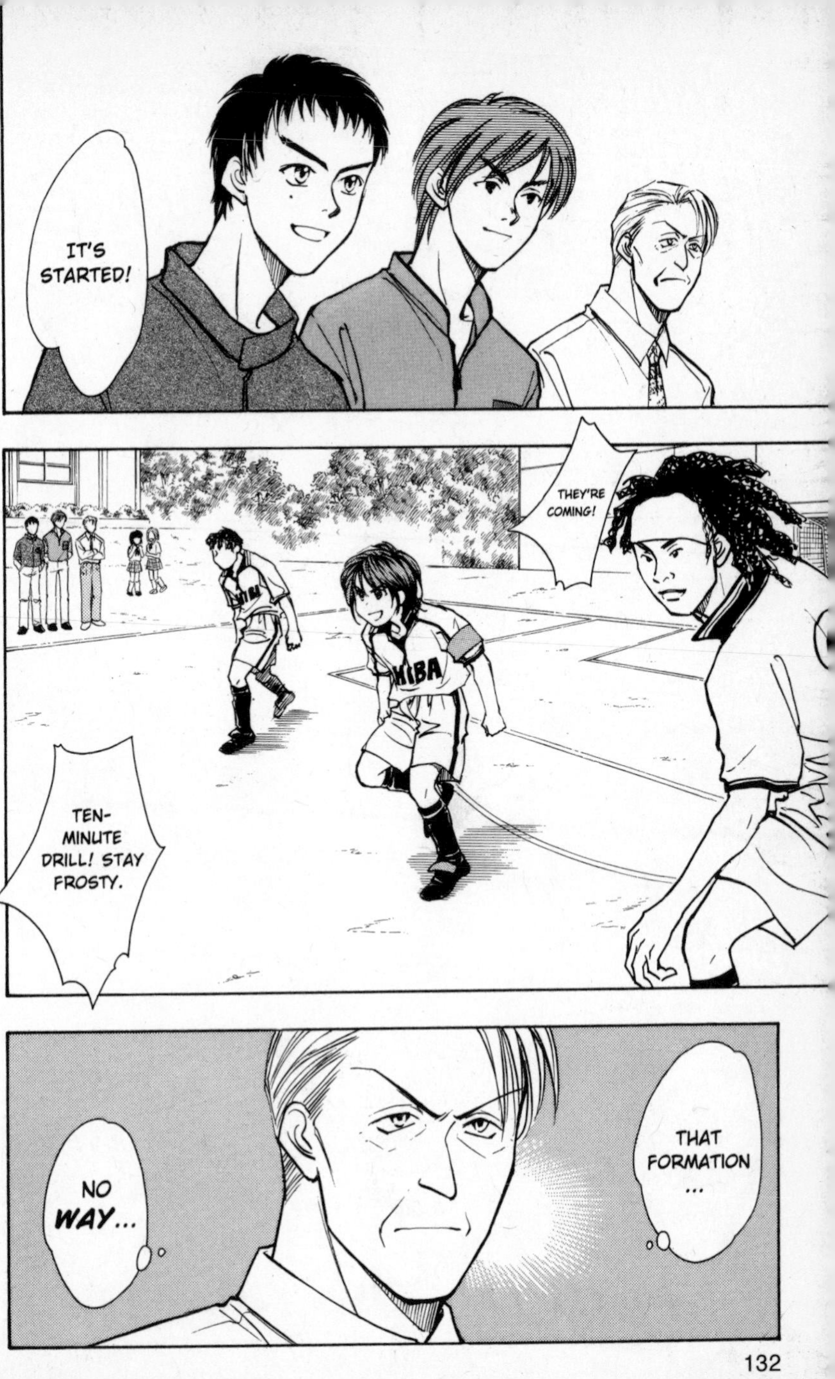
IT'S STARTED!
THEY'RE COMING!
TEN-MINUTE DRILL! STAY FROSTY.
THAT FORMATION ...
NO WAY...

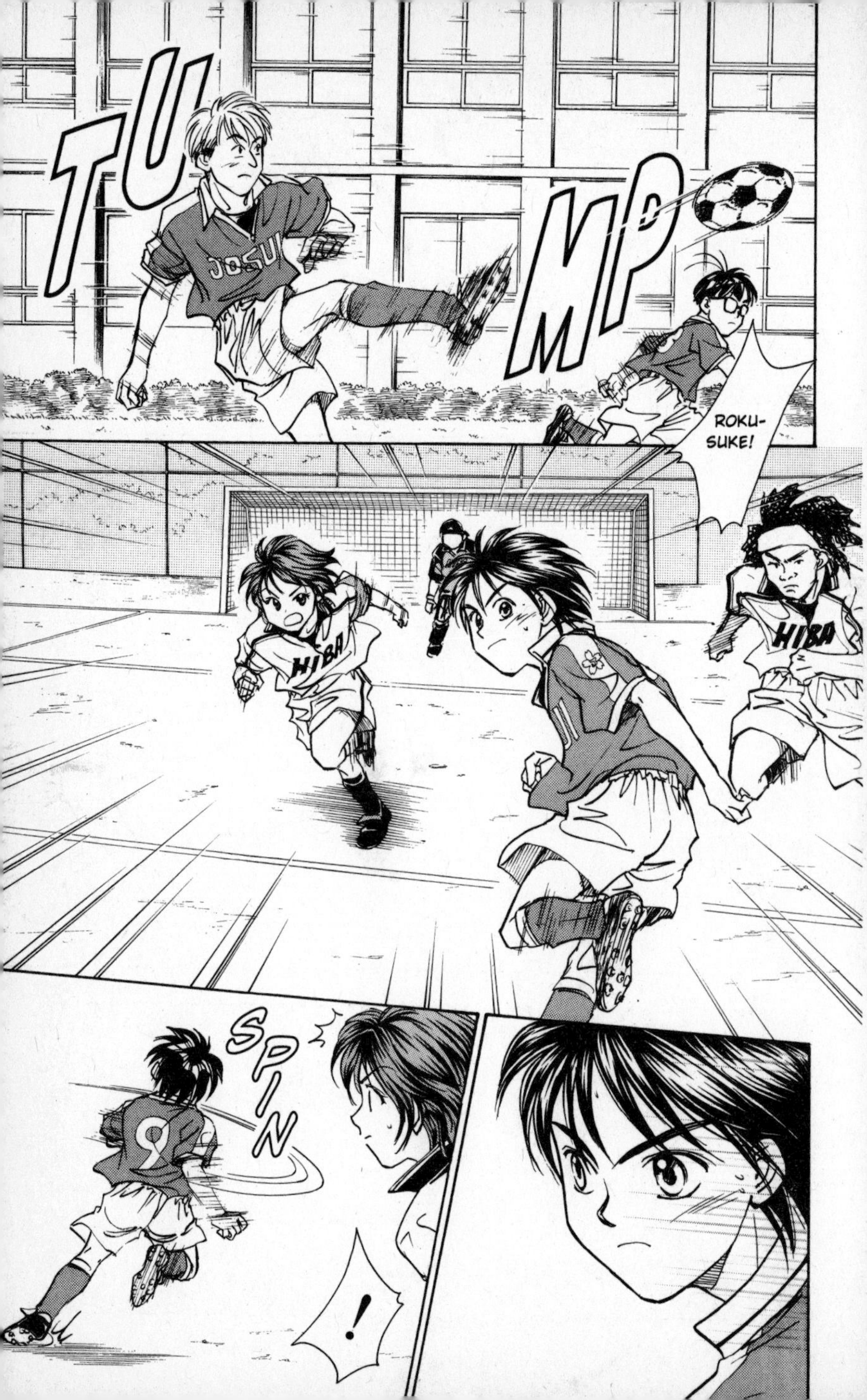
TUMP
ROKU-SUKE!
SPIN
!

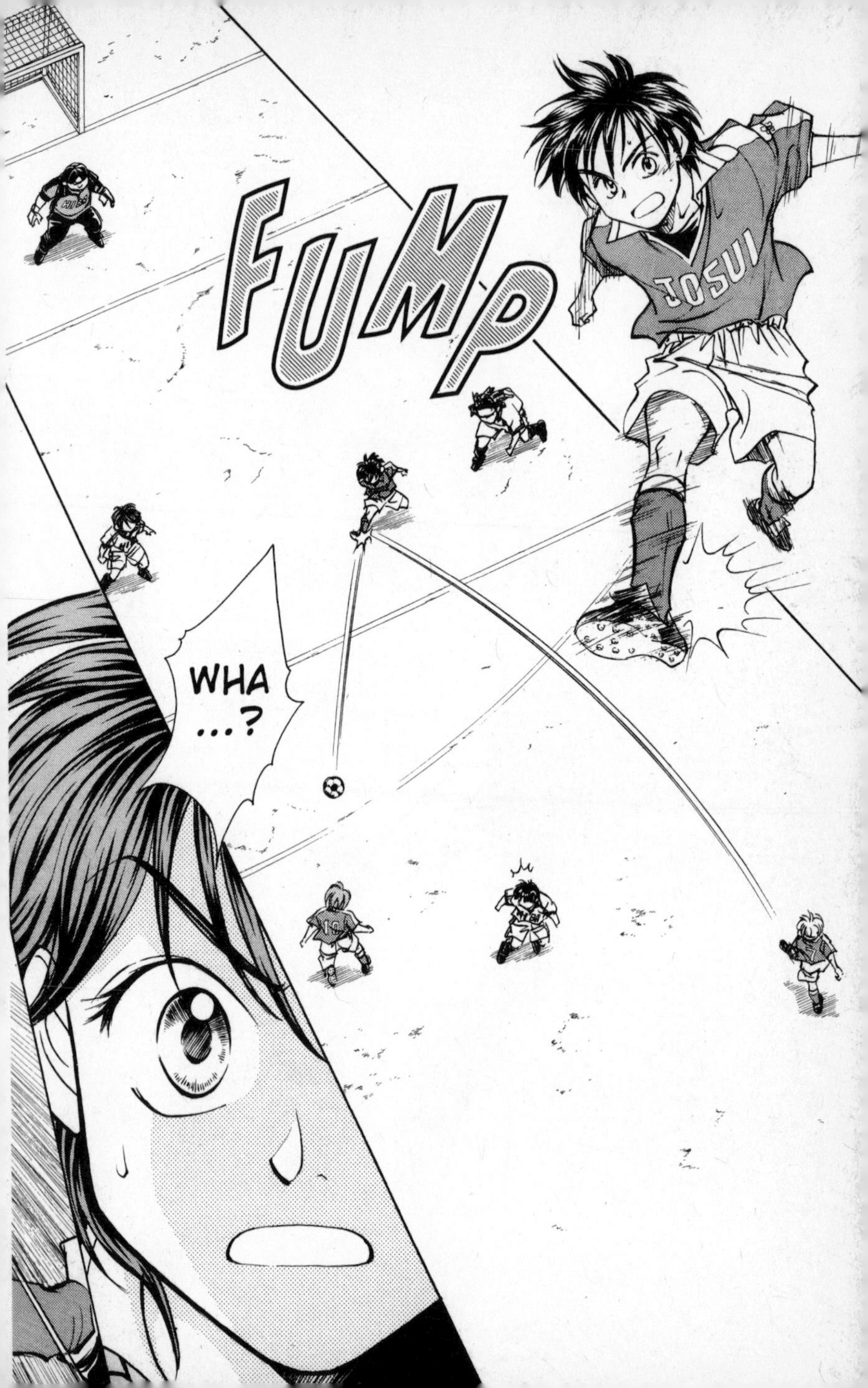
FUMP
JOSUI
WHA ...?

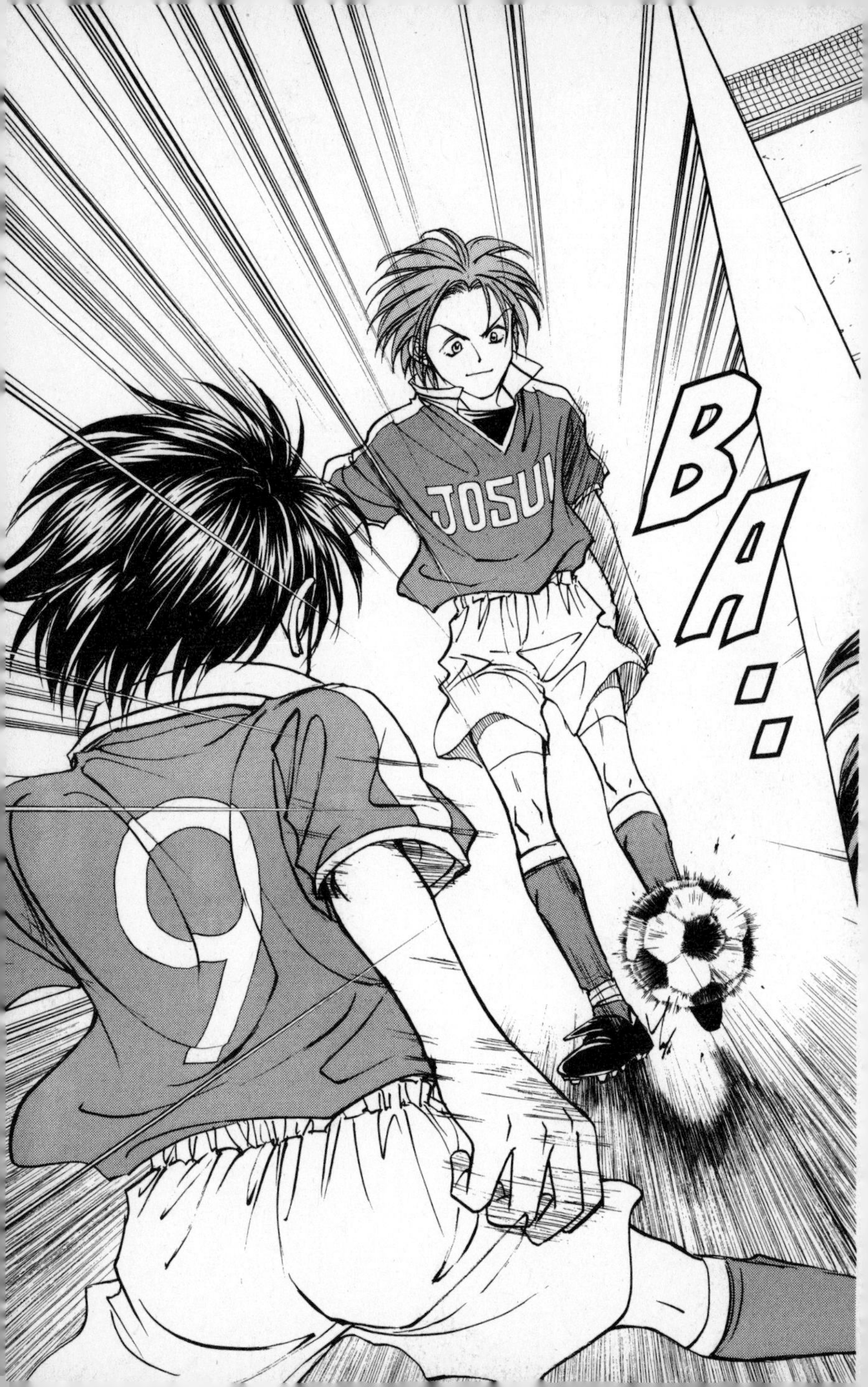
JOSUI
BA...

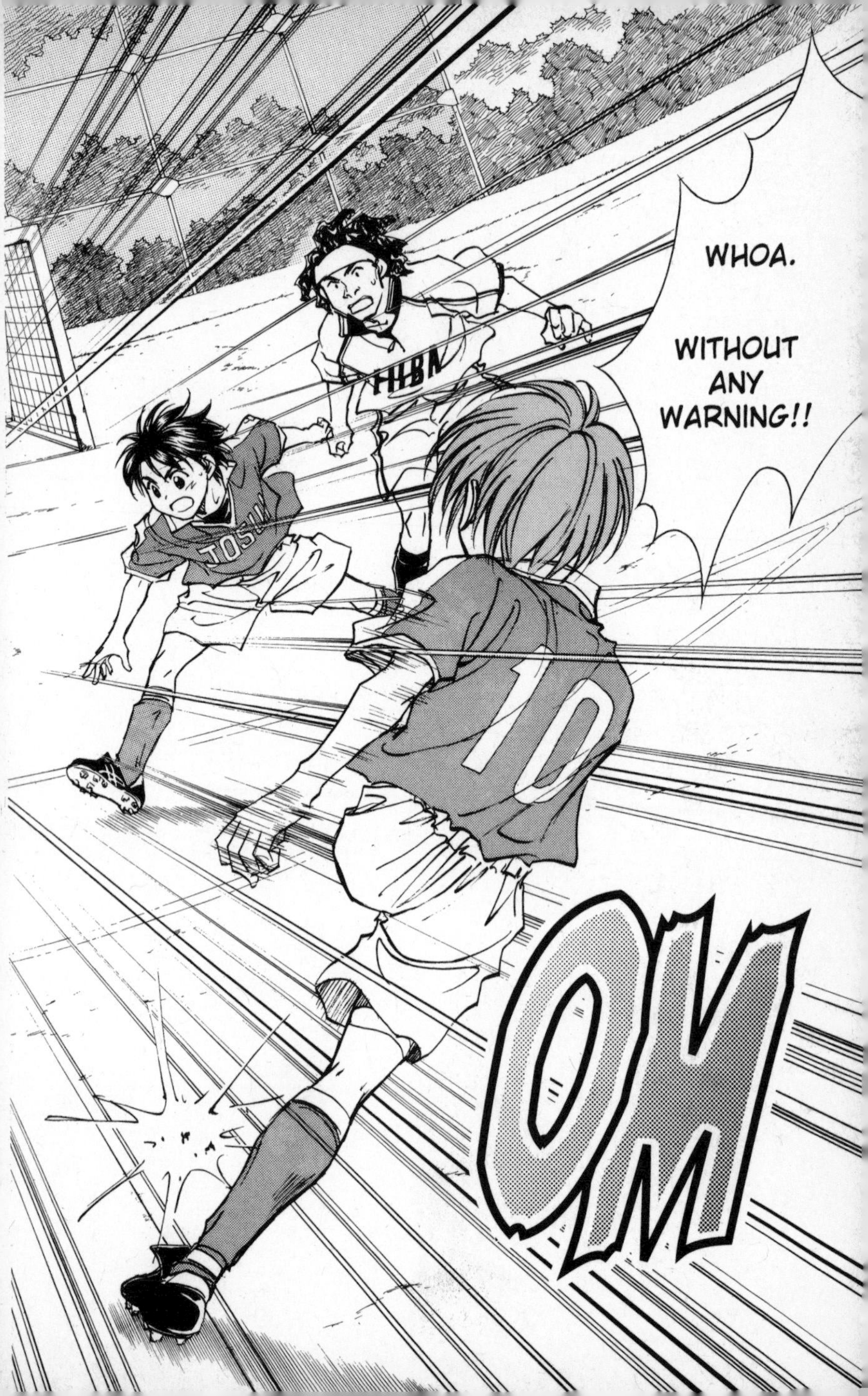
WHOA.
WITHOUT ANY WARNING!!
OM

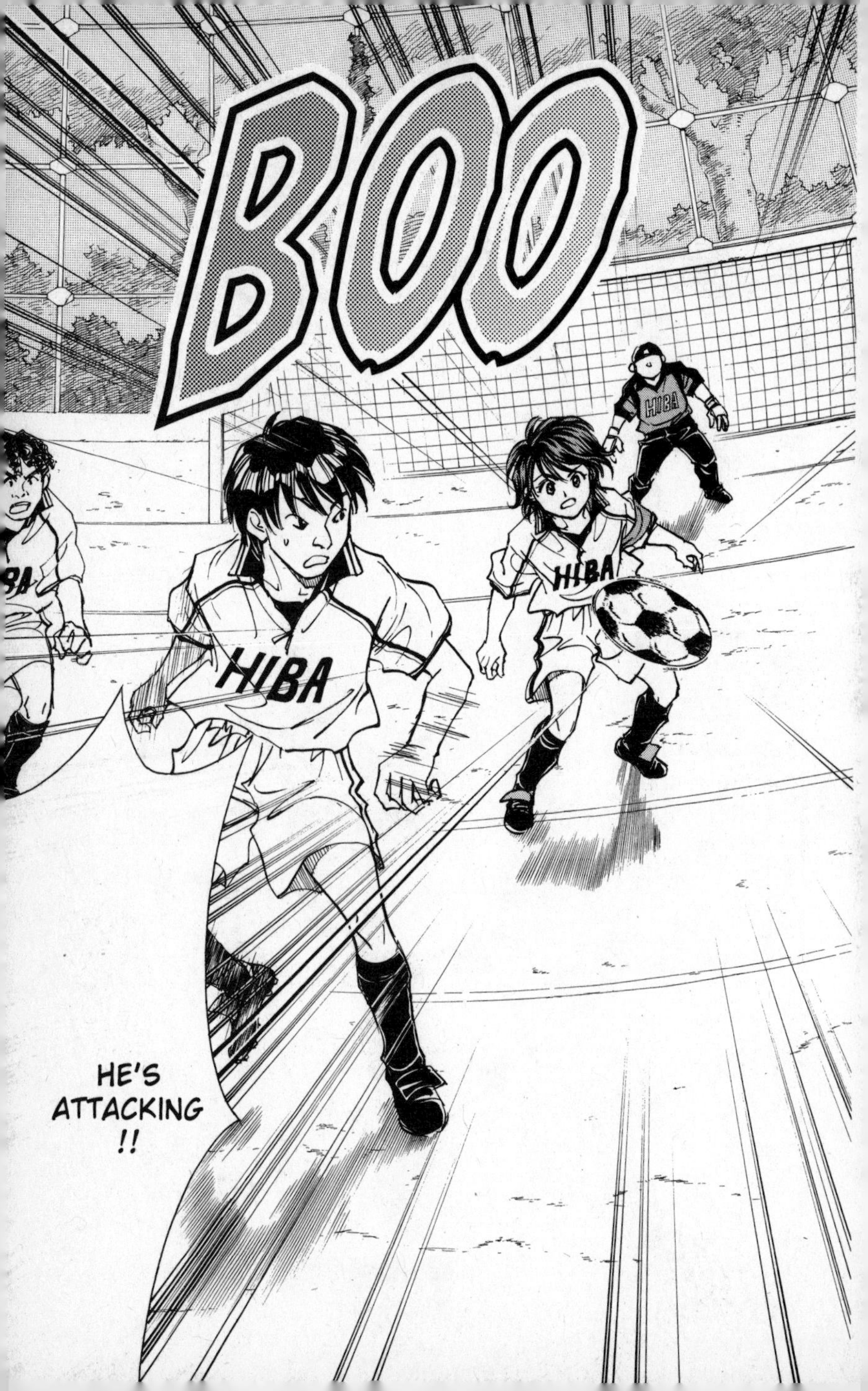
BOO
HE'S ATTACKING !!
HIBA
HIBA
HIBA

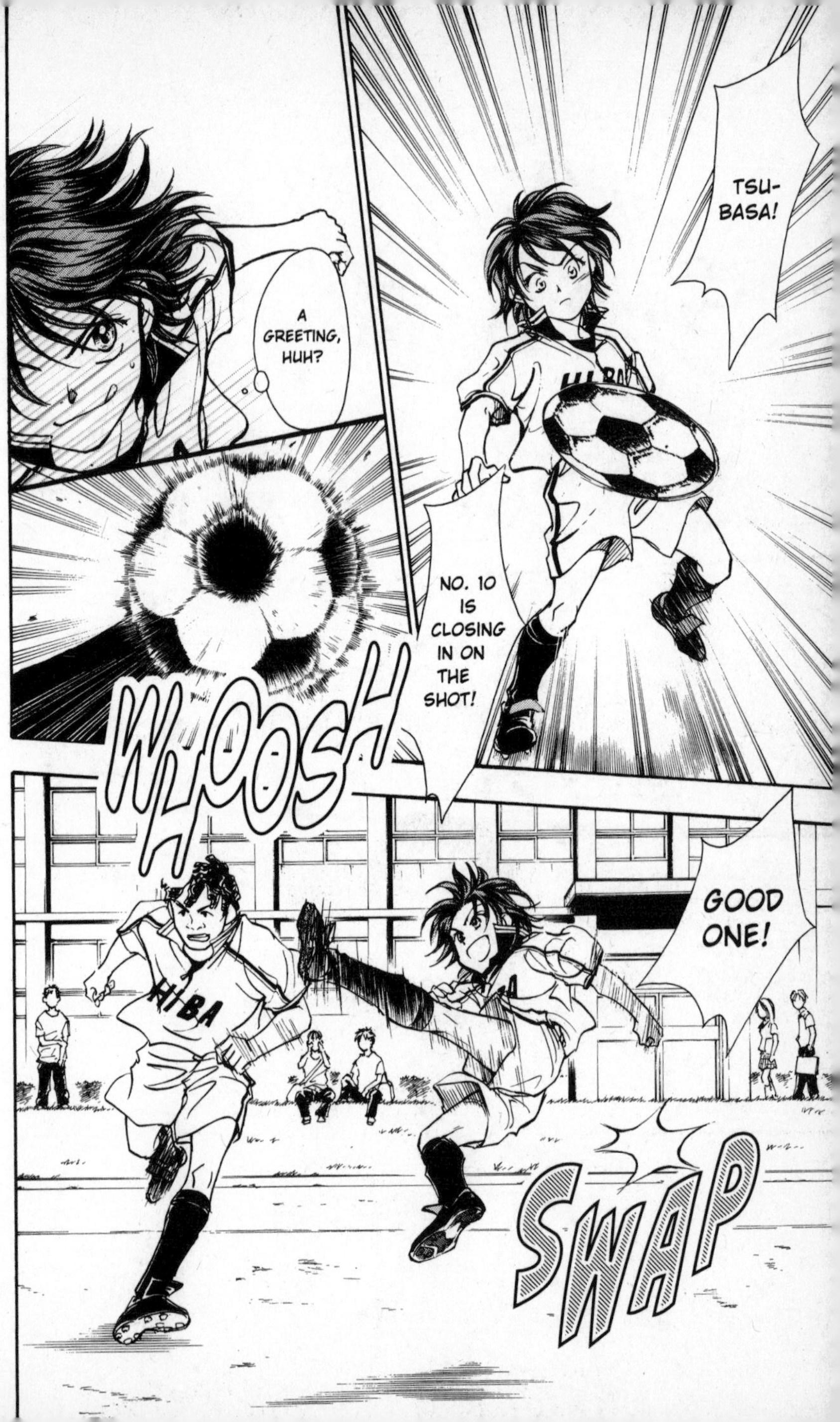
TSU-BASA!
NO. 10 IS CLOSING IN ON THE SHOT!
A GREETING, HUH?
WHOOSH
GOOD ONE!
SWAP

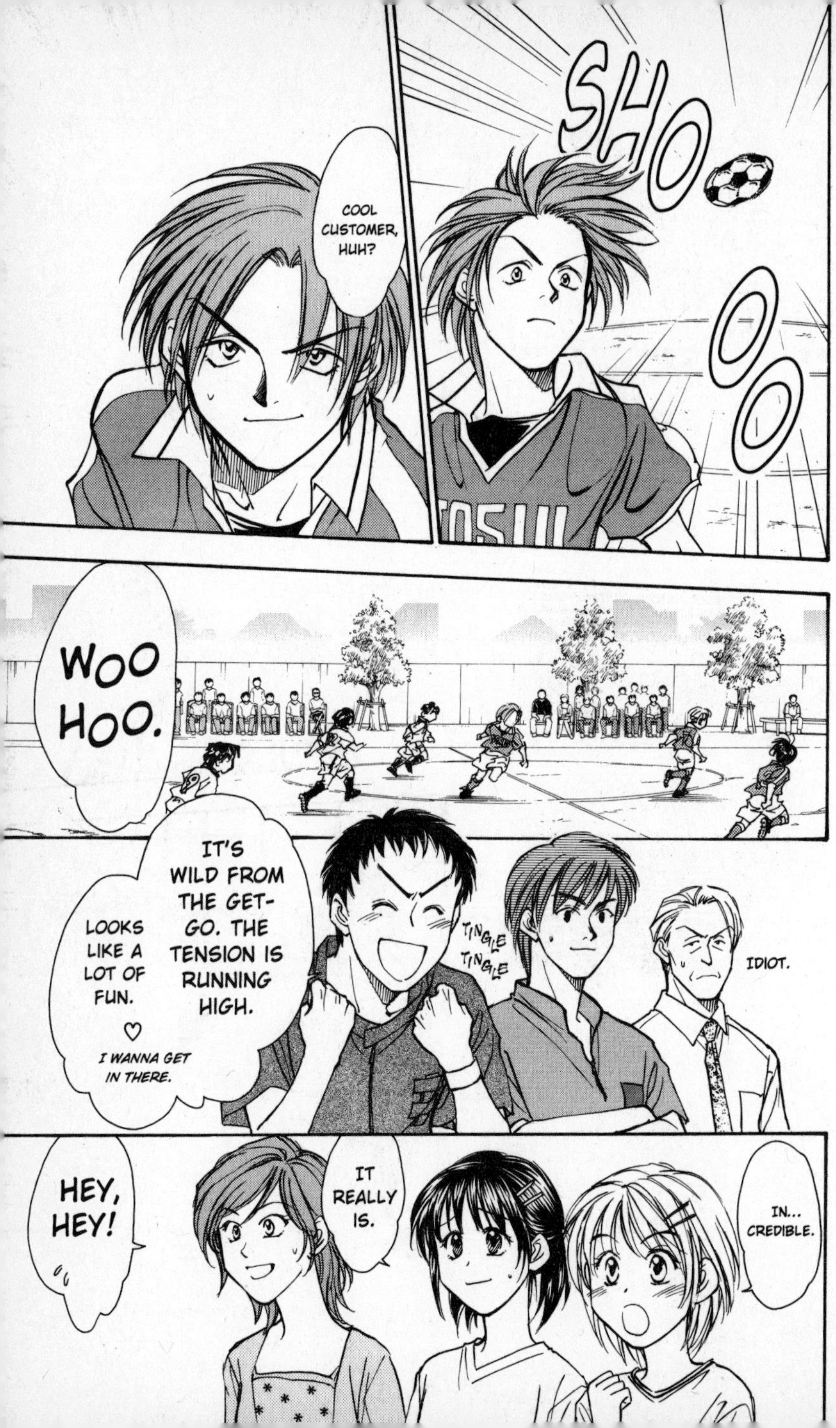
SHOOOO
COOL CUSTOMER, HUH?
WOO HOO.
IDIOT.
TINGLE TINGLE
IT'S WILD FROM THE GET-GO. THE TENSION IS RUNNING HIGH.
LOOKS LIKE A LOT OF FUN. ♡
I WANNA GET IN THERE.
IN... CREDIBLE.
IT REALLY IS.
HEY, HEY!

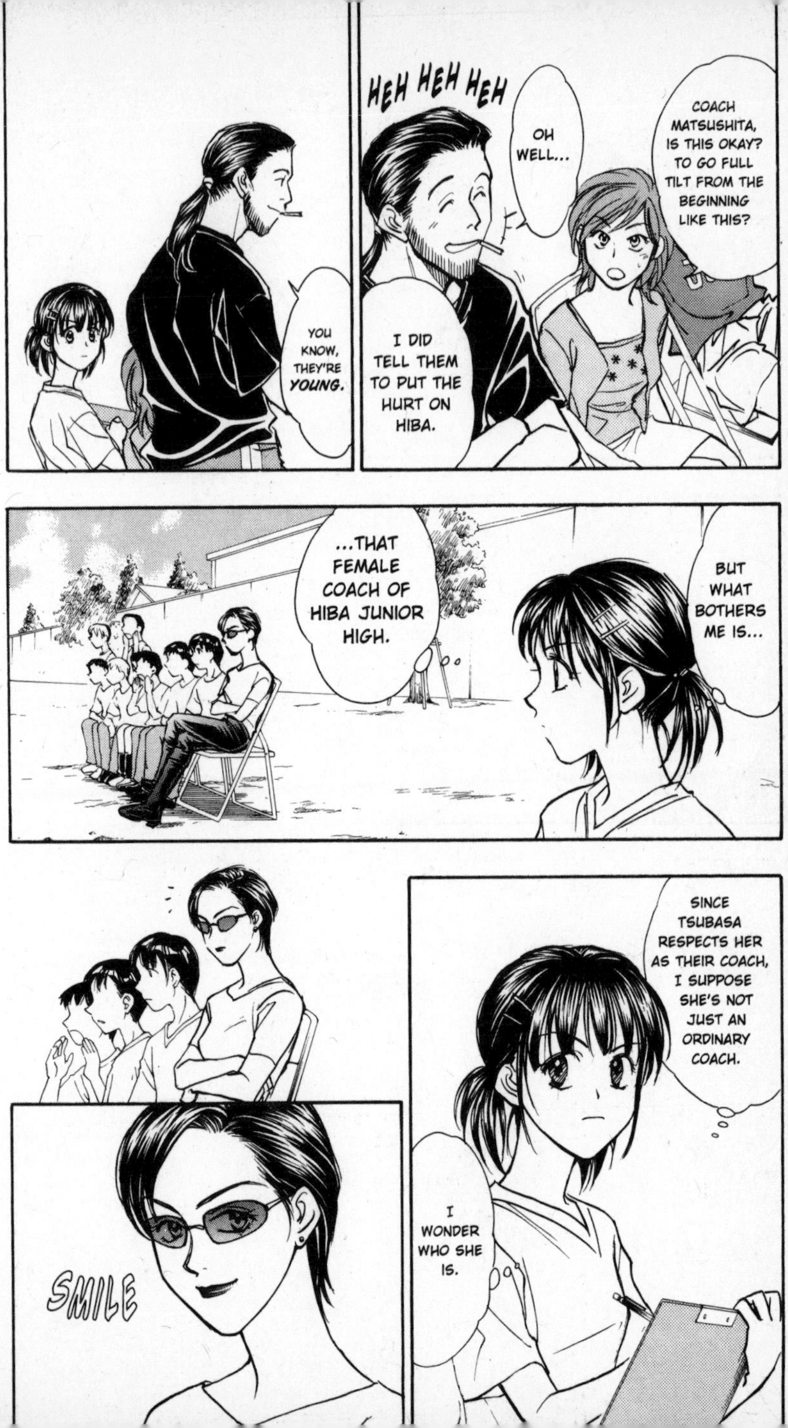
COACH MATSUSHITA, IS THIS OKAY? TO GO FULL TILT FROM THE BEGINNING LIKE THIS?
HEH HEH HEH
OH WELL...
I DID TELL THEM TO PUT THE HURT ON HIBA.
YOU KNOW, THEY'RE *YOUNG*.
BUT WHAT BOTHERS ME IS...
...THAT FEMALE COACH OF HIBA JUNIOR HIGH.
SINCE TSUBASA RESPECTS HER AS THEIR COACH, I SUPPOSE SHE'S NOT JUST AN ORDINARY COACH.
I WONDER WHO SHE IS.
SMILE

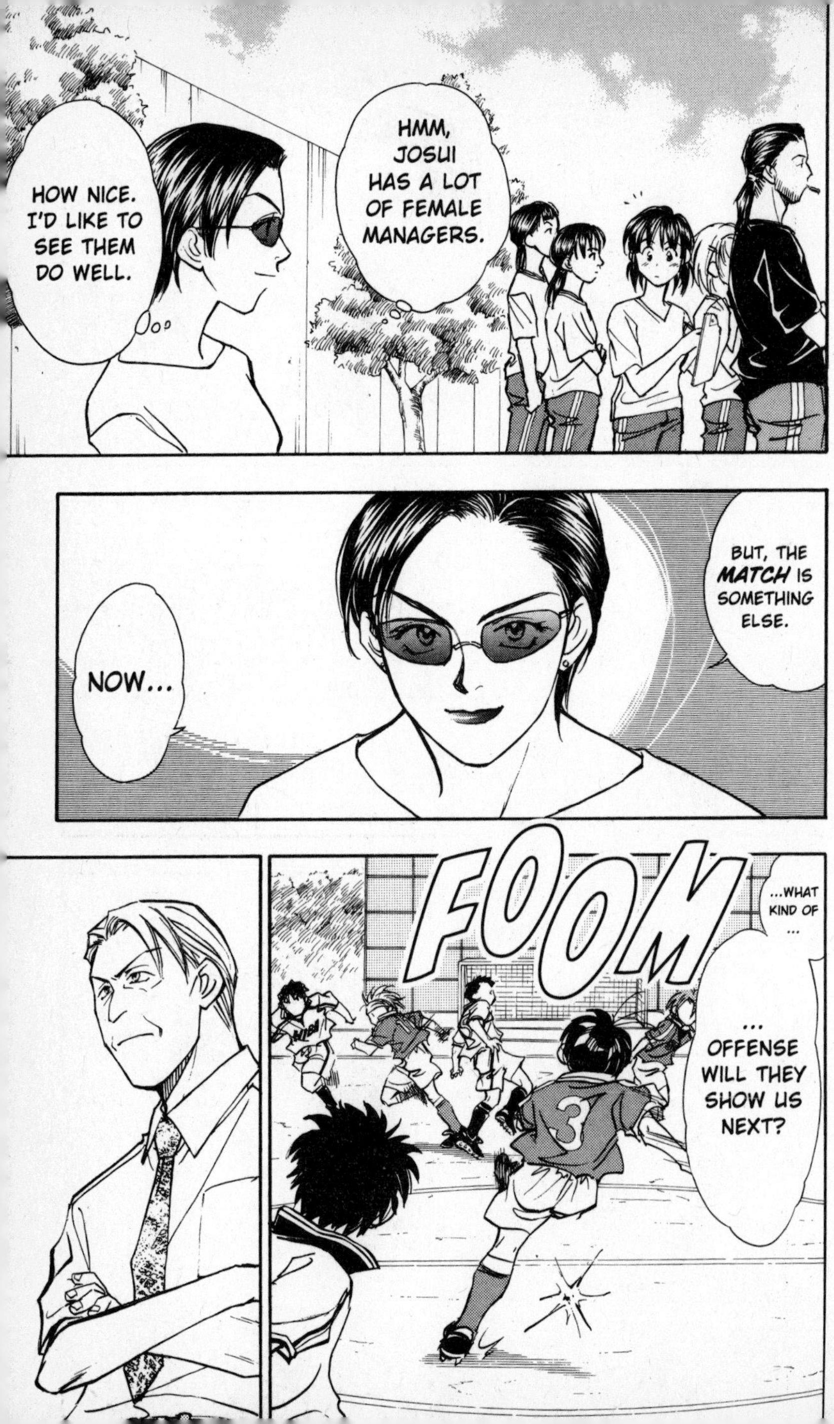
HMM, JOSUI HAS A LOT OF FEMALE MANAGERS.
HOW NICE. I'D LIKE TO SEE THEM DO WELL.
BUT, THE MATCH IS SOMETHING ELSE.
NOW...
FOOM
...WHAT KIND OF ...
... OFFENSE WILL THEY SHOW US NEXT?

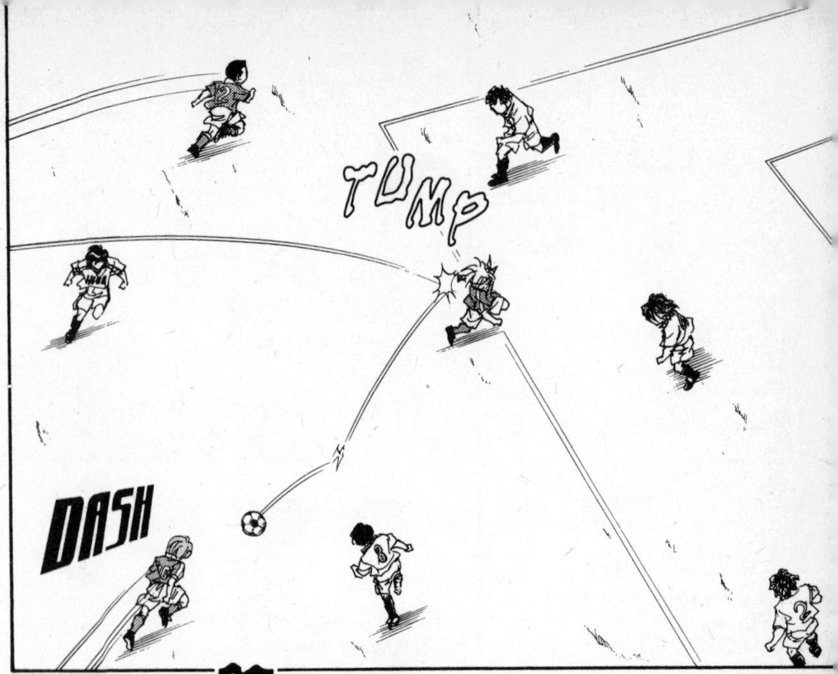
TUMP
DASH
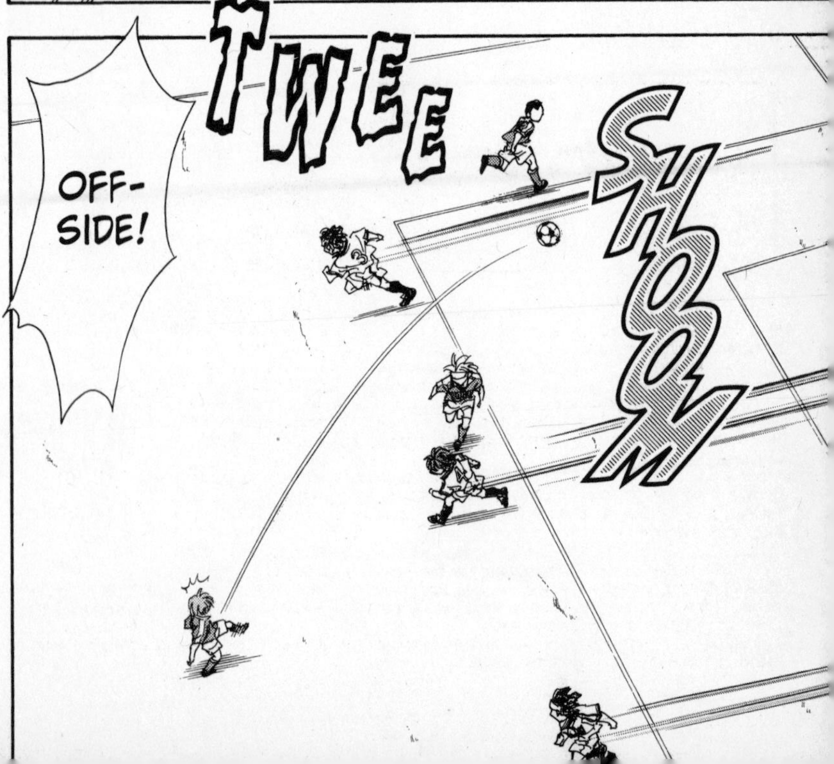
TWEE
SHOOM
OFF-SIDE!

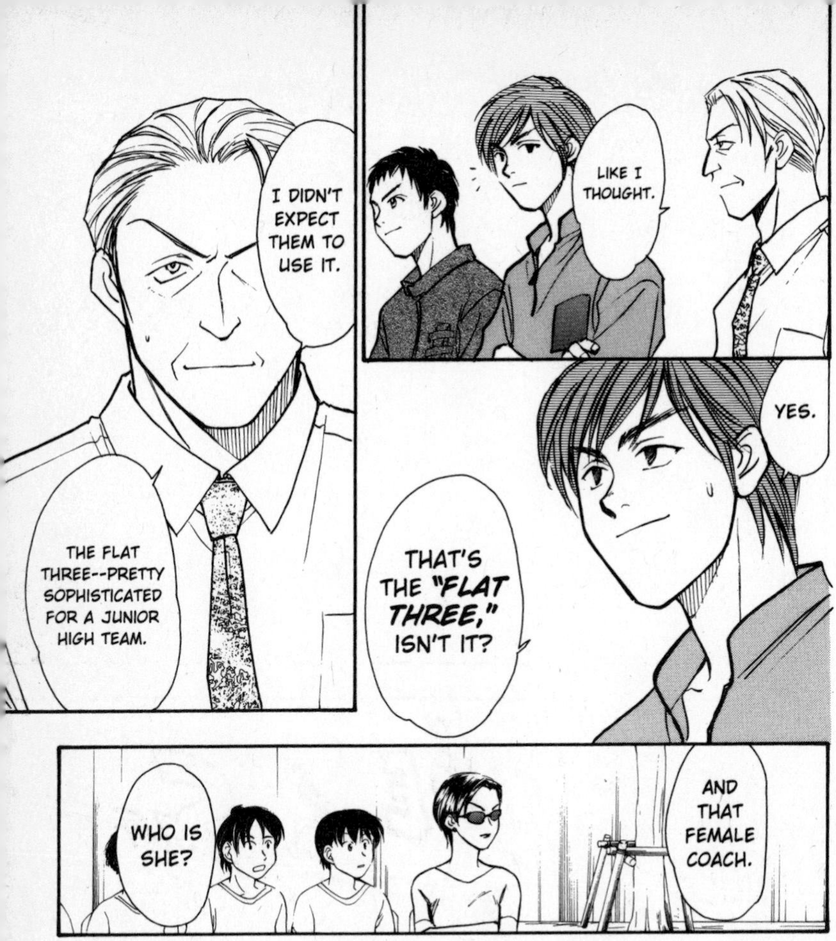
LIKE I THOUGHT.
YES.
THAT'S THE "FLAT THREE," ISN'T IT?
I DIDN'T EXPECT THEM TO USE IT.
THE FLAT THREE--PRETTY SOPHISTICATED FOR A JUNIOR HIGH TEAM.
AND THAT FEMALE COACH.
WHO IS SHE?

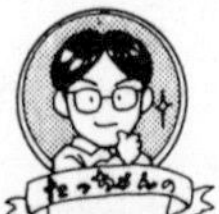

Tacchan's One Point Lesson

Flat Three

THREE DEFENDERS LINE UP STRAIGHT ACROSS THE WIDTH OF THE PITCH, AND EACH DEFENDS A ZONE INSTEAD OF GOING MAN-TO-MAN. THEY MUST CONSTANTLY KEEP THE DISTANCE BETWEEN THEIR OFFENSE'S FRONT LINE AND THE DEFENSE'S LAST LINE CLOSE TOGETHER: ABOUT 30 METERS OR SO. IF THEY MANAGE TO KEEP THE LINES TIGHT, THE DEFENSE AT MIDFIELD CAN BECOME STRONGER. SO WHEN THEY STEAL THE BALL, THEY CAN QUICKLY REVERSE GEARS AND ATTACK.

THUS, WHEN DEFENDERS DRAW BACK, THE STRIKERS MUST DRAW BACK, TOO. CONVERSELY, IF THE STRIKERS ATTACK, THE DEFENDERS MUST PUSH THE LINE UP ACCORDINGLY SO THAT NO MATTER WHERE THE BALL IS, THEY KEEP THE DISTANCE BETWEEN THE LINES AT 30 METERS. OTHERWISE, THE SYSTEM IS USELESS.

IF THE FLAT THREE IS USED CORRECTLY, THE DEFENSE CAN TRAP THE OPPONENT'S STRIKERS, AND EASILY GET OFFSIDE CALLS. OF COURSE, THE SYSTEM HAS WEAKNESSES, TOO. JUST THREE DEFENDERS MUST COVER THE WIDTH OF THE PITCH, AND THEY MUST ALWAYS BE READY TO RUSH BACK TO DEFEND THE GOAL.

THEREFORE, THE SYSTEM REQUIRES EXCEPTIONALLY TALENTED DEFENDERS: THEY ALL MUST HAVE GREAT SKILL, STAMINA, SPEED AND A KEEN EYE FOR THE FLOW OF THE GAME.

CURRENTLY, AMONG THE BEST EUROPEAN CLUBS, MOST TEAMS THAT USE THREE DEFENDERS EMPLOY THE FLAT THREE SYSTEM. MOST SWITCH BETWEEN THE FLAT THREE AND ANOTHER SYSTEM THAT ALLOWS FOR A "SWEEPER" OR "LIBERO": A DEFENDER FREE TO COVER THE ENTIRE PITCH.

IN JAPAN, AFTER TROUSSIER TOOK THE COACHING POST, THE OLYMPIC SOCCER TEAM SWITCHED TO THE FLAT THREE SYSTEM AND QUALIFIED FOR THE SYDNEY OLYMPICS.

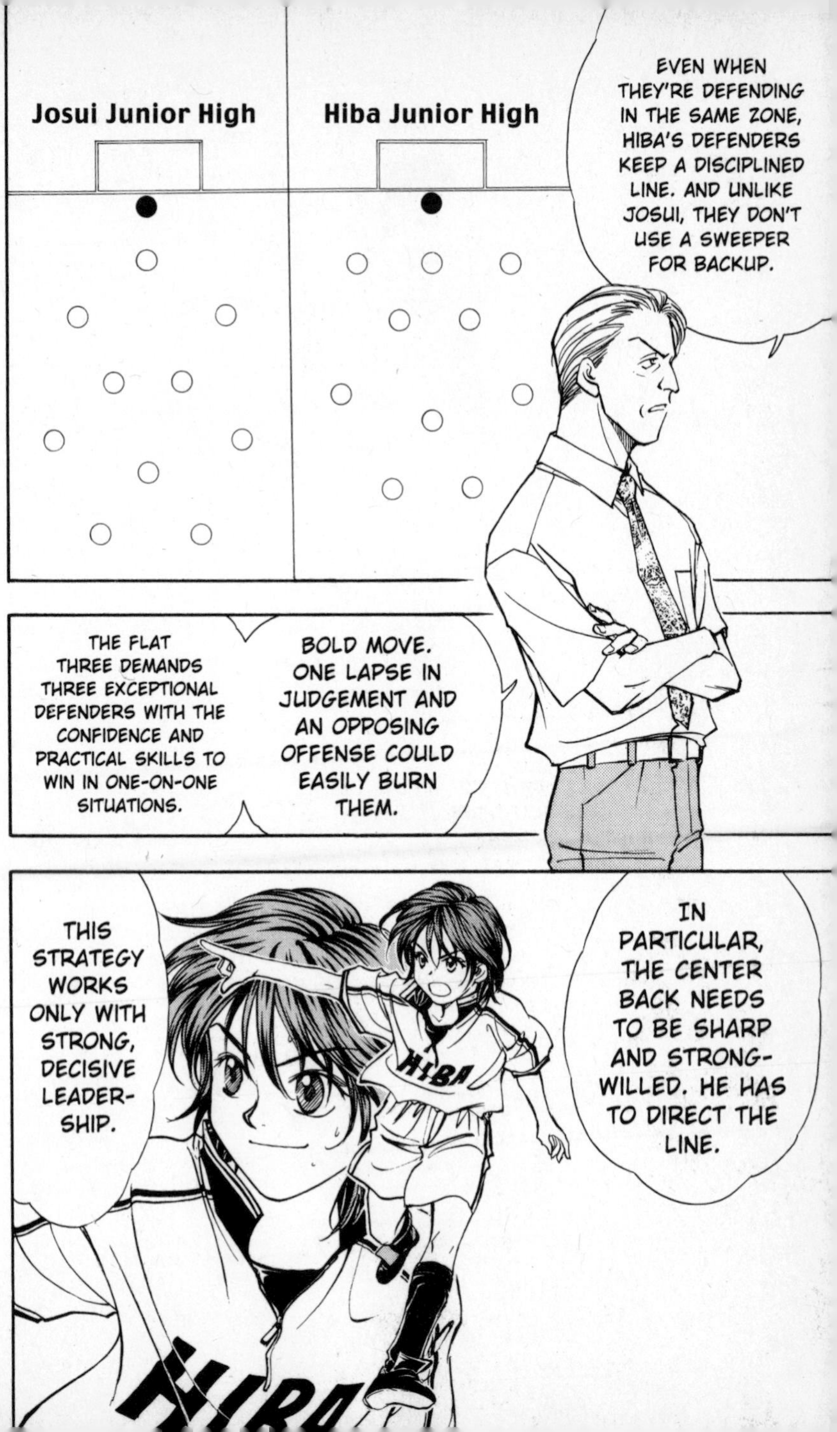
EVEN WHEN THEY'RE DEFENDING IN THE SAME ZONE, HIBA'S DEFENDERS KEEP A DISCIPLINED LINE. AND UNLIKE JOSUI, THEY DON'T USE A SWEEPER FOR BACKUP.
Josui Junior High
Hiba Junior High
BOLD MOVE. ONE LAPSE IN JUDGEMENT AND AN OPPOSING OFFENSE COULD EASILY BURN THEM.
THE FLAT THREE DEMANDS THREE EXCEPTIONAL DEFENDERS WITH THE CONFIDENCE AND PRACTICAL SKILLS TO WIN IN ONE-ON-ONE SITUATIONS.
IN PARTICULAR, THE CENTER BACK NEEDS TO BE SHARP AND STRONG-WILLED. HE HAS TO DIRECT THE LINE.
HIBA
THIS STRATEGY WORKS ONLY WITH STRONG, DECISIVE LEADER-SHIP.

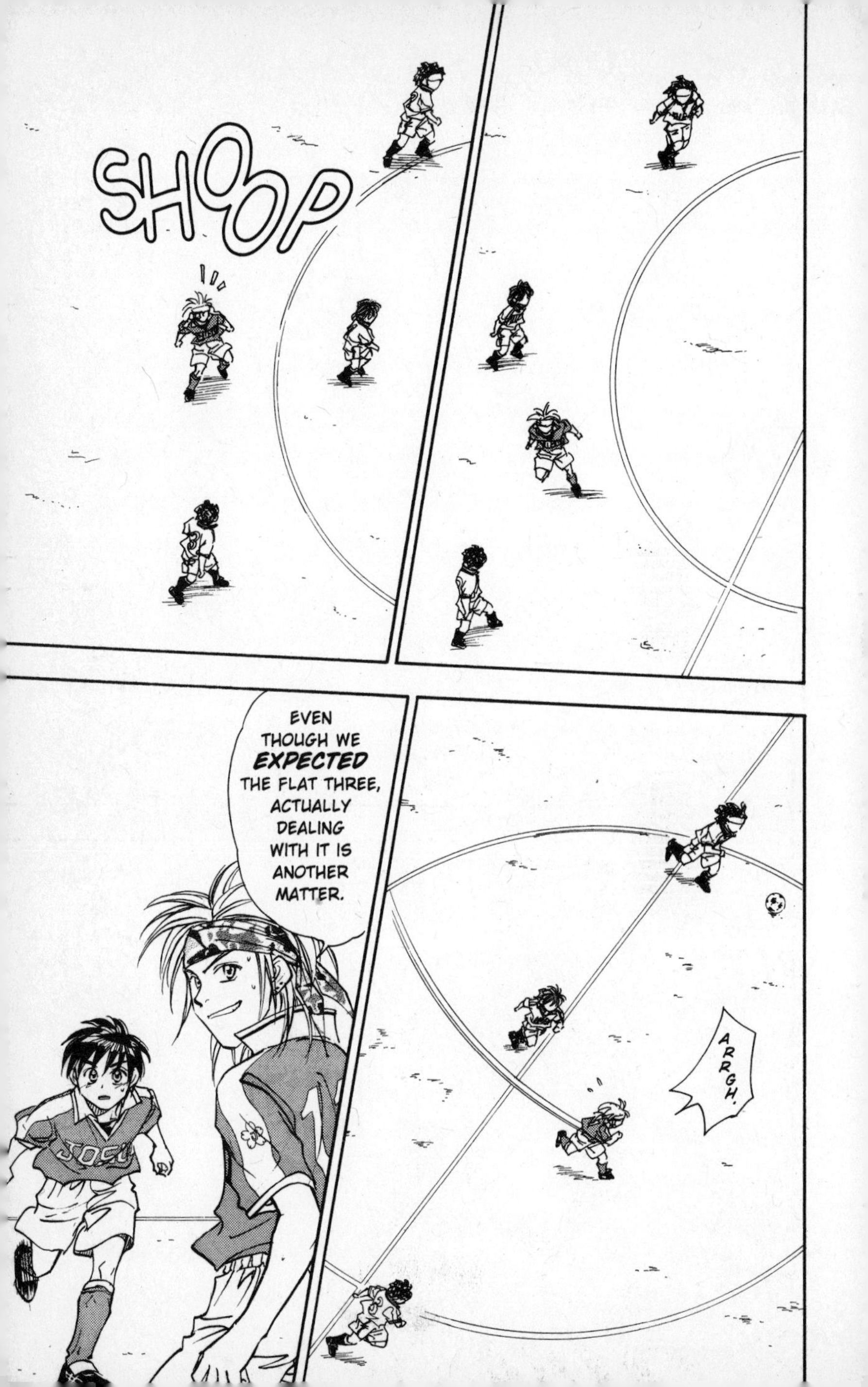
SHOOP
ARRGH.
EVEN THOUGH WE EXPECTED THE FLAT THREE, ACTUALLY DEALING WITH IT IS ANOTHER MATTER.

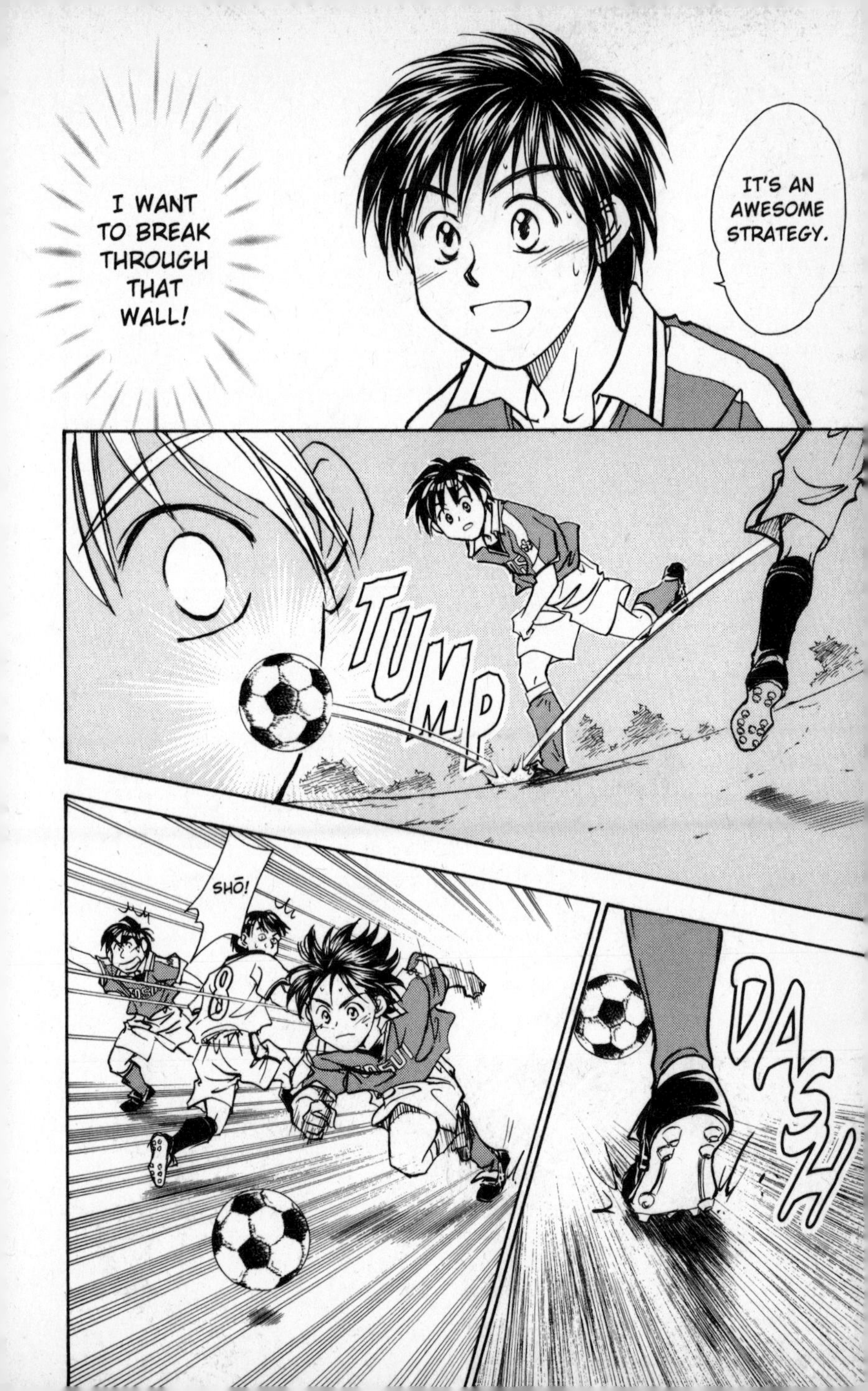
IT'S AN AWESOME STRATEGY.
I WANT TO BREAK THROUGH THAT WALL!
TUMP
DASH
SHŌ!

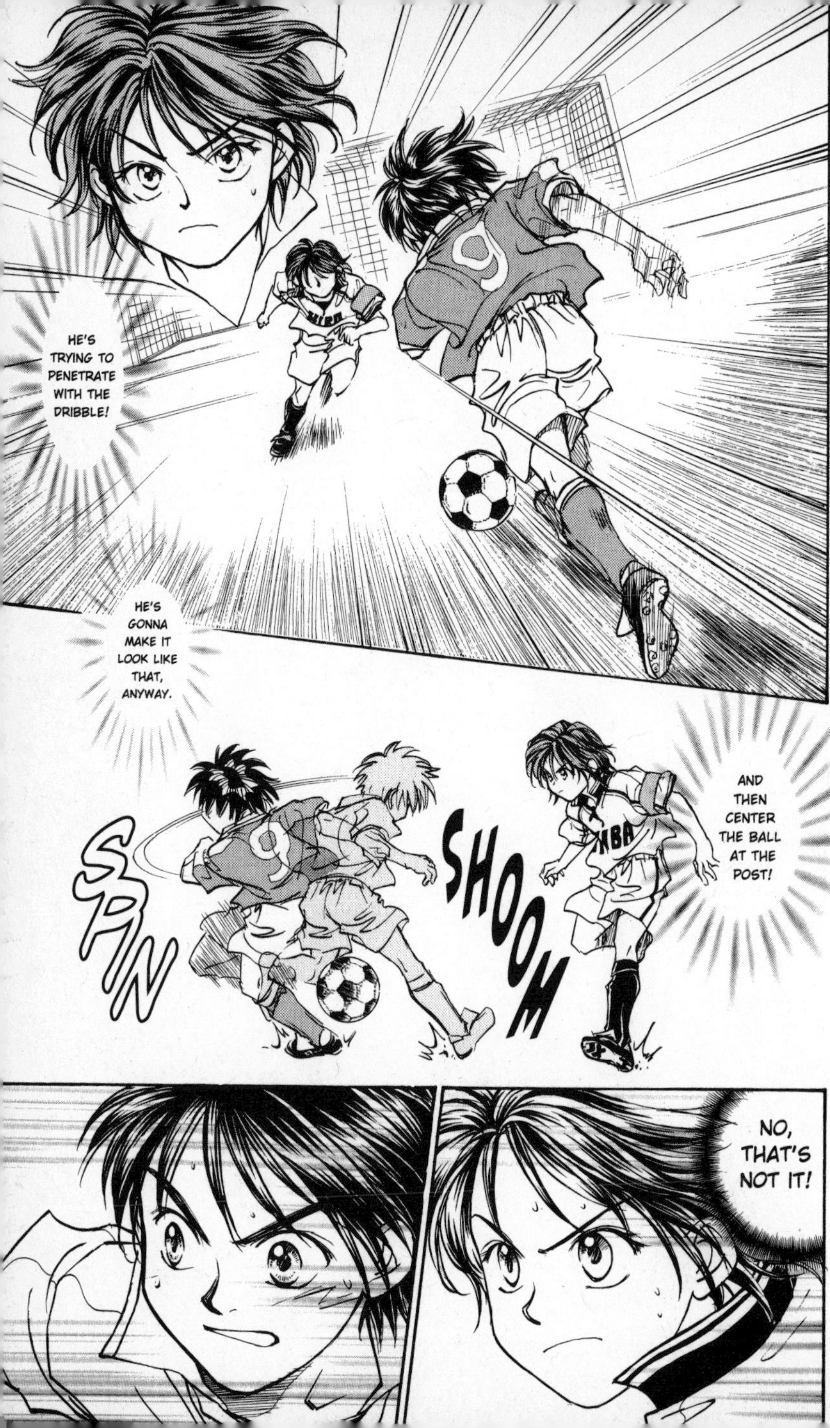
HE'S TRYING TO PENETRATE WITH THE DRIBBLE!
HE'S GONNA MAKE IT LOOK LIKE THAT, ANYWAY.
AND THEN CENTER THE BALL AT THE POST!
SHOOM
SPIN
NO, THAT'S NOT IT!

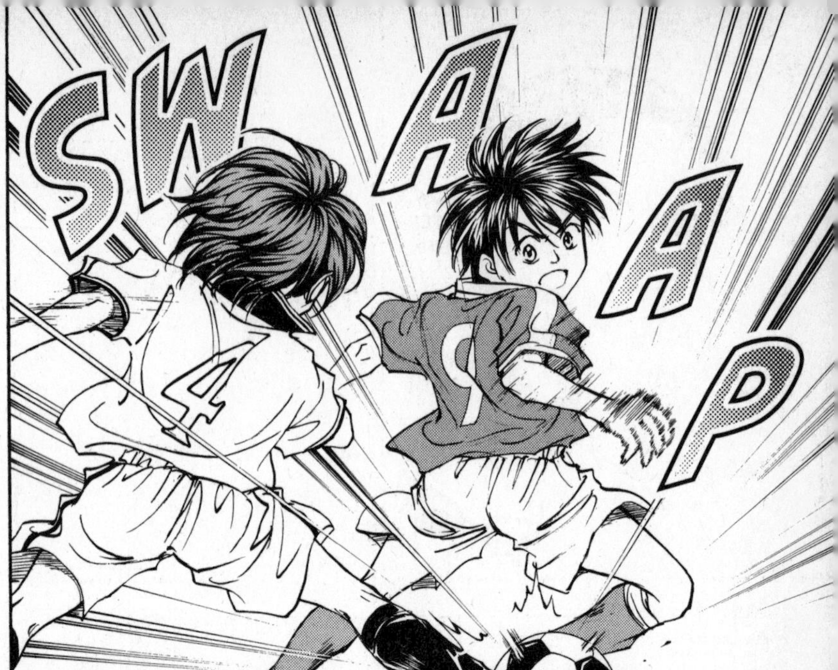
SWAAP
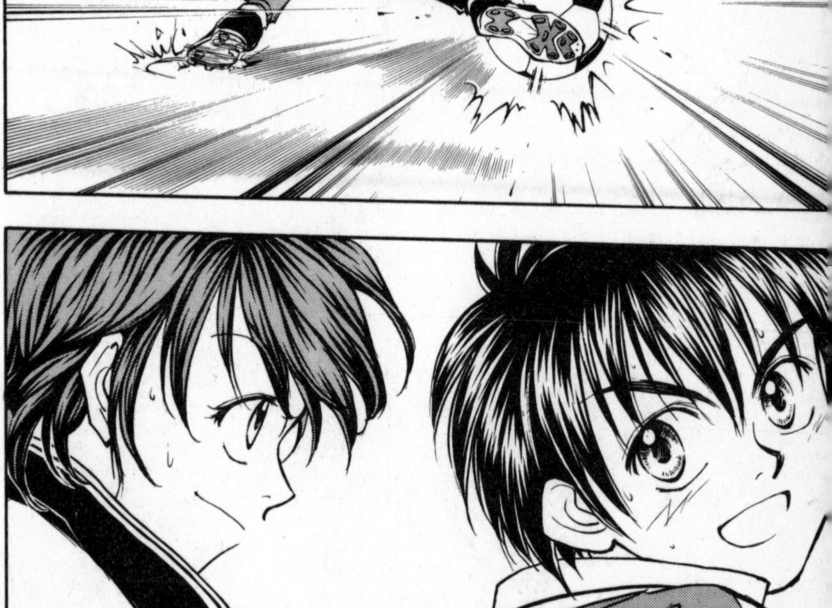

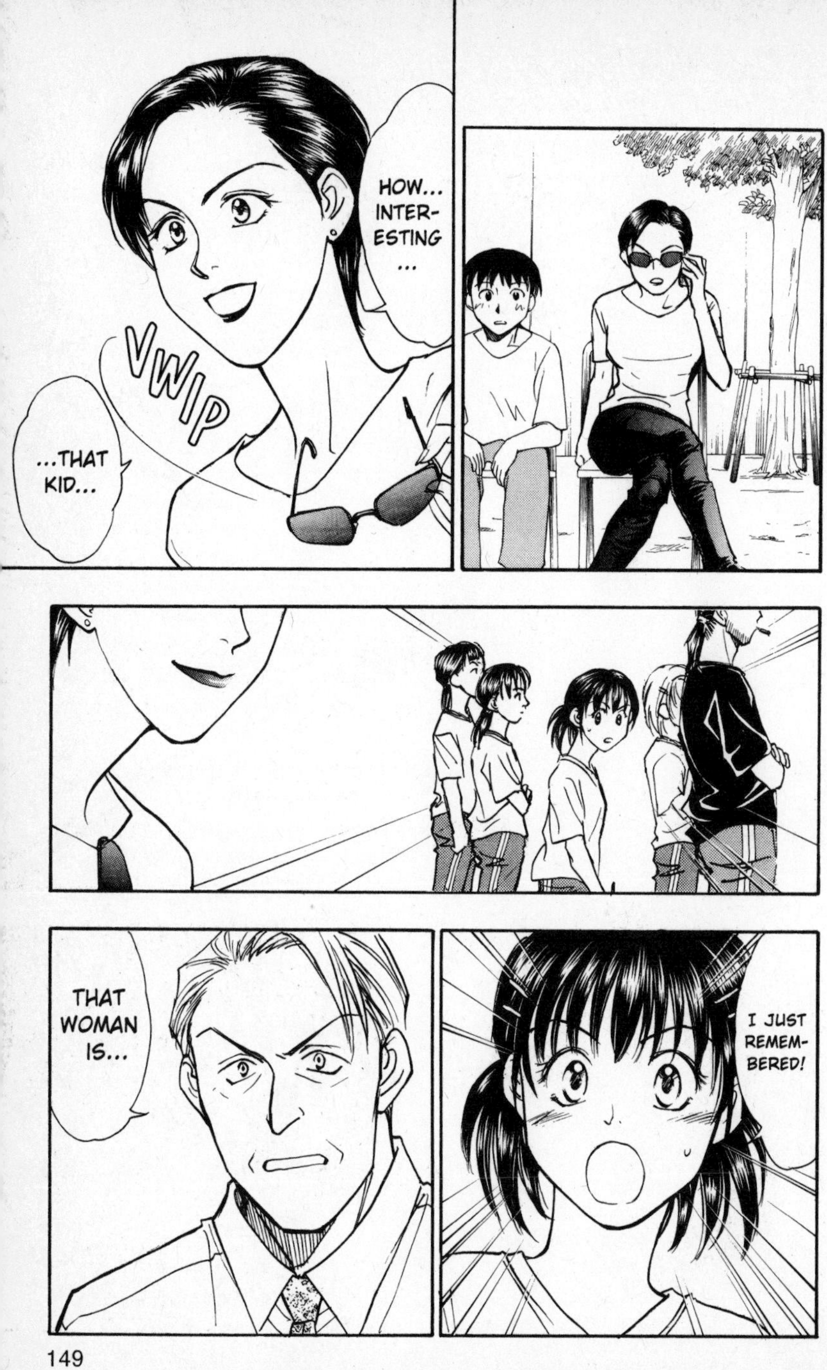
HOW... INTER-ESTING ...
VWIP
...THAT KID...
I JUST REMEM-BERED!
THAT WOMAN IS...

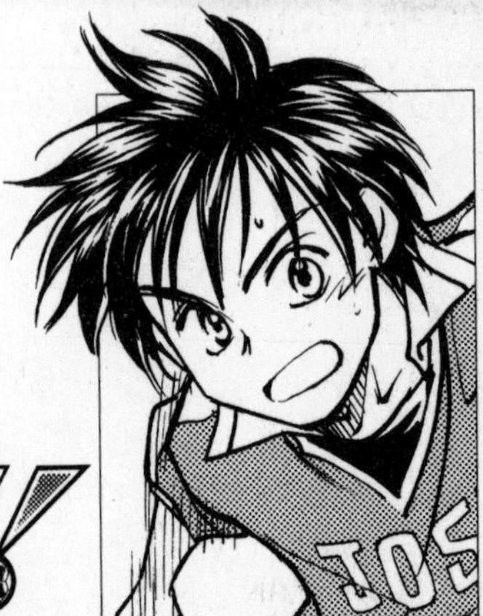

WHISTLE!

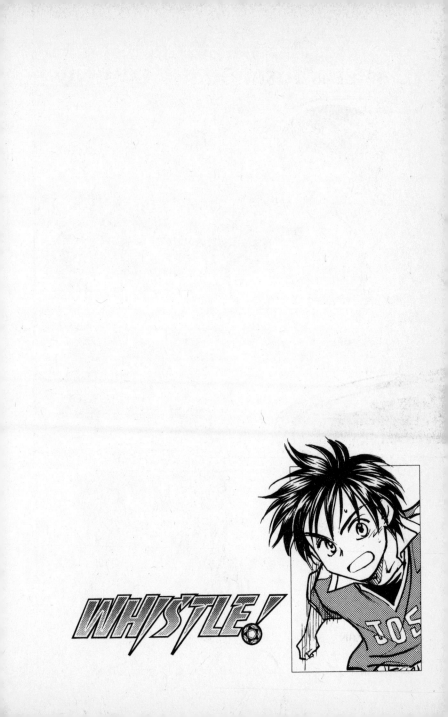

STAGE.88 Josui On the Offensive

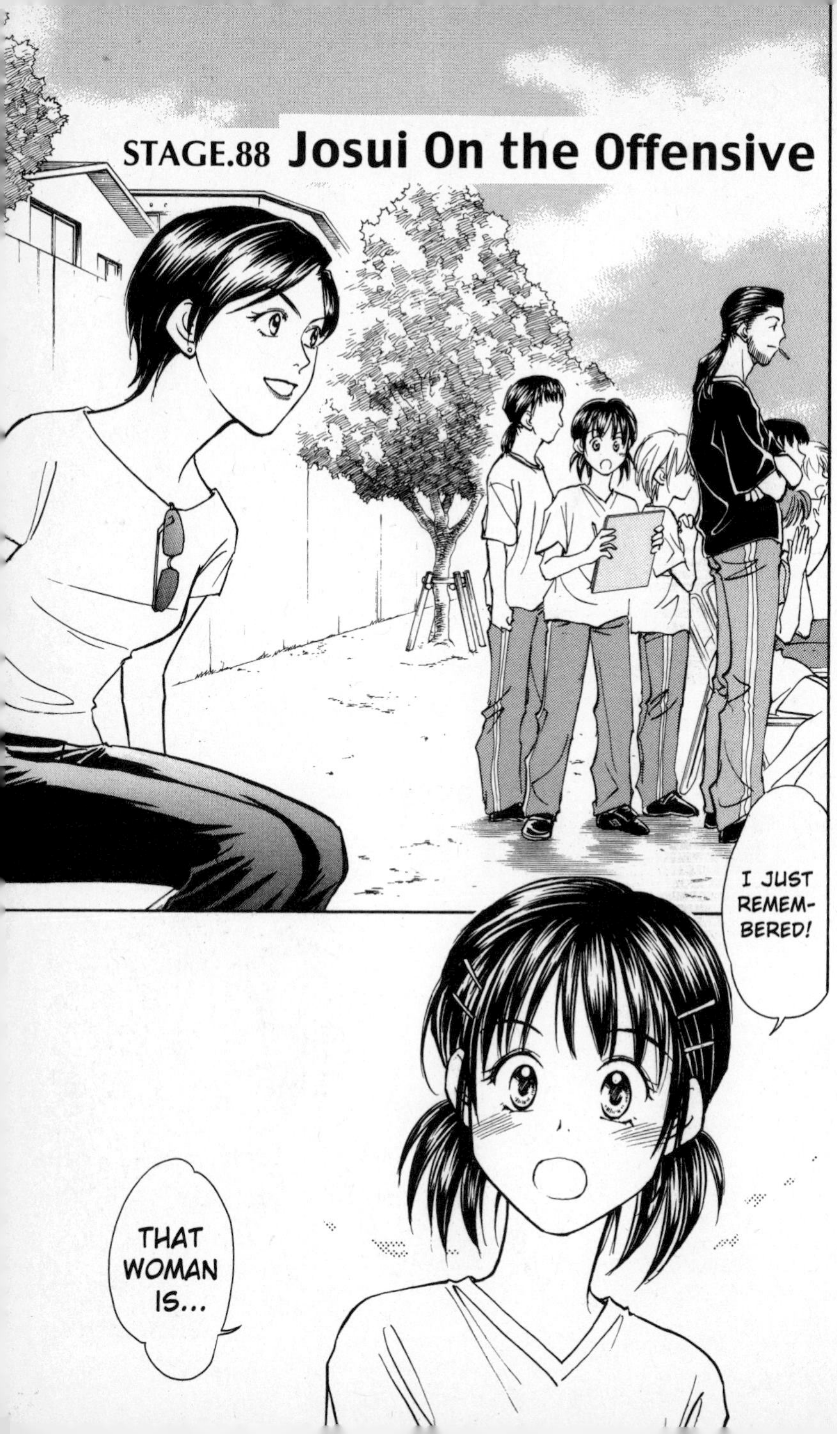
I JUST REMEM-BERED!
THAT WOMAN IS...

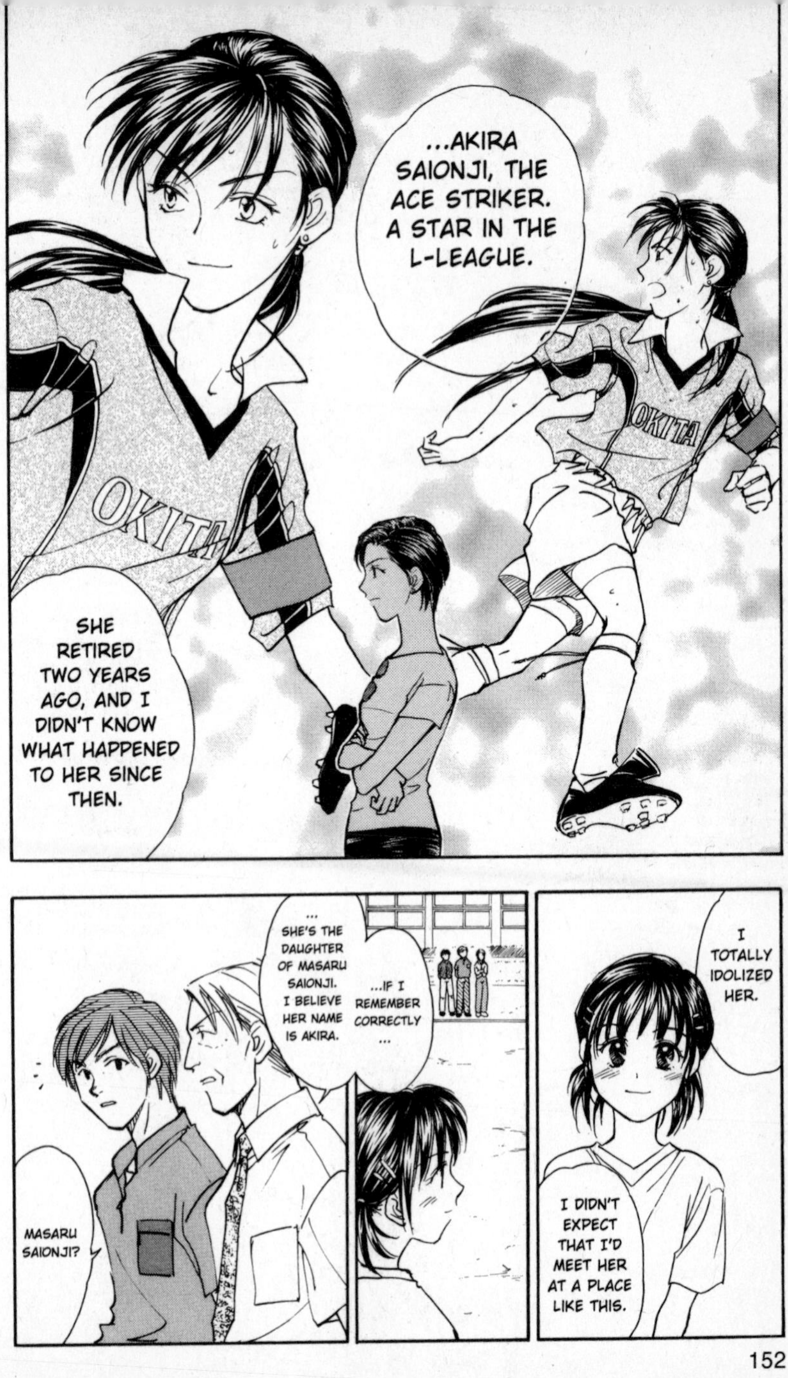
...AKIRA SAIONJI, THE ACE STRIKER. A STAR IN THE L-LEAGUE.
SHE RETIRED TWO YEARS AGO, AND I DIDN'T KNOW WHAT HAPPENED TO HER SINCE THEN.
I TOTALLY IDOLIZED HER.
I DIDN'T EXPECT THAT I'D MEET HER AT A PLACE LIKE THIS.
...IF I REMEMBER CORRECTLY ...
... SHE'S THE DAUGHTER OF MASARU SAIONJI. I BELIEVE HER NAME IS AKIRA.
MASARU SAIONJI?

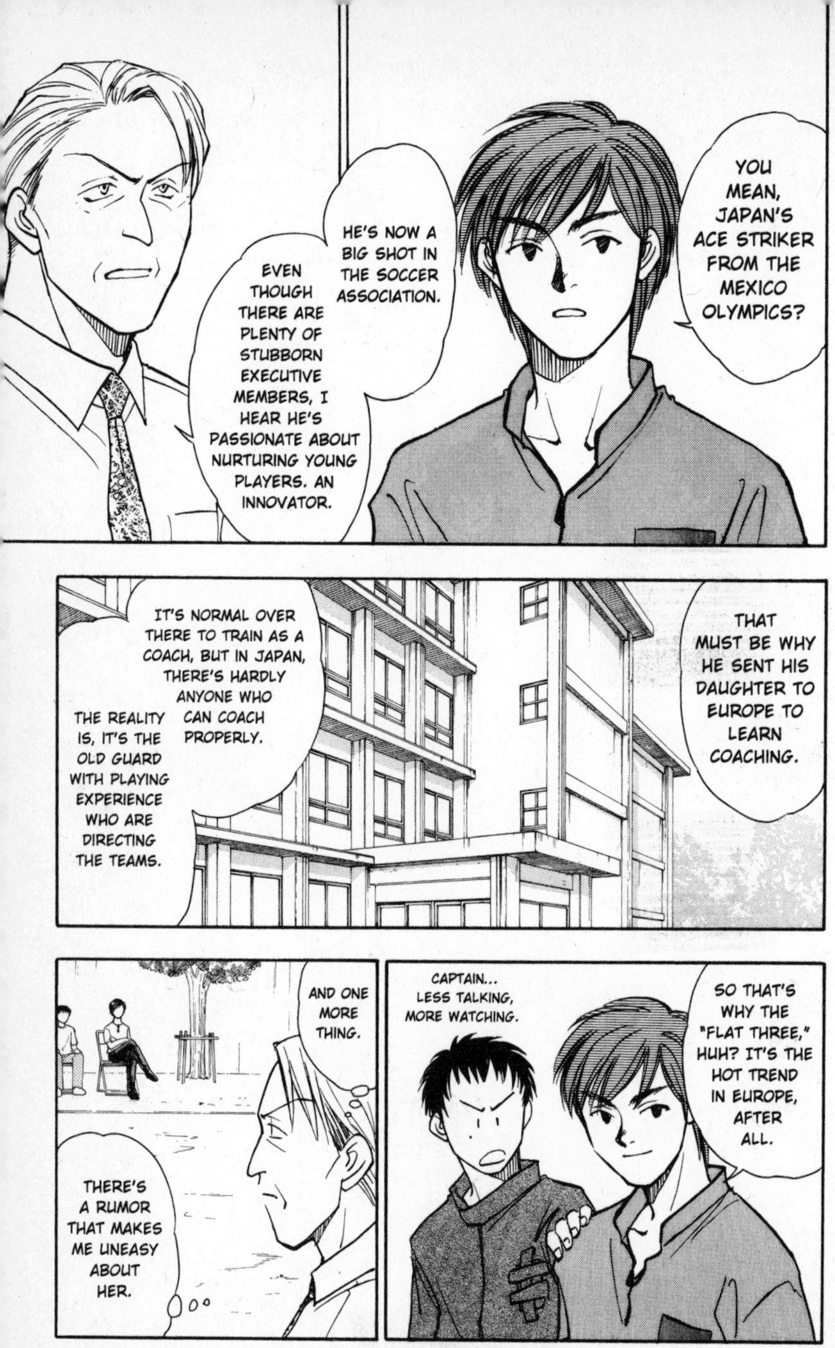
YOU MEAN, JAPAN'S ACE STRIKER FROM THE MEXICO OLYMPICS?
HE'S NOW A BIG SHOT IN THE SOCCER ASSOCIATION.
EVEN THOUGH THERE ARE PLENTY OF STUBBORN EXECUTIVE MEMBERS, I HEAR HE'S PASSIONATE ABOUT NURTURING YOUNG PLAYERS. AN INNOVATOR.
THAT MUST BE WHY HE SENT HIS DAUGHTER TO EUROPE TO LEARN COACHING.
IT'S NORMAL OVER THERE TO TRAIN AS A COACH, BUT IN JAPAN, THERE'S HARDLY ANYONE WHO CAN COACH PROPERLY.
THE REALITY IS, IT'S THE OLD GUARD WITH PLAYING EXPERIENCE WHO ARE DIRECTING THE TEAMS.
SO THAT'S WHY THE "FLAT THREE," HUH? IT'S THE HOT TREND IN EUROPE, AFTER ALL.
CAPTAIN... LESS TALKING, MORE WATCHING.
AND ONE MORE THING.
THERE'S A RUMOR THAT MAKES ME UNEASY ABOUT HER.

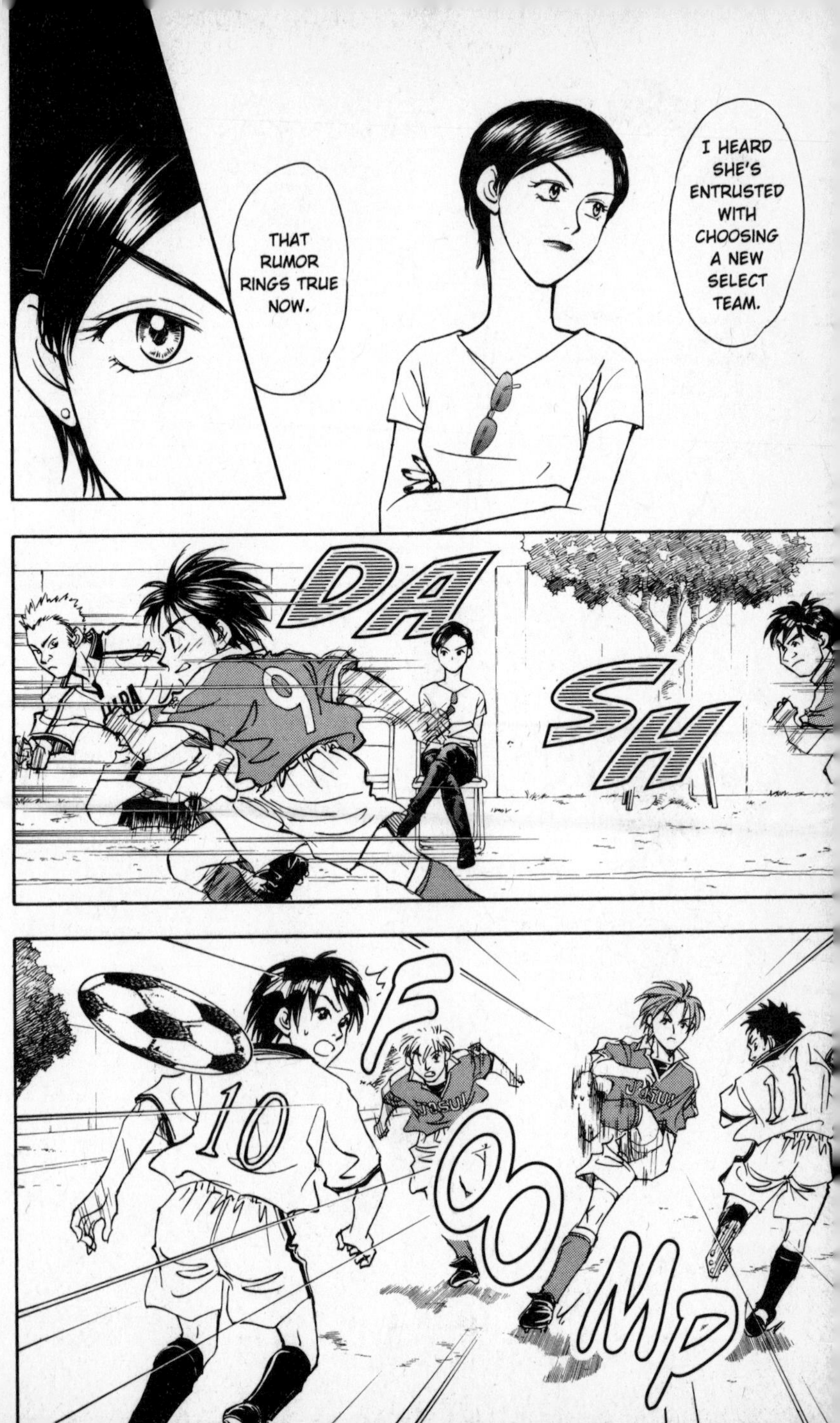
I HEARD SHE'S ENTRUSTED WITH CHOOSING A NEW SELECT TEAM.
THAT RUMOR RINGS TRUE NOW.
DASH
FOOMP

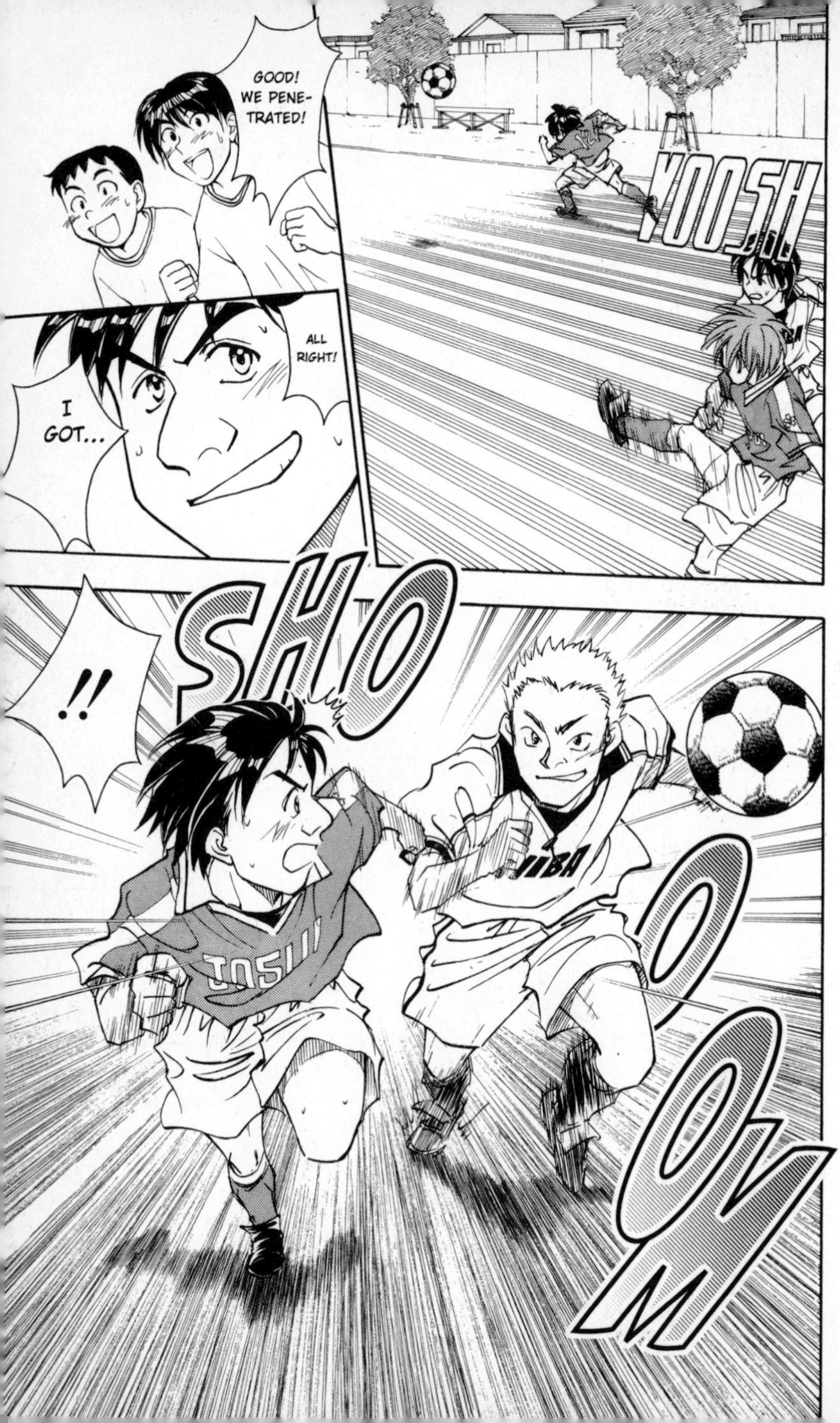
VOOSH
GOOD! WE PENE-TRATED!
ALL RIGHT!
I GOT...
SHOOOM
!!

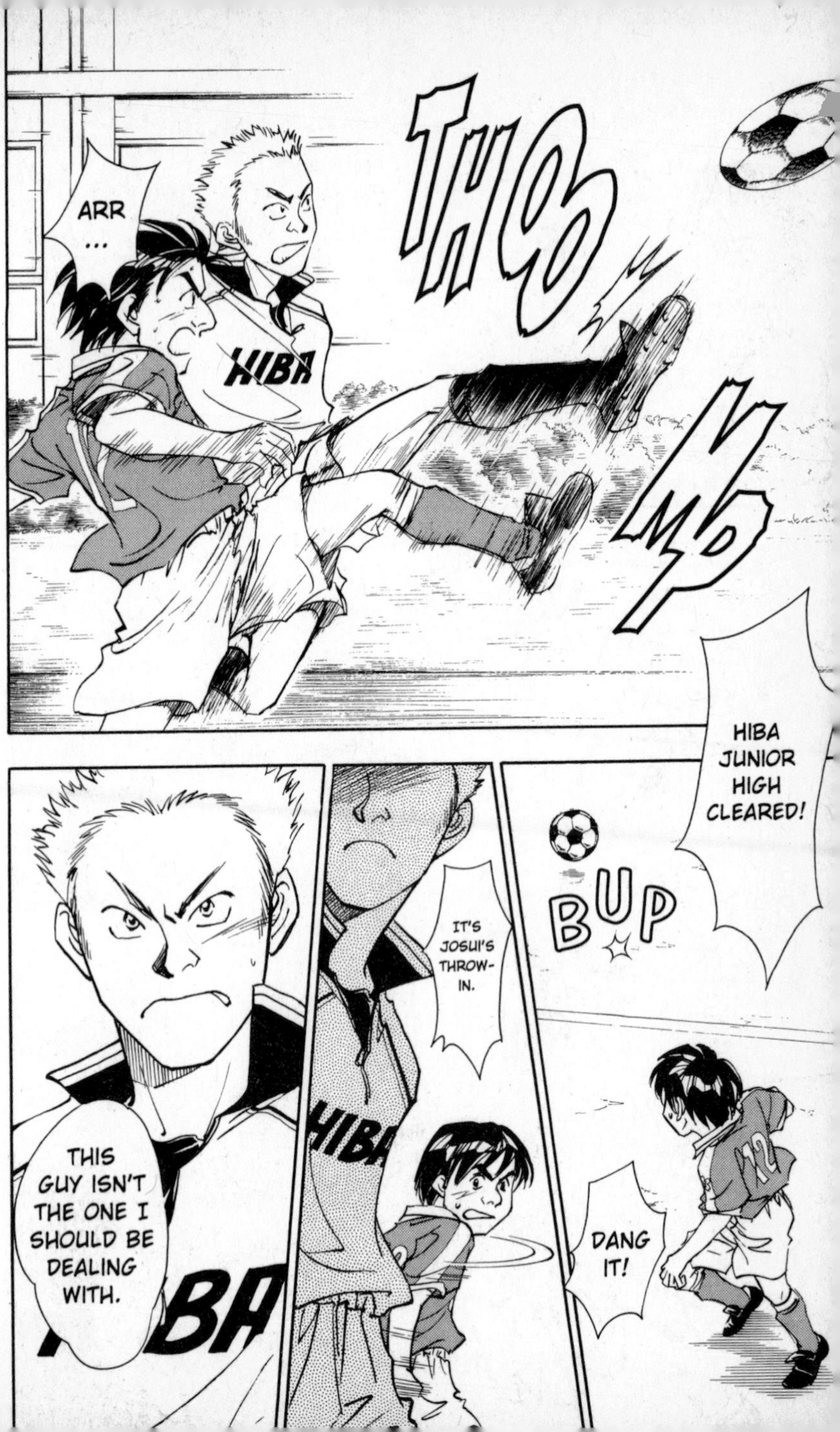
THOOMP
ARR ...
HIBA
HIBA JUNIOR HIGH CLEARED!
BUP
DANG IT!
IT'S JOSUI'S THROW-IN.
HIBA
THIS GUY ISN'T THE ONE I SHOULD BE DEALING WITH.
HIBA

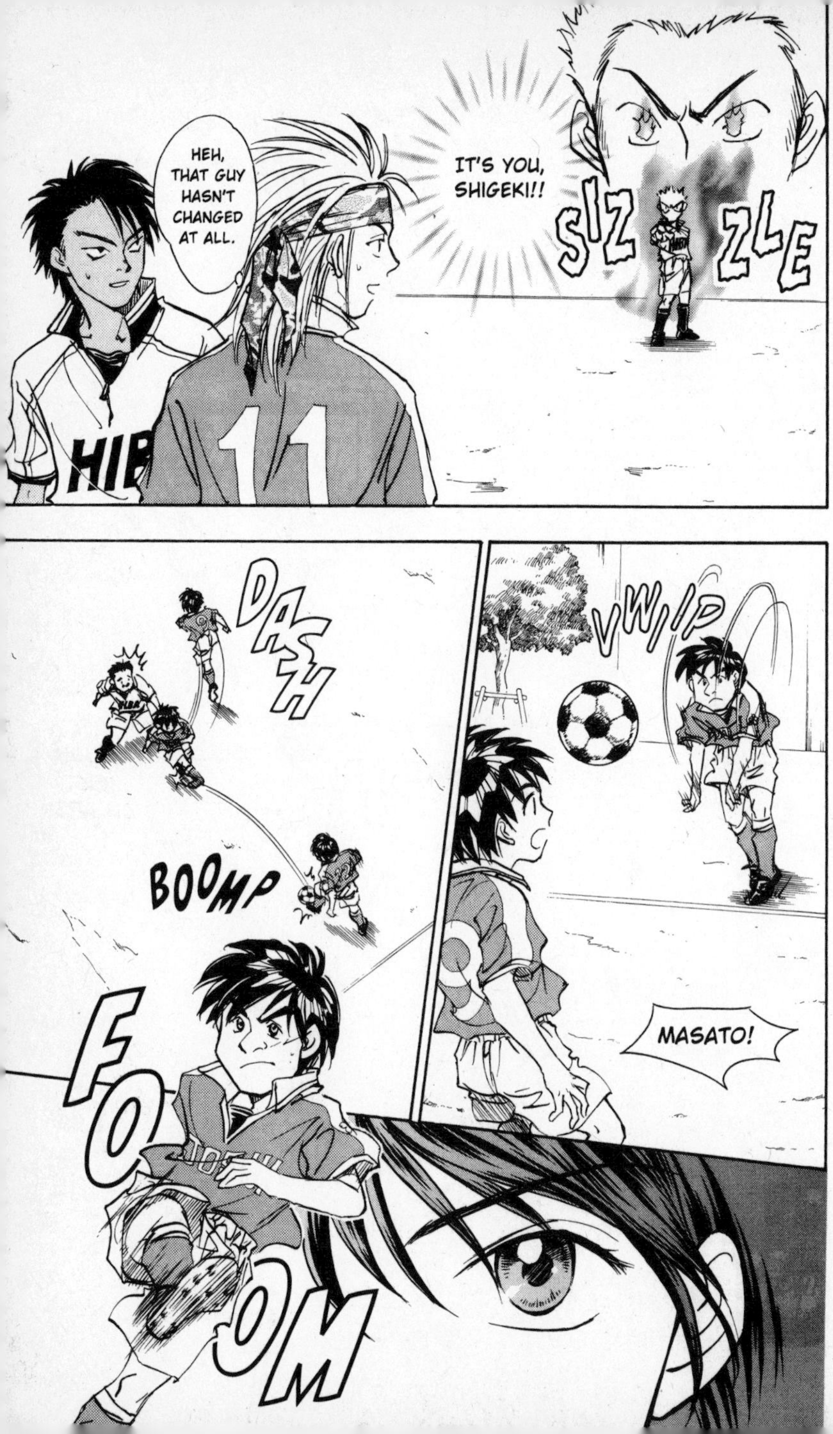
IT'S YOU, SHIGEKI!!
SIZZLE
HEH, THAT GUY HASN'T CHANGED AT ALL.
VWIP
MASATO!
DASH
BOOMP
FOOM

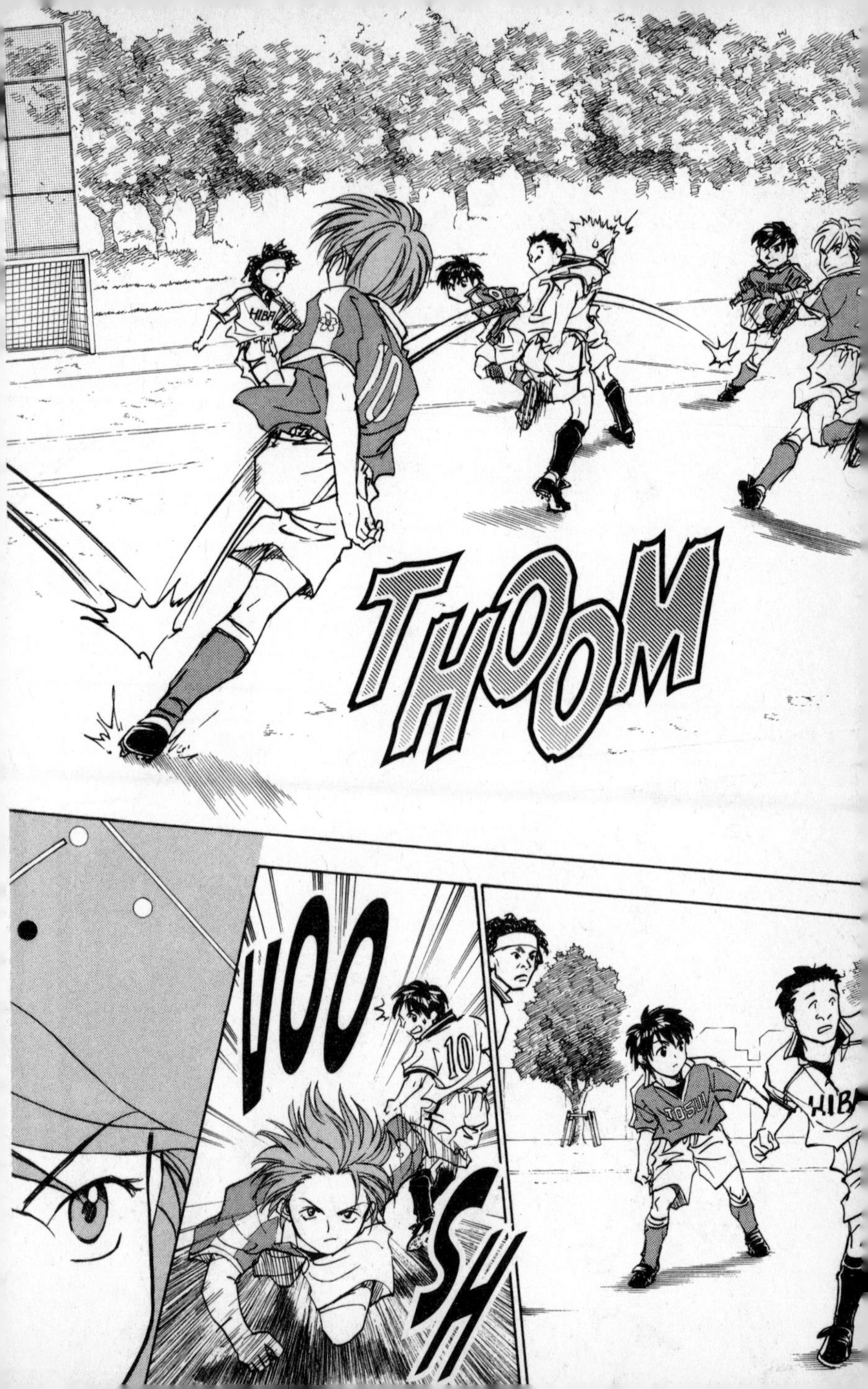
THOOM
VOOSH

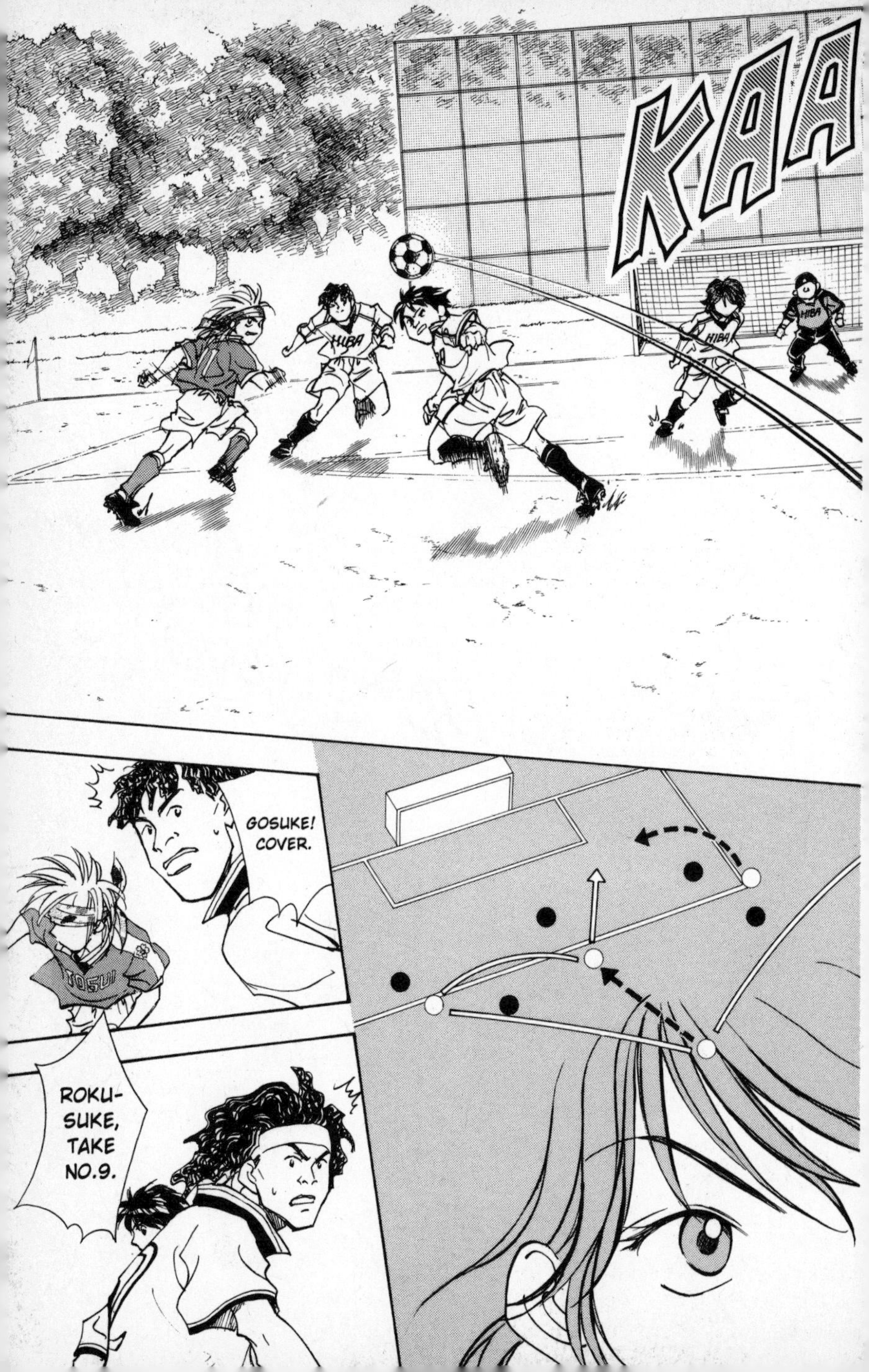
KAA
GOSUKE! COVER.
ROKU-SUKE, TAKE NO.9.

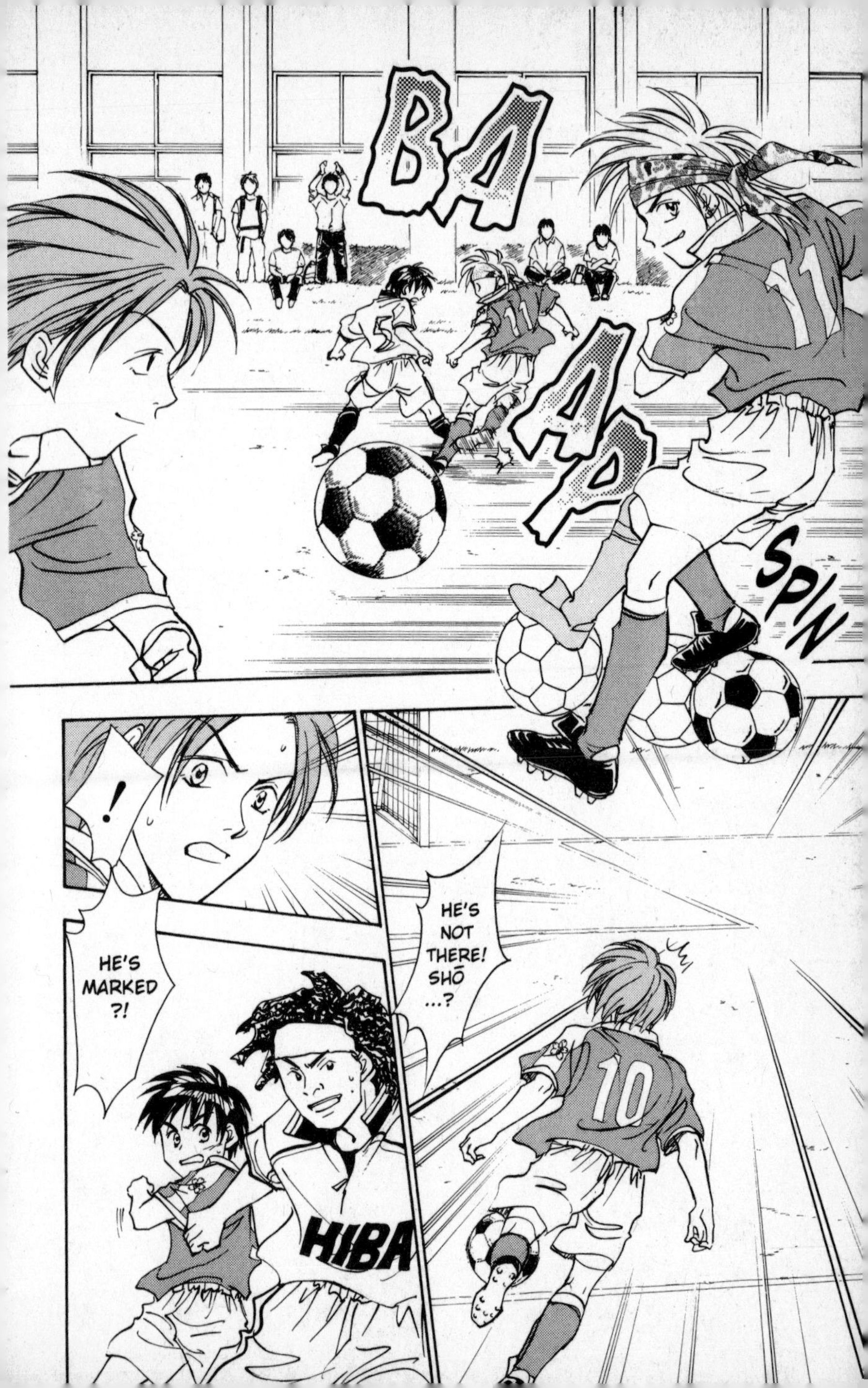
BAAP
SPIN
HE'S NOT THERE! SHŌ ...?
!
HE'S MARKED ?!
HIBA

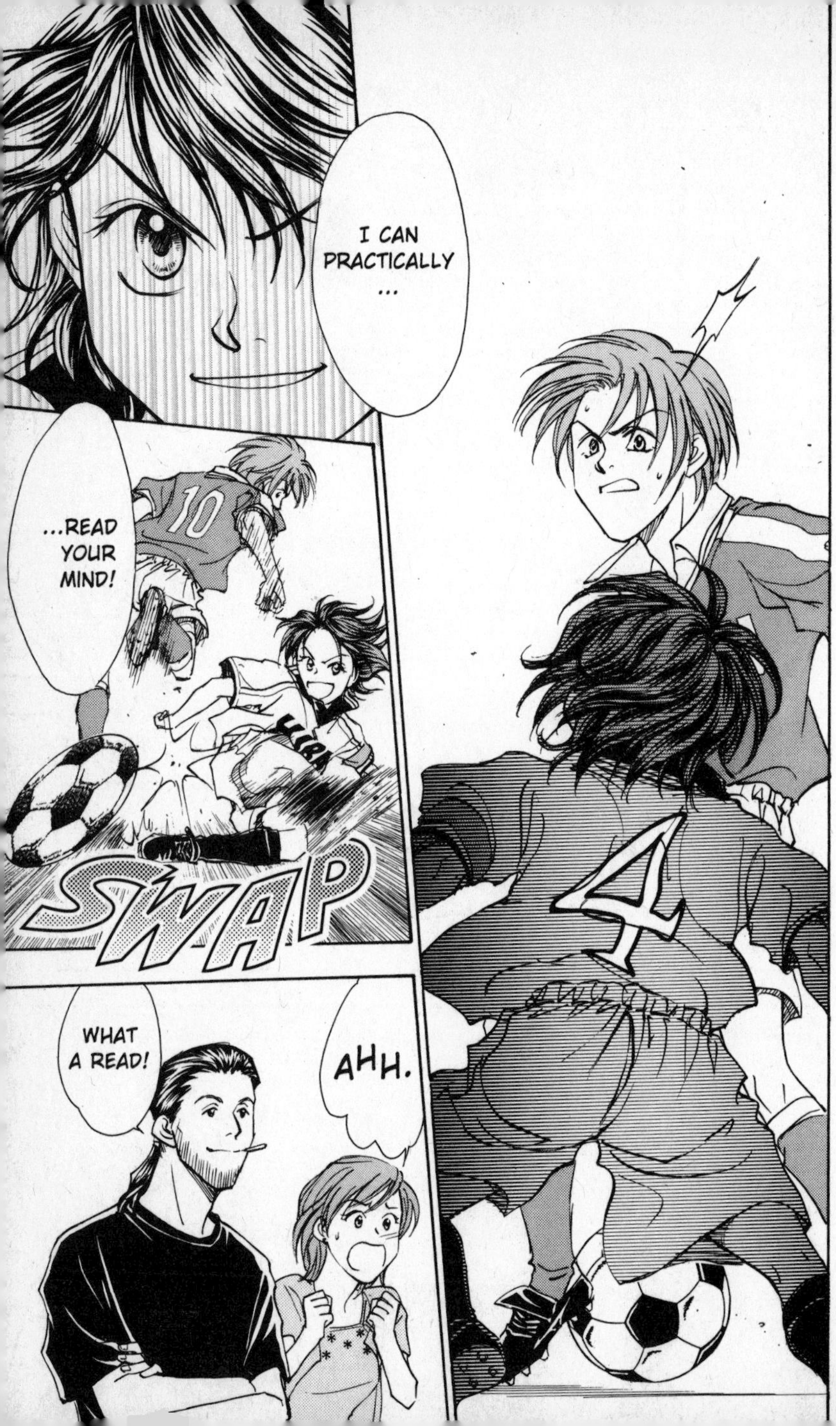
I CAN PRACTICALLY ...
...READ YOUR MIND!
SWAP
AHH.
WHAT A READ!

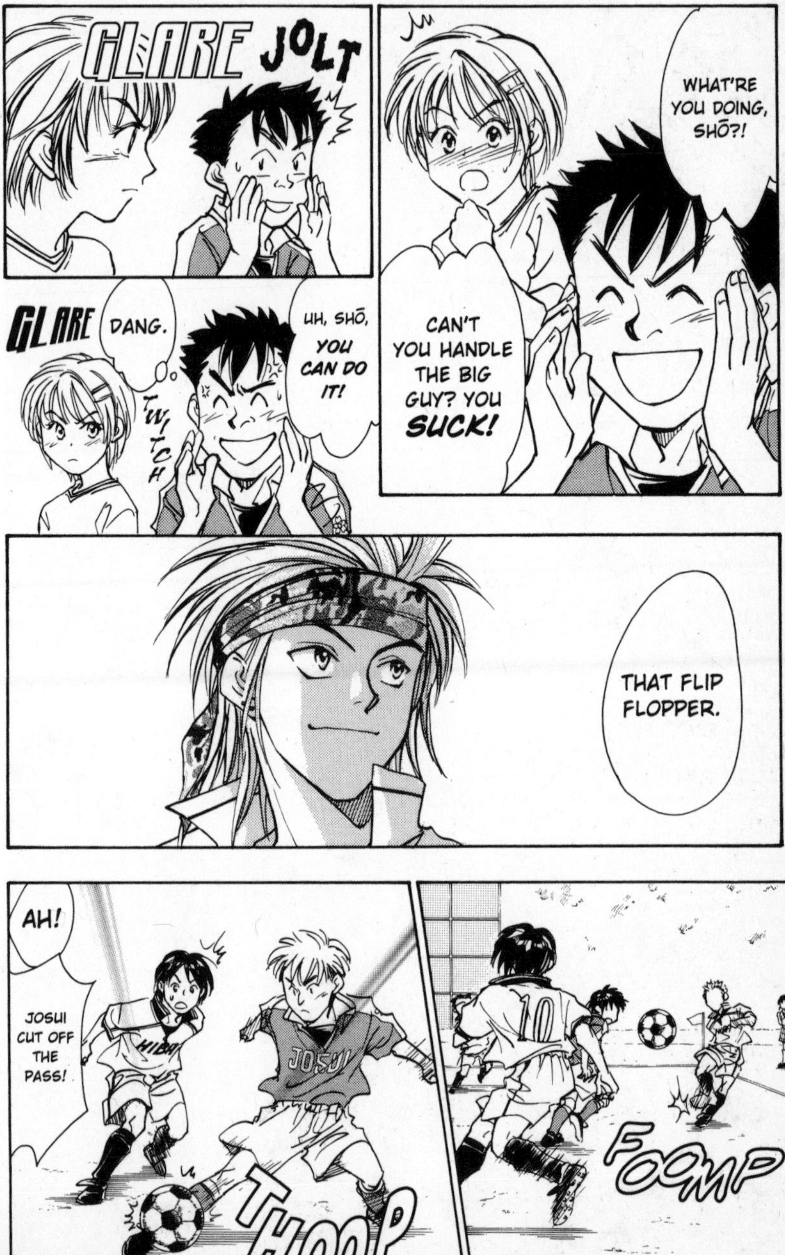
WHAT'RE YOU DOING, SHŌ?!
CAN'T YOU HANDLE THE BIG GUY? YOU SUCK!
JOLT
GLARE
UH, SHŌ, YOU CAN DO IT!
TWITCH
DANG.
GLARE
THAT FLIP FLOPPER.
FOOMP
AH!
JOSUI CUT OFF THE PASS!
JOSUI
THOOP

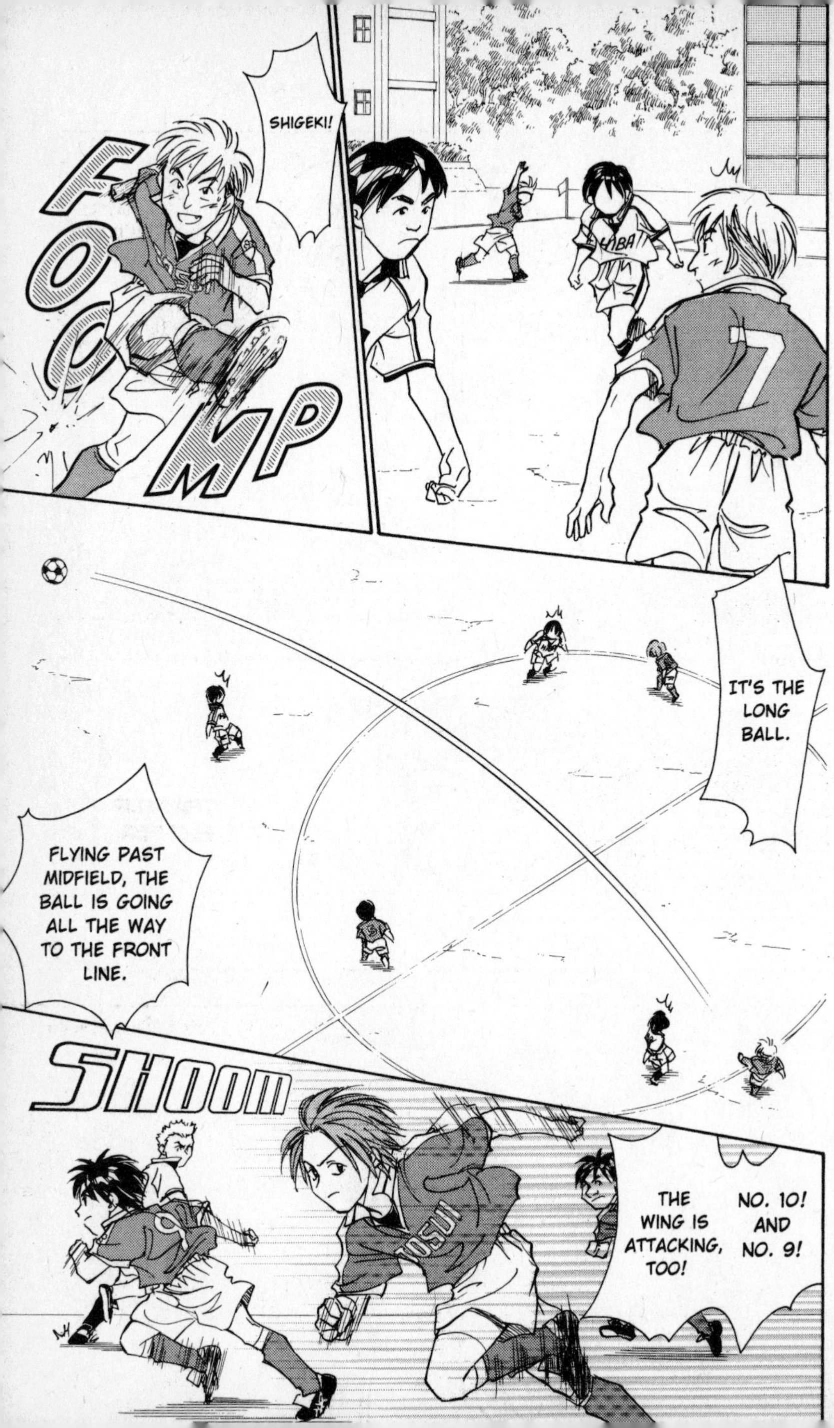
SHIGEKI!
FOOMP
IT'S THE LONG BALL.
FLYING PAST MIDFIELD, THE BALL IS GOING ALL THE WAY TO THE FRONT LINE.
NO. 10! AND NO. 9!
THE WING IS ATTACKING, TOO!
SHOOM

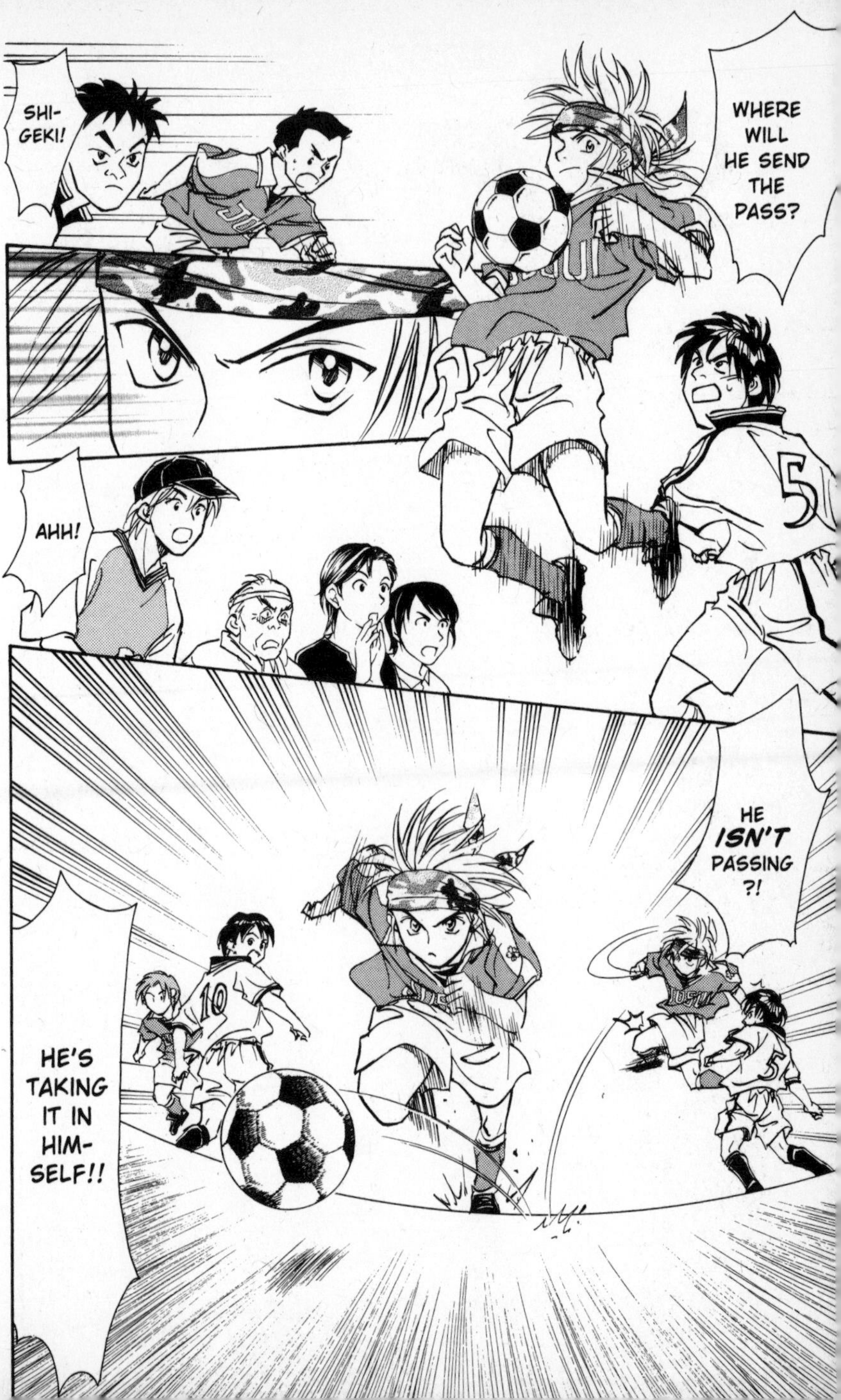
WHERE WILL HE SEND THE PASS?
SHI-GEKI!
AHH!
HE ISN'T PASSING?!
HE'S TAKING IT IN HIM-SELF!!

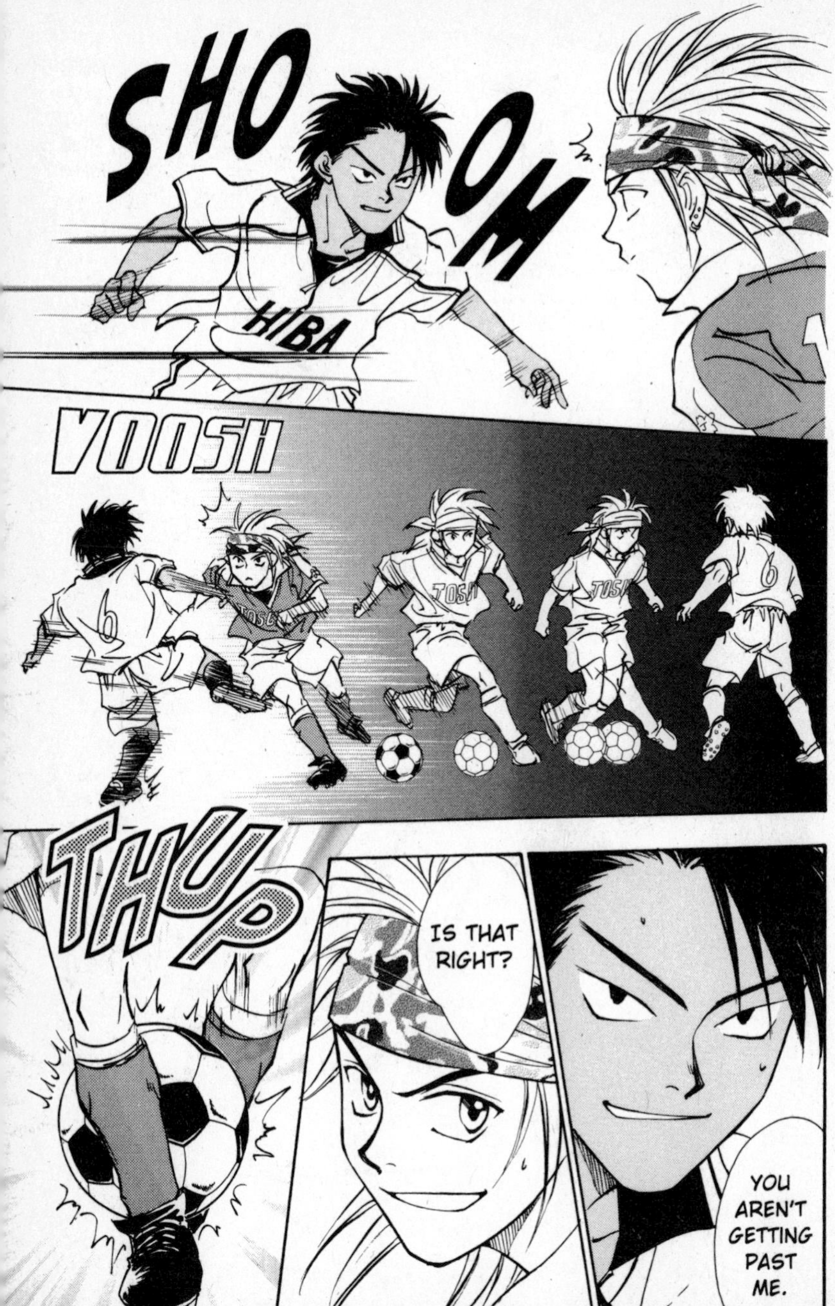
SHOOM
HIBA
VOOSH
TOSCA
YOU AREN'T GETTING PAST ME.
IS THAT RIGHT?
THUP

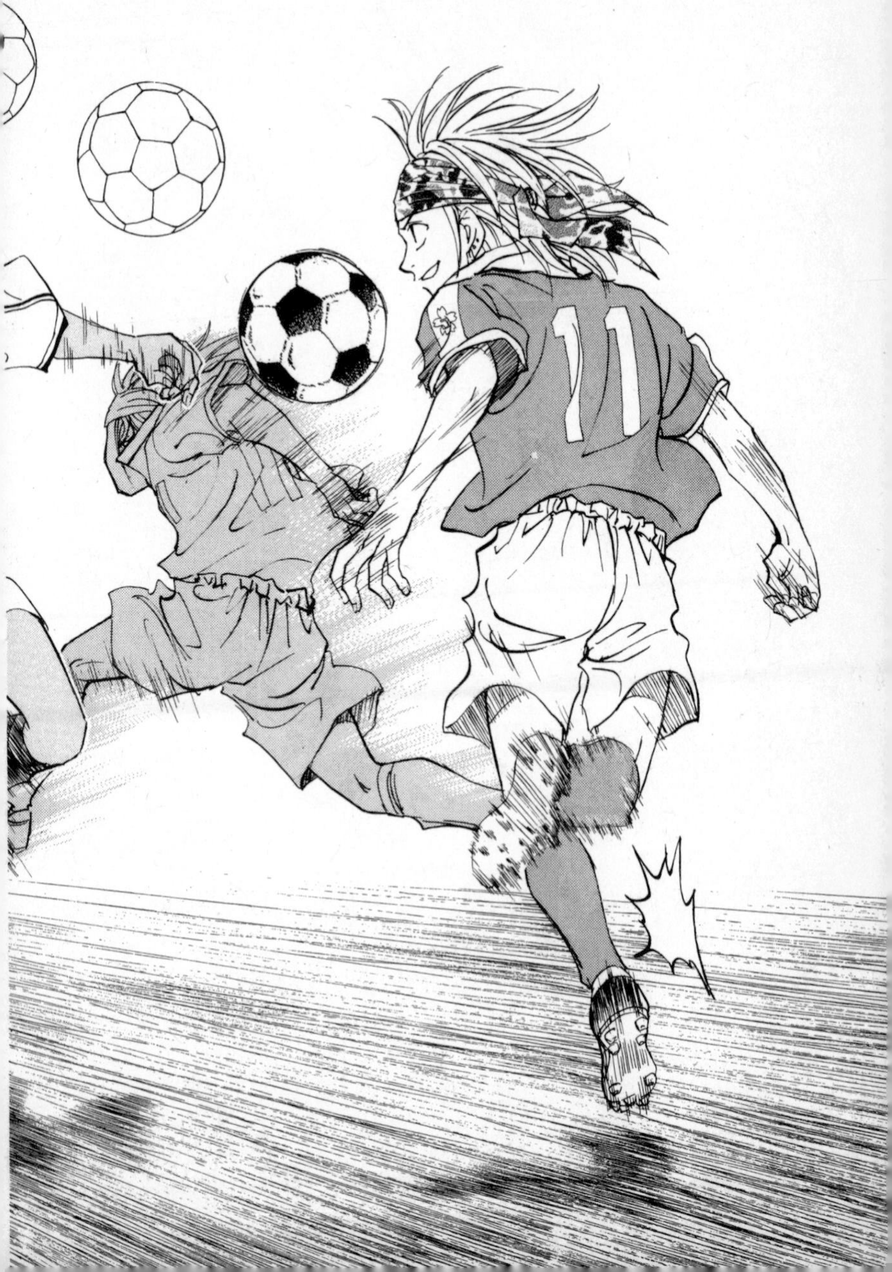

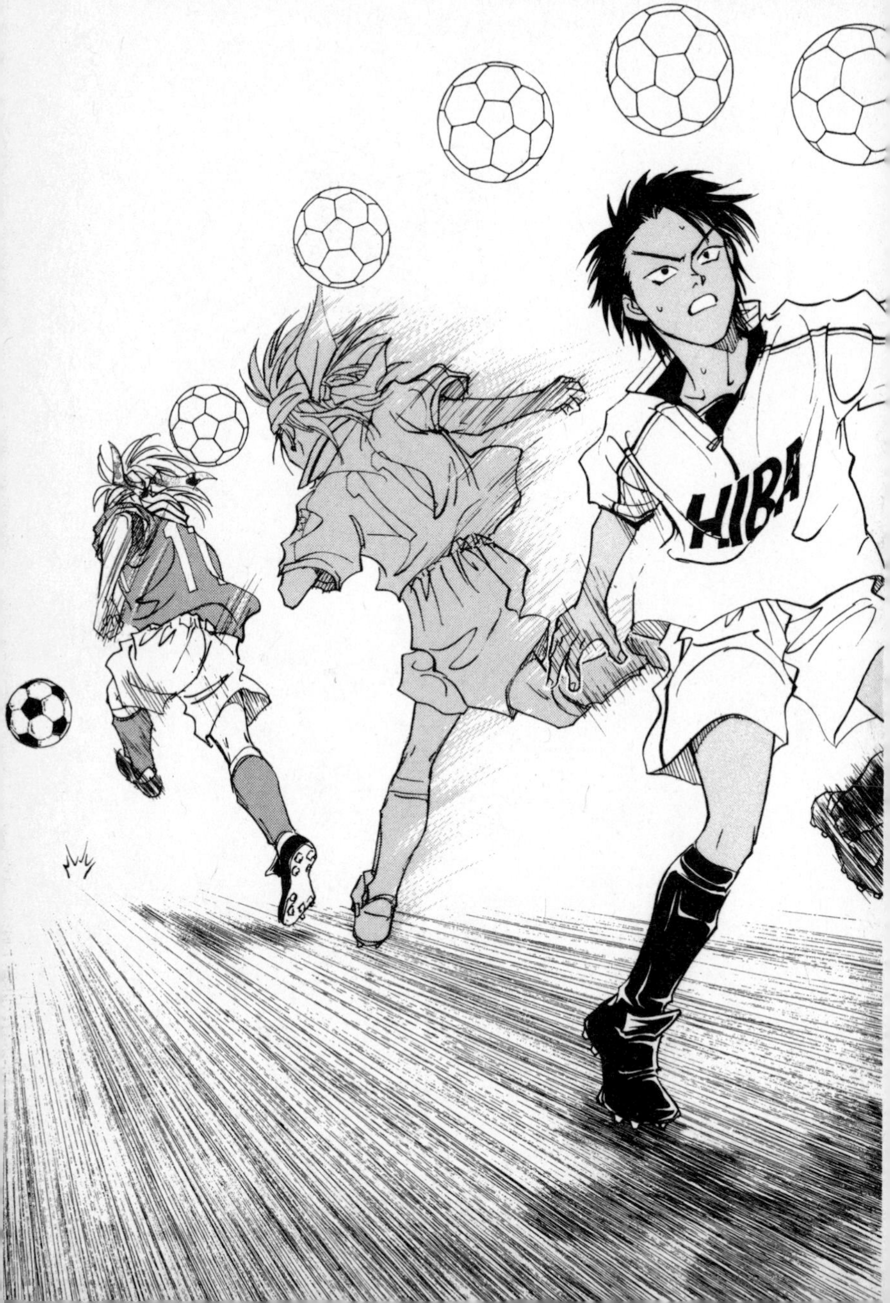
HIBA

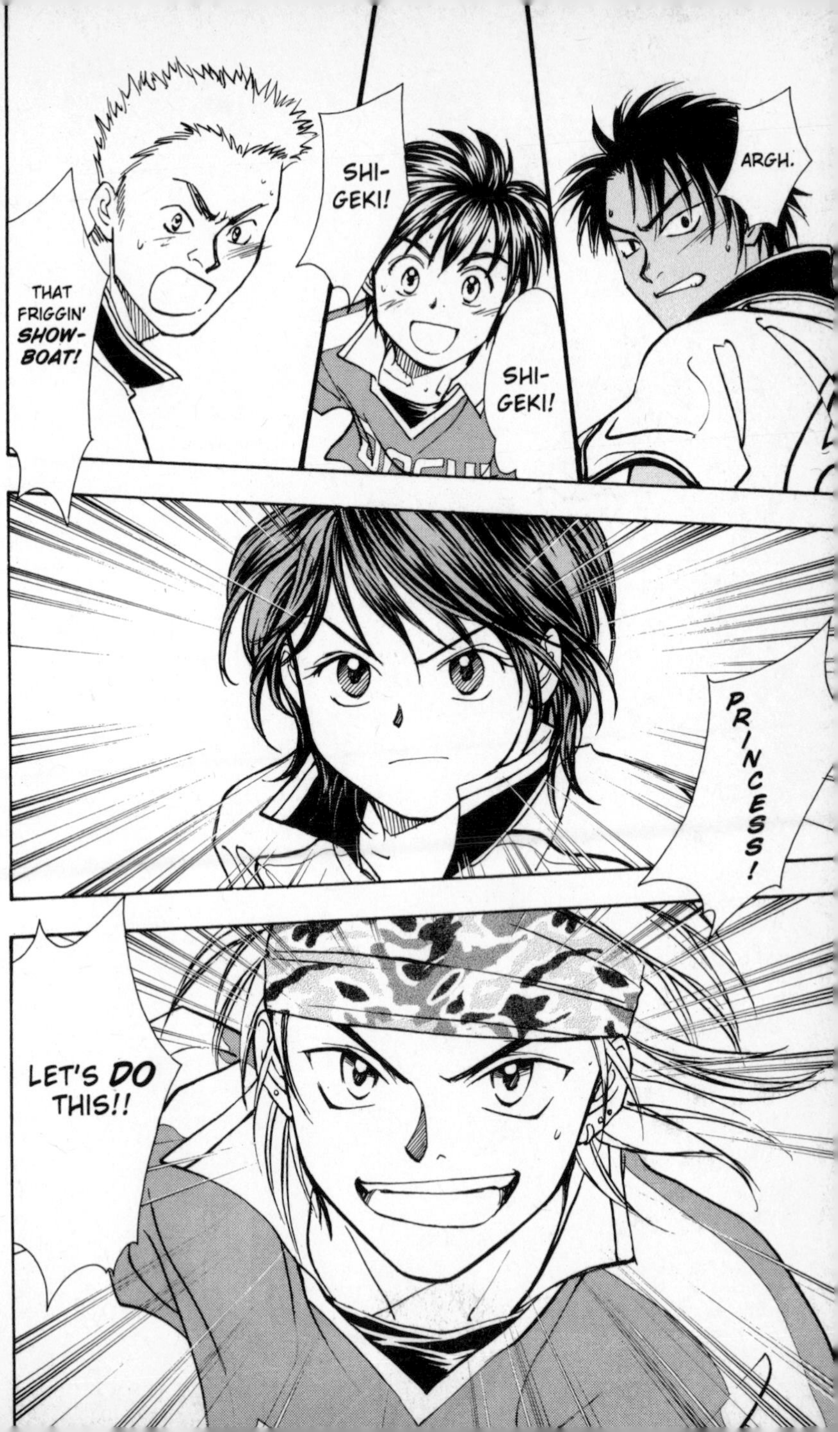
ARGH.
SHI-GEKI!
SHI-GEKI!
THAT FRIGGIN' SHOW-BOAT!
PRINCESS!
LET'S DO THIS!!

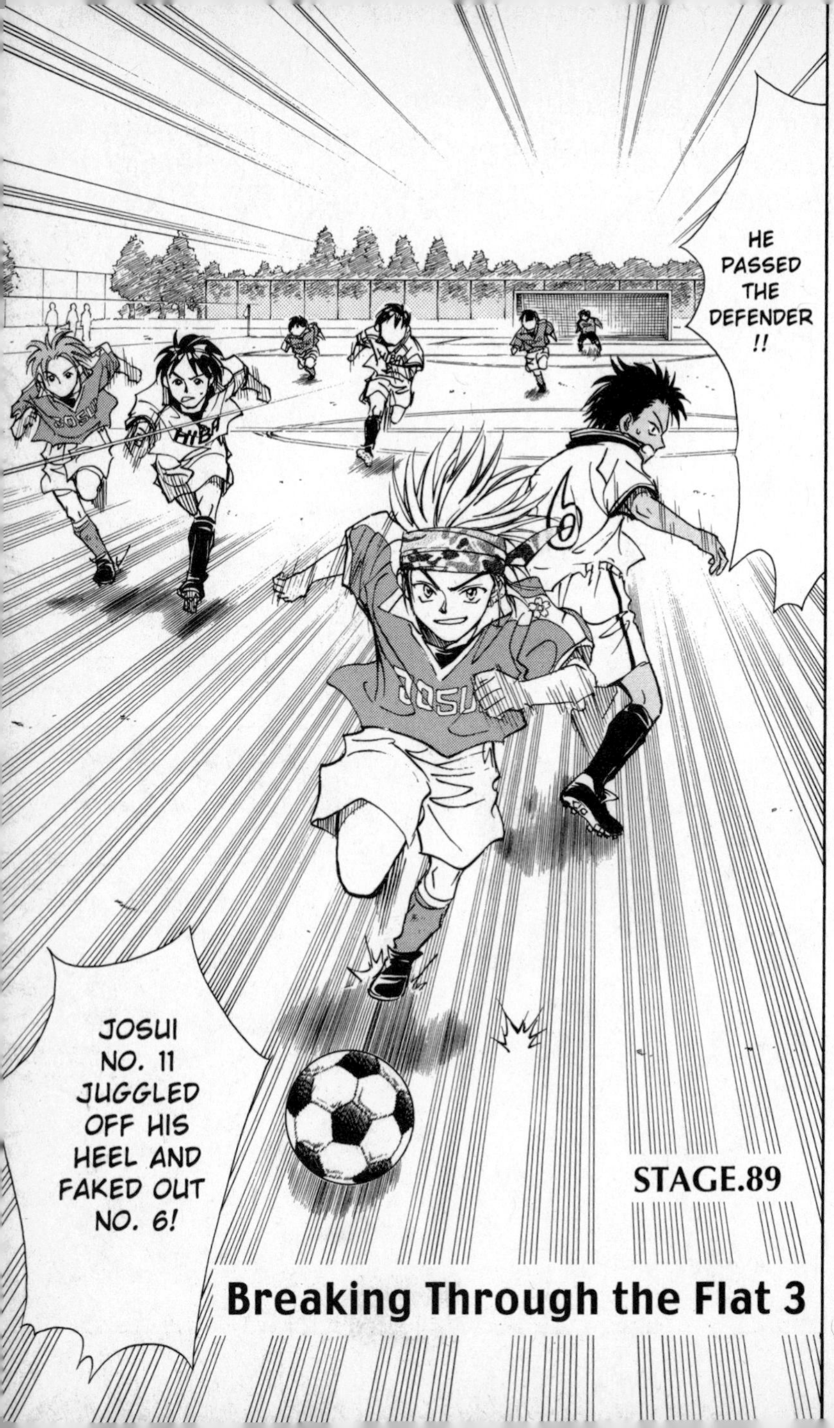
HE PASSED THE DEFENDER !!
JOSUI NO. 11 JUGGLED OFF HIS HEEL AND FAKED OUT NO. 6!

STAGE.89

Breaking Through the Flat 3

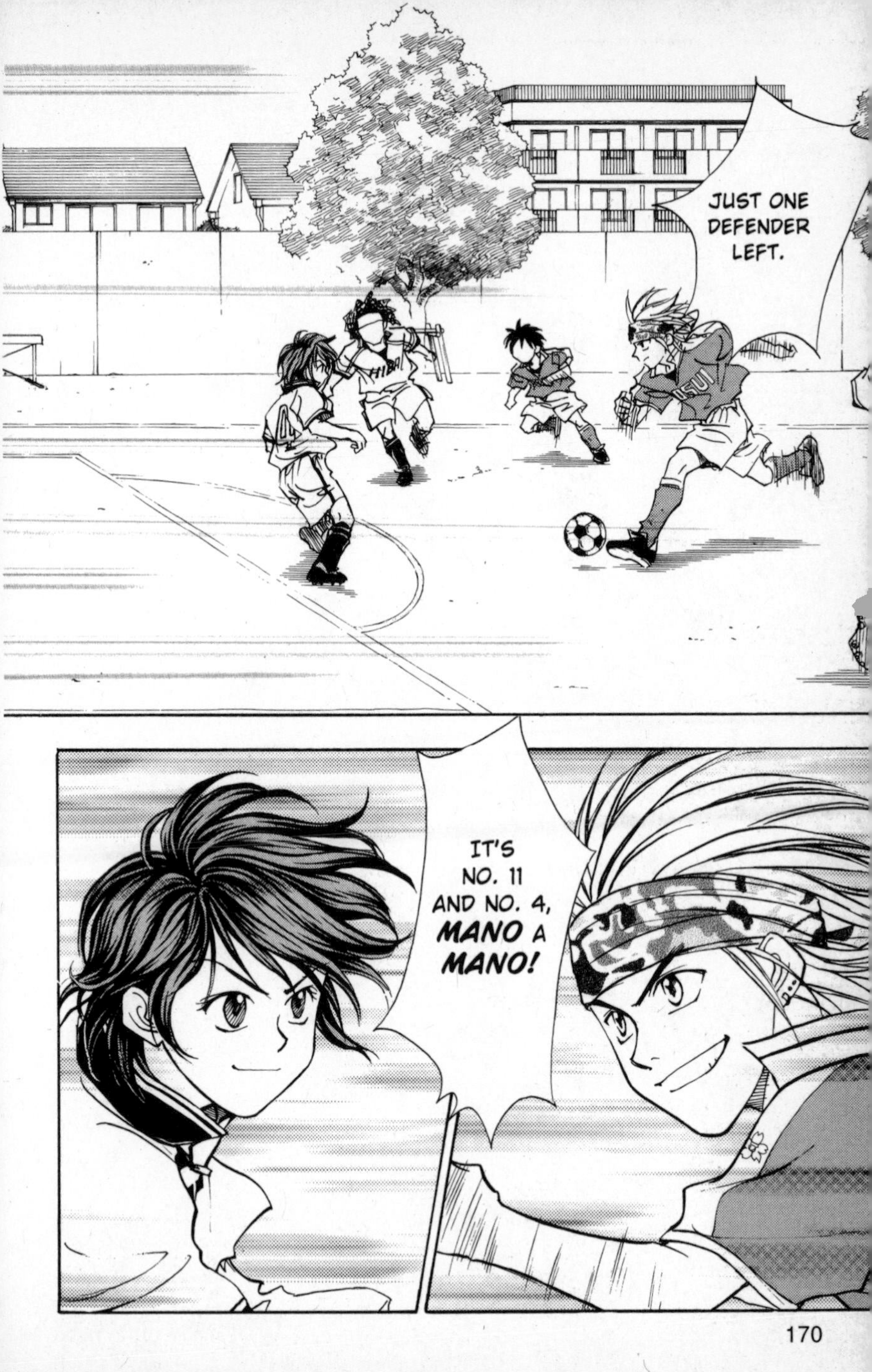

JUST ONE DEFENDER LEFT.
IT'S NO. 11 AND NO. 4, *MANO* A *MANO!*

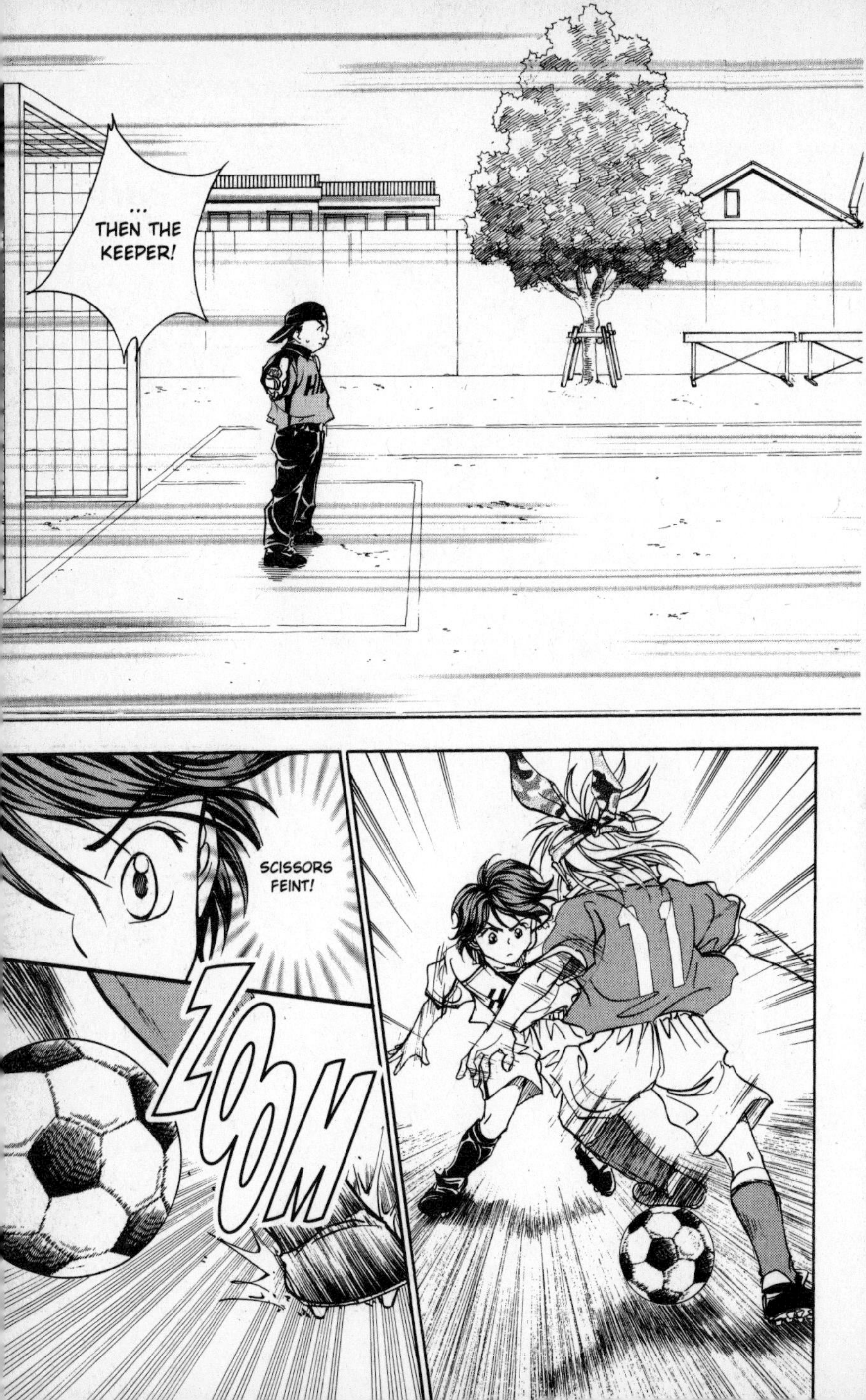
... THEN THE KEEPER!
SCISSORS FEINT!
ZOOM

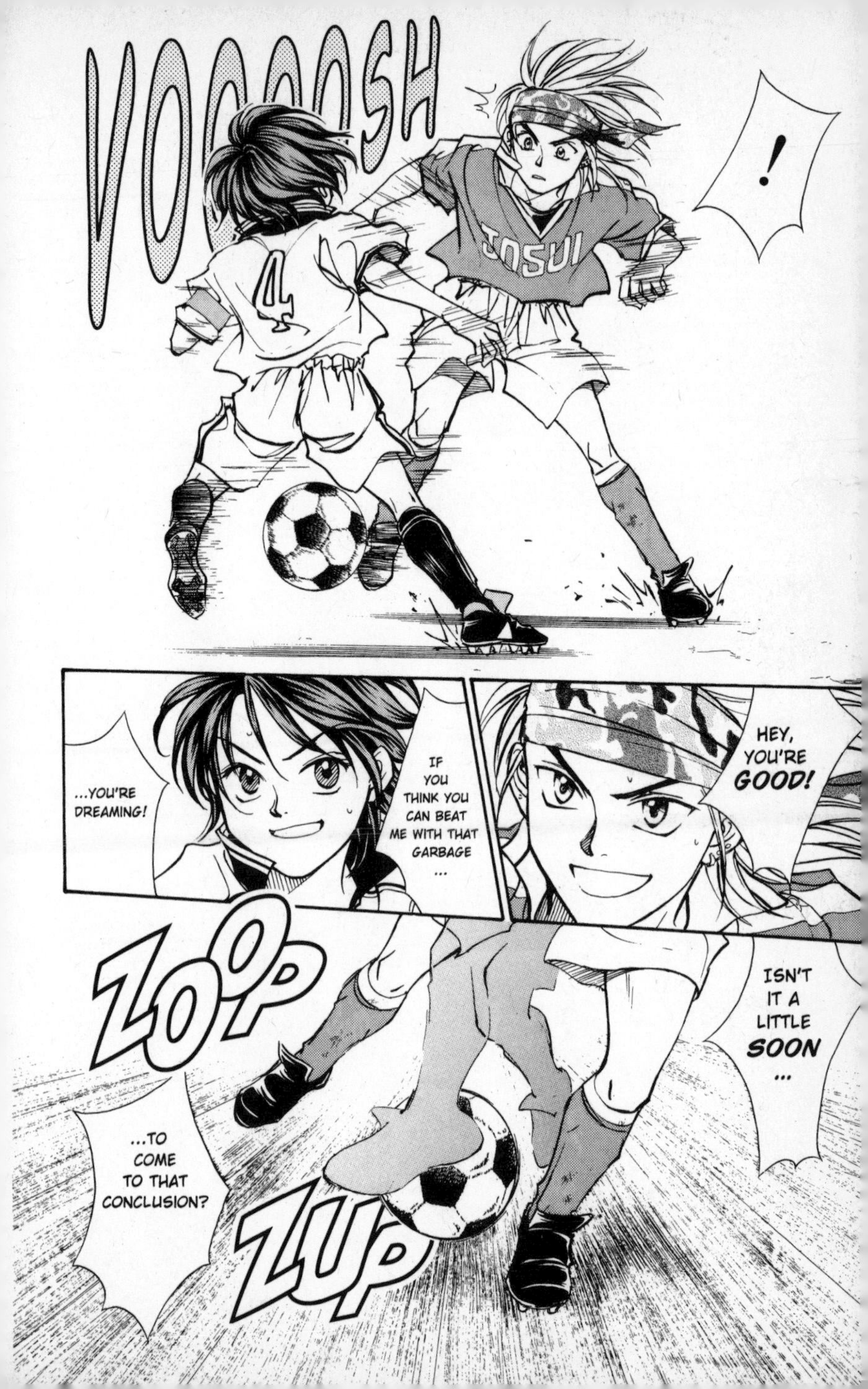
VOOOOSH
!
JOSUI
HEY, YOU'RE GOOD!
IF YOU THINK YOU CAN BEAT ME WITH THAT GARBAGE ...
...YOU'RE DREAMING!
ISN'T IT A LITTLE SOON ...
ZOOP
...TO COME TO THAT CONCLUSION?
ZUP

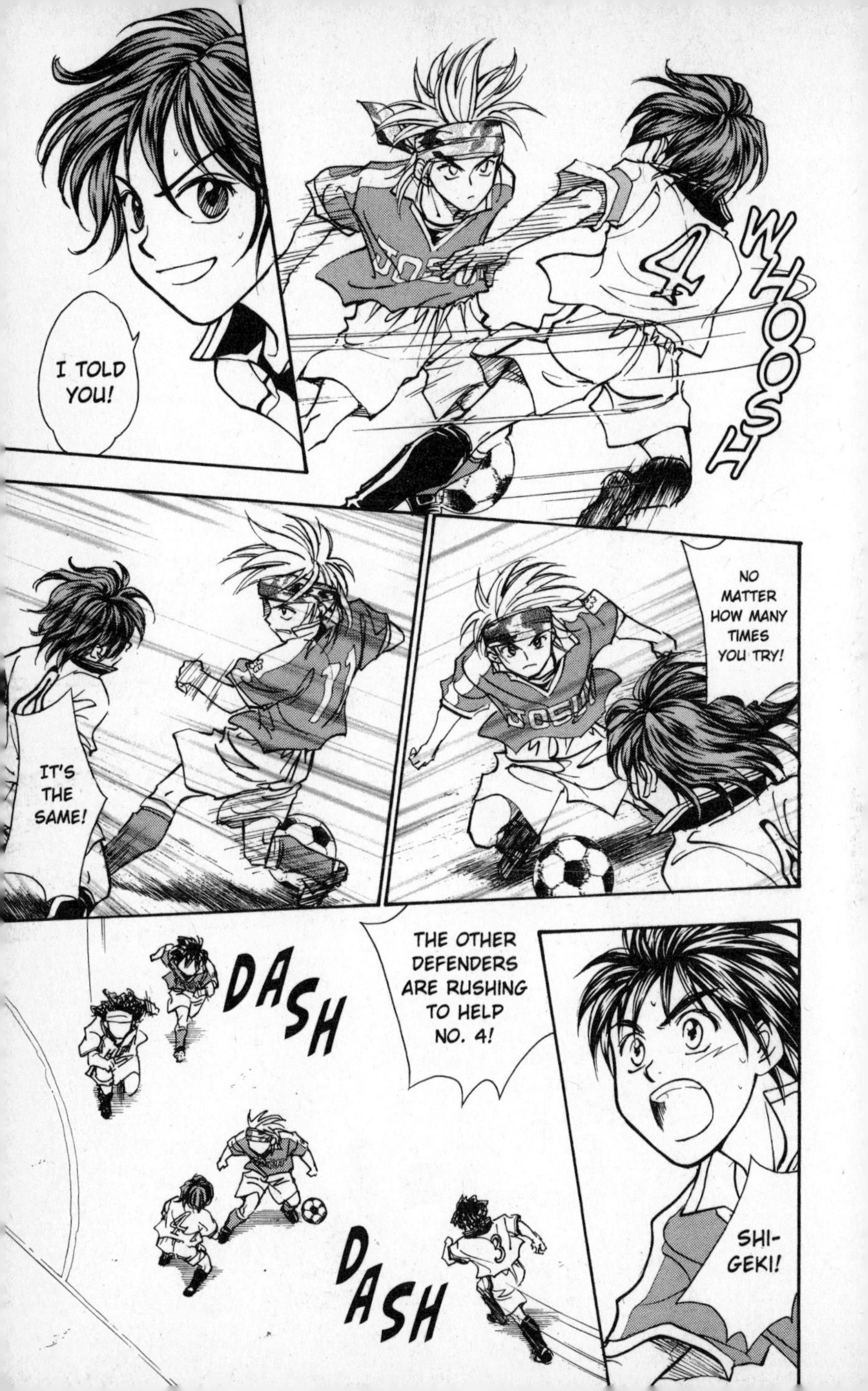
WHOOSH
I TOLD YOU!
NO MATTER HOW MANY TIMES YOU TRY!
IT'S THE SAME!
SHI-GEKI!
THE OTHER DEFENDERS ARE RUSHING TO HELP NO. 4!
DASH
DASH

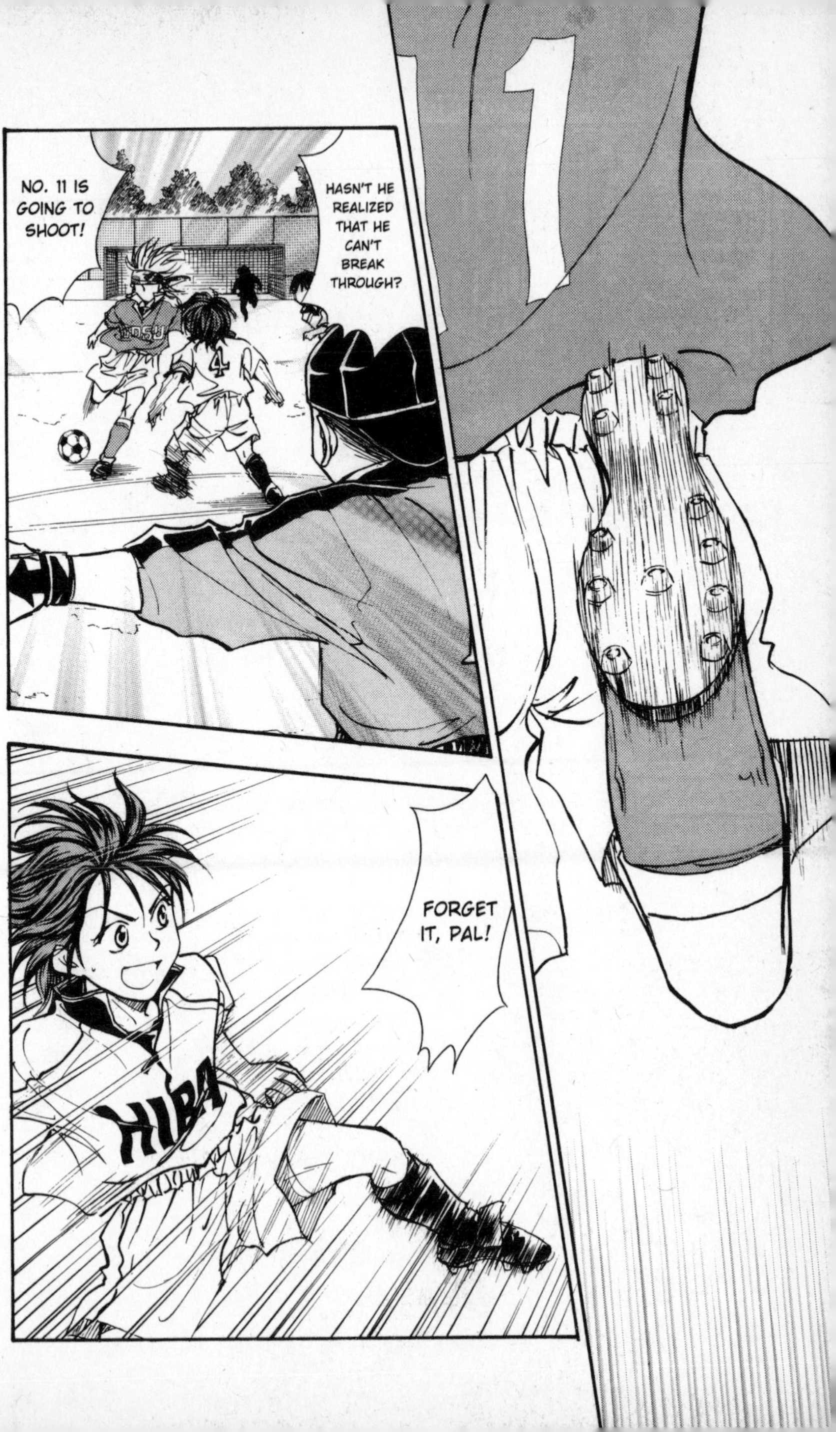
HASN'T HE REALIZED THAT HE CAN'T BREAK THROUGH?
NO. 11 IS GOING TO SHOOT!
FORGET IT, PAL!

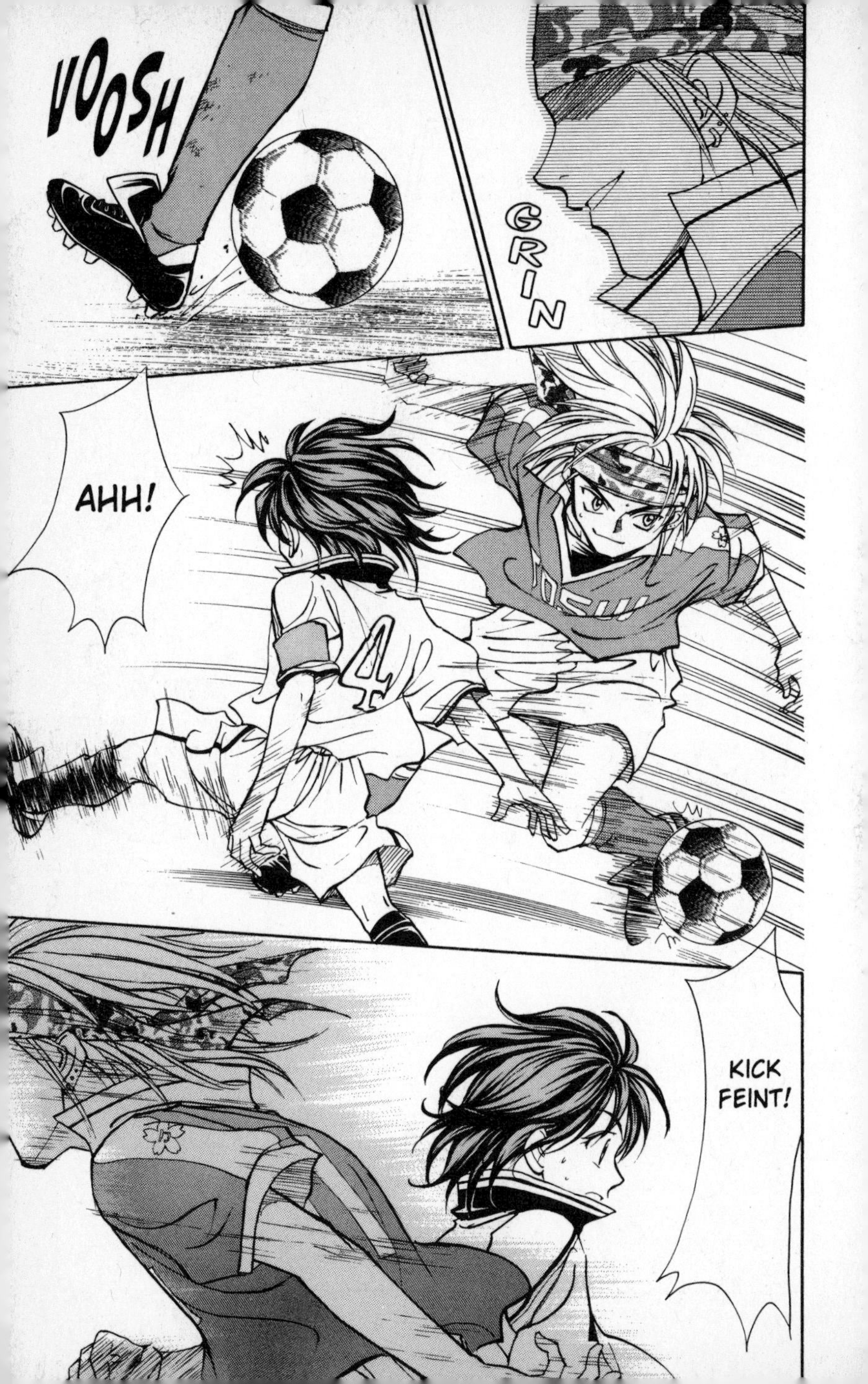
GRIN
VOOSH
AHH!
KICK FEINT!

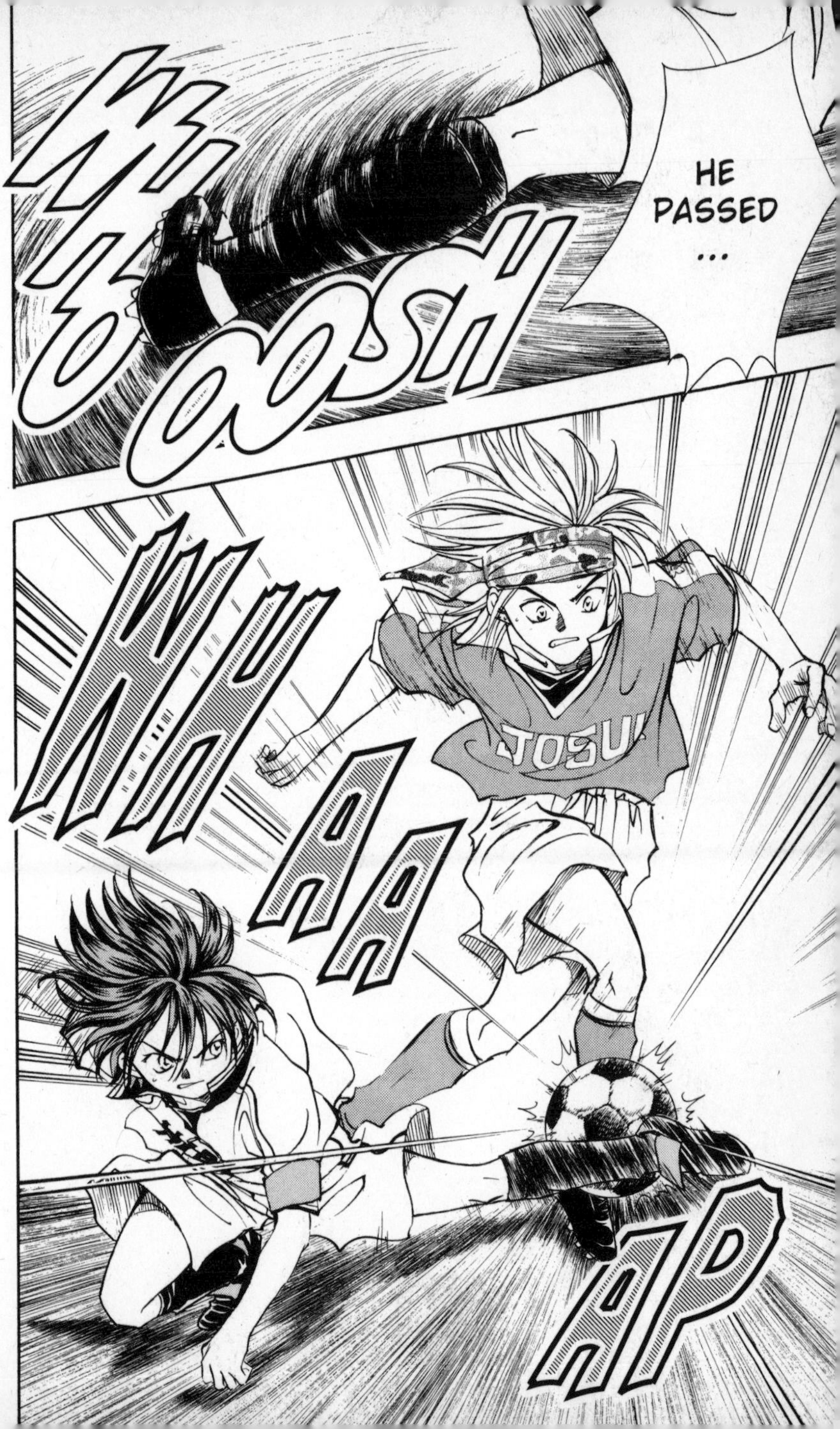
HE PASSED ...
Whoosh
WHAAAP

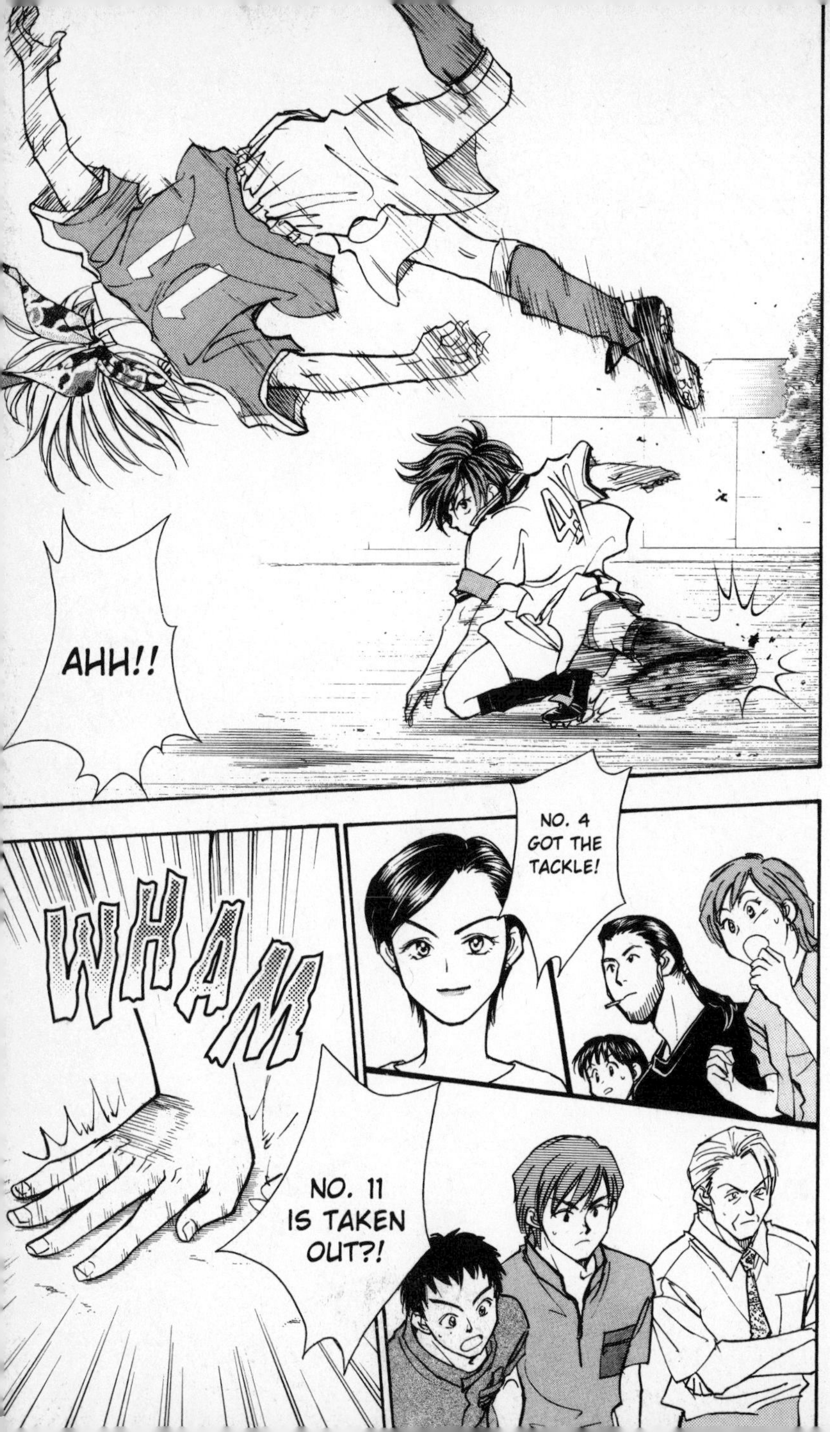
AHH!!
NO. 4 GOT THE TACKLE!
NO. 11 IS TAKEN OUT?!
WHAM

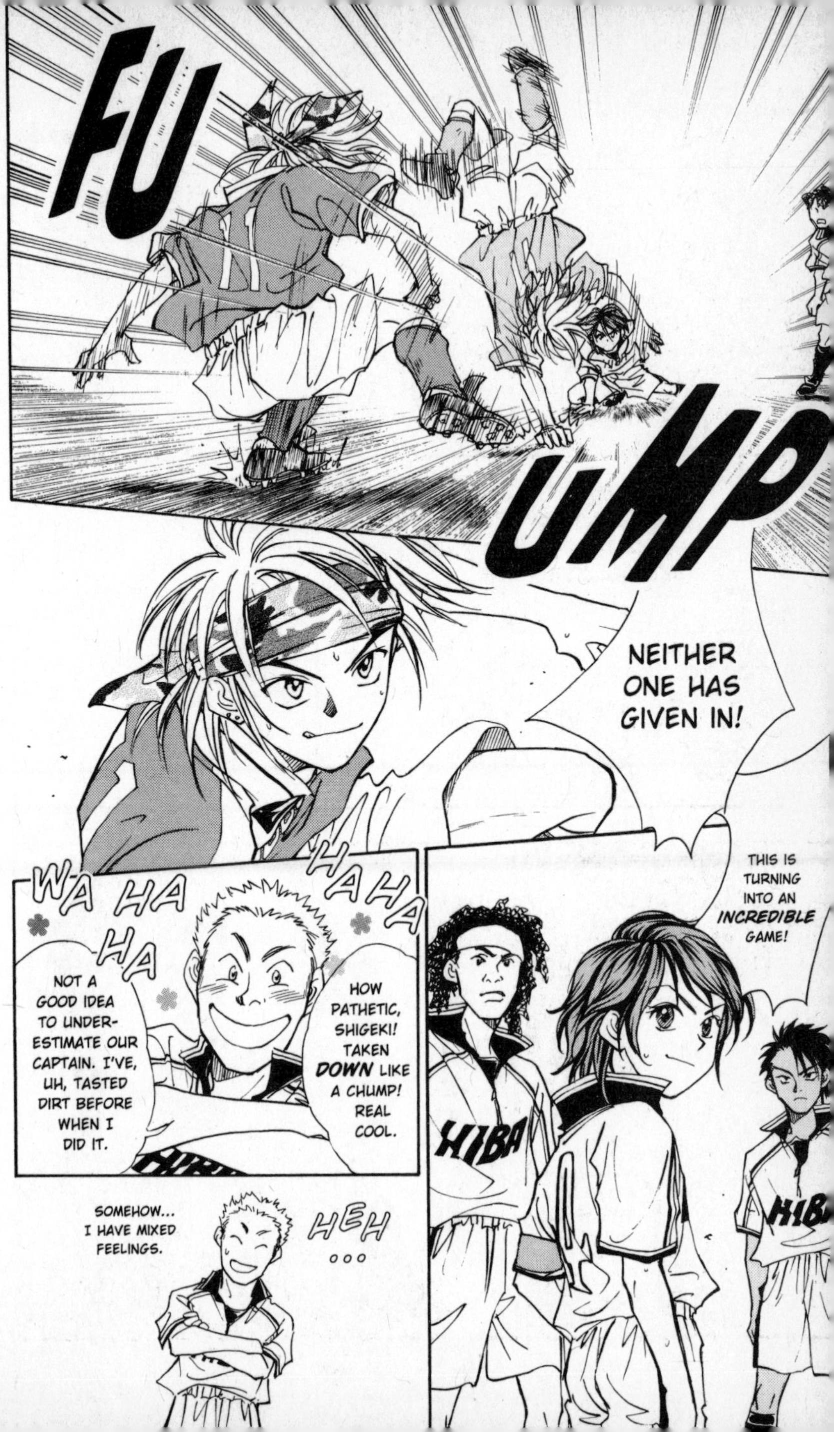
FU
UMP
NEITHER ONE HAS GIVEN IN!
THIS IS TURNING INTO AN INCREDIBLE GAME!
WA HA HA
HAHA
HA
HOW PATHETIC, SHIGEKI! TAKEN DOWN LIKE A CHUMP! REAL COOL.
NOT A GOOD IDEA TO UNDER-ESTIMATE OUR CAPTAIN. I'VE, UH, TASTED DIRT BEFORE WHEN I DID IT.
HEH...
SOMEHOW... I HAVE MIXED FEELINGS.
HIBA

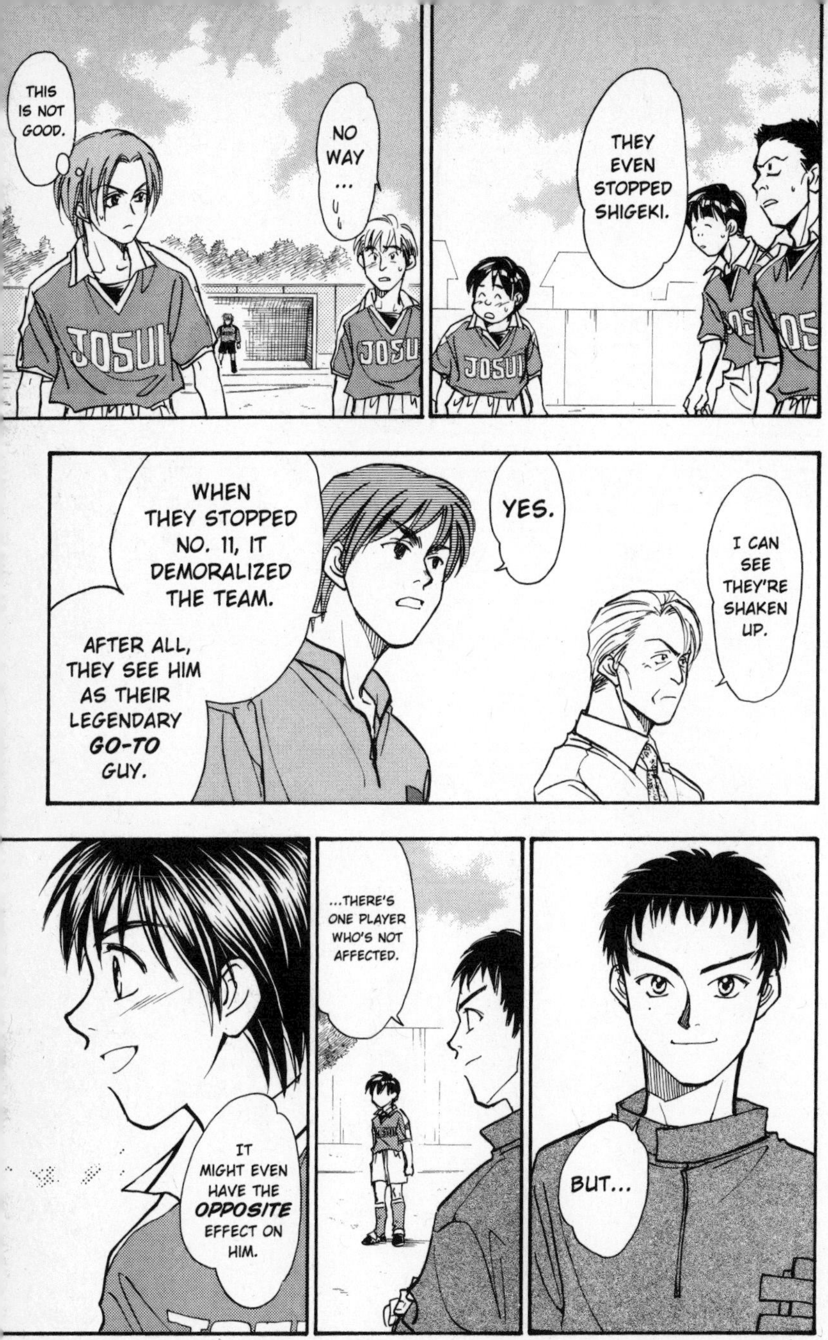
THEY EVEN STOPPED SHIGEKI.
NO WAY...
THIS IS NOT GOOD.
I CAN SEE THEY'RE SHAKEN UP.
YES.
WHEN THEY STOPPED NO. 11, IT DEMORALIZED THE TEAM.
AFTER ALL, THEY SEE HIM AS THEIR LEGENDARY GO-TO GUY.
BUT...
...THERE'S ONE PLAYER WHO'S NOT AFFECTED.
IT MIGHT EVEN HAVE THE OPPOSITE EFFECT ON HIM.

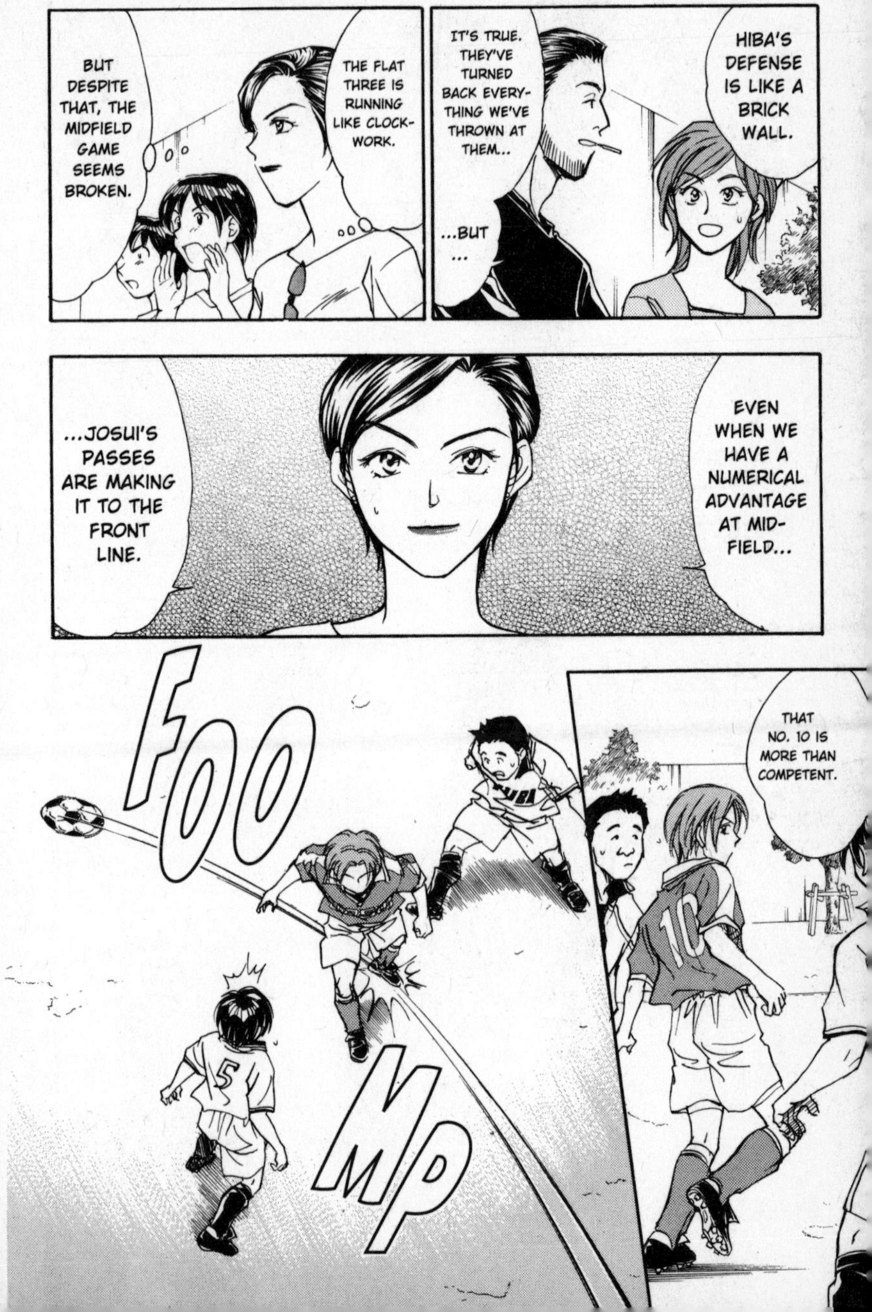
HIBA'S DEFENSE IS LIKE A BRICK WALL.
IT'S TRUE. THEY'VE TURNED BACK EVERYTHING WE'VE THROWN AT THEM...
...BUT ...
THE FLAT THREE IS RUNNING LIKE CLOCKWORK.
BUT DESPITE THAT, THE MIDFIELD GAME SEEMS BROKEN.
EVEN WHEN WE HAVE A NUMERICAL ADVANTAGE AT MIDFIELD...
...JOSUI'S PASSES ARE MAKING IT TO THE FRONT LINE.
THAT NO. 10 IS MORE THAN COMPETENT.
FOOMP

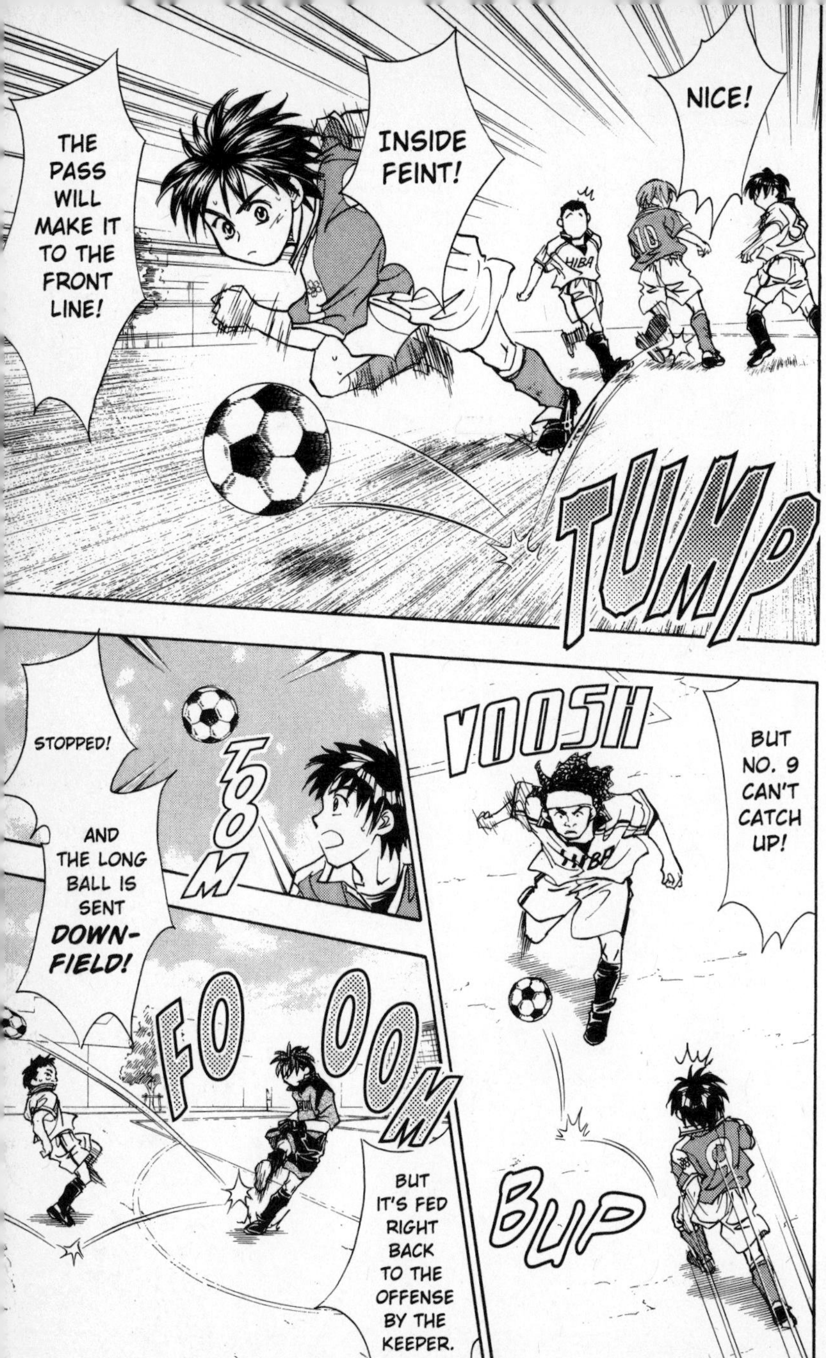
NICE!
INSIDE FEINT!
THE PASS WILL MAKE IT TO THE FRONT LINE!
TUMP
STOPPED!
78M
AND THE LONG BALL IS SENT DOWN-FIELD!
FOOOOM
BUT IT'S FED RIGHT BACK TO THE OFFENSE BY THE KEEPER.
VOOSH
BUT NO. 9 CAN'T CATCH UP!
BUP

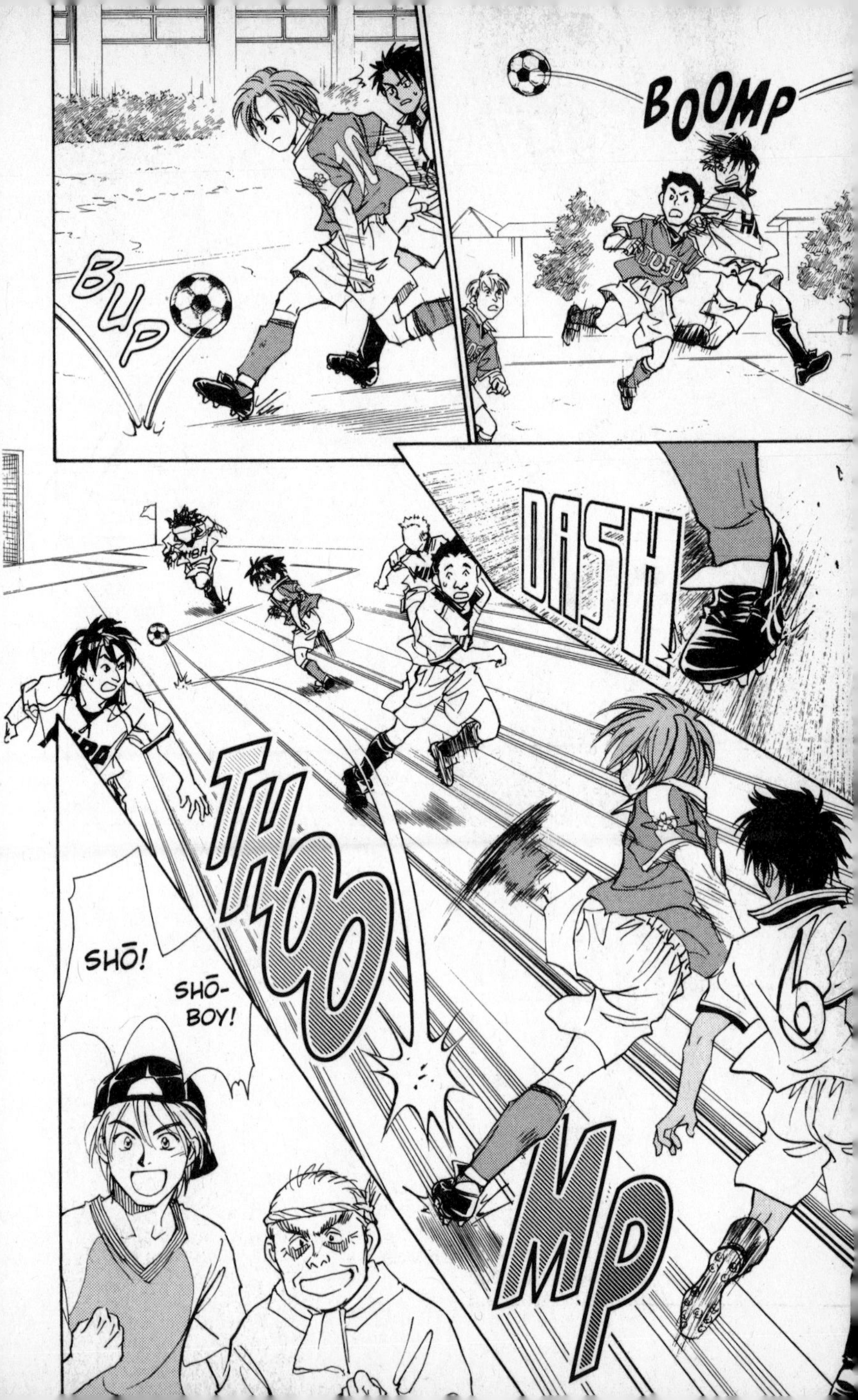
BOOMP
BUP
DASH
THOOMP
SHŌ!
SHŌ-BOY!

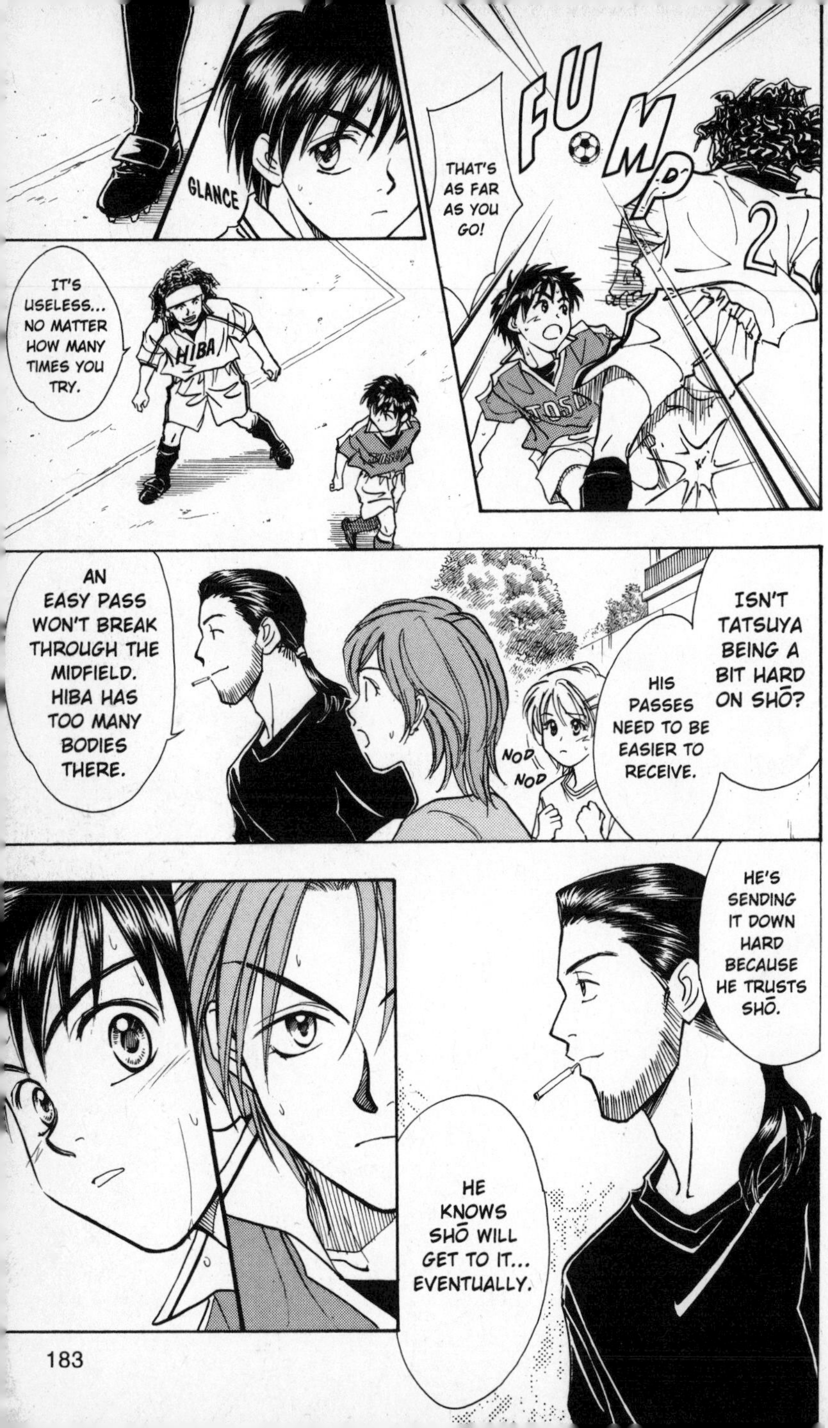
FUMP
THAT'S AS FAR AS YOU GO!
GLANCE
IT'S USELESS... NO MATTER HOW MANY TIMES YOU TRY.
ISN'T TATSUYA BEING A BIT HARD ON SHŌ?
HIS PASSES NEED TO BE EASIER TO RECEIVE.
NOD NOD
AN EASY PASS WON'T BREAK THROUGH THE MIDFIELD. HIBA HAS TOO MANY BODIES THERE.
HE'S SENDING IT DOWN HARD BECAUSE HE TRUSTS SHŌ.
HE KNOWS SHŌ WILL GET TO IT... EVENTUALLY.

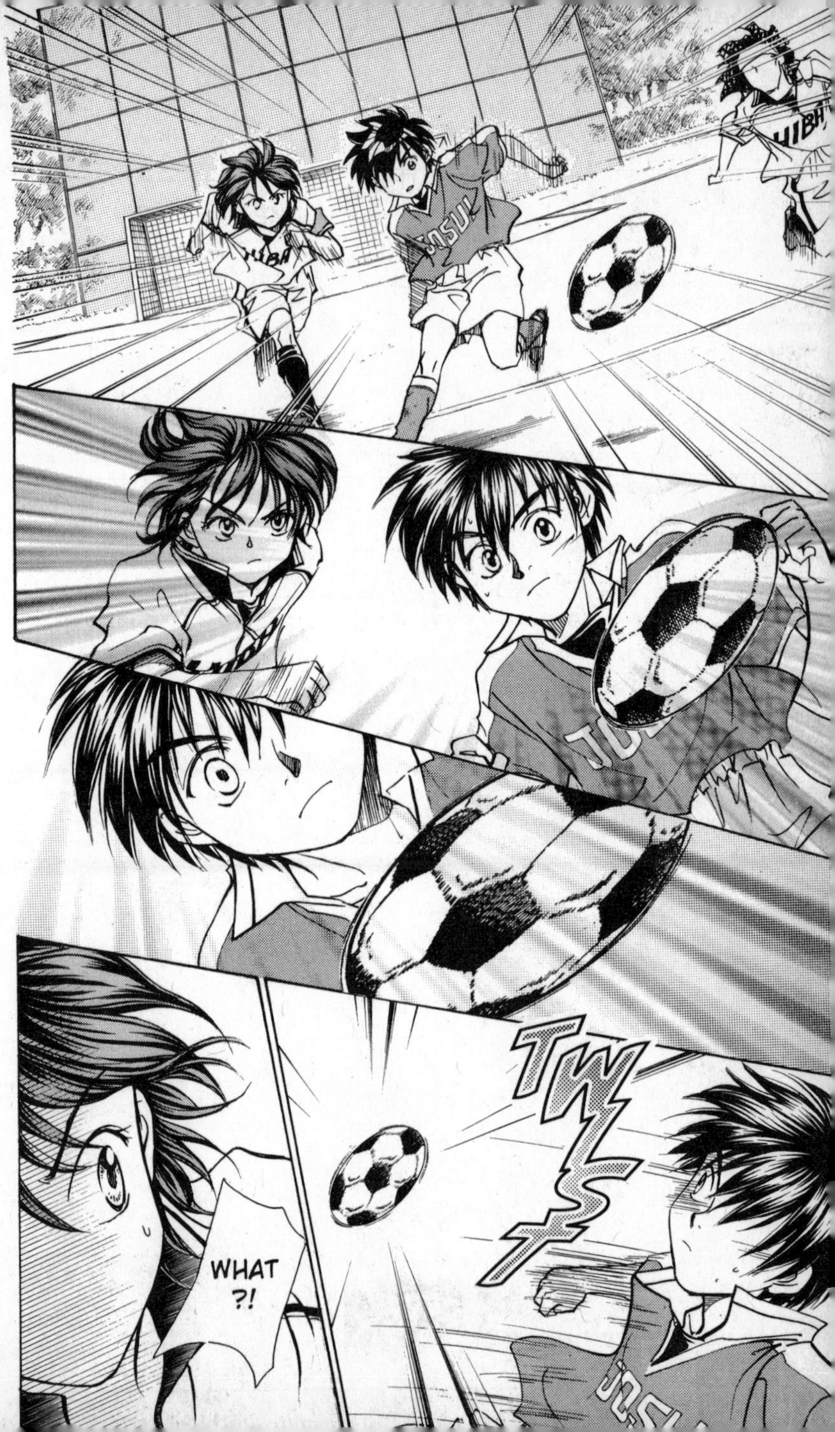
TWIST
WHAT ?!

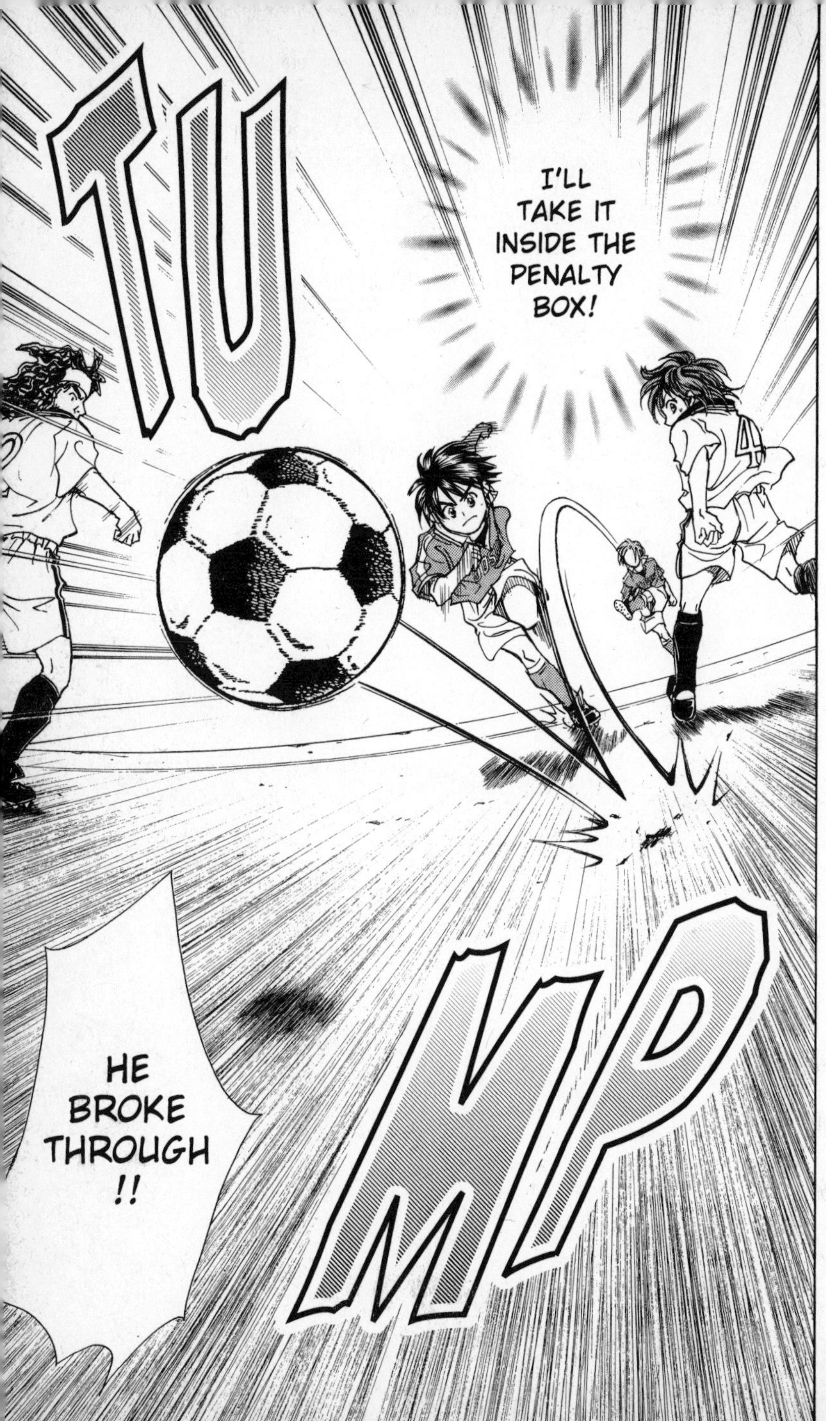

I'LL TAKE IT INSIDE THE PENALTY BOX!
TUMP
HE BROKE THROUGH !!

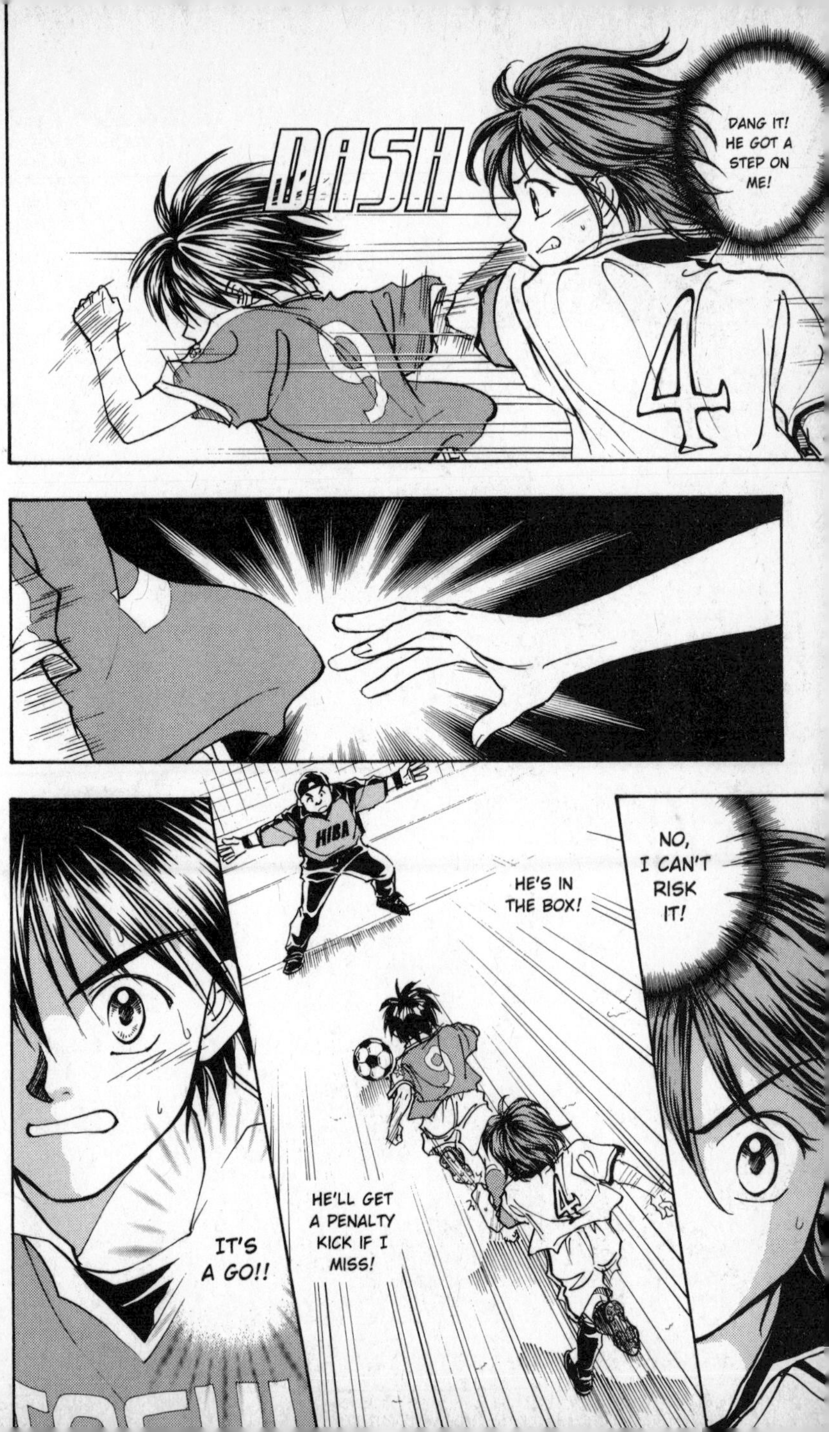
DASH
DANG IT! HE GOT A STEP ON ME!
HIBA
NO, I CAN'T RISK IT!
HE'S IN THE BOX!
HE'LL GET A PENALTY KICK IF I MISS!
IT'S A GO!!

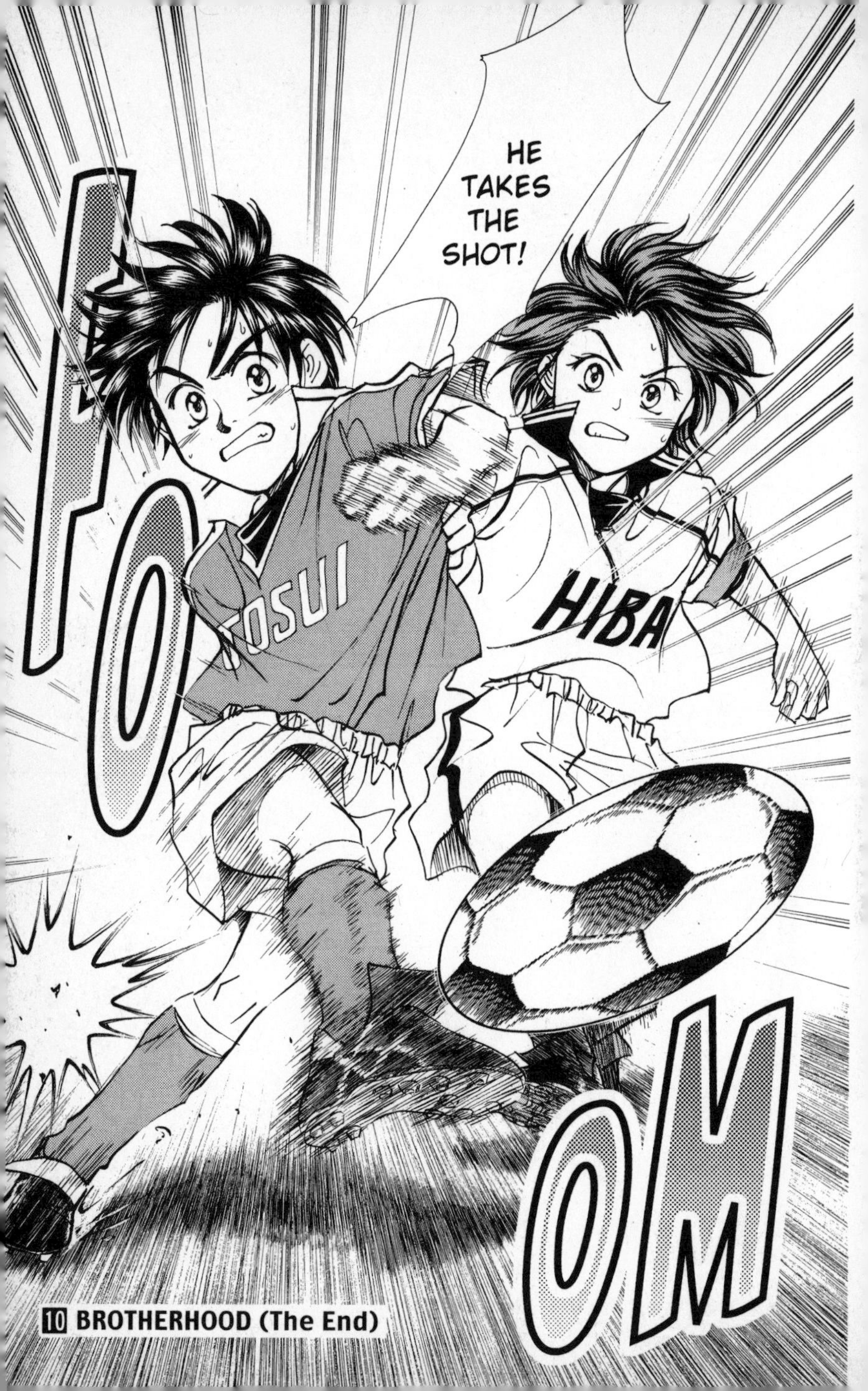
HE TAKES THE SHOT!
FOOOM
TOSUI
HIBA
10 BROTHERHOOD (The End)

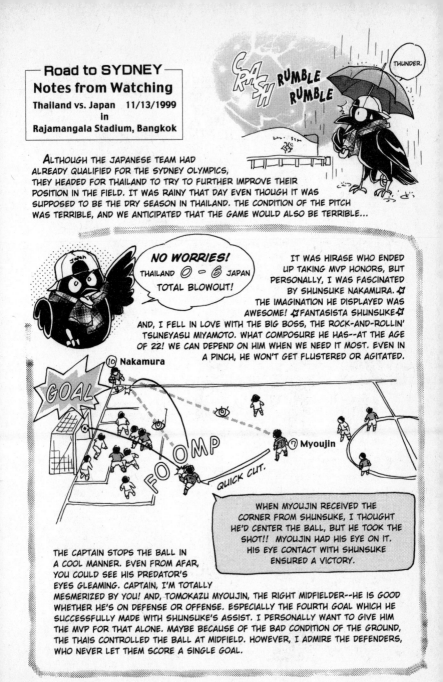

Road to SYDNEY
Notes from Watching

Thailand vs. Japan 11/13/1999
in
Rajamangala Stadium, Bangkok

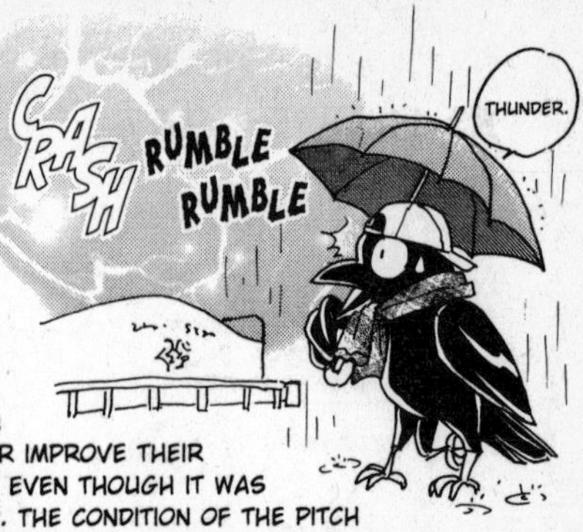
CRASH
RUMBLE
RUMBLE
THUNDER.

ALTHOUGH THE JAPANESE TEAM HAD ALREADY QUALIFIED FOR THE SYDNEY OLYMPICS, THEY HEADED FOR THAILAND TO TRY TO FURTHER IMPROVE THEIR POSITION IN THE FIELD. IT WAS RAINY THAT DAY EVEN THOUGH IT WAS SUPPOSED TO BE THE DRY SEASON IN THAILAND. THE CONDITION OF THE PITCH WAS TERRIBLE, AND WE ANTICIPATED THAT THE GAME WOULD ALSO BE TERRIBLE...

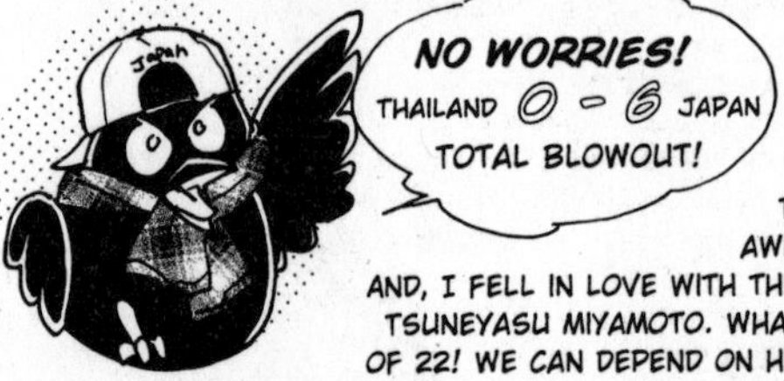
Japan
NO WORRIES!
THAILAND 0 - 6 JAPAN
TOTAL BLOWOUT!

IT WAS HIRASE WHO ENDED UP TAKING MVP HONORS, BUT PERSONALLY, I WAS FASCINATED BY SHUNSUKE NAKAMURA. ✩ THE IMAGINATION HE DISPLAYED WAS AWESOME! ✩FANTASISTA SHUNSUKE✩ AND, I FELL IN LOVE WITH THE BIG BOSS, THE ROCK-AND-ROLLIN' TSUNEYASU MIYAMOTO. WHAT COMPOSURE HE HAS--AT THE AGE OF 22! WE CAN DEPEND ON HIM WHEN WE NEED IT MOST. EVEN IN A PINCH, HE WON'T GET FLUSTERED OR AGITATED.

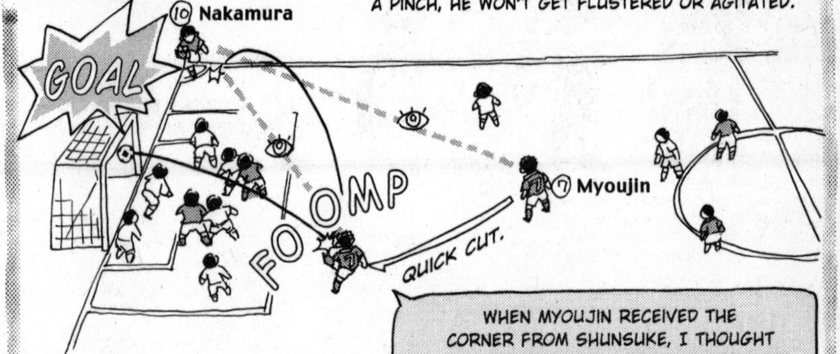
10 Nakamura
GOAL
FOOMP
7 Myoujin
QUICK CUT.

WHEN MYOUJIN RECEIVED THE CORNER FROM SHUNSUKE, I THOUGHT HE'D CENTER THE BALL, BUT HE TOOK THE SHOT!! MYOUJIN HAD HIS EYE ON IT. HIS EYE CONTACT WITH SHUNSUKE ENSURED A VICTORY.

THE CAPTAIN STOPS THE BALL IN A COOL MANNER. EVEN FROM AFAR, YOU COULD SEE HIS PREDATOR'S EYES GLEAMING. CAPTAIN, I'M TOTALLY MESMERIZED BY YOU! AND, TOMOKAZU MYOUJIN, THE RIGHT MIDFIELDER--HE IS GOOD WHETHER HE'S ON DEFENSE OR OFFENSE. ESPECIALLY THE FOURTH GOAL WHICH HE SUCCESSFULLY MADE WITH SHUNSUKE'S ASSIST. I PERSONALLY WANT TO GIVE HIM THE MVP FOR THAT ALONE. MAYBE BECAUSE OF THE BAD CONDITION OF THE GROUND, THE THAIS CONTROLLED THE BALL AT MIDFIELD. HOWEVER, I ADMIRE THE DEFENDERS, WHO NEVER LET THEM SCORE A SINGLE GOAL.

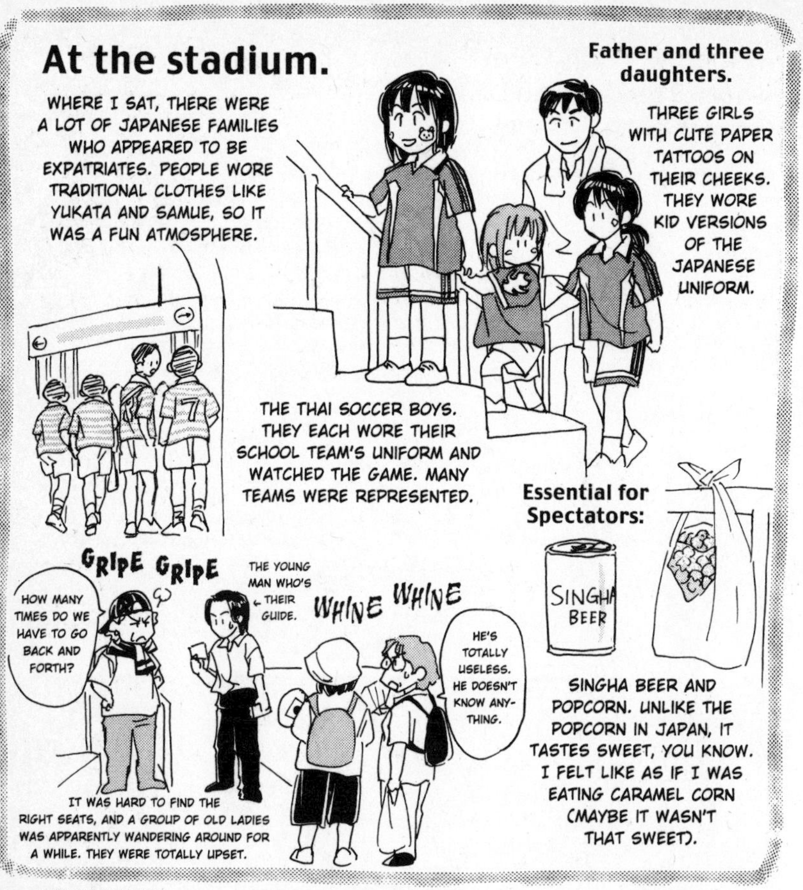
At the stadium.
WHERE I SAT, THERE WERE A LOT OF JAPANESE FAMILIES WHO APPEARED TO BE EXPATRIATES. PEOPLE WORE TRADITIONAL CLOTHES LIKE YUKATA AND SAMUE, SO IT WAS A FUN ATMOSPHERE.
Father and three daughters.
THREE GIRLS WITH CUTE PAPER TATTOOS ON THEIR CHEEKS. THEY WORE KID VERSIONS OF THE JAPANESE UNIFORM.
7
THE THAI SOCCER BOYS. THEY EACH WORE THEIR SCHOOL TEAM'S UNIFORM AND WATCHED THE GAME. MANY TEAMS WERE REPRESENTED.
Essential for Spectators:
SINGHA BEER
SINGHA BEER AND POPCORN. UNLIKE THE POPCORN IN JAPAN, IT TASTES SWEET, YOU KNOW. I FELT LIKE AS IF I WAS EATING CARAMEL CORN (MAYBE IT WASN'T THAT SWEET).
WHINE WHINE
HE'S TOTALLY USELESS. HE DOESN'T KNOW ANYTHING.
THE YOUNG MAN WHO'S THEIR GUIDE.
GRIPE GRIPE
HOW MANY TIMES DO WE HAVE TO GO BACK AND FORTH?
IT WAS HARD TO FIND THE RIGHT SEATS, AND A GROUP OF OLD LADIES WAS APPARENTLY WANDERING AROUND FOR A WHILE. THEY WERE TOTALLY UPSET.

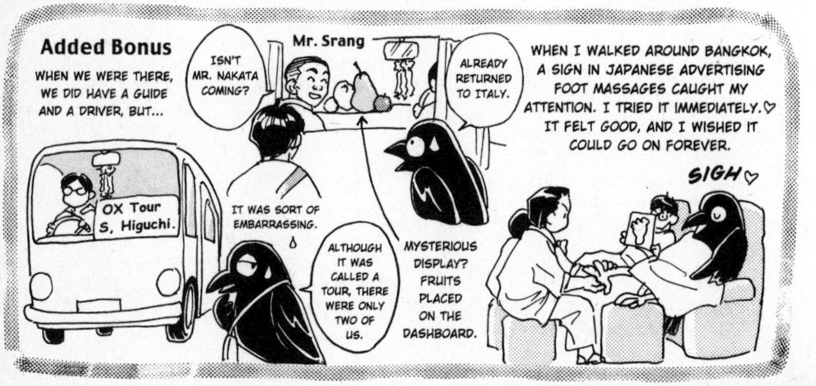
Added Bonus
WHEN WE WERE THERE, WE DID HAVE A GUIDE AND A DRIVER, BUT...
WHEN I WALKED AROUND BANGKOK, A SIGN IN JAPANESE ADVERTISING FOOT MASSAGES CAUGHT MY ATTENTION. I TRIED IT IMMEDIATELY.♡ IT FELT GOOD, AND I WISHED IT COULD GO ON FOREVER.
SIGH♡
Mr. Srang
ALREADY RETURNED TO ITALY.
ISN'T MR. NAKATA COMING?
MYSTERIOUS DISPLAY? FRUITS PLACED ON THE DASHBOARD.
IT WAS SORT OF EMBARRASSING.
ALTHOUGH IT WAS CALLED A TOUR, THERE WERE ONLY TWO OF US.
OX Tour S, Higuchi.

You may have wondered about this when you read this in serialization...

SOME OF YOU PROBABLY NOTICED THAT HIBA JUNIOR HIGH'S UNIFORM CHANGED HALFWAY THROUGH THE STORY. I CHANGED IT FOR VARIOUS REASONS... WHEN TWO SCHOOLS PLAY A GAME, AND BOTH TEAMS WEAR UNIFORMS WITH SAME COLOR, ONE OF THE TEAMS MUST WEAR A DIFFERENT UNIFORM WITH A DIFFERENT COLOR (OTHERWISE, IT WILL BE TOO CONFUSING TO PLAY). JOSUI'S UNIFORM IS BLUE, WHILE HIBA JUNIOR HIGH'S IS...RED (SEE THE COVER). IT SHOULDN'T BE A PROBLEM THEN, RIGHT? WRONG! IN MANGA, WHEN WE DRAW IT IN BLACK AND WHITE, THEY LOOK ALIKE. SO, ALTHOUGH THERE WAS ORIGINALLY NO PROBLEM WITH THE COLOR OF HIBA JUNIOR HIGH'S UNIFORM, WE HAD TO SUDDENLY CHANGE IT TO WHITE. IT'S NOT BECAUSE WE DIDN'T WANT TO TROUBLE OURSELVES WITH ADDING TONE THE UNIFORM...

◀ **Hiba Junior High 1999 ~ 2000 Season Away Uniform White + White**

WE'RE NOT SURE HOW MANY JUNIOR HIGH SOCCER TEAMS ACTUALLY HAVE TWO DIFFERENT UNIFORMS, BUT APPARENTLY, WHEN THEY HAVE TO USE UNIFORMS WITH A DIFFERENT COLOR, THEY BORROW THEM FROM A HIGHER GRADE IN SCHOOL. PROFESSIONAL CLUB TEAMS IN EUROPE HAVE A "HOME" OR "FIRST" UNIFORM, WHICH THEY USUALLY WEAR FOR HOME GAMES. WHEN THEY PLAY ELSEWHERE, AS LONG AS THE COLOR IS NOT THE SAME AS AN OPPONENT'S, THEY USE THE SAME UNIFORM. IF THE TWO TEAMS USE THE SAME COLOR, THE VISITING TEAM WEARS A DIFFERENT UNIFORM-- A "SECOND" OR "AWAY" UNIFORM. AND, IF THE COMBINATION OF THE "FIRST" AND "FIRST" OR THE "FIRST" AND "SECOND" UNIFORMS DOESN'T WORK, THEN THEY'LL WEAR A..."THIRD" UNIFORM! SO CLUB TEAMS USUALLY HAVE THREE UNIFORMS. ALSO, THEY SOMETIMES MAKE SPECIAL UNIFORMS FOR THE EUROPEAN CHAMPION'S LEAGUE OR "CUP" TOURNAMENTS, LIKE THE ENGLISH PREMIERE LEAGUE'S FA CUP.

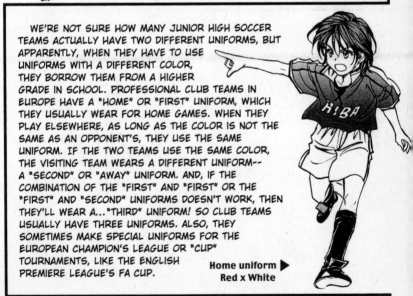

Home uniform ▶ Red x White

TEXT COLLABORATION / ASSISTANT N   THANKS ♡

WHISTLE! THEATRE!!

MANGA BY SEKI, ASSISTANT S

Secret Crib Note Story

After Shō left for the morning practice...
HMMM
OKAY, FOR SHŌ'S SAKE, LET ME WORK HARD ON THIS.
EVEN THOUGH I'M SLEEPY...
YES, YES, YES, YES, RIGHT HERE! IT SURE IS IMPORTANT!!
SIZZLE
IT'S SLOWLY COMING BACK TO ME.
FLIP FLIP FLIP
SCRATCH SCRATCH SCRATCH
URGH...I'M GETTING EXTREMELY SLEEPY...BUT...BUT... THE TEXT BOOK IS CALLING ME!!
SHŌ, BIG BRO WORKED HARD FOR YOUR SAKE...
BRO KŌ'S MEMO OF ESSENTIAL POINTS
AH, I CAN FINALLY GO TO BED, SHŌ...

Next in Whistle!

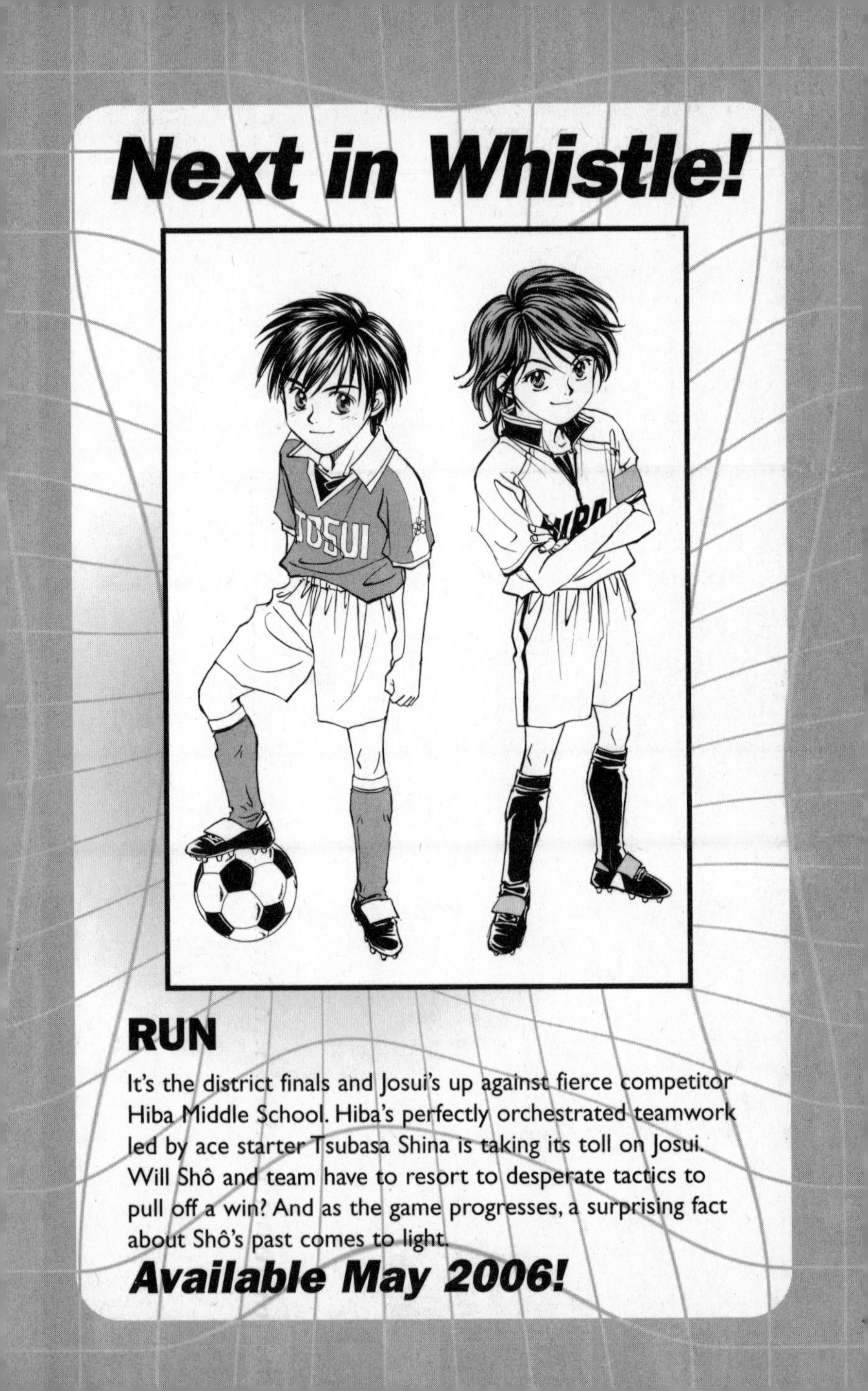
JOSUI

RUN

It's the district finals and Josui's up against fierce competitor Hiba Middle School. Hiba's perfectly orchestrated teamwork led by ace starter Tsubasa Shina is taking its toll on Josui. Will Shô and team have to resort to desperate tactics to pull off a win? And as the game progresses, a surprising fact about Shô's past comes to light.

Available May 2006!

Check us out
on the web!

www.shonenjump.com